DATE DUE			
SEP 2 0 1997			

Accounting History Classics Series

Other titles in this series

History of Public Accounting in the United States
by James Don Edwards

Evolution of Cost Accounting to 1925
by S. Paul Garner

ACCOUNTING EVOLUTION TO 1900

BY

A. C. LITTLETON, PH.D.
Certified Public Accountant (Ill.),
Professor of Accounting,
University of Illinois

The Academy of
Accounting Historians

The University of Alabama Press
University, Alabama

The University of Alabama Press Edition

Library of Congress Cataloging in Publication Data

Littleton, Ananias Charles, 1886-
Accounting evolution to 1900.

(Accounting history classics series)
Revised version of the author's thesis.
Reprint of the 1933 original ed. published by American Institute Publishing Co., New York.
Includes bibliographies and index, with a new foreword by V. K. Zimmerman.
1. Accounting—History. I. Title.
[HF5605.L5 1981] 657'.09 80-22353
ISBN 0-8173-0065-1

MANUFACTURED IN THE UNITED STATES OF AMERICA

EDITOR'S PREFACE

When the serious student of accounting history first approaches the subject, there is a very good chance that this work *Accounting Evolution to 1900* will be among the first encountered. It is difficult to appreciate the significance of Littleton's work fully because we are not all equipped with his masterly perception of the role of the past in conditioning our present state. Nevertheless, in part or in whole, the work provides the reader with a wealth of historical fact and perception.

The Academy is pleased to offer this as the third volume in its series. We call to your attention as well the fact that a hardback edition of this work is available from Atheneum Press. It may be of interest to researchers since it contains a short addendum written by Professor Littleton dated February, 1966—the time of that reprinting.

Our appreciation is expressed to S. Paul Garner for contributing the master copy volume for this reprint and to the Arthur Andersen & Co. Foundation for their financial support of the series.

October, 1980

GARY JOHN PREVITS, Series Editor
Case Western Reserve University

FOREWORD

Nearly fifty years ago the unique, pioneering book, *Accounting Evolution to 1900,* appeared. The author, A. C. Littleton, was an accomplished and productive accounting professor. His work provided both academic and professional accountants for the first time a historical perspective for the new and rapidly growing discipline of accounting.

Accounting Evolution to 1900 is a convincing historical study and interpretation of the long evolution of the practice of bookkeeping into an increasingly essential social science of daily practical importance. Professor Littleton's epic work reviews the history of accountancy from its earliest origins to the start of the present century—a century whose first eighty years have seen accountancy become a socially recognized and regulated profession, such as law, and also as an academic discipline of expanding social importance. This work provided the historical perspective necessary to identify the pragmatic economic market forces that generated the evolutionary development of accounting and from that identification to begin the long, difficult, and continuing search for the principles and standards that constitute the theoretical structure of this discipline.

Both accounting practitioners and academicians owe a major debt to the American Institute of (Certified Public) Accountants. This leading organization of practitioners agreed to publish this work on accounting history prepared by a former practicing accountant who had long since returned to the campus environment. It is especially noteworthy that the major American organization representing accounting practice enabled the publication of a work that had little apparent evidence of being of "practical value." Certainly the American Institute had a full and important agenda in the early 1930s. The American economic system was in disarray, and American auditors were under vigorous attack to perfect their own practices and to assist the American society with the major task of abolishing or revising certain prevailing market practices, particularly those related to the adequate disclosure of economic transaction data presented in published financial statements. Indeed, George O. May and other leaders of the American auditing profession were engaged in the essential, but difficult task of identifying and describing, coherently and logically, "generally accepted accounting principles." This book was an important and creative step in that ongoing effort because of the historical perspective it provided for the way accounting theory and practice existed and evolved.

In addition to our recognition of the important role of the American Institute in making this study available to accounting practitioners and academicians, we should also recognize the contribution of the author himself. A. C. Littleton, as mentioned, was already an established and respected accounting professor in the late 1920s when he recognized the need for the study of the history of accounting. Such a study was not necessary to advance his career. Yet, he sensed the academic need for a more complete intellectual base for the expanding accounting curricula. He and other colleagues at the University of Illinois (Urbana-Champaign) had already developed graduate accounting courses leading to a master's degree. It was Professor Littleton's special vision of the need for the development of doctoral work in this new academic discipline that was unique and important to the academic development of accounting in the United States.

In the late 1920s, Professor Littleton informed his academic supervisor, that he, although a tenured professor of accountancy, had decided to undertake a rigorous graduate program in economics leading to a Ph.D. degree while continuing his normal duties. Professor Littleton at this time had baccalaureate and master's degrees in accounting, but he correctly sensed that the development of a doctoral program in accounting would not be approved by a university if the staff members in that discipline did not possess an equivalent level of academic credentials themselves. He received little encouragement in his quest, but he perservered and earned his doctorate in economics. These efforts did provide the needed stimulus for the approval of the first doctoral program in accountancy in the United States. The first degree was awarded in 1939. The thesis supervisor for this graduate as well as twenty-three others was A. C. Littleton. Thus, this study of accounting history, which was in essence Littleton's doctoral research, itself helped to create history.

Accounting Evolution to 1900, a revised version of Littleton's doctoral thesis, recognizes the continuing vitality and relevance of this pioneer effort. The study of the history of accounting has slowly gained the attention of scholars. I am certain that Professor Littleton, a modest and unassuming person, would first speak of his delight that the growing importance of this area of accounting has been recognized in a significant number of books and articles and, particularly, that a journal specifically dedicated to accounting history now exists. This republication again makes available the knowledge of this early scholar and the continuing inspiration and challenge he provides to those who read and reread his seminal work.

July, 1980

V. K. ZIMMERMAN
Urbana, Illinois

TO

HENRY RAND HATFIELD

WHOSE

AN HISTORICAL DEFENSE OF BOOKKEEPING

PROVIDES THE INSPIRATION AND

MODEL FOR THIS BOOK

Wer tiefer in eine Wissenschaft eindringen
will, muss auch ihre Geschichte
kennen lernen.

ERNST JÄGER

CONTENTS

PART ONE

THE EVOLUTION OF DOUBLE-ENTRY BOOKKEEPING

I. RESPECTABILITY OF BOOKKEEPING*

LET us boldly raise the question whether accounting, the late claimant for recognition as a profession, is entitled to some respect. Must it consort with crystal gazing, chiropractice and palm reading?

Three elements, if not conclusively proving, at least presumptively establish respectability. These are, first, parentage and lineage; second, the company one keeps; and third, the services which one renders the community. Let us examine accounting in these respects.

Without raising the question as to accounting in antiquity, we look upon the Franciscan monk Paciolo as the father of modern accounting, as his *Summa,* published in 1494, was not only the first printed work dealing with algebra, but it also contained the first text on bookkeeping, a slender tractate entitled *De Computis et Scripturis.*

Not much can be said of Paciolo, aside from his writings, but his academic credentials are flawless. He was an important, if not a great, mathematician, teaching first at the University of Perugia and at various times at Naples, at Pisa, and at Florence and Bologna, and ending his career with his highest honor, for in 1514 Pope Leo X appointed him professor of mathematics in the *Sapienza* at Rome, a position in the "University of the highest standing in all Christendom."

His career at the universities was interrupted in 1496 when he was called to Milan by the reigning duke, Ludovico il Moro, whose court was a center of light and learning. To be established there was a signal honor—Adams in China, Hollander in Porto Rico, Bogart in Persia, Paciolo in Milan—all indications of deserved recognition of professorial eminence.

At Milan, Paciolo was brought into contact with many eminent

* An abridgment by permission from Henry R. Hatfield's little classic, *An Historical Defense of Bookkeeping.*

persons, the most significant being Leonardo da Vinci, at once the most eminent artist and the greatest man of his time. Between the two there grew up an intimate friendship. Da Vinci himself tells that he hastened to buy a copy of Paciolo's *Summa* as it came off the press, and he collaborated with Paciolo on a later book, the *Divina Proportione,* for which Paciolo furnished the text and Da Vinci the illustrations.

It is not necessary to outline the nature of Paciolo's treatise, which has been made available in English through Geijsbeek's somewhat paraphrastic translation and more recently through Crivelli's translation. The little book is interesting to read, not merely as a piece of technical literature, but because of its quaintness of expression, its naïve attention to detail, its exuberance of piety, its flavor of mediævalism.

It is seldom the case that a first book on a subject has dominated its literature as did Paciolo's *De Computis et Scripturis.* It is nearly true to say that for 150 years the texts appearing in England, France, Germany, Italy and the Low Countries were "at best, revisions of Paciolo, at the worst, servile transcriptions without even the courtesy of referring to the original author." But, further than that, many little matters of bookkeeping technique were followed for at least four centuries, merely because they were inculcated by Paciolo, persisting like buttons on our coat sleeves, long after their significance had disappeared.

Let those who vaunt the superior merits of other disciplines remember that this first presentation made by Paciolo was not crude and incorrect, but contained the essentials of bookkeeping as we know it today, despite the fact that it was written at a time when chemistry partook of the vagaries of alchemy, biology was a weird collection of errors, and medicine had more in common with the medicine man than it has even today.

It may be well to see how this discipline—(perhaps one should not venture to call it science)—compares in its antiquity with the more arrogant natural sciences. It is not necessary to go back to the feeble beginnings and adumbrations of learning to do this; it needs only a view of the position of bookkeeping, as it was first formulated in print by a mediæval university professor, in contrast with the formulation of natural science—not by some dim groper in far-off antiquity—but by an early member of Harvard College. A comparison thus made is surely more than generous to the natural sciences, despite their general illiberal attitude toward the social sciences, with which, in general, they admit no kinship.

Charles Morton, who, like Paciolo, was at once distinguished teacher and cleric, was brought to Harvard from England almost two hundred years after Paciolo had formulated double-entry bookkeeping. If not professor, he was at least made vice president, and his work on science was used as a text-book in the college.

But he explained* the problem of the migration of birds by saying that each autumn they flew to the moon, 200,000 miles distant, a two months' journey, and in his text-book earthquakes are explained as follows: "They come from choking up of wind below fermenting, bursting out, causing trembling and strokes." Or dropping into verse:

> "In subterreanean caverns winds do frolic
> When Mother Earth is troubled with the colic."

How marked a contrast to the teachings of the geologist at the University of California. It is told that when he appeared in court as an expert witness, the opposing lawyer, foolishly attempting to ridicule his pretension of knowledge, said: "And do you pretend to know what is going on in the bowels of the earth?" to which the geologist replied "I do not know that the earth has any bowels."

Only two hundred years ago, therefore, science—in the leading American college—was a futile and ludicrous display of ignorance. More than four hundred years ago, in the very first book published on the subject, bookkeeping was outlined in a form which still prevails around the entire world. Can not bookkeeping claim an honorable and ancient lineage? Is it indeed an upstart as compared with geology and chemistry and landscape gardening and social psychology and business English and physiology and olericulture and oto-rhino-laryngology and other cherished subjects of the university curriculum? Founded, like San Francisco, by a follower of St. Francis of Assisi, cradled in mathematics, with algebra as a twin,

* Meriwether, *Our Continental Curricula,* page 190ff.

established under the ægis of a great university—surely this is an origin sufficiently academic to give respectability to this subject.

The second book on bookkeeping was also written by a man of distinction, Grammateus or Schreiber. He, like Paciolo, combined algebra and bookkeeping, and his book, dated 1518, was the first work published in Germany dealing with either of these subjects.

Almost immediately following Grammateus was Jerome Cardan, that picturesque scapegrace and brilliant scholar, astrologer, physician, scientist, mathematician, professor of medicine first at Pavia, later at Bologna. He, too, wrote a book (1539) combining algebra and bookkeeping. This work, says Richard Garnett, marks an era in the history of mathematics, being the first in which the principle of cubic equations was fully explained. Everett says it is one of the most valuable contributions to the literature of algebra. As a physician Cardan was so eminent that he was called to Scotland—no mean journey in those days—to attend an archbishop; he was famous enough as an astrologer to visit the court of Edward VI to cast the king's nativity. But his chief claim to distinction is his general scientific attitude, so far in advance of his times. Says Garnett: "Alike intellectually and morally, Cardan is one of the most interesting personages connected with the revival of science in Europe. He possessed the true scientific spirit in perfection. As a mathematician he effected most important advances, and to complete the catalogue of his accomplishments he is no contemptible poet." And to add picturesqueness to his career he became involved in difficulties, was addicted to gaming, imprisoned for debt, banished from Milan, was later deposed from his professorship, imprisoned, released, prohibited from further teaching, but spent his latter years in Rome as a pensioner of the pope.

Of the first six writers three are thus seen to be men of eminent distinction—in fields other than that of bookkeeping—as judged by persons who are not themselves particularly interested in bookkeeping. Surely the early days—if not the unknown origin of bookkeeping—are so respectable that we need not be ashamed.

Extending somewhat the field of survey, we find that Brown lists only 150 names of writers on bookkeeping before 1800. But even the reduced list of those who have reputations in fields other than bookkeeping is too long to repeat in detail. These are not a group of narrow specialists. We find there authorities on algebra (as is to be expected), on navigation, on optics, a commissioner to settle the foreign exchange, the author of the French code of 1763, astronomers, a French grammarian, an authority on gunpowder and the historian of the Baptist church. To find these names in the *Encyclopædia Britannica* one does not look under accounting or bookkeeping (these articles are scant and unsatisfactory, and both contain misstatements concerning the history of the subject) but under the following rubrics: algebra, camera obscura, deaf and dumb, earth figure, fortification and siege craft, gravitation, infinitesimal calculus, insurance, logarithms, mathematical tables, Napier and navigation.

Three names from the list may perhaps be mentioned more specifically. There was Simon Stevin. Cantor describes him as a Dutch mathematician, but says his claims to fame are varied. He invented a horseless carriage which worked; he was first to solve some problems regarding polyhedra; he proved the law of equilibrium on an inclined plane; he discovered the hydrostatic paradox; he explained the tides by the moon; he devised new forms of fortification, was many times public officer, a soldier and statesman and the first to introduce decimals. Yet he thought it well worth his while in 1602 to write an extended treatise on bookkeeping for the express purpose of training his royal pupil, the Prince of Orange.

There was Charles Hutton, a colliery boy who became teacher of mathematics at eighteen and later professor at the Royal Academy at Woolwich, fellow and foreign secretary of the Royal Society (three others in the brief list were also fellows of that distinguished body), perhaps most famous for his computation of the density of the earth, an achievement recognized by LaPlace and said by various competent critics to show ingenious and important methods, which can hardly be improved, author, too, of a work on conic sections said by Montucla to be a model of precision and clarity, receiver of the Copley medal for his paper on gunpowder and doctor of laws of Edinburgh. And yet this man, who could weigh the earth as in a balance, condescended to write a text-book on bookkeeping, a subject which many think worthy the attention only of writing masters and proprietors of business colleges.

There was Robert Hamilton, who after some years' experience as a banker, betook himself to teaching and was professor, first of natural philosophy and later of mathematics, at Aberdeen. He was famed, however, more as an economist, for it was he who exposed the economic fallacies of Pitt's policy of the sinking fund. Yet this man, banker, merchant, mathematician, capable of confuting England's master statesman, thought it not beneath his dignity also to write on bookkeeping.

This survey has been generally limited to writers before 1800; only two persons since then are to be included. Augustus De Morgan, whose eminence needs no description, was so far interested in bookkeeping that one of the best elementary books ever written on the subject acknowledges that it is based on the suggestions of De Morgan. And finally, Arthur Cayley, who thirty years ago turned aside from his duties as professor of mathematics at Cambridge long enough to write a most excellent work, entitled *The Principles of Double-Entry Bookkeeping*.

These citations are of illustrious men who have written on bookkeeping rather than illustrious writers on bookkeeping. This selection was by design in order to establish the argument that bookkeeping is a subject worthy the attention of men of ability—not to be relegated to the ordinary business college.

But not every writer on the subject has succeeded. He may, like Grammateus, stand high as a mathematician, and yet, as a writer on bookkeeping, "deserve no praise beyond that of being the first German who ventured to write on that difficult subject," producing a book, which Row Fogo says is "so confused that it is extremely improbable that he himself knew much about what he was attempting to teach. . . ." He may, like Cardan, show originality and genius in science, yet as a writer on bookkeeping be worse than banal; he may, like Collins, hold an honorable position in the Royal Society, yet produce a work on bookkeeping which deserves no particular mention by the historian of the subject; he may, like Hamilton, deserve the encomium of McCullough, that he succeeded in the impossible task of opening the mind of the British public on an economic question, and yet have the *Encyclopædia Britannica* say that his work on bookkeeping is now forgotten. A man of distinction may write on bookkeeping; but his work in that field is not necessarily distinguished. Would it be fair to say that it takes a peculiar genius to make a success in that subject?

The third presumptive evidence of respectability is that one performs some important service in the world. Can this be said of accounting? Perhaps this can best be answered by showing that bookkeeping appeared, not as a chance phenomenon, but distinctly in response to a world need. This is true not only of the days of Paciolo, but, as can be shown, of that more important, almost present-day, revival.

It is not without significance that bookkeeping appeared at the end of the fifteenth century, nor that its birthplace was in the Italian republics. We all know of the marvelous awakening of that period, and particularly of the sudden expansion of commerce. Sieveking, one of the few historians who has paid attention to the subject, says that bookkeeping arose as a direct result of the establishment of partnerships on a large scale, a feature of the expanding commerce.

But bookkeeping dozed for several centuries, and it was not until about four hundred years after Paciolo's book that a startling awakening took place. New works in unheard-of abundance and of a new quality began to appear, and again the university seriously undertook instruction in a subject which had fallen into academic disrepute.

Why this new prominence in a subject taught before 1500? The answer is so obvious that explanation seems impertinent. The end of the nineteenth, even more than the end of the fifteenth century, was marked by a most extraordinary expansion of business. Then was the period of the organization of the great corporations (ordinarily called trusts), a phenomenon common to America, England and Germany. Then came that new appearance, the billion-dollar corporation, and just then—not a curious coincidence, but a necessary response—accountants woke up. Garcke and Fells began the list of works on cost accounts. Pixley, first, and then Dicksee began their voluminous writings dealing with the more refined problems of corporation accounts. England chartered the Institute of Chartered Accountants. New York set the example, since followed by every American state, of granting the title of Certified Public Accountant; the adding machine was invented; logarithms were placed beside the ledger; books were written; conventions were held; accounting *was.*

In part the new significance of accounting is due to subdivision of ownership and the severance of ownership and control so characteristic of the corporate form of business organization. If the substitution of a small partnership for the individual trader called for improvement in bookkeeping methods, how much more was improvement needed when the partnership was displaced by the corporation with its owners numbered by the tens of thousands?

But still more significant has been the great investment of fixed capital characteristic of modern production and made possible by the organization of corporations. The use of fixed capital on a large scale increased incalculably the difficulty of determining the profits earned in any given year. Paciolo made no serious effort to do this. Business in his day was a congeries of disconnected ventures. A ship went here, a caravan there, a joint venture was undertaken with Messer Juan Antonio in French wool, and a "flyer" was taken in *ginger bellidi.* As these ventures fell in, the profit gained in the completed transaction was ascertained—somewhat roughly, it is true, but fairly satisfactorily. But no attempt was made to deal with unfinished operations.

But today business is a continuum. Machinery serves for many years; the factory building stands for a generation; the railroad is built to last forever. The industrial process is made up of a never-ending stream of raw materials, goods in process and finished commodities. Expenses are incurred in common and not, like the expenses of a caravan, solely for one parcel of goods. But man is strangely agricultural in his traditions, even though society has become industrial. Time was when the recurring cycle of the year was of immense significance to him, for seed-time and harvest each came in the course of the earth around the sun. And man still thinks that he must reckon results in terms of the accidental period involved in such a circuit. We demand to know how much a concern makes in a year. We must know, because the reciprocal rights of preferred and common stockholders may be altogether changed, depending on whether profit is to be attributed to the month of December or to the following January. We must know in order to satisfy the demands of the income-tax collector. And so accountants are asked to perform the hopeless task of taking this economic continuum, of chopping it up into arbitrary and meaningless lengths called years, and apportioning to each such year a proper part of the cost of a building which will last fifty years, of a machine which will be used for twenty years, of a blast furnace which will last ten, and of a stock of coal bought in December which will all be consumed before spring again appears.

Nine tenths of the problems of the accountant are due to this demand to express results in terms of years. The accountant is wrestling with it. That it has not been solved is apparent to anyone who opens a text on the subject or enters into the intricacies of the income tax.

In these paragraphs an attempt has been made to remove the stigma attached to accounting by showing that in its origin it is respectable, even academic; that despite its present disrepute it has from time to time attracted the attention of men of unquestioned intellectual attainment; that it justifies itself in that it has arisen to meet a social need, for its function is to place responsibility, to prevent fraud, to guide industry, to determine equities, to solve the all essential conundrum of business: "What are my profits?", to facilitate the government in its fiscal operations, to guide the business manager in the attempt to secure efficiency. Are not these efforts worthy of any man's attention? Certain men whom all respect have thought so; Scott, the romanticist, declared the profession of accounting respectable; Goethe, the universal genius, speaks of bookkeeping as one of the fairest inventions of the human mind, and Cayley, scientist beyond question, even more significantly declared, "Bookkeeping is one of the two perfect sciences."

II. THE ANTECEDENTS OF DOUBLE-ENTRY BOOKKEEPING

The antecedents (or ingredients) of double entry—those factors which in time became so interwoven as to render double entry inevitable—are all familiar quantities. Some are very old and most of them very obvious, but all are, in my opinion, indispensable:

The *Art of Writing,* since bookkeeping is first of all a record; *Arithmetic,* since the mechanical aspect of bookkeeping consists of a sequence of simple computations; *Private Property,* since bookkeeping is concerned only with recording the facts about property and property rights; *Money* (i.e., a money economy), since bookkeeping is unnecessary except as it reduces all transactions in properties or property rights to this common denominator; *Credit* (i.e., incompleted transactions), since there would be little impulse to make any record whatever if all exchanges were completed on the spot; *Commerce,* since a merely local trade would never have created enough pressure (volume of business) to stimulate men to coördinate diverse ideas into a system; *Capital,* since without capital commerce would be trivial and credit would be inconceivable.

These elements are recognized as essential to the formation of double entry; had any of them not existed, its appearance would have been problematical. If either property or capital were not present, there would be nothing for records to record. Without money, trade would be only barter; without credit, each transaction would be closed at the time; without commerce, the need for financial records would not extend beyond governmental taxes. If either writing or arithmetic were absent, the vehicle of bookkeeping would not exist. These then are the *sine qua non* of bookkeeping—the elements without which there could be no double-entry bookkeeping. They furnish a material which needs reworking, that is, profitable exchanges of goods and transactions in credit; they provide a language by which to give expression to the material which is under active observation and control, that is, money as a medium of exchange, arithmetic for computing values, prices, profits, etc., and writing as a means of making permanent records. Outlined, these elements fall into groups as follows:

The Antecedents of Bookkeeping

1. A Material (something which needs to be reworked)
    a. Private property (power to change ownership)
    b. Capital (wealth productively employed)
    c. Commerce (interchange of goods)
    d. Credit (present use of future goods)

2. A Language (a medium for expressing the material)
    a. Writing (a means of making a permanent record)
    b. Money (medium of exchange, "common denominator")
    c. Arithmetic (a means of computation)

These elements, when energized by favorable economic and social circumstances, produce:

3. A Methodology (a plan for systematically rendering the Material into the Language)

This methodology is bookkeeping.

Essential as they are, even these elements could not produce bookkeeping by merely appearing together historically. All of them were present in some form throughout the era of ancient history, but the early civilizations failed to produce double entry as the term is now understood.

Writing, for example, is as old as civilization itself. Babylonian mortgages impressed in cuneiform characters upon clay tablets and Egyptian tax collections painted in hieroglyphics upon papyrus can still be read after more than 4000 years. But in none of this writing was there any sign of double-entry bookkeeping, for bookkeeping is more than a writing, although always written.

Arithmetic as we understand it—the easy and systematic manipulation of number symbols—did not exist in the ancient world, although the Greeks made great advances in geometry. Numbers could be expressed by the use of letters of the alphabet, it is true, but arithmetical manipulations, even addition and subtraction, were very difficult to perform. The lack of an easy means of computation must have been as strong a deterrent from organized financial record-making at this time as its later appearance was a favorable factor.

Property is a requisite antecedent to bookkeeping, of course; without the right to possess, enjoy and dispose of articles of property there would be little reason indeed to "keep books." But property rights under the ancient civilizations were not accompanied by the other conditions necessary to bookkeeping. Property acquired by conquest or obtained from slave labor is likely to be expended in lavish display or in further wars—in any case, unproductively. The highest conceivable need for bookkeeping under these conditions would be satisfied with a sort of "stores accounting," which would merely tell what property was available. The accounting of the Egyptians did not extend beyond this process, and the financial records of the Roman head of a family were little better—hardly more than a record of receipts and disbursements.

Even the addition of the factor "money" to the art of writing and private property could not produce double-entry bookkeeping. These three factors made possible a written record of private properties which could be expressed in money as a common denominator. But the stimulus to convert a possibility into an actuality was lacking.

Credit there was too, such as was extended by the ancient money-changers. But this offered little incentive to completely systematic record-making. Loans were for the most part based upon pledged valuables as in modern pawnbrokerage. In the ancient world money was not often lent commercially but rather against necessity—for consumption, rather than for production or trade. Indeed, lending could hardly be called a credit transaction until far into the Middle Ages. A loan upon pledged property was to the lender practically a completed transaction. If the borrower never reappeared to redeem his property it was his loss, not the lender's responsibility. There would be little need here for systematic records.

Nor was the commerce prevalent in the ancient world of the kind to give rise to bookkeeping. The Phœnicians were great traders along the coast of the eastern Mediterranean 3500 years ago and are said to have given us our alphabet of twenty-six letters, but it is doubtful whether they gave us double entry. Barter needs no bookkeeping. The antecedent of double entry which we designate "commerce" is not just a trading exchange; it must be an extensive commerce in order to produce the pressure of a great volume of trade. This sort did not exist in the era of ancient history. The demand for trade goods was small, because populations were relatively small and largely self-sufficing, as they consisted of many slaves, serfs and poor artisans with low purchasing power and only few people of wealth. Furthermore, the supply of trade goods was very limited and the means of transportation were inadequate. The commerce which was to assist in the formulation of double entry had to be a profitable commerce, for this is the best means of saving a fund of capital which can be re-employed productively and thus in turn create additional capital.

This lack may have been the principal reason why the ancient world did not produce complete bookkeeping. The idea of productive capital was not yet present; in that era of an agricultural stage of development there was no occasion to consider capital as a factor in production. This stage was to be followed long afterward by an era of handicraft and one of commerce and still later by an industrial era. These later stages were better suited to the development of bookkeeping, but neither of them had been reached at the time when recurrent waves of invading barbarians pushed the remnants of Roman civilization out of Europe into Constantinople and closed the doors upon ancient history.

There was capital, in the sense of wealth, in the ancient world, but the mere existence of wealth would not predispose other conditions to form double entry. Wealth in marble palaces and secret hoards does not create conditions favorable to the appearance of a coördinate system of financial records, but other forms of wealth could do so—wealth in the form of goods and ships which is active, turning over, ever changing in producing more. Wealth in such forms creates questions and doubts and hopes, and men, in striving to find answers to these, slowly evolve or adapt methods of record to serve their needs. In other words, wealth in the ancient world was not possessed of the energy to become "capital" in the sense necessary to make it a true antecedent of double entry.

In fact, all the elements which are here presented as indispensable antecedents of double-entry bookkeeping were already present, as has been said, in the ancient civilizations in recognizable form. Yet they failed to produce at that time what they later did produce, namely, bookkeeping. Why later? The answer very likely lies in the historical characteristics of the period which followed the Dark Ages—in the changes in outlook and surroundings, in men's varying aspirations and interests, and in the differences in the quantity of the wants and the quality of the ideas which were current.

Consider the background. The outlook for civilization was discouraging, to say the least, for more than eleven centuries of the Christian era. Rome, in the later days of the Empire, consisted of a government made up of a corrupt bureaucracy, void of either political ideals or enthusiasm and responsible only to a distant emperor, and of a population which was exhausting itself in trying to wrest a living from a depleted soil or was being crushed out of existence by grinding taxes. Poverty, weakness, decay—small wonder that the hardy barbarians from the provinces who made up the slave class and the army soon became the military officers and before long the governmental officials. By the last quarter of the fifth century a barbarian general was crowned emperor with barely a gesture of acknowledgment to Constantinople. The slowly loosening restraints of strong government were thus still further relaxed, and vast disorder reigned generally through Europe. It was a long dark period, full of violent individualism and petty group struggles, marked by conflict between barons and dukes, emperors and popes.

For centuries education was practically eliminated; intellectual life became morbidly centered upon the preparation for life after death since an earthly existence held so few attractions. Only the church held out any promise to mankind, and nothing but the church remained to civilize the barbarian and keep alive the spark of intellectual activity.* But in a thousand years of this existence much real progress was made. Europe had reached the mediæval era

* From the sixth to the eighth centuries all that survived of ancient thought in western Europe was preserved in the Benedictine monasteries. ". . . . to learn the use of the abacus, to keep accounts and to know the rule by which the date of Easter could be determined was all the science that the most studious aimed at." Ball, *History of Mathematics*, p. 123.

with its intense religious fervor, its feudal ties, its chivalrous idealism. Now for the first time in ten centuries, Europe was united enough to join hands in a common enterprise.

In 1075 the Turks captured Jerusalem, and in less than twenty-five years the cream of European manhood was moving southward in a common cause at the instance of the church to retake the Holy Sepulchre. For the next two hundred years a steady stream of humanity, increasing at times to mighty waves, ebbed and flowed across Europe in the crusades. That Jerusalem was won and lost and won again mattered less to civilization, as it proved, than did incidental results which formed no part of the original intention.

The unforeseen results of these great movements appeared first in the city-republics of northern Italy—Venice, Florence, Genoa—which had long carried on trade with the East. In this traffic they had prospered greatly, and Venice particularly had become a great maritime power, which not only made constant war upon numerous pirate fleets, but also established trading posts in strategic places, by treaty if possible, by force if necessary. Thus Venice and the other cities were ready when their services were needed for transport and supplies, and they profited according to the demand.

But more important to later developments than the business of transport was the great impetus given to the European demand for eastern goods and the stimulus given to handicraft work at home. Crusaders and camp followers returning from the luxurious East to their own rude countryside were no longer so easily satisfied with the old style of living. They wanted more of the products found in the East, and hence they set about developing goods which could be used in exchange and encouraging craftsmanship among their own people during the process.

Here were two elements which were to stimulate a commerce the like of which the world had never seen: on the one hand, a hardy, growing population in northern Europe, developing a taste for distant products and willing to work to get them; on the other hand, a source of abundant supply now made accessible in the Near East—an area which constituted a connecting link with far eastern countries where civilization had reached a peak only shortly before. There is nothing in ancient history to compare with this situation for potential commercial developments or in actual final results. Such a commerce as was then beginning could, because of its size and its freedom, accomplish much which had been impossible earlier.

Since ancient civilizations lived, for the most part, in an agricultural stage of economic development, with large slave or serf classes which had no purchasing power, barter was the usual method of exchange, and traders were hardly more than peddlers. Northern Italy in the Middle Ages, however, was populated by a nation of traders rather than by agricultural serfs and landed nobility. Commerce was the principal activity; wealth accumulated rapidly and with it scholarship and the arts flourished. Reading and writing, formerly the prized possessions of a few scholars, were now more common among the traders and bankers of Venice than anywhere else outside the monasteries. Scholars had long been able to write, but traders could now, for the first time, have some one write down whatever needed to be written in trade. Property rights, which in an earlier day had meant little to a slave population, now were freely enjoyed by freemen. In the prosperous city-republics of Italy, where there existed the most stable government of ten centuries, private ownership of property was widely diffused and amply protected. These cases of stable government proved an advantage in another respect, for they gave money as a medium of exchange a significance it had not known for long centuries. Thus was hastened the day of a complete money economy.

It is evident, then, that even the very ancient institutions of money, property and the art of writing took on a vitality in the new surroundings which had been impossible in the ancient world. The Renaissance was not an awakening of interest in the arts alone. New interest appeared in practical matters as well, for commerce, capital, credit, arithmetic were all antecedents of bookkeeping, and all absorbed the spirit of the Renaissance which surrounded them; they seemed animated by a new life in comparison with that shown in ancient history.

Transporting the numerous armies of crusaders between 1096 and 1272, as well as supplying these soldiers with necessities and equipment, was a profitable business. Here was commerce on a new basis. And when to these sources of profitable activities was added the trade in eastern commodities and articles of eastern manufacture which the crusades so largely stimulated and for centuries flowed through the cities of northern Italy, it is obvious that capital would accumulate rapidly in the cities most concerned, and, having accumulated, would seek employment, thus expanding again the productive cycle of trade.

The wealth of the ancient civilizations was stagnant in the form of palaces, rather than active in the form of ships. But in the city-states of mediæval Italy, between the years 1200 and 1500, capital was urged into productiveness. Trading was the vocation of large and small; wealthy traders owned their own ships and ventured their capital in goods to fill them; those in more moderate circumstances went adventuring as active partners upon the capital of silent partners. Others chose the safer road of lending money upon the security of the ships themselves or of lending to various governments. These are examples of early transactions in credit.

Loans to governments marked the beginning of investment banking—the participation of many persons in one loan. As early as 1178 the merchants of Genoa advanced funds to the government upon the security of the public revenues and the profits from military expeditions. This financing later developed into the famous Bank of St. George. The Bank of Venice had a similar origin when in 1171 the merchants were given transferable book credits for gold advanced to the government. The size of some of the early deals is staggering to contemplate. For example, in 1307 the merchants, acting as a group, lent the Republic of Florence seven million gold florins ($15,000,000), and a little later (1340) lent nearly $4,000,000 to King Edward III of England.

With the resulting accumulation of capital seeking employment, it is not surprising that the great merchant houses of the day added a rudimentary sort of commercial banking to their activities. Indeed, this soon became a practical necessity, because the sums involved in trade were often too large to be risked unnecessarily on unprotected roads. Even before the year 1200 bills of exchange had made their appearance, and in the next century their use spread so rapidly that the bankers became important enough to have a duly organized guild which regulated many of their practices. Members were required to keep records and to open them for surprise inspections by guild agents. Illegibility was severely censured as were also, of course, inaccuracies and falsifications.

By 1230 Florentine and other bankers had representatives scattered over the whole of Europe. These agents, among other activities, collected most of the papal revenues, remitting usually by bills of exchange through branch offices of their banking houses. How extensive these scattered connections had become by the next century may be judged from the example of the firm of Peruzzi, which had sixteen branch houses scattered over both European and Mediterranean countries and one hundred and thirty agents looking after its interests. Much of the firm's activity was trading, naturally, but besides this it carried on banking operations, for the two were seldom separated as early as this.

Throughout the three hundred years between 1200 and 1500 arithmetic had been quietly playing its appointed part with the other antecedents of bookkeeping. The ancient world had been greatly handicapped by inability to make computations easily; the literal symbols used for numbers by the Greeks, and the even more faulty system of the Romans, did not lend themselves readily to calculations. But in the Middle Ages Europe began to learn arithmetic from the Arabs, and this condition was in the way of being remedied.

There is small doubt that Italian traders knew the essentials of early commercial arithmetic before the material appeared in Europe in manuscripts—their contacts with the Arabs of Northern Africa and in Constantinople would insure this. And in 1202 Arabic numerals and methods of computation were introduced into Europe in book form by Leonardo of Pisa. The book had chapters on addition, subtraction, prices of goods, barter, partnership and the like, and it would be of interest to merchants on account of these topics, as well as because the book made use of the new system of ten numerals, including a zero.

Such a system lent itself naturally to computations, and had already been applied by the Arabs to a great many of the arithmetical problems of trade. This knowledge the Italians acquired early in the period, and it seems very probable (even though difficult to prove) that it opened the way for systematizing the record-keeping made necessary by bills of exchange as nothing else could have done. One historian of mathematics (Ball) says that, within a generation after Leonardo of Pisa, Arabic numbers were widely used with the Roman system by Italian merchants. It should be noted, however, that the rules of the bankers' guild invariably prescribed the use of Roman numerals in making ledger records. The idea prevailed for a long time that such numerals made fraudulent alterations more difficult. But there was nothing in this restriction by the guild to preclude other informal uses of Arabic numbers.

It is evident from all this that the conditions surrounding commerce, capital and credit in the Middle Ages were very different from those which accompanied the same elements in the period of ancient history. And it becomes increasingly apparent that these attendant circumstances so changed the size and extent of commerce and the purposes for which capital and credit were employed, that the latter elements could now become the vitalized antecedents of bookkeeping, whereas before they were without issue. They now led directly to the development of double entry.

III. THE CHARACTERISTICS OF DOUBLE ENTRY

DOUBLE-ENTRY BOOKKEEPING is a way of recording facts of surprising adaptability to modern conditions, in spite of the long time which has elapsed since men began to assemble its essential elements into a coördinated methodology. Relatively little is known of the actual process of its formulation. Yet enough fragments of old account books and descriptions of old practices are extant to indicate quite clearly that bookkeeping as it is today is not the invention of one man nor the product of a single generation, but that it is rather the result of a long evolution.

Bookkeeping has developed from very humble beginnings because of the fact that men, under the dictates of self-interest, were able to adapt and modify known ideas and methods to the new needs of their day. But just how and when they made changes in previous methods, the meager historical materials dealing with the commercial side of the ancient world and mediæval civilization do not clearly show. Inconclusive as it must be, an attempt to surmise the probable steps of the evolution and to place them in some sort of logical sequence may, however, constitute an acceptable substitute for a more definite knowledge of the facts. If the conjectures which follow seem unsupportable by full historical evidence, let it be remembered that they are offered solely as suppositions which are not wholly illogical in the light of what is known of the circumstances.

In turning to a consideration of the stages of evolution through which bookkeeping probably passed a preliminary question presents itself: How shall one know when double-entry bookkeeping has been achieved? By what criterion may it be recognized? If the basic characteristic of double entry is a simple one, the art may be found to have been quite completely formulated much earlier than would be the case if the essential characteristic is a complex one.

The first thought probably is that the name itself expresses the fundamental characteristic, i.e., double entry means duality of record. But would not this test be based on purely superficial indications? In America the word "bookkeeping" is so generally used for "double-entry bookkeeping" that the fact that two elements are involved is not always realized. "Bookkeeping" is a general term which should carry the meaning of recordings, reckonings,* account-keeping. The attached adjective, "double-entry," almost unconsciously leads to a bias in the direction of duality as bookkeeping's basic characteristic. But there is need to look deeper. This designation, given so long ago, may have been merely a superficial, rather than a fundamental, characterization. It was not the only term applied to the discipline now known by that name. A glance at the following list of freely translated and somewhat abbreviated titles of some of the earlier texts will reveal a variety of ideas:

Account Keeping (Paciolo, 1494)
Reckoning Book (Schreiber, 1523)
Book Keeping (Gottlieb, 1531)
Double Record Book (Manzoni, 1534)
Keeping the Reckoning called Debtor and Creditor (Oldcastle, 1543)
Account Books in the Italian Manner (Ympyn, 1543)
Double Bookkeeping (Schweicker, 1549)
Keeping Books of Account (Mennher, 1550)
Accounts of Debitour and Creditour (Peele, 1569)
Bookkeeping with Two Entries (Mellema, 1590)
Books of Account in the Italian Manner (Stevin, 1602)
Treatise on Double Books in the Italian Manner (Waninghen, 1615)
Double Accounts (Anonymous, 1624)
Keeping Double Books (Flori, 1636)
Merchants Accounts (Collins, 1652)
Merchants Accounts by Debtors and Creditors (Liset, 1660)
Debtor and Creditor Made Easie (Monteage, 1675)
Keeping Books by Double Entry (Giraudeau, 1700)

* Compare the German word *Rechnung* from *rechnen,* to compute. In seeking the essence of bookkeeping, not the essentials of "account-keeping" but the characteristics of *complete, systematic* account-keeping should be sought. The complete, unified system has come to be called "double-entry bookkeeping." Or put in another way, "double-entry bookkeeping" means complete, systematic, coördinated account-keeping.

Bookkeeping by Single and Double Entry (Donn, 1758)
A Defense of Double Entry (Collier, 1796)

Some of the titles refer merely to record keeping; others extend the idea somewhat by adding "in the Italian Manner," but many do not suggest more than "records" or "books of account." Several titles, however, reflect a concept of duality in such phrases as "Accounts by Debtor and Creditor," "Double Books," "Double Bookkeeping," "Double Accounts," "Double Entry." In these terms there are three kinds of "duality" expressed, (1) duality of books, as ledger and journal, (2) duality of account form, as debtor page opposing creditor page and (3) duality of entry or of the postings of an entry.

These phases of duality are indeed a characteristic part of double-entry bookkeeping, but to consider them as the criterion of double entry is, it would seem, to regard the form as the substance. As a matter of form, duality is perhaps peculiar to bookkeeping. Account-computation operates through "subtraction by apposition" or "subtraction by contra-position"— * i.e., it works toward *balances* rather than remainders. Bookkeeping (i.e., account-keeping) is indeed an instrument of classification as well as a mere record, but that is not its distinguishing peculiarity; various expedients could produce equally good classification, if nothing more than that were needed. Bookkeeping is more than classification; it unites the sorting of facts into accounts with "deferred balancing," if the term may be permitted. The purpose of most classifications would be fulfilled at once when the data were totaled, that is, fulfilled by mere segregation; but for the purpose of account-keeping the classification is not fulfilled until "likes and opposites" in each class are brought to a *balance.*

Yet duality—whether in the two-sided form of the account, in the existence of ledger and journal or in the double posting of each transaction—is not the essential criterion of complete, coördinated

* In his *History of Mathematics,* Ball points out that in mediæval arithmetic the most popular terms in subtraction were *debt* for minuend and *payment* for subtrahend (p. 96) and that Paciolo used the initial letter of the word *plus* to indicate addition and that of the word *æqualis* to indicate equality. Paciolo avoided the introduction of a symbol for minus in his algebra, however, by writing his quantities on the side of the equation which makes them positive (p. 189).

account-keeping. It is possible to conceive a complete (even though complicated) statistical procedure of classifying facts which could yield the same summarized data as bookkeeping without the use of formal duality. It is evident, also, that a considerable degree of duality of record probably existed long before double-entry bookkeeping was completely formulated. In fact, instead of being the *sine qua non* of bookkeeping, this duality of form is quite probably a mere reflection or result of a deeper, more basic characteristic.

Perhaps equilibrium of results may be the keynote of double entry rather than duality of form.

An examination of the balance-sheet seems to indicate that equilibrium within the statement (and within the accounts from which it was derived) is inevitable. In the balance-sheet there is an inescapable equilibrium, whether it is found in the antithesis of (a) positive and negative properties and (b) proprietorship (i.e., assets less liabilities equal net worth), or in the opposition of (a) capital kinds and (b) capital sources (i.e., assets equal owner's capital plus borrowed capital). But it must finally be evident that these peculiarities are, like the duality of form, the consequence of the fundamental characteristic of double entry rather than the element which gives bookkeeping its comprehensiveness and finish. It is, of course, axiomatic that the parts (positive and negative properties) are always equal to the whole (proprietor's net investment), and it is quite true that the sum total of the several kinds of property will always be equal to the sum total of claims by some one to those properties.

But it does not necessarily follow that *equilibrium* is that criterion the appearance of which indicates the existence of double-entry bookkeeping and the absence of which leaves us without complete, coördinate record-keeping. Equilibrium is an important element in modern bookkeeping and perhaps adds a certain uniqueness to the method as compared with statistical procedure in other fields. But there is possible—and in very large corporations this is very nearly attained—a complete financial information tabulation service yielding all the data now coming from double-entry bookkeeping without the conscious use of either duality of form or equilibrium of result.

On the other hand, it would be possible for equilibrium of entered transactions to exist without the framework's being complete double-entry bookkeeping. The Roman slave, for example, may have been made responsible for managing some of his master's business affairs and may have maintained an equilibrium within his records through the use of a "master's account" to stand in opposition to the various investments of the funds in his hands, but much of the master's business would remain outside this record. The mediæval commercial factor may have acted as agent to one or more large traders and may have found it advantageous to secure equilibrium within the records by keeping an account with his principal as well as accounts with the property in his possession and with debtors who owed him for goods they had bought. But this record-keeping, if it stood alone, would still be incomplete in comparison with true "double-entry bookkeeping." Mere equilibrium within the agent's records would not be enough to make incompleteness complete. As a forerunner to complete double entry, and perhaps as a bridge connecting an earlier and simpler method with a later and full discipline, agent's accounts undoubtedly made a large contribution to the final result. But they hardly constituted complete double entry unless, by definition alone, the term "double entry" is designedly made equivalent to equilibrium of entries and duality of form.

Strictly speaking, however, the term should have a broader connotation than this if it is to be suitable for designating the modern concept. Or perhaps two terms are needed, one to indicate a simple regime of internal equilibrium suitable to record agent's bookkeeping and another to designate a complete instrumentality adapted to recording modern corporate activities.

It would seem, therefore, that other features must be added to equilibrium and duality before complete double-entry bookkeeping is possible. This added element, no doubt, is proprietorship—that is, a direct ownership of the goods handled and a direct claim upon the income which emerges. Without this element account-keeping (bookkeeping) consists merely in recapitulating the details of a responsibility and casting them into a convenient form—a form which, it is true, lends itself remarkably well to certain later-perceived fundamental principles * but is insufficient to constitute of itself an instrumentality adequate to later demands.

The full performance of bookkeeping is not called for until it undertakes to serve the enterpriser. His interests are broader and deeper than the agent's. The former is not merely following directions, as is the latter. The enterpriser is continually advancing his own capital and later recouping it; he is not merely discharging a designated responsibility but is choosing risks for gain; his interest is centered upon learning what the gain was so that he may judge the wisdom of having risked his capital in that particular time, manner and place. Not until bookkeeping serves such a person and such problems does it achieve its destiny.

It is this service which is the province of complete, coördinated bookkeeping. It is called double-entry bookkeeping, but the wording of the name is only a reflection of the earlier tendency to emphasize form above substance and not a description of its function. The *form* of complete bookkeeping is the duality and equilibrium which derive from early record-keeping precedents; the *substance* consists of proprietary calculations of the gains (or losses) from ventured capital.

Thus it would seem that the essential criterion of double-entry bookkeeping, as the term is now understood, is commercial proprietorship, and especially those elements which are called "nominal accounts" or "economic accounts." "Proprietorship" expresses an ownership of property and its dedication to gainful activities; "economic accounts" are designed to measure and explain the tangible results of this ownership and dedication. This is the function of modern account keeping. Double-entry bookkeeping means the organized instrumentality for executing this function. When commercial proprietorship drew to itself and adapted to its own requirements the account-keeping methods of banking agents and trading factors, modern double-entry bookkeeping emerged. "Factor's bookkeeping" had become "proprietor's bookkeeping."

* Such as (1) the total of property is inevitably equal to the sum of its constituent parts and (2) a test of accuracy (as the trial balance, for example) is highly desirable for such a massing of data.

Having thus established the criterion by which to recognize the emergence of double-entry bookkeeping, the rest of this chapter is given over to an outline of the probable sequence of development by means of which simple account-keeping grew into a coördinate system of proprietorship bookkeeping. To debt (personal) accounts, goods (impersonal) accounts were added; to debts and goods, proprietorship (capital and expense) accounts were added. At that point the framework was complete; no basic elements have been added since then.

There are two possible starting points for tracing the development of a coördinated system of bookkeeping. One of these is a record of receipts and disbursements. Such records appear very early; in Egypt, Greece, and Norman England governmental taxes gave occasion for records of receipts and disbursements. But these records evolved in the direction of logismography and modern governmental accounting, in which the central concerns are (1) expected receipts and actual receipts and (2) expected expenditures and actual expenditures. This development obviously is not in the direction of double-entry (proprietary) bookkeeping, for it contains little to cause careful attention either to the calculation of profits or to the statement of present capital.

The other starting point, that is, the record of indebtedness, is recognized at once as more directly contributory to the later system. From this beginning there are two possible avenues of development. Personal accounts may have begun as simple, independent memoranda of the terms of agreements affecting the future. These would be memory aids more than anything else and, when disposed of in one way or another, could be eliminated by merely crossing the memorandum off the list, destroying the parchment, etc. Undoubtedly, such records existed; clay bricks from ancient Babylonia, papyri from Egypt, parchment documents of the Middle Ages—and even present day experience at the corner store—indicate that in all ages personal memoranda of debts have been kept in very informal ways.

But it is not so easy to see how these isolated notations might come to be given the characteristics of accounts and to be coördinated into a homogeneous system. Could the bi-lateral form so peculiar to ledger accounts have evolved from these simple memoranda? Perhaps part payments and the difficulties of properly anticipating the space necessary to record canceling entries would have brought forward the idea of placing the debt on one page and the payments thereon upon the opposite page. There is no way to know. It would seem now just as easy for the development to have been such that part payments would be recorded by crossing off the old memorandum and writing a new one for the revised amount. The length of time it would take to make an entry in one way or another would probably not have been a material element at such an early day. But even if simple, independent debt-memoranda could evolve directly into a bi-lateral account form, it is still difficult to see how that evolution gave debts receivable one characteristic (plus on the left, minus on the right) and debts payable quite the opposite.

The other avenue of development of debt-records offers fewer obstructions to a hypothetical reconstruction of the way in which changes may have occurred. This is the development founded upon Roman accounting methods, in which debt records were regulated by systematic practices under legal requirements. These show so many features which were later definitely associated with double-entry bookkeeping that one is inclined to feel satisfied that this line of development is the more plausible.

Debts were contracts, which, even before they had been made the subject of records in writing, had been reduced by the legal-mindedness of the Romans to set forms. A pledge (*sponsio*) was originally a moral obligation in the nature of an oath symbolized by a libation in wine. Later, as this religious oath came to be employed for legal purposes, it lost its religious aspects; the old phraseology of an oath became a formal question and answer—*spondesne? spondeo,* Do you pledge? I do pledge. Thus the *sponsio* was invested with legal effects and became the basis of the verbal contract (*stipulatio*) of Roman law.

Various agreements (*stipulationes*) had to be couched in certain words. In a suretyship, for example, the creditor asks: "Do you agree that the amount which T owes me is to be on your security? (*centum quae T mihi debet, eadem fide tua esse jubes?*)." The surety replies: "I agree this is to be on my surety (*fide mea esse jubeo*)." A vendor would say: "Do you agree to give me this amount? (*spondesne mihi centum dare?*)." The vendee replies: "I agree (*spondeo*)." A debtor discharging a debt would say: "Have you received what I promised? (*quod ego tibi promisi, habesne acceptum?*)." The creditor replies: "I have (*habeo*)."

In the later Empire, under the influence of Greek law, writing became a requisite of the *stipulatio*, and a memorandum was usually drawn up attesting that the promise had been made in the proper form of question and answer. But there was another way in which contracts of debt were made definite and effective; this was associated with the household records as then kept.

The head of every Roman family was required to keep domestic accounting records of which the most important was the cashbook (*codex accepti et expensi*). Originally this probably contained only entries relating to money actually received and paid (*nomina arcaria*). But later a second class of entries came into use—the *nomina transcripticia*—which represented the acknowledgment of a debt rather than an actual payment of cash. Thus a payment entry (*expensum* or *expensilatio*) might be either an actual cash disbursement or a fictitious payment having, by agreement of both of the parties concerned, the effect of creating a legal liability by thus becoming a literal (i.e., written) contract.

The procedure[1] was somewhat as follows: The creditor made an entry among the receipts as if the prior unwritten obligation (from a sale, loan, etc.) had been canceled; at the same time he entered that amount among the payments as if now paid to the debtor.* The two entries (*acceptilatio* and *expensilatio*) constituted a written contract; they had the effect of converting an amount previously due under a simple contract into an amount now due as a loan—somewhat the same change in relationship as is now seen when an account payable is converted into a note payable.

Just as the written obligation was produced only by the book entry, so the debt could be extinguished only by a canceling entry. The creditor's entry of an *acceptilatio* for the prior sum and prior

* The debtor usually (though in law it was unnecessary) made corresponding entries in his records.

person among the receipts indicated that the debtor was discharged from his debt. The entry was the same whether the debt was paid or whether one person was released as another took his place (novation). In the latter case the creditor made a further entry (*expensilatio*) in the payments side to bind the new debtor by a written obligation.

In summary form these entries would appear somewhat as follows:

LENDER L——'S CASHBOOK

Receipts	*Payments*
1. to cancel prior verbal agreement with A——.	2. to set up obligation running from A—— as if for a loan.
3. to cancel loan due from A—— now assumed by B——.	4. to set B——'s obligation in place of A——'s.
5. to cancel B——'s obligation when payment is received.	

BORROWER A——'S CASHBOOK

Receipts	*Payments*
2. to set up obligation running to L—— as if for loan.	1. to cancel prior verbal agreement with L——.
4. to set up obligation to B—— as if loan from him.	3. to cancel loan due to L—— now transferred to B——.

If one person made many loans which had to be recorded in this manner, it is clear that his cashbook would soon become a confused mixture of real cash transactions and fictitious cash transactions expressing debts. It would make matters still worse if the lender were also upon occasion a borrower and recorded his borrowing debts as well as his lending debts in his cashbook. Obviously, the thing now needed was a record of individual loans.

Up to this point the Roman practice had worked out carefully worded phrases in which agreements should be expressed and had systematized the treatment of debts, 1. by establishing a method of converting oral agreements into written obligations, 2. by providing for expressing the cancellation of a prior written obligation by mean of a contra entry and 3. by extending the use of the contra entry to include the transfer of an obligation from one debtor to another. But the practice as described had not set up the fourth element of systematic debt records, i.e., duality of entry, nor established the fifth element, i.e., the reversed plus and minus characteristics of debts receivable and debts payable. These missing elements, so necessary to the ultimate formation of double entry, may, however, have been present in the records wherein loans were classified by individual borrowers.

Surplus funds of wealthy Romans were carefully invested to produce an interest return and thus gave rise to many cashbook entries of the sort above described. To keep track of these debts (investments) special books of account (*ratio calendarii, liber calendarii* or *codex rationum*) were arranged, supplemental to the cashbook and put in charge of a special assistant (*curator calendarii*). It seems probable [2] that loans entered as fictitious (or real) payments in the cashbook were also separately entered according to borrowers' names. But this alone would not supply the fourth and fifth elements indicated above. The clue to these items may rest in the suggestion by P. Kats [3] that perhaps the *curator calendarii* was a well trained slave who acted as an agent for his master in the transaction of various business matters and felt impelled to keep a "master's account" in order to be better able to report intelligently upon the discharge of his responsibilities.

This is not unlikely. It was not only held beneath the dignity of a patrician to engage in trade, but he also ran the risk of losing his political rights as a Roman citizen as well. Obviously, therefore, practical matters of business would be delegated to others—probably to educated slaves. Such slaves might reasonably be expected to enter in a "master's account" the sum of money received for investment; when a loan was made, entry would follow in the cashbook (as above) and in the borrower's account in the *liber calendarii*. When a loan was repaid these entries would be reversed. When interest was received, entry was made in the cashbook and in the master's account; payments made on the master's instruction would reverse this entry.

If this methodology had been followed, it would have introduced the element of duality into the records incidental to the use of a "master's account." But the way the systematic arrangement of the plus and minus sides of the receivables and payables came about is not so clear. That the personal accounts in the *liber calendarii* would be bi-lateral seems probable from the precedent of the cashbook. That the master's account should be regarded by the slave as just another personal account is also quite natural, for it would operate very much like an account for money borrowed, upon instruction, from a third party by the slave.

With this as the probable background, it seems likely that the way the entries were placed upon the left or right side of the respective individual accounts would easily drop into a routine without any philosophical pre-arrangement. The idea of opposition of entries would already have been well established in cashbook usage, and its extension would, no doubt, suggest itself readily enough as *duplicate* entries were made: those duplicating, in the personal accounts, right hand (expense) entries in the cashbook would be placed on the left of the master's account; interest received in the left side of the cashbook would go to the opposite side of the master's account. The latter practice would plainly be correct, for there the item would meet other amounts due the master, such as the original sum entrusted by the master to the slave. Payment received from a loan paid off (left side of cash) would be duplicated in the personal account on the right side in order to cancel (by opposition) the previous entry which already stood on the left side. Granted an intelligent educated slave who had felt impelled to keep a "master's account," it seems quite reasonable to assume that he would presently perceive the self-contained scheme of dual entries in bi-lateral accounts, even though he might be unable to explain why the entries when made constituted a closed system.

The study of "agency bookkeeping" afforded so good a key to this part of the reconstruction of the formation of double entry that it may prove a profitable clue to follow into the Middle Ages. Historical continuity is broken, of course, by the fall of the Roman Empire and the Dark Ages which followed. And it is impossible to prove whether the Roman-like practices which appeared in the Middle Ages had been perpetuated and directly transmitted to Italy through the barbarians themselves or by way of Constantinople, or whether they came from a revival of Roman ideas when, after several centuries, the literature and law of Rome were opened for study.* But however that may be, mediæval banking shows many characteristics of the earlier days, and is of great interest in the development of bookkeeping.

The money changer (*argentarius*) of the Roman Empire may have been nearly forgotten during the Dark Ages, but as commerce began to revive, he reappeared as the *campsore* of the Italian trade cities. The need for his service was great, because the variety of coins in use demanded a wider knowledge of values than ordinary merchants were likely to possess. Furthermore, a merchant going into distant markets would usually take bars of bullion with him, change them into local coins during his stay and reconvert the coins into bullion when he departed. The risk attached to the transportation of precious metal in any quantity in those unsettled times must be quite obvious. It is not astonishing, therefore, to find assignments of debt, letters of credit and bills of exchange early taking the place of much of the bullion and coin in the transaction of commerce and the remittance of tax money.

Money changers by the beginning of the thirteenth century were becoming merchants of exchange (*bancherii de scripta*) who kept careful accounts under strict regulations of their guild and dealt in debts generally. As has already been indicated, credit instruments were in wide use in the middle of the century—there were eighty banking houses in Florence alone in 1338, and one hundred and twenty by the end of the century. By 1450 one firm, the Peruzzi, had sixteen branches in various parts of the world and one hundred and thirty widely scattered agents. Numerous other firms, which were in existence at the same time, greatly expanded the total.

* Conant, in his *History of Modern Banks of Issue* (p. 6), says that it was the opinion of Jannet (*Le Credit Populaire et les Banques en Italie*) that the organization of commerce and banking as it existed in the Roman Empire survived the invasions and persisted into the Middle Ages. Adams (*Civilization in the Middle Ages,* p. 30) hints at a similar conclusion when he says that Roman influences were perpetuated because the process of Romanizing the German conquerors was begun at once and succeeded wherever it had a fair chance. In the opinion of Sohm (*Institutes of Roman Law,* Ledlie, tr., p. 138) Roman law in its original form never completely lost its hold in Italy, for the traditions of Roman law continued among the people as well among the jurists.

Here was an excellent framework for bookkeeping, but account keeping did not continue to develop from the point to which Roman law and practice had brought it. It seems probable that the early accounts of mediæval exchange bankers were pretty definitely confined to records of debts and transactions in debts; the cashbook seems to have been missing and, at first, the self-contained system of dual entries as well. But in such ledger entries as have been preserved from the thirteenth, fourteenth and fifteenth centuries * it is evident that certain account characteristics had been retained intact. Entries were made for debts, all of them being carefully expressed in a similar phraseology, suggesting the influence of the standardized verbal contracts of early Roman law. The account form was generally bi-lateral, cancellation or novation being expressed by contra-entry.

The following hypothetical novation is presented to set in comparison the Roman methods already described and entries which, from later examples, appear representative of the type of ledger record used in the early Middle Ages.[4]

The banker, upon receiving a deposit, writes in his ledger, in the words of his promise to the depositor:

"Antonio shall have at his pleasure 200 ducats this day left with me in cash...... 200"

The banker, upon lending a sum of money to a borrower, enters in his ledger in the words of the latter's promise to him:

"Francisco shall give 200 ducats to me at my pleasure for cash this day lent to him... 200"

When sometime later the occasion arises for substituting Antonio as debtor in place of Francisco (perhaps since the latter can not pay), the banker makes two entries, one canceling the debt receivable:

"Francisco shall have 200 ducats of me this day placed at his pleasure by Antonio.... 200"

* See examples at the end of chapter VII.

This entry, though stated in language suggestive of an independent deposit, represents a cancellation of Francisco's prior debt and in the records would be written on the page opposite the earlier entry. The other entry is made at the same time and is stated in the same words as if it represented a loan to Antonio:

"Antonio shall give to me 200
ducats this day placed at the
pleasure of Francisco...... 200"

But since Antonio has previously made a deposit of this amount, and now agrees to look to Francisco for repayment of this sum, this last entry is written opposite Antonio's prior entry and in cancellation of it.

These transactions illustrate the "cross entries" which accompanied the use of bills of exchange between financial correspondents. Traces of such entries are found in the records of a Florentine banker dated as early as 1211. But cross entries do not complete a closed system of accounts. It seems not improbable that the element which was missing from banker's accounts (that is, a "master's account") would be supplied when the keeping of personal accounts was extended beyond finance into trading operations.

When the owner was his own trader he had little need for account keeping. But as trade continued to expand under the stimulus of the crusades and wealth kept accumulating in the Italian city-states, the practice of each man's being his own trader was largely replaced by the practice of trading through agents or partners.

Several conditions contributed to this development. The risks of long sea voyages or overland journeys to trading towns would deter some who might otherwise have desired to engage in trade. Capitalists who disliked travel could entrust their goods to experienced agents or form partnerships with younger and more venturesome men. Nobles and clerics who wished to enjoy the fruits of trade without actually engaging in business in their own name could accomplish their desire by contributing capital as silent partners. This arrangement also had the advantage of taking the capital transaction out of the category of a loan, for taking interest was prohibited by canon law and firmly disapproved by the church. The formation of partnerships was further stimulated by the fact that the regulations of the various guilds tried to keep foreign traders out of the trade centers by placing a tax upon all but local traders. This taxation of strangers could be avoided by taking a local merchant for a partner.[5] Probably the local merchant would be more accurately described in modern terminology as a consignment agent upon a profit-sharing basis.

The silent partnership (*commenda*)* was particularly well developed in sea-borne trade. The silent capitalist (*commendator*) entrusted his goods, and occasionally a ship of his own, to the active trader (*tractator*) upon a partnership basis. Naturally, in these circumstances the latter would have to make a careful and detailed report upon his return; especially if he had been trading with goods belonging to several silent partners. Here was a definite need for capital accounts comparable to the master's account kept by the Roman slave, and here too was a need for goods accounts, whereas the Roman needed only personal accounts for loans made.

The active partner would, no doubt, know the account-keeping methods practised by bankers, for banking and trading were often intermingled. To him, then, the investment by silent partners would appear the same as a deposit with a banker—an amount to the credit ("shall have" side) of the silent partner's personal account; expenses (taxes, provisions, seamen's wages) would easily be recognized as debts which the principal "shall give" (owes) to the agent—hence they were items to be entered in the latter's account as if he had borrowed the sums from a banker,† that is, on the left side.

It is easy to assume the beginning of goods accounts along similar lines. If three silent partners had each contributed different goods, the trading partner would feel it his duty to report to each upon his goods as disposed of at different prices and different places. This might at first have produced debt accounts, only when goods were sold and debts receivable had been created in distant towns. But the step could hardly have been a very great one from that to keep-

* For other terms of similar meaning see, Edler, *Glossary of Mediæval Terms in Business*, Italian Series, Cambridge, 1931.

† The canon against taking interest did not apply to Jews, therefore lending and banking were not entirely stifled by church law.

ing separate goods accounts for each partner's contributions, showing on one side in detail the goods contributed and on the other the amounts received for sales made at various places. Certainly the need for some such records would be present, and in the accounts kept by bankers there was a methodology available. If the two were united by shrewd trading agents, the latter could please their capitalist associates by being able to go over in convincing detail all that had happened to the goods invested—and satisfied associates would mean further trading ventures.

When goods accounts, cash accounts, customers' accounts and silent partners' investment accounts were associated in this manner, then there had appeared again a closed system of accounts in which it would be possible—and natural—for entries to be made in pairs and upon opposite sides. This would be account-keeping by dual entries, but, according to the criterion set up at the beginning of this chapter, it would not yet be double-entry bookkeeping as that term is generally understood. Proprietorship, profit-and-loss, expense accounts, etc., were still needed to present a complete framework for modern bookkeeping. But these elements were not far off. They would grow quite naturally out of these "agency" relations, as trading partnerships of more permanent nature replaced single ventures and occasional agreements.

As trading began to resemble a permanent business rather than a series of joint-ventures, the partners would keep accounts of their whole business; consequently, the point of view would shift from an accounting (a reporting) by a profit-sharing agent, at the end of a special venture, to the investment account-keeping of the capitalists (entrepreneurs) themselves. If they entered upon a venture, the capital would be recorded just as any investment in goods, but it would be only a part of their invested, and recorded, capital. They would need a profit-and-loss account for the convenient summarization of numerous separate gains and losses, so that periodically, or whenever a change occurred in the make-up of the partnership, the relative position of the partners could be properly ascertained. Once the practice of dual entries upon opposing sides of bi-lateral accounts had become established, it would not be difficult to extend it by analogy to new accounts. No one would have to stop and reason out the philosophy of the matter first. Accounts "must give" from some transaction and "must have" from others; and it is hard to understand why these "give" and "have" characteristics would not have been applied in expense accounts (i.e., the temporary profit-and-loss accounts) as well as in personal debts.

In any event the relationship was perceived sometime, somehow, for by the end of the fifteenth century this complete system had appeared in textbooks; and long before this, as the fragments of actual ledgers which remain show, the framework of accounts—debts, cash, goods, expense, profit-and-loss, capital, and all the rest—was well established, and a definite methodology of entry and transfer was regularly in use.

The process by which the necessities of the moment and the inventiveness of men combined to bring about the formation of complete double-entry bookkeeping is long drawn out, very halting in its progress and difficult to trace satisfactorily. Yet when an attempt is made to see bookkeeping in perspective, there is evidence that its formation must have been the result of slow social evolution. Those who search the records of the centuries find many clues to past practices. But these, even were all of them brought together, would not fill in the whole picture.

For example, they find financial agreements carefully framed in set sentences in the early Roman Empire and ledger entries in mediæval ledgers expressed in similarly exact forms of wording—and they try, very unsatisfactorily, to see just how these earlier ideas might have been passed on, gathering other ideas as they went. They find in Rome a well-defined practice of canceling prior entries by new and opposite entries and think they see in this one of the basic elements of later double-entry bookkeeping. They also know that duality of entry is an outstanding characteristic of double-entry bookkeeping, and when they find duality in the Roman slave's records through the use of a "master's account," and in the agents' accounts for mediæval joint-ventures they wonder if these contributed to the later formation of double entry. They accept proprietorship, expense accounts, profit-and-loss, etc., as part and parcel of double-entry bookkeeping, and attempt to find the circumstances in which these elements may have been added to all that had been so slowly accumulating before.

And when it is all put together, what do they have but a surmise as to how it all came about? But even a surmise, if it is supported at various points by acceptable evidence, can give a better perspective than fragmentary evidence badly disarranged by breaks in the continuity.

REFERENCES

1. Following Sohm's—*Institutes of Roman Law* (Ledlie, tr.) Sec. 81.
2. P. Kats, in *The Journal of Accountancy,* April, 1929.
3. *The Accounting Review.* December, 1930.
4. From "Two Fables of Bookkeeping," *The Accounting Review,* October, 1927.
5. Buhl, *Die geschichtlich begründete Kontentheorie,* p. 36.

IV. TRANSACTION ANALYSIS

Early writers on bookkeeping were intent upon giving instruction in the bookkeeping practice of the day; they indulged in very little theorizing. Even in transaction analysis, their underlying theory must be interpreted from the practices which they described. The writers did not enter into explanations of how transactions should be thought out or why one did thus and so, but they confined themselves strictly to telling in detail how to perform the acts of record-keeping. An attempt to formulate the early reasoning involved in analyzing transactions into debits and credits must therefore be hypothesized from the phraseology used by trying to read between the lines of the practical explanations of how the record was to be made.

The analysis of a few examples of ledger entries will show the presumable reasoning behind the wording used and open the way for a surmise about the probable basis of early transaction analysis. Three sets of entries are given below.

LEDGER ENTRY 1 (1436–1439)

From the ledger of *Fillippo Borromeo e comp.*, the London branch of a large Italian trading house (Milan): [1]

Giovanni Bindotti must give on 8th March s.4 d.4 per Giovanni Vanuzzi, to whom credited on folio 13 . . . . l0,4,4	Giovanni Bindotti must have on the 8th March l19.11.11 by the Borromei of London, to them fol. 4 . . . . l19,11,11

This entry is from the account books themselves and is in the bilateral form, as shown above, but uses Roman numerals.

LEDGER ENTRY 2 (1494)

From the only example of ledger entries given by Paciolo in the first printed work on bookkeeping: [2]

Francesco, son of Antonio Cavalcanti, shall give, on Nov. 12, 1493, l20, s4, d2 which he promised to pay to us at our pleasure for Ludovico, son of Pietro Forestani, page 2 .... l20,s4,d2.

Francesco, son of Antonio Cavalcanti shall have, on Nov. 14, 1493, for l62,s13,d6, which he brought himself in cash; posted cash shall give at page 2 .... l62,s13,d6.

This entry is Paciolo's illustration of the practices current in his time in Venice. While it does not purport to be copied directly from any actual book of account, yet one may easily feel satisfied that the form is representative.

LEDGER ENTRY 3 (1522)

Two items from the ledger (1519–1527) of Thos. Howells, a dyer of cloth in London:[3]

(a)

John de Lassys and John de Rowso of Muros in Galicia ought to give acc't of Broadcloth shipped in S't Maria de Rodys .... l74,0s,0d.

(b)

R. Donnington ought to have in barbing of a short Plonket that Th. Petter delivered you .... 8d.

These old entries call for several observations. In the first place it will be noted that each entry expresses a complete thought. Likely the wording is much as if the thought had been spoken; probably it would have been easily understood by anyone who heard it so phrased.

Perhaps the completeness of the thought expressed will be clearer if the old entries are rendered a little more freely than the more or less literal translations given above and are slightly modernized as to amounts, etc. The entries are therefore restated below.

THE 1436 ENTRIES RESTATED

B—— "must give" $4 to us (as proprietors or agents) because on March 8 he assumed the burden of V——'s prior debt to us ...... $4.

B—— "must have" back from us (as proprietors or agents) the $19 deposited with us on March 8 .... $19

THE 1494 ENTRIES RESTATED

F—— "shall give" $20 to us because on Nov. 12 he promised us he would pay on demand the debt which L—— owed to us.....$20.	F—— "shall have" back from us the $62 he deposited Nov. 14 with us in cash...................$62.

THE 1522 ENTRIES RESTATED

L—— and R—— "ought to give" me an accounting in money or in goods for the broadcloth shipped in their care . . . etc...........$74.	
	D—— "ought to have" $.50 from me for fuller's work done on my cloth.......................$.50.

In addition to their being framed in complete sentences, all the entries, it will be observed, contain certain "words of accountability"—that is to say, words which apparently were regarded as indispensable in making an accounting entry out of an otherwise straightforward sentence, in much the same way that words of negotiability are now regarded as essential in a bill of exchange. The words of technical significance in the above entries are repeated below.

For Debits:	For Credits:
Entry 1—must give	must have
Entry 2—shall give	shall have
Entry 3—ought to give	ought to have

These phrases all express the same basic idea; the differences are only variations in emphasis. Clearly the idea of "give" (i.e., return to the proprietor or agent) was directly associated with debits and "have" (i.e., receive from the proprietor or agent) with credits. The debit side of a bi-lateral account was the "give" side and the credit side was the "have" side.*

* It is interesting to note that this basic concept is preserved in the designations, undoubtedly based on the Latin, given to the two sides of an account in Italian, French, and German.

Latin		Italian		French		German	
Debent dare	Debent habere	Dare	Avere	Doit	Avoir	Soll	Haben

Thus it appears that the early ledger entries were fairly complete sentences expressing complete ideas. They were, in fact, memoranda of what the writer wished to avoid forgetting and probably were cast into the forms of expression of ordinary speech. These records in the old books give, therefore, some idea of how fifteenth century merchants thought their transactions through for recording purposes. The forms used were probably modeled on similar practices in much earlier use. The point of view was always personal, as is evidenced by the personal pronouns expressed or clearly implied in the entries.

From the wording of the entries it is also to be observed that the records were stated in words which look to the future. "Must give," "shall have," "ought to give," are phrases which look to the future. This sense of futurity is brought out more clearly in the entries as restated.

The old ledger entries, then, contain these three characteristics:

1. The entries are complete sentences expressing complete ideas.
2. The entries are written from the point of view of the proprietor or agent in question—i.e., his accounts with others.
3. The entries are definitely stated as memoranda of expected future occurrences, not of present happenings.

How would these ideas of framing ledger entries be stated in a general rule? No one knows; none of the earliest writers tried to reduce the process to a general rule. Their nearest approach was to have rules for specific accounts such as: "Goods account is debited for purchases." Even though they stated no general rules, some rules may be derived from an analysis of their transaction records.

The following hypothetical rules are offered in the attempt to reduce to simple concise statements the ideas of transaction analysis which seem to have been at the base of double-entry bookkeeping.

Each term used for debit and credit either is, literally, "give" and "have" or can be traced to these verbs. Note also that the rule of thumb for analyzing debits and credits which was so much used by later writers is not unrelated to these technical terms. The rule was in two parts: (1) "Debit what is received," that is to say: what I now receive I *must give* back; (2) "Credit what is given," that is to say: what I now give I *must have* returned to me.

(a) a sum is to be entered in the record as "shall give," if the person involved is obliged to return to me at a later date an equivalent of the sum which he has just now received from me.

(b) A sum is to be entered in the record as "shall have," if the person involved is entitled to receive from me at a later date an equivalent of the sum which he has just now given me.*

These statements of principle may be abbreviated somewhat as follows:

(a) X shall later give what he now receives—(i.e., Dr. X.)
(b) Y shall later receive what he now gives—(i.e., Cr. Y.)

The characteristic form of the ledger record was well established at an early date, before there was much evidence of records beyond personal accounts. How that record was first expanded to include impersonal accounts is unknown. But it does not seem improbable that the impulse came from traders rather than from bankers, although the two occupations merged into each other much more then than now. As has already been indicated, it seems quite reasonable to suppose that when the use of ledger accounts was extended into trade, the incompleteness of the record would become much more apparent, for it was necessary to keep track of a variety of goods and accounts were required for the partners' investments as well as ordinary accounts with persons.

But when these new accounts came into use there was an additional difference beyond the mere increase in number of accounts. Whereas the banker, keeping accounts with persons, made double entries only when transferring one person's debt to another (simple loans made or deposits received requiring only a single entry each in a personal account), the trader, with impersonal accounts also in his scheme of records, must record all transactions in double, for otherwise some of the accounts in his ledger would not receive a record of all the transactions which affected them.

* Compare with this the following German explanation of the technical terms "debit" and "credit":

"Der Empfänger eines Wertes wurde als Schuldner, der einen Gleichwert geben soll, mit 'Soll,' der Geber eines Wertes hingegen als Gläubiger, der einen Gleichwert zu empfangen hat, mit 'Hat,' Besw. 'Haben,' bezeichnet."—Stern, *Buchhaltungslexikon*, 3d ed. (1927), p. 346.

The relation of the proprietor to the scheme of accounts was new, and it complicated the analysis of transactions beyond the simple logic of memorandum-making, which was implied in the wording of the old ledger accounts. It was difficult to consider accounts abstractly; all were viewed in the same light as if they were personal accounts, that is, as records which showed what should be given back or received by the original party to the transaction recorded. In simple deposit or loan accounts this was easy enough: X shall give back to proprietor (who has just made X a loan). When cash and goods accounts were introduced the same reasoning would apply. For goods bought from Z on credit, the reasoning would become: Goods shall give to proprietor (who now places the responsibility upon that account), Z shall have or receive from proprietor (what Z now places in his hands).*

In trying to frame a memorandum in terms of *shall give* and *shall have* in order to record the above transaction, the trader would have to decide who "shall give" and to whom, also who "shall have" and from whom. The trader's own goods account, it is clear, could no more have a direct responsibility to an outsider (as Z) than B, a borrower of money from A, could have a direct responsibility to a depositor, D, who lodged the money with A. In a similar way, Z could not be conceived as entitled "to have" from any one other than the proprietor to whom he had given the goods; Z could not pass the proprietor and reach the goods themselves or the person who now had them. One debt was from proprietor to Z; the other debt was from goods account to proprietor. Thus it would have been impossible in those days to reason out a two-sided ledger entry (such as is used today) which would debit goods and directly credit Z, who supplied them on time, since there was no privity between these two. The reasoning of that time produced a four-element expression of the transaction; the modern type produces a two-element form. Their analysis, however, reaches

* Perhaps early journal entries tried to express at the same time the reciprocal rights of the creditor and the obligations of the debtor. Goods account has an obligation to give (restore), the proprietor has a right to receive; Z has a right to receive, proprietor has an obligation to give (repay). The interdependence of right and duty (in regard to debts) was clearly worked out in Roman law (see Sohm's *Institutes of Roman Law*, Ledlie, tr. p. 379). Knowledge of so fundamental a relationship would be very apt to survive through the Dark Ages or be revived early thereafter.

the same conclusions in regard to the accounts involved when the contrasting "proprietor" items are canceled against each other.

This is theory which is not stated in the early bookkeeping texts; in a sense it is deduced theory, for the early writers did not explain the logic behind their transaction analysis. They did, however, mention certain bits of technique which by themselves are quite mysterious but fit in marvelously well with some such scheme of transaction analysis as the one suggested. Two of these matters may be mentioned.

The old practice was to separate the debit and credit elements of the journal entry by two symbolic marks, such as ≷ or //. These, it is concluded, may represent the omission of the two proprietor items which were needed in reasoning out a transaction but were useless in the written record. Apparently it was expected that the mental process of transaction analysis would be communicated by the teacher rather than by the text, for the texts did not explain these symbolic marks; or else bookkeeping by that time had already become so formalized in the hands of its practitioners as to include technical methods to be carefully followed by novices, in spite of a lack of clear understanding.

The other item in the old books which shows, when the key is found, that the writers had a reasoning theory of transaction analysis is from Manzoni (1534), who writes that the four principal things appertaining to buying, selling, receiving, paying, exchanging, lending, and gifts are:

1. The one who gives
2. The one who receives
3. The thing given
4. The thing received *

* Jehan Ympyn Christophle (1547) stated the matter thus:
"And to enter to the first part you must consider that in all accounts there are two special parts, as a debtor that owes and a creditor that lends. These things considered, then follow also two other points, which are the sum of money that is owing and the cause and reason why it is ought [owed]. These specially remembered, you may then by this exemplar easily draw out and enter all your reckonings." (Reproduction by P. Kats in *The Accountant,* August 20, 1927, p. 264.) Contra entries of four items in the Roman cashbook are noted by H. Herskowitz, *The Journal of Accountancy,* May, 1930.

The application of this classification to the above transaction in which goods are bought on credit from Z would give the following:

Item 1—the one who gives=Z (who gives goods to the proprietor)
Item 2—the one who receives=proprietor (who receives goods from Z)
Item 3—the thing given=proprietor's (promise to pay Z)
Item 4—the thing received=goods (brought to the business by Z)

This classification placed in a hypothetical journal entry of the early form would be:

(a) "Goods" *shall give* to proprietor (what proprietor intrusted
    (item 4)   (item 2)   to the goods account)
(b) from proprietor, Z *shall have* (what the latter gave for
    (item 3)   (item 1)   proprietor's promise)

Somewhat modernized the entry becomes:

(a) G owes (P)
(b)   (P) owes Z

After canceling the opposing and unnecessary "proprietor items," the transaction finally assumes the rather modern technical form of journal entry:

Goods owes Z

In fifteenth century terminology it would read:

by Goods // to Z

In strictly modern form, in which the position of the words relative to each other and a double column for figures are the technical devices for indicating debit and credit items in an entry, the record would be: *

Goods xx
    Z   xx

* For a somewhat less detailed discussion of the significance of the parallel lines in the old journal entries and of the meaning of the "four principal things" mentioned by Manzoni, see Hardcastle, *Accounting for Executors* (1903) lecture 1; and Geijsbeek, *Ancient Double Entry Bookkeeping* (1914) pp. 15, 85.

In the present analysis the attempt has been made to associate the fourfold classification of the elements of a transaction with the system of transaction analysis previously developed from the technical ledger terms "shall give" and "shall have."

This hypothesis may not have succeeded in showing what the actual reasoning process was, but it may indicate that the incompleteness of the textual explanations of the early writers did not conceal the possibilities which existed even at that early date that a real reasoning process was involved in double-entry bookkeeping.

It has already been pointed out that the first bookkeeping texts did not generalize upon transaction analysis to the extent of stating a general rule for resolving transactions into debits and credits. But later such rules became the mainstay of text writers. It is doubtful whether the early authors resorted to the direct personification of impersonal accounts in their explanations. But this too became prevalent later. With the use of the old terminology personification would be quite unnecessary, for the term "shall give" is clearly equivalent to "yield up" or "render back." Thus even an impersonal "chest" (for cash) could yield up what had been placed in it and could receive back what had earlier been abstracted, without having to be thought of as a person owing or being trusted. No personification would have been necessary to make the meaning clear. But when the left side of every account came to be rendered, in some languages, as "debitor" or "debit" and the right side as "creditor" or "credit," personification soon became necessary. Accounts then lost the statistical character implied in the Italian technical words and took on the single significance of records of debts owed or owing. Thus was lost some of the clear logic of Italian double entry through bookkeeping's reversion to the single-entry usage, which was logical enough except when applied to impersonal accounts.

At first personification was apparently not needed in order to analyze transactions; later it seems implied in the use of words relating to debts and owing; and finally it is given specific mention in the texts.

Simon Stevin (1604) gives the following explanation involving an impersonal account:

> "Suppose that someone by the name of Peter owed me some money, on account of which he paid me 100 £, and I put the money in a cash drawer just as if I gave it the money for safe keeping. I then say that the cash drawer owes me that money,

for which reason (just as if it were a human being) I make it debtor, and Peter, of course, becomes a creditor because he reduces his debt to me. This I put in the journal thus: 'Cash debit per Peter.' "[4]

Richard Dafforne (1636) in the following dialogue makes a very similar phrasing of the explanation of the entry for cash invested:

Q—"How booke you the Ready Money after the way of Debitor and Creditor?

A—"Cash Debitor to Stock.

Q—"Why make you Cash Debitor?

A—"Because Cash (having received my money unto it) is obliged to restore it again at my pleasure: for Cash representeth (to me) a man, to whom I (only upon confidence) have put my money into his keeping; the which by reason is obliged to render it back, or to give me an account what is become of it: even so if Cash be broken open, it giveth me notice what's become of my money, else it would redound it wholly back to me."[5]

Dafforne's indebtedness to Stevin is obvious and is no doubt intended to be acknowledged when in his preface the former speaks of Stevin as "our master."

Another bookkeeping text (Abraham Liset, 1684)[6] makes personification quite plain in the descriptive titles given to certain ledger accounts. Cash account is thus headed:

"Cash is Debtor at present under Custody of Mr. Richard Goldcoin, Jeweller in Lumbard St."

In another instance a heading is as follows:

"John Faithful, Steward of the Household, is Debtor"

for an account which is credited with goods, money or rents received and is charged with provisions bought, wages paid, etc.

Impersonal accounts in an early day would unquestionably have been hard to teach as abstractions. Hence it is quite understandable that they should be discussed in a simpler way. Cash as an abstraction, or as a more or less statistical subdivision of total property, would be difficult to grasp. This would be especially true after bookkeeping had evolved some distance beyond its early simplicity.

The simple logic of the (apparently) early Italian manner of analyzing transactions became much obscured when the conscious inclusion of the proprietor in every transaction fell into neglect, and when the ledger terms *de dare* (must give) and *de havere* (must have) were replaced in translation by others much less suitable for implying mere statistical or record responsibility in an account.

Cash as an abstract account would be puzzling, but *Cash,* considered as a person—perhaps as a trusted employee—who "owes" what is now given him and who "trusts" others to restore to him what is now taken from him, could be fitted into transactions on a basis similar to that of other personal accounts. Thus the desired simplicity of transaction analysis was achieved even though logic suffered in the process. But this was a sort of artificial simplicity, for no amount of fiction can render a fundamentally complex thing actually simple.

The artificiality of transaction analysis had for a time a cumulative effect; it was soon accompanied by the formulation of many rules of thumb for determining debits and credits and the formation of almost endless lists of varieties of possible transactions as a means of teaching the pupil how to deal with the bookkeeping situations he might later meet. The seventeenth and eighteenth centuries particularly seem to have witnessed this development; in the nineteenth there was a rather pronounced reaction, which is reserved for later consideration.

Several texts well distributed throughout the seventeenth and eighteenth centuries have been chosen as sources of examples to show the extent to which the "formalization" of bookkeeping reasoning into the application of rules of thumb was carried in that period.

One of the early writers (Joannes Buingha, 1627) presents his rules in the following compact tabulation:

Who the Debitor is, or oweth	*Who the Creditor is, or must have* [7]
1. What we have.	1. Whence it arriveth.
2. Who so receiveth.	2. Who so giveth out.
3. What we buy.	3. Of whom we buy.
4. Unto whom we sell.	4. That which is sold.
5. For whom we buy.	5. They of whom we buy.

Who the Debitor is, or oweth	*Who the Creditor is, or must have* [7]
6. Who so must pay.	6. They that must have.
7. For whom we pay.	7. Wherewith we pay.
8. What we cause to be insured.	8. The assuror.
9. For whom we insure.	9. Insurance reckoning.
10. Whither-wards we send.	10. What we send away.
11. That which is gained upon.	11. That which is lost.
12. Profit and Losse.	12. Profit and Losse.

After explaining in detail the opening entries to be made from an initial inventory, Dafforne (1636) states thirty rules for analyzing transactions into debits and credits. A few of these are given below:

"First I will book some exquisite rules of aid, very requisite in Trade's continuance, to be learned without book——

1. Whatsoever cometh unto us (whether money or wares) for Proper, Factorage, or Company account, the same is....... *Debitor*	1. Whatsoever goeth from us (whether money or wares) for Proper, Factorage, or Company account, the same is....... *Creditor*
2. Whosoever Promiseth, the Promisor is............. *Debitor*	2. Unto whom we Promise, the Promised man is........ *Creditor*
3. Unto whom we pay (whether with Money, Wares, Exchanges, Assignations) being for his own account, that man is...... *Debitor*	3. Of whom we receive (whether Money, Wares, Exchanges, Assignations) being for his own account, that man is...... *Creditor*
4. Unto whom we pay [as above] for another man's account; the man whose account we pay is...................... *Debitor*	4. Of whom we receive [as above] for another man's account; the man for whose account we receive is................ *Creditor*

* * * * * * * * *

15. When we lose by gratuities given, whether great or small, or howsoever, then is Profit and Loss .... *Debitor*	15. When we gain by gratuities received, whether great or small, howsoever, then is Profit and Loss .... *Creditor*

The greater part of the text following these rules consists of rehearsing individual transactions in great variety and expressing them in terms of debitors and creditors. There is no analysis of the nature of the transactions, only a statement of the facts and a statement of the journal entry which results. The student had to learn transaction analysis not by reason but by rote. A natural inference is that the pupil of that time might have been somewhat at a loss if a transaction should appear for which he had had no previous example. The developments which in the nineteenth century led directly to modern transaction analysis tended to free the student from the use of unreal "fictions" (i. e., personification of accounts) and to enable him to reason out entirely new bookkeeping situations upon logical grounds rather than upon the bases of rules of thumb and memorized examples.

Much the same condition with respect to rules and examples continued throughout the eighteenth century, as the following selections from three important texts of that period will show.

Thomas King (1717) [8] lays down one basic rule and then applies this to a large number of situations. His rule for debiting and crediting is this:

> "That whatsoever you receive must be made debitor in the journal and ledger to the person from whom it was received, or to anything or things for which it is received, and on the contrary, whatsoever you deliver is in the journal and ledger made creditor by what you have received, whether money or wares, if neither, by the person to whom it was delivered." (p. 5)

Then there follows a brief statement of a number of "cases" or types of transactions, thirty-seven of them being transactions "in domestic trade" and twenty "in foreign trade." The author's analysis of one transaction will illustrate his method.

(Transaction) "If the goods you insure are lost.

Waste Book, December 17, 1715.

"I have received advice that the goods I insured for Mr. K—— are lost, value.................£500

Journal, December 17, 1715.

"Insurance account Debitor to Mr. K—— £500 being for goods insured to him on board the Thomas and Mary, John Seaman, master, are now lost.

Ledger, December 17, 1715.

"Insurance account is Dr. to Mr. K—— £500
"Mr. K—— is Cr. by insurance account .... £500"

These "explanations," then, are mere examples; that is, they are the same matter as appears in the account books without the account-book arrangement as to form. There is no instruction in the manner of reasoning out debits and credits; the general rule is given and large numbers of typical transactions are solved (not analyzed). Presumably the teacher is expected to explain orally how to apply the rule, or the pupil is to apply it blindly.

William Weston (1754) [9] makes use of a large number of rules; he has forty-five rules for journalizing transactions and his application of these occupies thirty-four pages of the text. A few of these "rules" will suffice to indicate the method which this eighteenth-century author followed.

"Rule 4, Bartering Goods of Unequal Value.

"Make the goods you receive in exchange, Dr. to the person with whom you barter; making one journal entry: then drawing a line, make the person with whom you barter, Dr. to the goods you deliver in Exchange." [Requires two complete journal entries.]

"Rule 9, of Legacies.

"If they are immediately paid you, debit cash for the money received, to Profit and Loss.
"If they are not paid, Debit the Executors to Profit and Loss for the money left you, and when such money is received, make Cash Dr. to the Executors for the sum received."

"Rule 22, Concerning Repairs of Ships.

"The ship must be made to Dr. to Cash for the money paid, or to the person or persons whom you employ, if they credit you, for the work."

In spite of the wide variety of transactions presented (including bills of exchange, consignments, partnership ventures, etc.) the teaching is by precept and example. It is interesting to note in passing that legacies (rule 9) would be more logically credited to capital account than to profit-and-loss, and that the old practice (rule 22) of charging expenses into the asset account concerned (to be later cleared by an inventory entry) is now abandoned in favor of separate expense and asset accounts.

John Mair (1765),[10] whose text on bookkeeping ran through many editions, formulates his rules as follows:

> "From the preceding remarks it is evident that Debtors and Creditors are of three kinds, viz., personal, real, and fictitious . . . I shall now sum up the substance of these remarks in the six following rules.
>
> "I. A thing received upon trust, is Debtor to the person of whom it is received.
>
> "II. The Person to whom a thing is delivered upon trust, is Debtor to the thing delivered.
>
> "III. A thing received, is Debtor to the thing given for it.
>
> "IV. In antecedent and subsequent cases, parts that are the reverse of one another in the nature of the thing are also opposed in respect of terms.
>
> "V. In cases where personal and real Debtors and Creditors are wanting, the defect must be supplied by fictitious ones.
>
> "VI. In complex cases, the sundry Debtors and Creditors are to be made out from the preceding rules jointly taken."

Following these rules, the author devotes fifty pages to applying the rules to many different situations, including transactions in domestic and foreign trade, factorage (consignments) and partnership. The aim apparently is to cover every conceivable type of transaction. In applying the rules of debit and credit to purchase transactions, Mair distinguishes seven distinct situations which may be met: goods bought (1) for ready money, (2) by bill, (3) on time, (4) part money, part bill, (5) part money, part time, (6) part bill, part time, (7) part money, bill and time. In each case the reader is shown how to make the necessary entry, but there is no logical analysis of the situations. In the same way the rules are applied to sales transactions (seven different situations), to barter (four situations), to money received (twelve cases) and to money paid (fourteen cases).

From what has been stated, it will be evident that early bookkeeping practices rested upon rudimentary theory. Whether or not the theory entered into the teachers' explanations and the bookkeepers' reasoning is by no means clear. Very likely the subject seemed tremendously complicated in the fifteenth century, when solving a problem of long division was work for a professor of mathematics. Probably also learning the mysteries of bookkeeping and following its methods proceeded more by rote than by reason. Certain it is that subsequent writers (e.g., Dafforne, 1636, and others of this later period) laid much stress upon rules of thumb for analyzing transactions and resolving them into debits and credits.

Their work was an attempt to simplify an inherently complex matter. Trial-balance equilibrium can be explained from the careful equalization of debits and credits in each separate transaction, but the relation of profit to capital is not so easily described. The resort to personification of accounts and to rules of thumb for transaction analysis is evidence of an inability to explain bookkeeping practices in abstract terms. This limitation could not prevail, however, without stimulating inquiry and speculation. Here and there the abstract side of bookkeeping received scraps of attention from a few authors (especially in the nineteenth century). In these fragmentary comments, the beginning of modern accounting theory takes more definite form.

NOTES ON RULES AND PERSONIFICATION

The entanglements which may result from trying to see the logic in bookkeeping rules of thumb are so slyly presented by Thomas Jones in his endeavor to replace rules by reasoning that a considerable extract of his dialogue between Mr. Rule and Mr. Logic is reproduced here.

In the second extract Charles E. Sprague, another ardent advocate of reason vs. rule, deals with personification in much the same spirit.

A LESSON ON THE PRINCIPLES OF DOUBLE ENTRY [11]

Mr. Rule. For your guidance in debit and credit you must apply literally the following rule:

"Whoever or whatever owes you is Debtor,
Whoever or whatever you owe is Creditor."

Mr. Logic. That would certainly seem a very simple guidance indeed. Having always supposed there was nothing in Bookkeeping but to distinguish what I owed from what was owing, I treated it as a subject requiring no serious study, but when I came to try to separate debit and credit according to that view, I found myself befogged, and came to the conclusion that bookkeepers must attach some meaning to those two words differing from their ordinary acceptation.

Mr. Rule. You probably regarded one thing as being debtor to another thing instead of being debtor to you, and you being debtor to the other thing, which was the creditor. In that case you would be befogged.

Mr. Logic. I see the distinction, sir, and am quite encouraged with the prospect of having the difficulty so easily removed. I am quite anxious to try the rule under this new aspect.

Mr. Rule. I give you then the following transaction, and require the Journal entry. Bought Merchandise, for which I paid Cash $500.

Mr. Logic. I debit Cash because it owes me for so much property gone. I credit Merchandise because I owe it for increasing my property.

Mr. Rule. No, sir. You have reversed the rule. You must debit Merchandise because it owes you the value that is in it.

Mr. Logic. Excuse me, sir, for saying that I cannot see why I should consider Merchandise debtor because there is value in it, rather than credit it for increasing my property; but if you tell me that it is a law of your science to make things debtor because there is value in them, I submit and make note of it, not doubting that the reason why I do so will hereafter appear.

Mr. Rule. That is the law of the subject, sir.

Mr. Logic. I will note it, sir. (He therefore notes: "Things are debtor because of the value in them.") But how about the Cash?

Mr. Rule. The Cash is creditor because you owe it for producing that value. (Mr. Logic notes also "Things are creditors because of producing value.")

Mr. Rule. We abate $15 for damaged goods in John Brown's bill of 10th inst. Required the entry.

Mr. Logic. Do you sometimes make loss owe you?

Mr. Rule. Certainly. Profit & Loss is the title to give to losses and gains.

Mr. Logic. Then I suppose I may debit Profit & Loss, though it seems not to agree with my note above, as the value is not in it, although it seems to have gone or disappeared in it. It moreover appears to me that when I gain there must be value in it, therefore I must put gain and loss both as debit. It also seems to have something to do with Merchandise, but I cannot see how I can owe Merchandise for producing the loss.

Mr. Rule. You will be surprised when you are told how simple the entry is. You must credit John Brown for the $15 which you now owe him, and debit Merchandise for causing you to owe him.

Mr. Logic. You must permit me, sir, to remind you that I enter upon the subject totally ignorant of all matters of business, and consequently what may be a perfectly lucid explanation to most of your pupils may be the reverse to me. But on the other hand, I am myself a teacher of some years' practice, and have diligently and closely studied the art of teaching. I have always strictly refrained from putting any question to my pupil, the answer to which was not to be found by reference to some rule or principle I had previously taught him. The explanation that fails to satisfy and instruct me, I cannot possibly offer to instruct another; so you must indulge me while I point out to you what appears to me as inconsistent and strange in your interpretation of debit. I first note down as the reason why something owed "because of the value that is in it," now I debit Merchandise or Profit & Loss *because the value is not in it.* It is, therefore, evident that there must be more than one reason for things owing, or in other words, you make one thing owe you for one reason and another thing for an opposite reason. It strikes me that you must use the term debtor in an arbitrary way, and not, as your rule implies, for indebtedness in a literal sense. You say in your rule, "debit what owes you." Now as all things do not appear to owe me for the same reason, could you give me any further rule or principle that would help me to find what does owe me in your sense of the term? Either there must be some one reason which makes things owe me, or there must be several. If only one, the whole difficulty is easily cleared up by stating it. If there are many, they must all be ascertained before the term can be applied. For all you have stated to me so far, I see no better reason for Cash owing me when I receive it, than when I pay it.

Mr. Rule. I have shown you that Cash owes you for the value that is in it, and which you are to look to cash for.

Mr. Logic. Yes, but you have also shown me that Profit & Loss owes me for the value that is not in it, and which I am to look to Profit & Loss for, but consider it lost.

Mr. Rule. Still it may be considered to owe you, though it never pays.

Mr. Logic. That may be, but it brings me no nearer our uniform reason for owing, which can alone make your rule of any service to me. What makes things owe me, is the question I want to solve. I care not whether it has one reason or many. If several, my first business is to learn them all.

Mr. Rule. You will acquire them practically by repeating the application of the rule.

Mr. Logic. If the rule throw no light on one transaction, I cannot possibly suppose it to do better with another. If I am to understand that you expect me to get into the habit of considering certain things debtor or creditor, you still leave me the task of finding out what is the theory or principle by which I am guided, before I can pretend to teach, for teaching implies directing the mind to the principles or theory in opposition to learning or finding it out.

TRANSACTION ANALYSIS BY PERSONIFICATION [12]

One method of explaining all the relations of transactions to accounts was the allegorical, or personifying, plan. Let us suppose a merchant named STOCK, who desires to keep his books hereafter by double entry. He already has accounts with all the persons with whom he deals, and he employs Mr. BALANCE as his bookkeeper, and requests his aid and counsel as to the new method. The chief clerks in STOCK's employ are ordered to come to the office and told that they shall hereafter assume certain functions, or roles, in the drama of business, which we may thus detail in the playwright's manner:

DOUBLE ENTRY

A REALISTIC DRAMA

Scene: A Counting-house

DRAMATIS PERSONAE

Stock, a merchant.
Balance, his accountant.
Cash, keeper of the money-chest.
Merchandise, a salesman.
Wm. Receivable, protector of the portfolio.
Profit-and-Loss, the economical business-manager.
Expense, his subordinate, a spendthrift, but good-hearted.
Smith, Jones, Brown, Sundries, Wm. Payable, and others, friends and customers.

BALANCE finds that there are appropriate accounts in the old books for all the persons with whom STOCK has had dealings, but that Mr. STOCK has opened no account for himself. This omission must be remedied. If SMITH, JONES and others are his debtors, he must be their creditor. But at the same time let us distribute among the various clerks, according to the part assigned to each, the effects which STOCK has on hand:

> "Cash! unto thee is given thy master's purse:
> See that thou guard it truly. Merchandise!
> Thine be the task to watch the heaped-up wealth
> Brought from far lands by many a gallant ship:
> Let not the moth corrupt, nor thieves break through;
> Sell not below that price by wisdom fixed—
> The Plimsoll-mark of safely-floating trade.
> Bill-R.! to thee our documents I trust:
> Agreements, warrants, vouchers for our dues,
> (*Vide* the Colonel's lengthy disquisition,)
> Keep them in order just, and when matured,
> Like Shylock, thou shalt say, 'I'll have my bond.'
> Profit-and-Loss shall o'er you all preside,
> For e'en his losses lean to profit's side."
>
> (Exeunt omnes except BALANCE.)

BALANCE (soliloquizing): "Now my master's effects are all reduced to indebtedness, and I can record them by debitor and by creditor.

"SUNDRIES are debtors to STOCK; to wit:

"CASH, for amount of ready money;

"MERCHANDISE, for goods on hand, as per inventory;

"BILLS-RECEIVABLE, for written evidences of value to be received; and

"Messrs. SMITH, JONES, and others, for amounts of their several indebtedness.

"I will open accounts in my new ledger for each of these, and chronicle them each indebted to Mr. STOCK for the proper amount. Then, as he must be a creditor for the total amount, I register it to his credit.

"But hold; again he owes! but of these debts I have a list, and thence will I transcribe each creditor and the amount he claims; debit my Master, STOCK, for all he owes, without enumeration of details.

" 'STOCK debitor to SUNDRIES'; this will serve to wake the memory in after-days."

Now our hero's books are fairly opened. He is debtor to all he owes, and creditor by all that owe him—really or constructively. If his account were balanced it would show, theoretically, how much the world owes him. Then the transactions of business are brought upon the stage. If goods are sold, MERCHANDISE is credited; but who owes him? Either some customer is the debtor, or the head of some department of the business, to which he has delivered an equivalent value, is debtor in his stead. Thus we have the entries, "Cash Dr. to Mdse.," "Bills-Rec. Dr. to

Mdse.," or "Smith Dr. to Mdse." When value is parted with, the chief of the appropriate department is credited, and some one else is correspondingly debited—either a real debtor, or a make-believe one.

In the last scene, PROFIT-AND-LOSS makes an inspection of the entire establishment. BALANCE—with the ledger under his arm, and the journal in his pocket, ready to take notes—accompanies PROFIT-AND-LOSS. Visiting MERCHANDISE, it is found that the goods unsold (when carefully valued at purchasing prices) amounted to more than his account called for. MERCHANDISE is charged with this additional value, and PROFIT-AND-LOSS takes credit for it, as the representative and agent of STOCK. BALANCE assumes possession of the goods at the new valuation—temporarily relieving MERCHANDISE, who is therefore credited, and BALANCE is charged. CASH is found to have just the amount called for by the account; he is also given a momentary vacation; his keys are turned over also to BALANCE, who charges himself and discharges the faithful CASH from his responsibility. BILLS-RECEIVABLE is found to have one note which is overdue and protested: it is a hopeless case. He turns over to BALANCE the other notes ("Balance Dr. to Bills-Receivable"), but delivers this one to PROFIT-AND-LOSS ("Profit-and-Loss Dr. to Bills-Receivable"). EXPENSE has nothing to show for his indebtedness, except receipted bills. PROFIT-AND-LOSS, adjudging these to have been properly incurred, assumes the responsibility therefor, and, accordingly, relieves EXPENSE ("Profit-and-Loss Dr. to Expense"). Finally, all the personal debtors and creditors are transferred to the account of BALANCE, who stands in their place for the final adjustment. If any of the debtors, however, should be considered as insolvent, PROFIT-AND-LOSS must be charged, for he scrutinizes all sales on trust. Now, the two chief clerks, BALANCE and PROFIT-AND-LOSS, are the only ones holding direct relations with STOCK. PROFIT-AND-LOSS reports the course of business for the past term. He has to his credit a certain balance, which, he claims, has been realized in the increase of various departments. With thanks for his faithful services, STOCK commands the bookkeeper to transfer this net profit to his (STOCK'S) credit, because it was gained by PROFIT-AND-LOSS merely as his agent. This closes one more account, and leaves STOCK and BALANCE to settle it between them. BALANCE says: "My values, less claims to be settled therefrom, are hereby transferred to you; if your account is equalized, if your claim is satisfied, then all must have been correctly recorded." The test is made—STOCK finds that the supposed settlement satisfies his actual claim.

(Curtain.)

REFERENCES

1. From a monograph *Archivo Storico Lombardo, Giornale della Società Storica Lombarda* by Dr. Gerolamo Biscaro, Milan, 1913, quoted by P. Kats in "Double Entry in England before Hugh Oldcastle," *The Accountant* (London), January 16, 1926. Also see an article by B. Penndorf in *The Accounting Review,* September, 1930.

2. *Ancient Double Entry Bookkeeping* by John B. Geijsbeek (Denver, Colorado, 1914), wherein the original book is photographically reproduced and translated.

3. Quoted in *The History of the Worshipful Company of Drapers of London* by Rev. A. H. Johnson, Vol. II, p. 253.

4. Geijsbeek, *op. cit.,* p. 15. See also "Simon Stevin" by P. Kats in *Institute of Bookkeepers Journal* (London), September, 1927.

5. P. 9 of Dafforne's *Merchants Mirrour* bound in Gerard Malynes' *Lex Mercatoria,* London, 1636.

6. Bound with others in Malynes' *Lex Mercatoria,* 3d ed., London, 1686.

7. H. J. Eldridge, *The Evolution of the Science of Bookkeeping,* London, 1931, p. 34.

8. Thomas King, *An Exact Guide to Bookkeeping,* London, 1717.

9. William Weston, *The Complete Merchant's Clerk,* London, 1754.

10. John Mair, *Bookkeeping Methodiz'd,* Edinburgh, 8th ed., 1765.

11. From: *Paradoxes of Debit and Credit Demolished,* Thomas Jones (New York, 1859).

12. From *The Bookkeeper* (N. Y., Dec. 5, 1882) probably written by Charles E. Sprague, assistant editor.

V. THE COMPLETED STRUCTURE—PACIOLO

Introductory Note. In order to outline the procedure of double entry bookkeeping as it appeared after the system had been completely formulated, this chapter presents most of the text of the first printed work on bookkeeping. This was written by a Franciscan monk, Luca Paciolo, as a part of a larger book on mathematics, and was published at Venice, in the year 1494.

For present purposes the text follows the Geijsbeek translation. (*Ancient Double Entry Bookkeeping,* Denver, 1914.) In order to condense the material into its essentials, however, Paciolo's work has been edited by the omission of certain sections and here and there a few sentences. The original chapters have also been somewhat re-arranged as to sequence in order to bring closely together Paciolo's explanations of the basic procedure of double entry. Other important sections, which are, however, collateral and secondary to the main theme, are presented toward the end of the chapter. Marginal indications are given of Paciolo's chapter numbers to show where the sequence has been interrupted.

PACIOLO'S TEXT

(Ch. 1) This treatise will adopt the system used in Venice, for by means of this one can find his way in any other.

(Ch. 2) To begin with, the merchant must make his inventory [*inventario*] in this way: He must always put down on a sheet of paper or in a separate book whatever he has in this world, personal property or real estate, beginning with the things that are most valuable and most likely to be lost, such as cash, jewels, silver, etc. Then all the other things must be put down one after another.

(Ch. 3) As an example for you, I have written down systematically this inventory of all my property, personal and real, what is owed to me [*debiti*] and what is owed by me [*crediti*]:

> First item: I find myself possessed in cash, in gold and coin of so many ducats, of which so many are Venetian, and so many gold Hungarian; of so many large florins made up of Papal, Siennese, Florentine, etc.
>
> * * * * * * * *
>
> Fourteenth item: I have so many debtors [*debitori*]: one is so-and-so, who owes me [*me dee dare*—shall give me] so many ducats, and so on, putting down all the names and how much they owe you [*te debbono dare*—shall have to give you]. In total I have so much ducats to collect, you will say, of good money, if the money is due from good people, otherwise you will say of bad money.

(Ch. 5) Immediately after the Inventory you need three books to make the work proper and easy. One is called Memorandum (Ch. 6) [*Memoriale*], the second Journal [*Giornale*], and the third Ledger [*Quaderno*]. The memorandum book is a book in which the merchant shall put down all his transactions, small or big, as they take place, day by day, hour by hour. This book is kept on account of volume of business, and in it entries should be made in the absence of the owner by his servants, for a big merchant never keeps his assistants idle. They must enter every transaction as well as they can in this memorandum book, naming simply the money and weights which they know; they should note the various kinds of money that they may collect or take in or that they may give in exchange. As far as this book is concerned, it is not as important to transfer to standards the various kinds of coin handled as it is with the journal and ledger.

(Ch. 7) These memorandum books should be taken and shown to a certain mercantile officer such as the Consuls in the City of Perosa employ, and to him you should state that those are the books in which you intend to write down all your transactions, and also state in what kind of money the transactions therein should be entered. The clerk should mention all this in the records of the said officer and shall write down on the first page of your books, in his own handwriting, the name of the said officer, and will attest to the truth of everything and shall attach the seal of that office to make the books authentic for any case in court.

The second common mercantile book is called the Journal. There are two expressions used in the said Journal each of which has a meaning of its own; the one is called "per," the other "a." "Per" indicates the debtor and "a" the creditor. At the beginning of each entry, we always provide "per" because the debtor must be given first, and immediately afterward the creditor, the one separated from the other by two little slanting parallels, thus //. (Ch. 11)

EXAMPLE OF MAKING AN ENTRY IN THE JOURNAL

Per Cash // A—Capital of myself so and so. In cash I have at present, in gold and coin, silver and copper of different coinage as it appears in the first sheet of the inventory in cash. All this in Venetian money is worth: L——, S——, G——, P——, (Ch. 12)

Per Silver // A ditto—by which capital is understood —for several kinds of silver which at present I possess: L——, S——, G——, P——,

In this way you can continue to enter all the other items as the Inventory shows. Indicate only one kind of money to which you reduce the estimated values. As you transfer an entry into the Journal from the memorandum book, you shall draw a single diagonal line through it; this will show that this item has been entered in the Journal.

After you have made all your entries in the Journal in an orderly way, you must transfer them to the third book called Ledger [*Quaderno Grande,* i.e., big book]. On the first page you shall enter cash as debtor [*debitrici*]. It is customary to reserve the whole of the first page to cash, because the cash entries are more numerous than all others. (Ch. 13)

For each one of all the entries that you have in the Journal you will have to make two in the Ledger. That is one in the debit [*in dare*] and one in the credit [*in havere*]. The debitor entry must be at the left, the creditor one at the right; and in the debitor entry you must indicate the number of the page of the respective creditor. In this way all the entries of the Ledger are chained together and you must never make a credit entry without making the same entry (Ch. 14) with its respective amount in the debit. Upon this depends the obtaining of a trial balance [*bilancio*] of the Ledger.

Since for one entry of the Journal you make two in the Ledger, you shall draw two diagonal lines as you make the transfer. At the side, in the marginal part, you shall write down two numbers before the beginning of the entry, the one under the other. The upper indicates at what page of the Ledger the debit entry is and the lower indicates the page of the Ledger where the credit is. You always try to put the said creditor immediately after its debtor on the same line,* or on the line immediately following without entering anything else in between, for whenever there is a debit item there must exist at the same time a credit item. For this reason, get the one as near as possible to the other.

(Ch. 15) After having told you these things for your instruction, we write now the first entry of the cash in the debit column, and then the first entry of the capital in the credit column, in the Ledger. Thus, you shall put it this way:

Jesus............ MCCCCLXXXXIII

Cash is debtor [*dee dare*—shall give] on November 8, "per" capital. On this day I have in moneys of different kinds, gold and other coins; page 2: L——, S——, G——, P——,

After you have made the entry in this way, you shall cancel in the Journal as I have explained to you. Then in the credit side you write down this way:

Jesus............ MCCCCLXXXXIII

Capital of myself, so and so, is creditor [*dee havere*—shall have] on November 8, "per" cash. On this day I have in cash, in gold and other kinds of money; page 1; L——, S——, G——, P——,

If there are other items to be entered in the same account, it will be enough to say, on ditto, "per" such and such, as has just been shown. Then you will cancel, by drawing a line, the credit entry in the Journal. In the margin, opposite the entry, you shall write down the two numbers of the pages where the debit and credit entries are.

(Ch. 17) I shall not give you any more rules for the other items, for each of which you shall make entries in the Journal and

* Referring to the form of the journal entry.

Ledger, carefully writing down everything and checking off, without forgetting anything, because the merchant must have a much better understanding of things than a butcher.

(Ch. 22) Besides the entries so far mentioned you shall open these accounts in your books: that is, mercantile expenses, ordinary household expenses, extraordinary expenses, and account for what is cashed in [*entrata*] and what is paid out [*uscita*]; one for profits and loss [*pro e danno*] which accounts are very necessary at any time so that the merchant can always know what is his capital and at the end when he figures up the closing [*saldo*] how his business is going.

The account named "small business expenses" is kept because we cannot enter every little thing in the account of the merchandise that you sell or buy. We cannot do without the account of ordinary household expenses. By these expenses we mean expenses for grains, wine, wood, oil, salt, meat, shoes, hats, stockings, clothes, tips, expenses for tailors, barbers, bakers, cleaners, etc., kitchen utensils, vases, glasses, casks, etc. Many keep different accounts for all these different things so that they can see at a glance how each account stands, and you may do so and open all these different accounts, and any accounts that you like, but I am talking to you about what the merchant cannot do without. For small accounts, as meat, fish, boat fares, etc., you shall set aside in a little bag one or two ducats and make small payments out of this amount. It will be impossible to keep an account of all these small things. If you wish you can include in the household expenses the extraordinary expenses, as those that you make for amusements or that you lose in some game, or for things or money that you might lose, or that might be stolen or lost in a wreck or through fire, etc., for all are classified as extraordinary expenses. If you want to keep a separate account for them, you may do so, as many do, in order to know at the end of the year how much you have expended for extraordinary expenses, under which title you should include also gifts and presents that you might make to anyone for any reason.

(Ch. 27) After the other accounts there must follow one which is named variously according to different localities, Favor and Damage, Profit and Damage, or Increase and Deficit. Into this other accounts in the Ledger have their remainders. You should not put these entries in the Journal, but only in the Ledger, as they originate from overs or shorts in the debits and credits, and not from actual transactions. If you had sustained a loss in a special line of merchandise and if this account in your ledger would show less in the credit than the debit, then you will add the difference to the credit so as make it balance, and you shall enter as follows:

> Credit, per Profit and Loss, so much, which I enter here in order to balance on account of loss sustained—and so on.

Then you go to the Profit and Loss account and in the debit column you shall enter as follows:

> Profit and Loss debit, on this day, to such and such loss sustained, so much,—which has been entered in the credit of said merchandise account in order to balance it.

If the account of this special merchandise would show a profit instead of loss—that is, more in the credit than in the debit—then you will proceed in the opposite way.

This account (Profit and Loss) must then be transferred for its closing into the capital account, which is always the last in all the ledgers and is consequently the receptacle of all other accounts.

(Ch. 32) After all we have said you must know now how to carry forward the accounts from one Ledger to another if you want to have a new Ledger for the reason that the old one is all filled up or because another year begins, as is customary in the best known places, especially at Milan where the big merchants renew every year their Ledgers.

This operation, together with the operations of which we will speak, is called the balancing [*bilancio*] of the Ledger, and if you want to do this well you shall do it with great diligence and order. That is, first you shall get a helper as you could hardly do it alone. You give him the Journal for greater precaution and you shall keep the Ledger. Then you tell him, beginning with the first entry in the Journal, to call the numbers of the pages of your Ledger where that entry has been made, first in debit then in credit. Accordingly, in turn you shall obey him and shall always find the page in the Ledger that he calls and you shall ask him what kind of an entry it is, that is, for what and for whom, and you shall look at the pages to which he refers to see if you can find that item and that account. If the amount is the same, call it out. If you find it there the same as in the Journal, check it or dot it so that you can readily see it. You ask your helper to make a similar mark or check in the Journal at the same entry. Care must be taken that no entry will be dotted either by you without him, or by him without you, as great mistakes might be made otherwise, for once the entry is dotted it means it is correct.

After you have proceeded in this way through all the accounts of the Ledger and Journal and found that the two books correspond in debit and credit, it will mean that all the accounts are correct and the entries entered correctly.

(Ch. 34)

Then you will proceed with all the accounts of the Cross [i.e., the old] Ledger which you want to transfer to Ledger A [the new one]: cash account, capital account, merchandise, personal property, real property, debtors, creditors, public officers, brokers, public weighmen, etc. But as to those accounts which you should not care to transfer to Ledger A, as, for example, your own personal accounts of which you are not obliged to give an account to another, as, for instance, small mercantile expenses, household expenses, income and expenses and all extraordinary expenses, etc.,—all these accounts should be closed in the Cross Ledger into the profit and loss account. You shall enter them in the debit column as it is rare that these expense accounts show anything in the credit side. As I often have told you, add the difference to the column, either debit or credit, which shows a smaller total, saying: Per profit and loss in this account, see page—, etc. By doing so you have closed all these different accounts in the profit and loss account through which then, by adding all the debit and all the credit entries, you will be able to know what is your gain or loss, for with this balance all entries are equalized; the things that had to be deducted were deducted and the things which had to be added were added proportionately in their respective places. If this account shows more in the debit than in the credit, that means that you have lost that much in your business since you began. If the credit is more than the debit, that means that in the same period of time you have gained.

After you know by the closing of this account what your profit and loss is, then you shall close this account into the capital account in which, at the beginning of your management of your business, you entered the inventory of your worldly goods. You shall close the account in this way: If the losses are in excess—from which state of affairs may God keep every one who really lives as a good Christian—then you add to the credit in the usual manner. Then you shall cancel the account with a diagonal line in the debit and credit, and put in the total amount of all the debit entries as well as of the credit entries, which should be equal. And then in the capital account, you shall write in the debit column: Capital debit on such and such a day, per profit and loss account on account of losses as marked down in the credit column of said account in order to close. If instead there should be a profit, which will happen when the profit and loss account would show more in the credit than in the debit, then you should add the difference to the debit side to make the equalization, referring to the capital account and respective page. You should credit the same amount to the capital account, making the entry on the credit side where all the other goods of yours have been entered, personal or real. Therefore, from the capital account, which always must be the last account in the entire Ledger, you may always learn what your fortune is, by adding together all the debits and all the credits, which you have transferred in Ledger A.

Then this capital account should be closed and carried forward with the other accounts to Ledger A either in total or entry by entry. You can do either way, but it is customary to transfer only the total amount, so that the entire value of your inventory is shown at a glance.

In order that it may be clearer that the books were correct before the said closing, you shall summarize on a sheet of paper all the debit totals that appear in the Cross Ledger and place them at the left, then you shall write down all the credit totals at the right. Of all these debit totals you make one sum total which is called the Grand Total, and likewise you shall make a sum total of all the credit totals, which is also called Grand Total. Now if these two grand totals are equal, then you shall conclude that your Ledger was very well kept and closed. But if one of the grand totals is bigger than the other, that would indicate a mistake in your Ledger, which mistake you will have to look for diligently with the industry and intelligence God gave you and with the help of what you have learned. Therefore, take good care and make all efforts to be a good bookkeeper, such as I have shown you fully in this sublime work how to become one. And remember to pray God for me so that to His praise and glory I may always go on doing good.

[Branch Store]

(Ch. 23)

If you should have a store outside your house (branch store) and not in the same building with your house, but which you have fully equipped, then for the sake of order you should keep the accounts in this way: You should charge it in your books with all the different things that you put into it, day by day, and should credit all the different merchandise that you put in it also each one by itself, and you must imagine that this store is just like a person who should be your debtor for all the things that you may give it or spend for it for any reason. And so on the contrary you shall credit it with all that you take out of it and receive from it as if it were a debtor who would pay you gradually. Thus at any time that you so desire, you may see how the store is running. There are many who in their books charge everything to the manager of the store. This however can not be properly done without his knowing it, nor put him as a creditor under certain conditions without his consent.

Accounts are nothing else than the expression in writing of the arrangement of his affairs, which the merchant keeps in his mind, and if he follow this system always he will know all about his business and will know exactly whether his business goes well or not. Therefore, the proverb: If you are in business and do not know all about it, your money will go like flies—that is, you will lose it.

[Banking transactions]

(Ch. 24)

If you put money in the bank, then you shall charge the bank or the owners or partners of the bank and shall credit your cash. And you will have the banker give you some kind of a written record for your surety. In case you should withdraw money, the banker shall have you write a receipt. It is true that at times this kind of receipt is not given because the books of the bank are always public and authentic; but it is better to require this writing, because as I have told you things can't be too clear for the merchant. When you should withdraw money from a bank either to pay somebody else as part payment or payment in full, or to make a remittance to parties in other countries, you shall do in this case just the opposite of what we just said—that is, if you withdraw money you shall charge your cash and credit the bank or owners of the bank for the amount withdrawn. If you give an order on the bank for somebody else, you shall charge this party and credit the bank for that much, stating the reasons.

If on the contrary you are the banker you have to do in the opposite way; when you pay you charge the man [*fa debitori*] to whom you pay and credit cash. If one of your creditors, without withdrawing money, should issue a draft to somebody else, you shall say in the Journal as follows:

> Per that special creditor of yours // A the man to whom the money was assigned.

In this way you just make the transfer from one creditor to another and you still remain as debtor and act as a go-between, as witness or agent of the two parties.

[Books when traveling]

(Ch. 26) Trips are made usually in two ways, either personally or through somebody else; therefore, two are the ways to keep their accounts and the book always ought to be in duplicate whether the trip is made by you personally or it is in charge of somebody else. One Ledger is kept at home and the other one is taken along and kept on the trip. If you conduct the trip yourself, for the sake of order and system, you must take a new inventory also a small Ledger and small Journal and follow the instructions above given. If you buy or sell or exchange, you must charge and credit according to the facts, persons, goods, traveling capital, traveling profit and loss, etc. If, however, you entrust the trip to some other party, then you should charge this party with all the goods that you entrust with him, and you should keep an account with him as if he were one of your customers, for all goods and moneys, keeping separate accounts, and he on his part will set up a little Ledger in which he makes you creditor for everything. When he comes back he will balance with you.

[Brokerage]

(Ch. 18) In doing business with the office of the *Messetaria* (exchange), you shall keep the account in this way: When you buy any merchandise through brokers, you shall credit the said office of the *Messetaria* with the 2% or 3% or 4% of the whole amount, and shall charge it to the specific merchandise, for you are thus paying for it, etc. The brokers make a report of the transaction, how and what for and with whom made, in order to have things clear in case any questions should arise, which may happen. If any question should arise and the parties wish to settle it, they would go and examine the records of the transaction made by the broker, to which records, according to the public decrees, as full faith is given as to a public notarial document, and according to these records very often the office of the Consuls of the merchants issues its judgment.

[Barter]

(Ch. 20) I say, therefore, that no matter how you make a record of the trade in your books, you shall first enter it in the memorandum book, stating in detail all about it, its terms and conditions and whether it was made through a broker. After you have so described it, you then at the end shall put a money value on it; and you shall put down such price in accordance with the current value which the things that you have traded have; reckoning in any kind of money in the memorandum book. Afterwards the bookkeeper, when he transfers the entry to the Journal and Ledger, will reduce that money to the standard money that you have adopted. This is done because, without entering the value of the things that you have traded, you could not, from your books and accounts, learn, except with great difficulty, what your profit or loss is. The merchandise must always be reduced to actual money value in order to take care of it (in the books).

[Partnership]

(Ch. 21) You should credit the partners for the amount which each of them contributes, and you shall debit cash with the same if you keep the account with your own. But it is better for the business if you keep this cash account separate from your private one when you are the one at the head of the business, in which case you should have a separate set of books in the same order and way we have shown previously. However, you might keep all these accounts in your own personal books opening new accounts which, as we have said, are referred to as well-known accounts because they are kept separate from all the others.

(Ch. 29) It is always good to close the books each year, especially if you are in partnership with others. The proverb says: Frequent accounting makes for long friendship.

[Abstract of Account]

(Ch. 30) The following is the way you have to proceed in adjusting your own business with the business of your employer. But if you should act for others as an agent or commissioner, then you will make out a statement for your employer just as it appears in the Ledger, crediting yourself from time to time with your commission according to your agreements. Then at the end you shall charge yourself with the net remainder, or you shall credit yourself if you had to put in any money of your own. Your employer will then go through this statement, compare it with his own book, and if he finds it correct he will like you better and trust you more. For this reason, of all the things that he gave or sent you, you should with your own handwriting keep an orderly account when you receive them.

[Summary]

(Ch. 36) All creditors [*creditori*] must appear in the Ledger on the right hand side, all the debitors [*debitori*] at the left.

All entries made in the ledger have to be double entries [*doppie*]—that is, if you make one creditor, you must make some one debtor.

Each debit and credit entry must contain three things, namely: the day, the amount, and the reason for the entry.

The last name in the entry of the debit (in the Ledger) must be the first name in the entry of the credit.

On the same day that you make the debit entry, you should make the credit entry.

By a trial balance [*bilancio*] of the Ledger we mean a sheet of paper folded lengthwise in the middle, on which we write down all the creditors of the Ledger at the right side and the debtors at the left side. We see whether the total of the debits is equal to that of the credits, and if so, the Ledger is in order.

The trial balance of the Ledger should be equal—that is, the total of the credits [*credito*]—I do not say creditors [*creditori*]—should be equal to the total debits—I do not say debtors.

The cash account should always be a debtor or equal.

You must not and cannot make anyone debtor in your book without permission or consent of the person that has to appear as debtor; if you should, that account would be considered false.

The values in the Ledger must be reckoned in one kind of money.

Of all the cash that you might have, if it is your own, you shall make yourself creditor and make cash debitor.

Of all the real property that you might own, as houses, lands, stores, you make cash debitor and estimate their value at your discretion in cash and make creditor yourself or your personal account. Then you make debitor an account of that special property by giving the value, as I have said above, and make yourself creditor.

If you should buy merchandise or anything else for cash, you should make a debitor of that special merchandise or thing and like creditor cash.

If you should buy merchandise or anything else partly for cash and partly on time, you shall make that special merchandise debitor and make a creditor of the party from whom you bought it on time. After this you will have to make another entry—that is, make a debitor of the party from whom you bought it for the amount of the cash that you have given him and make creditor cash or the bank which might have paid that much for you.

If you should sell merchandise or anything else, you should proceed as above with the exception that you should proceed in the opposite way.

If you should loan cash to some of your friends, you shall charge the friend to whom you have given it and credit cash.

If you should borrow cash from some friend, you will have to debit cash and credit your friend.

If you have received 8 or 10 or 20 ducats in order to insure a ship or a galley, or anything else, you should credit the account "ship insurance," and shall charge cash account.

If anybody should send you any goods with instructions to sell them or exchange them on commission, I say that you have to charge in the Ledger that special merchandise belonging to so and so with the freight, or duty, or for storage, and credit the cash account.

NOTE ON THE SPELLING OF PACIOLO'S NAME

In some places the name of the author of the first printed textbook on bookkeeping is spelled with a final "i," in others, "o." Those who use *Pacioli* are: Geijsbeek, Crivelli, Murray (in English), Kheil, Sieveking, Jäger, Penndorf (in German); those who use *Paciolo* are: Row-Fogo, Woolf, Kats, Hatfield (in English), DuPont (in French), Volmer, De-Waal (in Dutch), Augspurg, Hügli, Drapala, Gomberg (in German), Bariola, Gitti, Brandaglia, Vianello, Luchini, Besta (in Italian). On the mural tablet erected in 1878 at San Sepolcro, Italy, to Paciolo's memory the final letter is "i."

After interest in Paciolo's work had been awakened by E. Lucchini in 1869, the book was published in German by Professor Ernst Ludwig Jäger (Stuttgart, 1876); in modern Italian by Professor Vincenzo Gitti (Torino, 1878); in Russian by Waldenberg (St. Petersburg, 1893); in Bohemian by Professor Karl Peter Kheil (Prag., 1896); in Dutch by Professor J. G. Ch. Volmer (Rotterdam, 1896); in English by J. B. Geijsbeek (Denver, 1914), and by Pietro Crivelli (London, 1924); and in German by Professor Balduin Penndorf (Leipzig, 1933).

VI. ANCIENT AND MODERN BOOK-KEEPING COMPARED

THE careful reader of Paciolo's text is likely to be amazed to note how little basic change there has been in bookkeeping, and to be more than ever convinced that the underlying principles of double entry are as simple and as fundamental as addition and subtraction, and therefore not at all subject to change. The accountant is apt to feel not a little elated in the thought that the foundation of what later became accountancy was already firmly laid at a time when some of the basic processes of arithmetic were still chaotic.

On the other hand, one should not turn to Paciolo's book with the expectation of finding modern practices completely foreshadowed. Nineteenth and twentieth century conditions have of course brought about many modifications of original methodology and have, in some cases, forced the introduction of practices which were of necessity entirely foreign to fifteenth-century conditions. This is what one would naturally expect; yet, on the whole, bookkeeping has changed less than society has—not that bookkeeping has been a laggard, but that it was closer at that early date to its ultimate condition, and thus has had less distance to traverse to the present. It is, therefore, quite as instructive to consider what there was in Paciolo that is still modern as to note what has been added since his day.

From the very beginning (say, somewhat before the middle of the fifteenth century) certain basic peculiarities of method and form have been associated with bookkeeping. These fundamental characteristics still persist, and, being peculiar to double-entry bookkeeping, they form the principal means of setting it apart from other fact-manipulating systems. Ever since personal account-keeping was expanded to suit the impersonal aspects of mercantile affairs, bookkeeping has possessed a characteristic *theory,* a characteristic *form,* and a characteristic *technology.*

But underlying theory must be read, so to speak, between the lines of the old book, for Paciolo takes up no space in philosophizing. His purpose was practical: "To give sufficient rules to enable them to keep all their accounts and books in an orderly manner" (p. 1).* He was describing the manner in which records were kept by the method employed in Venice.

On the surface the bookkeeping described seems to hinge upon the duality of the entries. "Thus for each entry in the Journal you will write two in the Ledger," he says (p. 33). "Of this entry, as we have said, and of any entry in the Journal, a duplicate must always be placed in the Ledger twice, that is, first to debit and the other to credit——." (p. 42). Or it seems to rest upon the opposition of debit and credit. "The debitor's entry is placed on the left side and that of the creditor on the right" (of the ledger). (p. 32).

But this is not theory; this is not the essence of double entry; it is simply methodology. The double posting and opposition of debit and credit are merely incidental to a test of mechanical accuracy. They produce an equilibrium of amounts, it is true, but the true virtue of bookkeeping does not consist in this weak insurance against errors. Its real essence lies far deeper.

Beneath the surface of the methodology which fills the little book is the unquestionable recognition of the fact that every transaction has a dual aspect, just as a coin has "heads and tails." This is much more fundamental than the mere recording of facts "in double" in order to get an equality of totals as a test of accuracy. Indeed, this is the essence of a theory of transaction analysis which pervaded (unexplained) all the fifteenth-century practices and is still the most basic concept of bookkeeping. The mere search for means of increasing mechanical accuracy could hardly have produced impersonal accounts and nominal accounts in that day when few records beyond personal accounts were in existence. It is unlikely that a mere desire for standards of accuracy would at that time have been sufficient to prompt the devising of such an artificial thing as a mercantile-expense account. But this could easily result when the

* This and subsequent page references are to the Crivelli translation (Harper Bros., New York, 1924) from which the quotations are taken.

interest of traders in accounts brought them to see that all transactions presented two aspects.

It is very probable, as has been explained in a previous chapter, that the application of personal-account methods to trading affairs brought into prominence the fact that the proprietor was a frequently recurring factor in the transactions; that he owed one person and was owed by another; that certain transactions brought him gains and others brought losses or constituted merely equivalent exchanges at such advantages as the future should determine. This consciousness of the proprietor and of proprietorship is much more fundamental than equality of debit and credit. As has been suggested, a well-worked-out statistical methodology could conceivably sort all the necessary financial elements into properly classified records without the intervention of "debit and credit" at all. But no procedure which did not make use of the proprietorship concept can be conceived as being capable of bringing all the financial elements of trade into the record.

Paciolo does not theorize about proprietorship; but throughout he shows a clear consciousness of that element; it underlies every mention of "capital," "profit and loss," "mercantile expenses," and every intimation of their relations. Here one should note the following quotations: "Besides all the entries* spoken of, you will also have all these entries* in all your books; viz., mercantile expenses, ordinary and extraordinary; household expenses, one for each for what is cashed in and out; and one for profit and loss, which entries* are very necessary in any mercantile body so that the merchant will always be able to show his capital, and, at the closing of his business, how it is progressing." (p. 64). "After every other account, an account called Profit and Loss will follow, into which all other accounts must be adjusted. . . . This account must finally be closed and transferred to capital, which is always the last account of all in the Ledgers, and consequently is the receptacle of all other accounts, as you will understand." (p. 82). Here the relation of nominal accounts to the capital account, as well as the necessity for expense accounts, is clearly indicated.

* Geijsbeek translates the word as, "accounts."

The treatment of the nominal and the capital accounts is so consistent that it is obvious that, although he did not dwell upon theoretical explanations, Paciolo had a very clear concept of their relation. His exposition raises the feeling in the reader that the merchants who kept accounts as he described must have rested their transaction analysis primarily upon a consciousness of the dual aspect always present in every occurrence.

This is the theory which underlies fifteenth-century double entry and is still just as fundamental as ever. The characteristic form attached to double-entry bookkeeping from the beginning is another peculiarity which has undergone no basic change with the centuries.

In its operation, bookkeeping is essentially a classifying mechanism, but it is more, because simple classification (a sorting into pigeon-holes) does not go far enough. Simple classification is fully accomplished when segregation is complete; that is, classification has served its purpose by bringing like things together. But the mere segregation of like quantities is not sufficient for bookkeeping; both "likes and opposites" must be brought into the classes (accounts) to fulfill the requirements of bookkeeping. Classification looks toward class totals; bookkeeping requires class balances. In bookkeeping every class (account) may receive an increasing element or a decreasing element; in ordinary statistical sorting there are no decreasing elements.

This peculiarity of the data of business, this fluctuating, up-and-down characteristic of a "class," makes a bi-lateral form in the basic record practically inevitable, one side to group together like elements, the other to group together related, but opposite, elements; and yet the item of primary importance is always the balance. In working thus for balances, subtraction comes to be indicated by contra-position, that is, items placed in such a position are thought of as having an "oppositeness" which leads to subtraction. Thus a matter of mere "form," or arbitrary arrangement, comes to have an implied or understood meaning, just as the figures 2 and 3 come to have an imputed meaning when one is written above the other ($\frac{2}{3}$) with a line between. This fraction is a conventionality, an abbreviation, the meaning of which is learned early and never forgotten; it is a part of everyone's mental equipment. But the bookkeeping technicality of form, this "subtraction by opposition," is not often learned with the multiplication tables; in fact, in many minds it is quite vague even after some work in accounting at college. Yet this is still a most characteristic bit of bookkeeping form as it has been from the very beginning.

In Paciolo's summary of rules for the "keeping of a merchant's book," the first item emphasizes this bi-lateral characteristic. "All the creditors must be placed in the book at the right-hand side, and the debtors at the left-hand side." (p. 107). And throughout the text he is most particular to get the postings made correctly to left and right in the ledger.

The clearness with which this "subtraction-by-opposition" technicality was held in mind in the fifteenth century is best illustrated in Paciolo's statement about correcting errors. "And so to take out the entry you shall carry on in this manner; viz., when, for example, you have placed the entry in the debit, and it should have gone to the credit, then to take it out you shall make another entry opposite to this one in the credit for the same amount,—as soon as you have posted it per contra it is just the same as if it had never been placed in the debit. You will then place it in the said credit as it should have been placed, and it will be right." (p. 88). The same thought is made plain also wherever the closing of nominal accounts or the transferring of balances to new ledgers is discussed.

The trial balance as a test of equilibrium has been a part of the technology of double entry from the beginning; its description varies little after more than four hundred years. "You shall summarize on a sheet of paper all the debit items of the Ledger and place them on the left hand side, and summarize all the credit items and place them on the right—now if the two sums are equal you will infer that your Ledger has been well kept and closed. . . ." (p. 100).

The same careful noting of posting references in the books such as we adopt and the same calling back of postings to find mistakes are present in Paciolo's instructions; and, what is even more significant, the sequence of bookkeeping operations was the same then as now: viz., (1) an opening entry from an inventory; (2) an original record of transactions (in a memorandum book at first, now in various documents); (3) an analysis and entry of the debit and credit elements (formerly in the journal by individual transactions, now in many specialized, columnar books of original entry); (4) a posting into a classified record (whether in ledgers with bilateral accounts only, or, as in modern days, in columnar ledgers with their sub-columns and colored inks); (5) a test of accuracy (to the early trial balance have been added controlling accounts); (6) a closing of nominal accounts through profit and loss to capital (whether in the case of the simple proprietorships so typical of the old days, or the complex corporations of the present).

Although the essential steps in bookkeeping have changed little, many details have been modified under the urge for efficiency and greater accuracy. This, it would seem, explains the substitution of documents for memorandum book, the subdivision of the journal into a number of separate posting media, as well as total posting, controlling accounts and all other similar surface changes.

The elements which may be called additions to, rather than modifications of, bookkeeping can not be explained, however, merely on the basis of a desire to increase efficiency and accuracy. An increasing refinement of the classification—an increase in the variety of accounts—has appeared, especially in the area covered by expense accounts. The closing process has become a definitely periodical matter, and the old "balance account" has been replaced by separate financial statements constructed upon information supplied by the trial balance and the inventories. These are the principal new elements in bookkeeping. They arise, in all probability, from the modern need for administrative data—that is, facts by which to judge operations which can no longer be personally supervised. The large increase in the number of accounts reflects the modern desire for more specific data and for the resulting increase in illuminating and detailed knowledge as to what has occurred; the strict periodicity of the present record makes the classified data still more comparable and thus more informative regarding changes; the appearance of carefully constructed tabular statements of bookkeeping data indicates still more definitely the modern reliance upon "figure" information in place of personal observation and oral reports. In a word, modern bookkeeping tends to approach accounting; perhaps some day the distinction may no longer be necessary. There need then be, on the one hand, only a quasi-statistical procedure for dealing with certain kinds of facts and, on the other, a skilled manipulation and a professional criticism of data thus analyzed.

Lest the impression might be given from this discussion that Paciolo's description of bookkeeping accords with modern practices only in the basic peculiarities, brief mention is made here of some other details which have a modern ring.

In speaking of the opening inventory: "he must first of all write on a sheet of paper all that he has in this world—and always begin with the things that are more valuable and easier to lose." (p. 4). This sounds much like "the most liquid first," a rule frequently followed in modern financial statements. "Have also deposited with the Office of Loans, or elsewhere, so many ducats in Venice." (p. 8). This suggests bank deposits. Entries are also outlined for the use of cheques in transferring accounts and of drafts for remittances to distant cities. (p. 74).

"Summing up the debtors, I must receive so many ducats of good money, if from reliable persons; if others, you will call their money bad." (p. 9). Here are bad debts. Paciolo, however, does not reach the modern financial device of a reserve for uncollectible accounts. But he does have a pretty fair system of petty cash. A bag of one or two ducats is charged to expense and set aside "for small payments because it would not be possible to keep account of these things one by one. . . . (p. 66). He recommends separate accounting for a shop "outside of your house," that is, at a distance and in charge of a deputy, because (p. 68) "he who does business without knowing all about it sees his money turn into flies"—and take wing, no doubt. He would charge the shop with the fixtures given it as well as the salable goods, and he would require a proper inventory by him who keeps the shop—in a word, branch-house bookkeeping. Much the same advice is given to him who travels for the purpose of trade—but here Paciolo would go so far as to have a small journal and ledger with accounts for traveling capital, travel expenses, travel profit and loss, etc. (p. 79).

The preceding paragraphs have dealt with those principles and practices of the fifteenth century which have carried down to the present time. Now attention is directed to some aspects of modern accounting which are not reflected in Paciolo's work. Certain practices have carried forward for more than four centuries; what, then, have these four centuries added?

As one thinks back over the hundred or more pages of this reprint of Paciolo's work, the modern note most lacking could probably be concisely covered by the one word "theory." Bookkeeping at that time was essentially a recording procedure and there was no necessity for labored explanation of why one does thus and so, or for philosophic argument concerning refinements of classification.

Bookkeeping as such has not changed a great deal. We have already seen what has been retained; to this little of recording technique has been added, and little has been dropped from it. The form of the ledger account (as will be shown presently) is changed only in the direction of simplification; the ledger now is much more abbreviated in its record—a tabulation of figures with posting references, in place of a rather complete copy in the accounts of the several transactions concerned. The form of the journal entry is changed only in the direction of further abbreviation—technical phrases like "per" and "a" are replaced by a technology of position which gives significance to the mere indention in the writing of the certain items or to the location of figures in columns. To these changes there have been added: the subdivision of the books of original entry; the introduction of loose-leaf practices; and the principle of total posting. Otherwise double-entry bookkeeping is much as it has been for centuries.

But time has not left the recording functions of business unaltered even though the technique of recording is little changed. As business has grown in size and complexity, its records have taken on added importance. Simple records, for so long entirely adequate to all managerial uses, are no longer satisfactory, and lately, within the last one hundred years or perhaps even a shorter period, important refinements have been added—refinements not so much of method as of theory.

It will be noted in reading Paciolo that his practice makes no provision for financial statements. The reason for this omission is not far to seek: proprietors were in personal contact with their affairs and the occasional computation of a profit-and-loss account in the ledger was ample for their needs. This means that a modern importance was not attached to "periodical closing" or to the careful apportionment of costs and income as between successive comparable periods. When these things began to receive attention, "theory" followed as a matter of course. Out of financial statements emerged the theory of organized accounting data—that is, making a sequence of items a thing of significance and a grouping of like elements or a contrasting of opposites a matter of consequence. Out of "periodicity" grew those refinements of apportionment which produce deferred charges, accruals and the like, and all the modern problems of burden distribution as well.

Moderns have produced the business corporation whose far-flung ownership and limited liability place burdens upon accounting quite outside the ancients' vision. To give only one example, the objections to dividends out of capital are of recent origin, and because of these objections much added importance is now attached to properly determined periodic profits. This is a source for much of modern accounting theorizing.

Business is now regarded as a continuous process rather than as a group of disjointed transactions. This is expressed by the development of the terms "earnings" and "income" in contrast with "profits." No such abstractions were thought of until recent times. Management is anxious to associate with earnings the cost of producing those specific returns. Consequently cost accounting is used extensively and due recognition is given to depreciation as a cost. The ancients did neither. In fact, fixed assets themselves played very little part in the old books, and wages were of minor importance. Today wages and salaries count heavily in all computations of cost and expense; and the breakdown of expense into sub-classes far outdoes anything thought of in the earlier period.

Some of Paciolo's comments about expense follow:

"If you wish to keep separate accounts for each item of expense, it would be too long and not worth the expense, for *'De minimis non curat Praetor'* *—therefore you open this account called Mercantile Expenses Account, which is always used in debit. . . ." (p.

* "The magistrate does not busy himself with unimportant matters."

64). "We cannot do without recording the ordinary household expenses. By this is understood such expenses as grains, wines, wood, oil, salt, meat, boots, hats, coat fashioning, under-waistcoats, stockings, tailors' expenses, drinks, tips, barbers, bakers, water carriers, woolen cloths, kitchen utensils, vases, glasses, window panes, and all the buckets, baths, tubs and barrels. It happens that many persons keep separate account for these similar things—but I show you those which business cannot do without." (p. 66).

The inclusion of these household expenses in the records of business affairs indicates how closely the business of trading and the business of living were associated. The modern, however, is somewhat astonished to learn on the next page of the book that this same account may receive entries "when you spend money in playing various kinds of games, or money or things which you might have lost or have stolen from you or lost at sea or through fires, etc. . . ."

Attention to refinements in definition and to extensive subdivisions of the bookkeeping data are modern additions. The distinction between fixed and current assets is an interpretive element associated only with modern financing; capital and revenue expenditures grew out of the desire to determine net profits carefully; reservation of surplus appeared only after conservatism became a virtue in corporation finance. These things troubled Paciolo and his contemporaries not at all; and there was no need that they should.

New times have brought new conditions, and these in turn have wrought some changes. We may note how different accounting is from the bookkeeping practices of the fifteenth century, how broad is its modern field, how closely refined its definitions and concepts. But it is seldom realized that we have added little to the structure but a body of theory; outside the technique of auditing, cost finding and budgeting, moderns have contributed relatively little on the practical side. And all of this—the best and most that can be shown—can not compare, as a real contribution, with the first steps taken so long ago.

The modern may perhaps feel a little superior at recent achievements and at bringing out only now the latent possibilities of bookkeeping. But it should be noted that we have been working upon long established foundations, and that we have not successfully improved upon the basic fundamentals of methodology devised over four centuries ago. We are not working with whole cloth and no pattern as the ancients did. Reading Paciolo's description of the "method of Venice"—for he invented none of the procedure himself—may help us to realize, as no modern work could, our debt to the Middle Ages.

VII. CHANGING TYPES OF LEDGER ENTRIES

THE fundamental nature of business transactions and the necessity for their systematic recording have not changed for centuries. The idea that the grouping of related occurrences (supplementing merely chronological memoranda) would add to the information contained in the record is so fundamental that without it there would be no ledger; and without the ledger there would be no bookkeeping, as we understand the term. The other unchanging essential of double-entry bookkeeping is the recognition of the existence of two inevitably equal and opposite aspects in every business transaction. This last is what closes the circuit, so to speak, and transforms account-keeping into a unified system.

These principles are now more consciously perceived than was the case in the fifteenth century, but their relation to bookkeeping has not changed. They are the essence of the art. But, however unchanging the basic elements of double entry may be, there has been no lack of progress. Here as elsewhere evolution has been at work. The present conceptions of accounts, transactions, entries, are not original with the twentieth century but are the result of a steady growth in the ability to think clearly and reason closely and to recast methods to suit changing conditions. Thus, without altering the basic concepts upon which double entry rests, the manner of thinking about and recording business transactions has changed from time to time.

Among other elements, ledger entries have shown evidence of a development from an early form in which fully detailed expression was given of the complete transaction concerned into the modern practice of a highly abbreviated tabulation of the values involved. The evolution of the ledger account has included both the form of the record and the wording of the entry. Generally speaking the two elements are closely interrelated. But in the early examples the wording is the more significant, while in modern practice form is the more important. A particular wording of ledger entries has now disappeared.

Ledger entries from early in the fourteenth to the middle of the sixteenth century were in a general way much alike. Yet there were internal differences which make it possible to group the examples into several types. In a formative period, such as this was, there is apt to be more variety in the expression of similar ideas than would be the case after practices have become more crystallized into customary forms. In order properly to reflect the ideas of the period, therefore, these differences should be noted.

The following examples will show the form and wording of typical early ledger entries. They fall into three groups according to variations in the phrasing used.

TYPE 1

A LEDGER ACCOUNT OF 1340 *

November 7, 1340	April 7, 1340
W—— V—— clerk of the Commune of Genoa owes us (*debet nobis*) that which [is credited] in the same [sum] to us in [page] 142 .... 0 0 0	We have received (*recepimus*) through A—— C——, warder of the Chateau of Arculus, account of which [is debited] by us in [page] 147 .... 0 0 0

The difficulties of expressing in English the complete thought of the entry are indicated by the phrases which are interpolated in brackets. As presented each entry states both the debit and credit involved and thus constitutes in effect a complete "journal entry" written in the ledger account. This and other characteristics are shown even more clearly in the later examples.

TYPE 2

A LEDGER ACCOUNT OF 1396

MCCLXXXXVI	MCCLXXXXVI
Joint gains and losses of the firm of J—— D—— and M—— S——	[Joint gains and losses] should have (*debet habere*) for partable

* For the original of this and other examples of ledger accounts in chronological order, see the note at the end of the chapter. Personal names are represented by initials and the amount of money by ciphers.

at C——, should give (*debet dare*) for joint expenses incurred on behalf of the firm on Dec. 28, written in the credit (*scriptos in credito*) of M—— S—— at folio 6....000

gains in Milan from 46 bales of cloth sent to L—— D—— in exchange, on Dec. 28; written in the debit (*scriptos in debito*) of M—— S—— at folio 6..............000

This extract contains a charge to joint account for certain expenses incurred by one of the partners and a credit for certain merchandise gains. The account shows no heading, yet it is clear from the words used at the beginning of the paragraph what kinds of transactions are classified in that place. The words serving the purpose of a title, "Joint gains and losses," are not repeated on the credit side in the original but are here inserted in brackets for clearness.

It will be observed also that, with the exception of the title on the credit side, the entries are stated in full detail in complete sentences and contain clear-cut references to both aspects of the transaction. The debit entry, for example, is a complete statement of the occurrence, including an indication of the account debited (should give) and the location of the contra-credit; the credit entry is likewise a complete statement of a full transaction, including, by implication, the name of the account which is credited (should have) and the location of the contra-debit. Thus this ledger entry is essentially a complete journal entry also and not merely the posting of one side of a complete transaction, as would be the case in modern practice.

The terms which have particular technical significance are translated literally, the Latin of the original being shown in parentheses. *Debet dare* (should give) was used to indicate the debit; the words are merely the verb portion of the "transaction sentence" in which the subject of the sentence is the account debited. On the credit side the verb is *debet habere* (should have, or should receive).*

* Note the difference of terminology in the 1340 and the 1396 examples. The former *debet nobis* becomes, in the later case, *debet dare*. It is not clear whether this variation expresses different ways of thinking of transactions or merely reflects an ellipsis with a word omitted. *Debet* is translatable either as "owes" or as "should" (i.e., must), hence *debet nobis* could be "owes to us" and *debet dare* could be "should give." But at this time Italian was in the process of developing out of Latin and bookkeeping entries might easily have been customarily expressed in hybrid phrases interspersed with frequent ellipses. It would not have been impossible, therefore, for these two apparently different phrases to have been identical in meaning. Thus the one could have meant *debet* [*dare*] *nobis* (should [give] to us) and the other *debet dare* [*nobis*] (should give [to us]). This might easily have been the case if *debet* was then being used in the sense of *deve* (Italian "should").

The same words are used in their technical significance in entries for 1356, 1385, 1387 and 1416 also (see the note at the end of the chapter). It should be noted, too, that the contra reference in a debit entry does not make use of *debet habere* as a modern might expect. Instead the contra is covered by the phrase, *scriptos in credito* (written in the credit) together with the title of the account concerned. The entry on the credit side refers to its contra by the phrase, *scriptos in debito.* Thus it appears that *debito* and *credito* were used as nouns naming the respective sides of the account, but that *debet dare* and *debet habere,* being verb forms, were used in the entry to indicate the action expected of the account.

TYPE 3

A LEDGER ACCOUNT OF 1392

1392	1392
Ready money must give (*de dare*) as of the thirteenth day of March to Z——; posted in the latter [account] must have (*debba avere*) in p. 7 .... 0 0 0	Ready money must have (*de avere*) eighteenth of March by N—— G——; posted in the latter [account] must give (*deba dare*) in p. 6 .... 0 0 0

Some small differences in wording appear in this type, but there is little change in form. What were Latin terms in the 1392 type, in the 1396 example are expressed in Italian:

Debit in Latin: *debet dare* (should give) *
Debit in Italian: *de dare* (must give)
Credit in Latin: *debet habere* (should have)
Credit in Italian: *den avere* (must have)

This is interesting as evidence that the Italian language was still in the process of development from the Latin. It will be observed that the Latin word *debet* is replaced by *de, dee, den, die,* etc., in the Italian. However varied the spelling may be, this form can be related to the Italian *dovere* (should). *Dare* (give) remains the same

* In modern Italian bookkeeping the left side of a ledger account is called *Dare* ("give" or Dr.) and the right, *Avere* ("have" or Cr.). In the French the terms are *Doit* ("should" or Dr.) and *Avoir* ("have" or Cr.); in the German the words become *Soll* ("should" or Dr.) and *Haben* ("have" or Cr.).

in Italian as in Latin. With respect to the credit terminology, however, the Latin *habere* becomes the Italian *avere*. The two are obviously related. The development of Italian words from the Latin produced many cases in which a Latin "b" became an Italian "v," as in these words, and many cases in which a Latin initial "h" was dropped.

Other examples of this type of ledger entry are found in the specimens for the years 1436, 1459, 1520 and 1566 given in the note at the end of the chapter. Some differences will be noted in the spelling of the keywords but these variations do not change the meaning.*

The phrases which express the contra are also different from those used in the example of types 1 and 2. They, too, vary slightly among themselves, showing that the terminology had not stabilized as yet in either form. The phrases, *posto in questa deba dare, posto debi dare in questo, posto dare,* all say the same thing, i.e., posted as "shall give" to the latter [account], posted as "shall give," etc. The contra phrases in the 1436 and 1566 examples are somewhat more like type 2: *a lui in credito* (to him in the credit), *crediteur caisse a* . . . (creditor cash a . . .), thus showing some measure of overlapping in practice even though in other particulars the wording differs.

An example from the thirteenth century (1273) belongs to this type, even though there is one noticeable variation in the wording. This entry is as follows:

* In a period when the spoken language was just beginning to be used in written form, it was natural that spelling should be "by ear" so to speak. The following list shows the variety of spelling for identical terms found in the examples of old ledger accounts.

	(shall give)	(shall have)
1211	di dare	di avire
1273	deono dare	a dato (has given)
1356	debet dare	debet havere
1383	de dar	deono avere
1392	deba dare	. . . . .
1409	die dar	de avere
1417	die dare	di aver
1430	deno dar	die haver
1436	den dare	die aver
1458	debbe dare	deno aver
1478	divi dare	divi haviri
1494	die dare	die havere

S——, B—— & Co. must give (*deono dare*) in florins in the month of April..................................... o o o
according to the account balance in B——'s book.

S——, B—— & Co. has given (*a dato*) in florins in the month of April..................................... o o o
which is posted must give above on page 2.

Even though two or three hundred years older than many of the examples cited, this entry has most of the characteristics of the latter. Only the phrase indicative of the credit is different ("has given" instead of "must have"). In a sense "has given" as a credit phrase carries the same idea as *"recepimus"* in entries of type 1. Both of these plainly suggest cancellation of a prior item (i.e., the debit) much as if we were to mark "paid" across an item in a personal memorandum book. "Must have" as a credit phrase does not of itself directly suggest cancellation, for it applies equally well to a first entry as a credit (liability) and to a subsequent credit in discharge of a prior debit (debt).

Another group of examples (viz., 1383, 1406, 1409, 1417, 1430, 1436, 1458, 1478 and 1537 in the note) closely approximate type 3 in the characteristic repetition of full journal details in each ledger entry, in the phrasing of the reference to the contra account, and in the debit and credit words used. In one particular there is a small difference, that is in the use of "by" (*per*) on both sides to indicate the contra account instead of "to" on the debit and "by" on the credit as used in some of the others. This is a matter of more importance to the journal entry, however, than to the ledger. It is mentioned here principally to reinforce the statement that journal entries were completely reproduced in the ledger, even to the inclusion of variations in the wording. The ledger entry of 1537, for example, goes so far as to include the parallel lines as in the journal entry:

Cash must give // to capital *
.... etc.

In a few cases among the examples the paging reference to the

* This inclusion of slanting lines to separate the debit and its contra in a ledger entry is also illustrated from Angelo Pietra's text of 1586. See Geijsbeek, *Ancient Double Entry Bookkeeping*, p. 100.

contra is not clearly indicated. But this, it is probably fair to assume, is an indication of careless practice rather than a difference in type.

The entries outlined above represent the practice of almost three hundred years (1273-1566). They are expressed in Latin or Italian and fall into three general types according to differences in the wording.

	Debits	*Credits*
Type 1	.........*debet nobis* .... *valent nobis in isto*	*recepimus* .... *valent nobis in isto* ....
Type 2	.... *debet dare* .... *scriptos in credito*	........*debet havere* .... *scriptos in debito* ....
Type 3	.... *de dare* .... *posto debbono avere in questo*.....	...........*de avire* .... *posto debi dare in questo* ....

The differences in wording need not be considered of much basic significance, for the meaning is little changed whatever phrases are used.* This was before terminology had been standardized and variations are to be expected. Yet in essentials the entries are much alike throughout the whole period. Each entry is in effect a record of a complete transaction indicating both the account debited and the account credited. In form the accounts were generally bi-lateral, and the entries consisted of descriptive sentences formed into separate paragraphs full of details.

* This is further illustrated by a much earlier example. In the museum of the University of Pennsylvania, there is a clay tablet from Nippur recording a mortgage made about 429 B.C. and signed by several witnesses as well as the scribe. The translation reads as follows:

> "Thirty gur (bushels) of dates are due to Enlilnandin-shumi, son of Murashu from Belbullitsu and Sha-Nabushu, sons of Kiribiti and all their bow tenancy. They shall deliver these thirty gur of dates in the month of Tishri in the 34th year and in accordance with the measure of Enlilnandin-shumi in Bitbalatsu. Their planted orchard is pledged to Enlilnandin-shumi in security for payment of the dates. No other creditor has power over it."

Perhaps the phrase "they shall deliver" is the distant antecedent of the mediæval phrase "shall give" as a technical indication of a debt receivable, or debit.

In outline each ledger entry would usually contain the following in more or less detail:

Year (Roman numerals) at top of page.
Name of the account involved (in first entry only).
Technical words of debiting or crediting.
Statement of the amount involved and dates.
Occasion of the transaction, full details.
Name and page of the contra account.
Amount restated at the end of the paragraph.

Subsequent entries in the same account were quite similar except that the year and the account named were not repeated. In place of the latter, later entries began "to ditto. . . ." One of the changes to be observed later is the appearance of the account name at the head of the page instead of at the beginning of the first entry.

Now comes a period of transition and change as double entry is brought over into English. A book (*Nouvelle Instruction*) by a Dutch writer, Jehan Ympyn Christophle, appeared in French in 1543 and in English in 1547. A translation of some of the examples of ledger entries in the French edition [1] shows the use in one book of a variety of terms to indicate debiting and crediting. For example:

(a) J—— L——, jeweler *is debtor*. . . . .
(b) Expenses of Household *owe* to cash. . . . .
(c) Profit and Loss *must have* by Jewelry. . . . .

A similar mixed usage appears in the text by John Mellis (England, 1588) wherein an entry [2] is worded as follows:

1587

Aug. 8 Chest or Ready Money *ought to give* me (or *is Debtor* to Stock) for so much ready money in gold and silver I have this day in stock, as in credit, folio. 0 0 0

In his ledger Mellis translates the technical terms *de dare* and *de havere* quite literally into English as "ought to give" and "ought to have." Yet, feeling no doubt that such a translation might not clearly carry the meaning to English readers, Mellis * also uses the very different alternative phrase "is debtor to. . . ." This rendition of the older authors lays the groundwork for the inept English terminology of the future † which makes it necessary to use the same word "debit" as a noun, verb and adjective. It is rather doubtful whether the older writers in saying "cash shall give to Peter" meant to imply that cash *owed* Peter. It is more likely that their thought was, as has been suggested in an earlier chapter:

Cash shall give [to the Proprietor and]
Peter shall have [from the Proprietor]

The only *debt* was from proprietor to Peter for money borrowed; the relationship of "cash" to proprietor is a mere abstraction. Any direct relationship between "cash" and Peter (an outsider) is an impossibility.

Earlier writers did not themselves make the mental processes of their transaction analysis as clear as they did the small details of recording procedure. Hence, the writers who followed, such as the Dutch and English, had to do the best they could in making the essential processes of the foreign methods clear to readers of their own nationality.

The example from Mellis brings the development down to the end of the sixteenth century. The outstanding characteristics of the ledger accounts of this time can be reduced to two in number: First, there was little evidence of form as such except the contra-position of debit and credit paragraphs and a certain formality in the wording of the entries. Second, the transaction was twice duplicated completely in the ledger, once in the account debited and once in the account credited. The ledger therefore was not a compilation of classified debits and credits but rather a classified grouping of entries (whole transactions).

Early in the next century occurred certain modifications in the

* Or Hugh Oldcastle, for there is some reason for thinking that perhaps Mellis merely republished an earlier book (of 1543) written by Oldcastle.

† The preference of some authors for the phrase "is debtor to. . . ." in the ledger may perhaps be related to a certain style (1491–1559) of journal phrasing, viz., "I make T—— debtor and B—— creditor." See journal entries of the second type in the next chapter.

form of the ledger account which suggest that there was a tendency for account evolution to move in the direction of a more simplified and abbreviated arrangement. The style of ledger account introduced at this time prevailed for practically three hundred years with little further alteration. As will appear presently, the differences between the ledger accounts of Mellis (England, 1588) and those of Stevin (Holland, 1604–8) were much more marked than were the differences between the accounts of Stevin and any of his successors for nearly three centuries. The later ledger accounts were more like those shown by Stevin than Stevin's were like those of Mellis and other predecessors.

A LEDGER ACCOUNT OF 1604–8 [3]

Notes Debet			Year 1600			Notes Credit			Year 1600		
0	Jan.	Per capital fol. 3	144	0	0	30	May	Per Peter DeWitt fol. 10	334	16	0
28	Mar.	Per David Roels fol. 15	95	4	0	4	Aug.	Per Pepper fol. 16	620	0	0

Here for the first time the account begins to take on a modern arrangement—to have less of the appearance of narrative paragraphs and more of the effect of tabulations.

The title of the account is definitely separated from the body of the entry and placed above the details. Together with the title stand the technical terms *debet* and *credit,* now clearly "labels" of the respective sides of the tabulation and no longer merely the verbs of complete sentences. Yet, it is to be noted, the words and phrases employed are not entirely without grammatical relationship in spite of their altered spatial relationship. If we substitute for "debet" the original verb form, "shall give," the left entry may be made to read: "Notes shall give per capital on page 3, for 144," and the right side: "Notes shall have per Peter DeWitt on page 10 for 324." So the essence of the older practice of using complete sentences is still present, although perhaps somewhat obscured by the altered location of the significant words and by the substitution for *de dare* of "debet" and for *de avere,* "credit."

The body of Stevin's ledger entry contains only the date, the contra account reference and the amount; many details which found a place in the text of the older ledger entries are here missing. This brevity within the entry forms as marked a contrast to the earlier practice as does the placing of the account titles.

The next example is from the English again and shows similarities to both Mellis (English) and Stevin (Dutch), although the author, Richard Dafforne, refers directly in his preface only to his indebtedness to Stevin. The book went through several editions between 1636 and 1648, and probably definitely influenced later writers. The following ledger account is from the first edition.

A LEDGER ACCOUNT OF 1636[4]

[left folio]

Fol. 1 Anno 1633 in London

Cash is Debitor	£	s	p
1 Jan. to Stock for several coynes of money	1000	15	7
27 Feb. to Jacob Symonson his account current	328	10	111
etc.			

[right folio]

Cash is Creditor	£	s	p
4 Jan. By George Pinchback payd in part	144	—	—
13 Mar. By Figs in Company, 3/5 R.R., 2/5 for me	8	7	6
etc.			

Dafforne uses the same English terminology in his ledger accounts as did Mellis, namely, "Cash is Debitor to Stock," but does not, like Mellis, use also the literal translation ("ought to give" and "is due to have") of the older terms. In arrangement, however, Dafforne's account is much more like Stevin's; but Dafforne does not use the preposition "by" (*per*) to introduce both the ledger debits and credits as does Stevin. He follows Mellis and the later Italian practice in the use of "to" with the debits and "by" with the credits.

It is clear from this example that the account title, even though set apart as a heading, is to be read with each entry, thus still making a complete sentence which states not only the debit but the contra credit as well. The first entry on the debit side may be read:

Cash is Debitor	to Stock
(in title)	(in entry)

Reading the heading of the credit side with the entry gives:

Cash is Creditor	by George Pinchback
(in title)	(in entry)

This is as much as to say for the credit: Cash is trusted by Pinchback; and for the debit it is as much as to say: Cash is indebted (owes) to stock (capital). However, Pinchback can not truly be said to look to (my) cash directly for payment, but to me, the proprietor. We can now see that it would be incorrect theory to say that Pinchback has entrusted (my) cash account with anything; he has in fact entrusted me, the proprietor, and not one of my accounts; if any one has entrusted anything to my cash account, it is I, the proprietor, who have done so. Here is another illustration of the point made before, that the translation of early bookkeeping works from the Italian into Dutch and English failed to carry over the real essence of the transaction analysis which lay within the originals.

From this point the story moves rapidly. The English practices were now fixed, and for the next two hundred years changes were few and unimportant. The accounts were kept upon two folios, the left for the debit and the right for the credit; account titles were now definitely established as headings; and the arrangement in general was less narrative in form and more in the nature of tabulations than formerly, although each entry still carried a page reference to the contra account.

Early in the eighteenth century, however, two minor changes appeared in the account headings. The account title was dropped from the heading of the credit folio and the phrase "per contra" took its place. At the same time the words "debit" and "credit" were abbreviated as "Dr." and "Cr.," these abbreviations standing at the head of the respective folios. The following example* will serve to illustrate these distinctions:

THE 18TH CENTURY TYPE OF LEDGER HEADING

Dr. William Smith				per contra Cr.		
	(left folio)			(right folio)		

Technically it was only a step from this form of account to the next, but in point of time the older form prevailed for nearly a hundred years. By the middle of the nineteenth century both sides of the account were shown upon a single page and a single title applied to both sides in the modern manner. This form was as follows:

THE 19TH CENTURY TYPE OF LEDGER ACCOUNT

Dr. Bills Receivable Cr.

1847 May 10	6	to Wm. Johnson	150	00	1847 Nov. 10	12	By Cash	150	00

For over fifty years this was the prevailing type of account.† Indeed it may be said to be still in use, for the simple omission of the Dr. and Cr. abbreviations in the title and the contra references in the explanation columns will produce the ledger account in the form used in most ledgers in this country today.

Clearly there was a growing tendency during the later period to treat the account as a tabulation of facts related to the title. Such details as were still entered in the body of the account seem to have been used more as a brief explanation of the amounts rather than as avowedly cross references to the contra account concerned.

* These characteristics were typical of the accounts shown in the text books of King (London, 1717), Weston (London, 1754), Dilworth (London, 1792), Jackson (New York, 1816), Kelly (London, 1833), and no doubt many others.

† Accounts of this kind are used in the illustrations in the following texts: Thos. Jones (New York, 1841), Duff (New York, 1848), Bryant and Stratton (Chicago, 1861), Mayhew (Detroit, 1870), Bandy (New York, 1885).

With the disappearance from most ledgers some twenty-five or thirty years ago of the explanations, "to so and so" and "by so and so," there passed out of sight the last tangible suggestion in the ledger itself that each entry in an account expresses a complete thought resolvable into a grammatical sentence.

This, perhaps, is the most significant change in the evolution of the ledger account. Although at first sight it seems a simple and natural alteration, yet it definitely marks the transition from a personification concept of accounts to a statistical concept. Accounts with cash, notes, etc., are no longer "debtors," much less "debtor to stock" or "debtor to John Doe" and the like. Accounts now show on their face nothing but title, date, posting reference and amount. They are little more than the resting place of certain data, accumulated and tabulated perhaps by persons who did not have much knowledge of bookkeeping as such.

Indeed, in some cases twentieth-century practice goes even beyond this and abandons the ledger account as a form entirely. In its place are statistical summaries which bear not the faintest physical resemblance to left-sided and right-sided ledger accounts. On long sheets with columns for sub-classifications, figures are tabulated and thought of as "blacks" and "reds," instead of "debits" and "credits." Yet the results appear finally in financial statements which are indistinguishable from statements differently derived.

The twentieth century thus seems to be much less concerned with form than with substance; modern accounting is less formal and yet more technical than the bookkeeping of an earlier day. As a result, bookkeeping no longer aims at classifying debt-relationships, but at statistically tabulating the changes occurring in a great variety of financial elements which will reveal financial condition and the course of economic progress. This important change in the point of view of bookkeeping is no doubt largely attributable to the searching analysis into bookkeeping method and philosophy made during the last quarter of the nineteenth century by such men as Charles E. Sprague in the United States and J. F. Schär in Germany. Without a loosening of the chains of formalism and rule of thumb, it seems doubtful whether the bookkeeping of a generation or two ago would have proved elastic enough to have served modern conditions effectively and to have facilitated the development of such aids to management as cost finding, budgetary control and the like.

NOTE ON REPRESENTATIVE LEDGER ACCOUNTS

(1273)—Bariola, *Storia della Ragioneria,* p. 553.

1. Guidingho Saverigi e Iachopo Bonizzi e chonpangni deono dare in fiorini in k(alendi) aprile nel lxxiij .... o o o
per ragione salda di su'libro di Baldovino.

2. § e deono dare per prode di quessti denari infino in ka(lendi) apirile nel lxxiiij ° .... o o o

3. So'ma, lib' ccccIxxxvi in k(alendi) apirile.

4. § À dato Guidingho e chonpangni medesimi in fiorini in ka(lendi) apirile nel lxxiiij .... o o o
p(osto) che deono dare innanzi due charte.

(1340)—Besta, *La Ragioneria,* III, p. 275.

Guillielmo Vacha, notarius debet nobis pro Commune Janue unde nobis in isto in *cxxxxij* .... o o o

Recepimus, accipiente Andrea de Castellione castellanus castelli Arcule, in racione unde nobis in *cxxxxvij* .... o o o

(1340)—Bariola *op. cit.,* p. 331.

1. Jacobus de Bonicha debet nobis pro Anthonio de Marinis valent nobis in isto in LXI .... o o o

2. Item die quinta septembris pro Marzocho Pinello valent nobis in isto in LXXXXII .... o o o

Recepimus in racione expensae Comunis Janue valent nobis in isto in CCXXXI et sunt pro expensis factis per ipsum Jacobum in exercitu Taxarolii in trabuchis et aliis necessariis pro comuni Janue, et hoc de mandato domini Ducis et sui consilii scripto mano Lanfranci de Valle notarii MCCCXXXX die decimanona augusti .... o o o

(1356)—Besta, *op. cit.,* III, p. 288.

Guillelmus Bagarotus debet dare scriptum in credito Beltramo Leccacorno in isto folio die *iiij* martij .... o o o

Debet habere scriptum in debito Domino Gasparo Vice-comitj in isto in fo. *clxv* die *xiij* februarij ...... o o o

(1359)—Besta, *op. cit.*, III, p. 289.

Sozius Picollus debet dare scriptum in credito Communi Placentie in isto in fo. *lxj* die secundo julij....... o o o

Debet habere scriptum ei in debito in fo. *lxxij* die *xxv* junij .... o o o

(1383)—Besta, *op. cit.*, III, p. 319.

Nicholò di Francesco e fratelli da Firenze de dar a di *xvj* di maggio fior. quatrociento d. *j*. demo per lui a messer landuccio bonchonti portò simone di francesco a uscita *b* a carte 13.. o o o

Nicholò di Francescho e fratelli da Firenze deono avere a di *xiiij* di maggio prossimo fior. quatrociento d. -j-i quali gli prometemo a di *viiij* di febraio per piero del pueri chatalano posto a dietro in questo a c. 82 piero de dare.......... o o o

(1385)—Besta, *op. cit.*, III, p. 291.

Camera illustris principis et magnifici domini nostri domini comitis virtutum, etc. debet dare numeratos per Masotum de Aribertis massarium communis Regij... scriptum in credito dicto Masoto thesaurario in isto in folio *xxiij* f. *clx*........ o o o

Camera predicta debet habere pro provisione prefacto domino promissa per am baxiatores communis Regij incipiendo ...... scriptis in debito communi *Regij* in isto in folio *xi*.... o o o

(1392)—Besta, *op. cit.*, III, p. 320

La chassa dei chontanti de dare a di *xiij* di marzo a Zanobi di Taddeo Ghaddi posto in questo Zanobi debba avere nel c. 2.......... o o o

La chassa dei chontanti de avere *xviij* di marzo da Noro Guidi posto in questo deba dare nel c. 5........ o o o

(1396)—P. Kats in *The Accountant*, March 27, 1926

Lucrum et perditae cummunes quae fiont pro sotietate in Catalogna et que sunt communes inter nos Johanninum de Dugnano et Marchum Serrainerium, quilibet nostrum pro medietate, debent dare scriptos in credito Marcho Serrainerio in fo.

Debet habere scriptos in debito Marcho Serrainerio in fo. 6 die *xxviij* decembris videlicet qui paxiti sunt pro lucro in Medilano ball *xlvj* fustanei, missarum Lanfrancho de Dugnano pro cambio fl................. o o o

6 die *xxviij* decembris qui sunt pro expensis communibus factis causa sotietatis in summa per eum .... o o o	
(1406)—Besta, *op. cit.*, III, p. 304.	
Debitori e chreditori tratti del l'estratto fato per ser Jachomo Boltremo de dar per ser Donado Soranzo proprio fin di 19 agosto, par in quello k. 76, in questo k. 3 .... o o o	Debitori e chreditori tratti del l'estratto fato per ser Jachomo Boltremo de aver per la chamera da imprestidi, par in quello k. 75, 78 in questo. k. 2 U. *cxxvj* ...... o o o
(1409)—Besta, *op. cit.*, III, p. 283.	
Die *xxvij* marcij Bartholomeus de Mari debet nobis pro Francisco Iustiniano et socio massariis in *cclvj* .... o o o	Recepimus die *xxvij* maij in Martino de Mari in *ccccxxij* .... o o o Item die *viij* maij in sua racione temporum in *dcxiij* .... o o o
(1417)—Besta, *op. cit.*, III, p. 303.	
Ser Marcho da Ponte de Venizia die dar per uno quarto de la gastaldia de Arquà, messo debbe aver in questo car. 11 .... o o o	Ser Marcho da Ponte de Venizia die aver .... E a dì dito [dui aprile 1417] per suo quarto de la gastaldia de Arquà, messo debia dar in questo car. 11 .... o o o
(1430)—Bariola, *op. cit.*, Part II, Note 7.	
Debitori et creditori trati de libro bianco picolo A deno dar adi 2 zenaro per Andrea Barbarigo che fui de miser Nicholo come apar in questo in ...... K. 2 .. o o o	Debitori et creditori contrascriti deno aver adi 5 zenaro per ser Piero soranzo fo de ser Antonio apar in questo in ...... K. 7 .... o o o
(1436)—Besta, *op. cit.*, III, p. 327.	
Ghaleazo Borromei e Antonio di Francesco e comp. di Londra den dare a di 8 di marzo lir. 19.11.11 come appare al quaderno di Gio.	Ghaleazo Borromei e Antonio di Francesco e comp. deno avere a di 17 di marzo per li nostri di brugia a loro in debito a fo. 14 .... o o o

Bindotti a fo. 3 a lui in credito a fo. 5 .... o o o

(1436)—Alfieri, *La Partita Doppia,* p. 88.

Ser Piero soranzo fo de ser Antonio die dar adi 3 settembre per ser Jacomo marzelo de ser Cristofalo per due letere de chambio ch' a pagado al dito l'una de Duc. 250 a pp. 3 k. 8 el Duc. l'altra de Duc. 250 a perperi 3 k. 9 el Duc. monta in tuto K. 2 .... o o o

Ser Piero soranzo die aver adi 5 settembre per ser Felipo marzelo fo de ser Fantin per Duc. 300 d'oro che i mandai a pagare al dito ser Filipo per la galia chapitan ser Piero contarini a pp. 3 per Duc. segondo el suo hordene K. 2 .... o o o

(1458)—Bariola, *op. cit.,* p. 566-7.

Antonio di Guido Giuntini de' dare adì 2 di settembre 1458 s. xvi d. vi da ser Gabriello Lioni in credito a consoli del mare .... o o o

Comune di Firenze de' avere adì 31 di Gennaio 1458 lb. trentotto posto Antonio Giuntini cassiere di Camera debbi dare in questo c. 70 .... o o o

(1459)—Besta, *op. cit.,* III, p. 329.

La cassa de contanti de dare a di *xxv* di marzo fio. ventiquattro migliaia conti dalle eredi nel modo e forma che gli apare posto in questo *m* debbono avere c. 2 .... o o o

La cassa de contanti contro scritta de avere a di *xxvj* di marzo fio. venti-quattro mila, conti fino a questo dì in pezzi 19700 . . . . a Carlo Baronelli posto debi dare in questo c. 4 .... o o o

(1478)—Bariola, *op. cit.,* Note 9.

Lu banchu di gugliermmu ajutamicristu pir cuntu di lu donativo di la seconda tanda XI ind. DIVI DARI a XXIII di marzu pir restu daltru cuntu chomu appari jn quistu .... o o o

Lu banchu di gugliermu ajutamicristu pir cuntu di li dinari di lu donativo di la secunda tanda di lannu passatu XI ind. DIVI HAVIRI a di XXX di marzu ...... o o o

(1520)—Bariola, *op. cit.,* p. 351.

Lo illustri spectabili D. Federico Patella magistru Portulano per conto di corti DEVI DARE a dì XX di

Lo illustri spectabili D. Federigo Patella DEVI HAVERE per comto di Corte per resto daltro suo conto luglio unzi XXXX per sua petro zafarana al numero 238 posto .... o o o

posto dare in p.° 224 ...... o o o

(1524)—Bariola, *op. cit.*, Part II, Note 8.

Sier Mathio da Spalato die dar adi 24 marzo per l. 60 de filadi a rason de s. 12 la 1. monta l. 36 s. o e per l. 25 da rame a s. 8. la 1. monta l. 10 s.o. suma in tutto .... o o o

Sier Mathio da Spalato alicontro de aver adi 16 avosto contadi da lui per parte de le contrascritte robe l. 17 s. 14 .... o o o

Adi primo novembrio contadi da lui per resto de le contrascritte robe l. 28 s. 6 .... o o o

(1537)—Besta, *op. cit.*, III, p. 350.

29. Cassa die dar a dì primo zener // A Cavedal che me trovo haver fin questo zorno duc. 820 .... o o o

Cassa controscritta die haver .... o o o

(1566)—DeWaal, *Van Paciolo tot Stevin*, p. 152.

Gaings & Pertes doibuent donner ce 7 Novembre 200 £ baillé comptant a Marc Antoine Millanois pour jnterest a 2½ pour 100 de 8000 £ pour vne letre de change de 1111 £ 2 s 2 d de gros qu'il m'a faicte pour Anuers. Crediteur Caisse a f. 18 .... o o o

Gaings & Pertes doibuent auoir ce 24 d'Octobre 256 £ 10 s pour autant proffité sur les camelots de l'Isle a f. 5 .... o o o

Le 4 Januier 390 £ 5 s 5 d pour autant proffité sur le Vogage de Lion a f. V 6 .... o o o

REFERENCES

1. By P. Kats in *The Accountant* (London), August 27, 1927.

2. From a reproduction of John Mellis, *Brief Instruction*, by P. Kats in *The Accountant*, May 1, 1926.

3. Geijsbeek, *op. cit.*, p. 128; see also *The Institute of Bookkeepers' Journal*, December, 1927, p. 324.

4. Richard Dafforne, *The Merchants Mirrour*, bound with Gerard Malynes, *Lex Mercatoria* (London, 1636).

VIII. EVOLUTION OF THE JOURNAL ENTRY

THE journal entry is an important bookkeeping mechanism which serves as a means of converting a non-technical statement of a transaction into a species of technically-formed, intermediate statistical records. It is, moreover, particularly characteristic of double entry—more characteristic perhaps than the ledger entry—because it so clearly expresses the inevitable duality which is present in all transactions.

The importance of the journal entry in modern practice seems to be somewhat on the decrease, at least in America. Whether or not the processes of evolution will finally remove it altogether, no one knows. But one can say that it is not indispensable, and consequently it might conceivably disappear altogether from bookkeeping practice.

It is easy to become curious about this element of bookkeeping method, which probably was added to the structure after double-entry account keeping was quite well worked out and might sometime drop off the structure again—an outgrown appendage like a polliwog's tail.

The earliest journal entries were not what one would perhaps be inclined to expect in view of the early characteristics of the ledger account. Ledger entries, as has already been pointed out, were at first complete sentences—whole transactions entered twice *in toto*. But the earliest journal entries that we know of were not sentences to be rewritten in the ledger. On the contrary, they were, even in the first appearances, quite technical in form and phrasing. The uninitiated might understand a ledger entry, for the wording expressed a complete thought, but they could hardly grasp the meaning of a journal entry unaided, for the expression of thought was very much abbreviated.

Before speculating upon the origin of the peculiarities of journal-entry form, let us examine some typical journal entries of the fifteenth and sixteenth centuries.

JOURNAL ENTRIES OF THE FIRST TYPE *

ORIGINAL		TRANSLATION	
(1430)			
1. *Per* Cassa de contadi *a* ser franzesco baldi e fratelli—per resto de zafaran..................	0 0 0	1. *By* ready money *to* Franzesco Baldi and Brothers —for balance of saffron..	0 0 0
(1494)			
2. *Per* Ser Zuan d' Antonio da Messina: *A* Cassa contati a lui per parte de'sopra ditti zuccari secondo la forma del mercato....................	0 0 0	2. *By* Zuan Antonio of Messina: *to* cash, paid to him for part of the above mentioned sugar according to the terms of the agreement.............	0 0 0
(1525)			
3. *Per* Bancho di Cappelo e Vendramine, *a* chavedal i quali me trovo aver nel detto bancho come per suoi libre apar.........	0 0 0	3. *By* Cappelo and Vendramini's Bank, to Capital, which I find I have in the said bank per their books.................	0 0 0
(1540)			
4. *P(er)* Pro e Danno // *A* spese diverse per piu spese fatte l'anno presente, come in esse appar, per saldo suo..........	0 0 0	4. *By* Profit and Loss, *to* Sundry Expense, for various expenses made in the present year, as appears in the balance of that account	0 0 0
(1543)			
5. *Per* profyt ende onprofyte / *aen* Capitael van my Nicolaes Forestain somma sommarum dat ick bevinde gheprofiteert te hebben binnen den tijt gheduerende disen boek	0 0 0	5. *By* profit and loss *to* capital of myself Nicholas Forestain, the sum total that I have profited within the period of this book	0 0 0

* Sources are cited at the end of the chapter and numbered to correspond with the entries.

(1549)

6. *Für* Ingwer // *an* nutz und Schaden für nutz und gewin ich an dem Ingwer gehabt......... o o o	6. *By* Vinegar, *to* Profit and Loss, for loss and gain I have had on Vinegar... o o o

All these examples, in whatever language they are written, exhibit the same technical characteristics. The typical form in all of them is:

By A——, to B——
(with more or less detail of explanation).

This is a technical form, first, because the meaning is not obvious in the wording—something is left to be implied or understood; and, second, because the prepositions "per" and "a" have been given a special significance not in common usage. The old textbooks are very careful to point out that "per" must come first in the journal entry and that it indicates, or labels, the debtor. The creditor is always to be named next and is indicated by "a." Thus a rule explains the usage but not the significance. The writers do not explain how "per" and "a" came to be associated with "debtor" and "creditor" respectively.

The absence of any authority showing how these technical meanings came about throws the matter open to conjecture and inference. The question is interesting enough to be discussed.

A hint of a possible starting place may be found in the phrasing of some of the early German journal entries. Even though the German examples are dated later than many of the Italian entries in the established form, these particular German entries are not cast into the same earlier technical form. The following is a sample entry by Mathew Schwartz, the chief bookkeeper for the famous Fugger family of German merchants. It is dated 1516.

ORIGINAL	TRANSLATION
Uns soll herr Jacob Fugger duc. 85, die *sollen wir* a Cassa, umb souil hat Matheus Schwartz hie zu Venedig für sich gebraucht......	*To us* Mr. Jacob Fugger shall [give] 85 ducats, which *we shall* [give] to cash, for as much as Mathew Schwartz has used here at Venice......................

The words in italic type are the ones which have technical significance; the words in brackets in the translation are added to the original to complete the obvious meaning. Thus completed, the journal entry assumes the form of a simple sentence quite devoid of technicalities and therefore understandable by anyone who reads it. The word "give" is not in the original entry of 1516, and without that word even this entry becomes semi-technical, since a missing word is to be implied.

Back in 1440–1444, however, unsystematized memoranda of the time (as Penndorf shows in his *Geschichte der Buchhaltung in Deutschland*) contained the phrases *"er sol geben," "ich hab im gegeben"* ("he shall give," "I have given him") and the like. Thus it seems clear that the Germans had started with complete sentences, but by 1516 had begun to drop words out of the bookkeeping entry so that the record was already becoming technical. But the process had not yet gone so far as to make the full sentence hard to reconstruct.

On the other hand, the entry given above (No. 6) was only thirty-three years later (1549) and, it will be noted, its form was already so technical as to have been hard for the uninitiated to understand. It is not a whole sentence, whereas the entry of 1516 was very nearly a complete sentence. The entry of 1549 is, moreover, identical with the Italian form. This leads to two suggestions. The first is that the established Italian form probably did not make itself felt in Germany until some time later than its early use in Italy (1430). The second suggestion here is that the technical Italian form of journal entry might possibly be experimentally reconstructed into a complete sentence which could have been so changed in the course of time by dropping out words as to produce in the end the brief, technical expression used in the Italian entries, namely:

By A——, to B——

In order to follow up this thought, it is necessary to start with a hypothetical ledger account in the early Italian manner.

On the cash page, debit side, it might read:

"Cash shall give the stated amount

> to Francisco at his pleasure for coins this day deposited."

On Francisco's page, credit side, it might read:

> "Francisco shall have (i.e., receive) the stated amount at his pleasure for cash this day deposited in coins."

Certain conditioning factors must now be taken into consideration:

1. The journal was developed *after* the ledger, presumably for the purpose of systematizing the daybook memoranda preparatory to entry in the ledger. Consequently, journalizing would be then as now a process of translating the occurrence into ledger terms. Therefore it would have been natural at first to state the journal entries in phrases used in the ledger.

2. The only words in the ledger entries which do not vary according to the details of the transaction are: "shall give" and "shall have," and "to" and "for" (*per* = for or by). Therefore these words at least would have to appear in every journal entry to put it into association with the ledger.

3. The debit item (here "cash") appears twice in the old form of ledger entry: once as the first part of the entry on the debit page and again as the second part of another entry (the contra). The same is true of the credit item, reversed of course. Thus in the above example, "Cash shall give" appears again as "for cash" in the other account, and "to Francisco" appears a second time as "Francisco shall have" in the contra account.

4. The modern entry for the receipt of cash on deposit from Francisco would be

Cash............ o o o
    Francisco............ o o o

But in the old ledger both debit and credit from the journal were shown twice, that is to say, the *whole transaction* was written in both of the accounts concerned. Therefore, the old journal entry would need some unmistakable indication of a "four-element posting." Consequently, the old journal entry would have to have two elements not shown in the modern journal. In essentials, the only thing the old entry had that the new has not are the words "by" (or "for") and "to." These constitute the third and fourth elements, and produce the form:

By cash, to Francisco.

On the basis of these factors the situation seems to be as follows. It is possible to reconstruct a fully worded journal entry to express the facts of the transaction in accordance with what would seem from the German examples to have been a very probable form of entry before technical omissions began to be made. This hypothetically reconstructed journal entry is as follows:

> For cash deposited this day, Francisco shall have the stated amount, etc. and to Francisco, cash shall give the stated amount at his pleasure.

If omissions or reorganization of the wording then appeared, the entry might next have been reduced to the type:

For cash, Francisco shall have;
To Francisco, cash shall give

And if still later the duplicated phrases were neglected, the form might result in this type:

For cash, to Francisco

This form expresses the technical essentials of the journal entry of 1430 and for a long time thereafter. Why such a change should take place it would be hard to say; perhaps it seemed to simplify the record and reduce the work of recording—a reason no doubt as satisfactory to scribes of that day as it still is to bookkeepers now. The essential facts for the ledger—to anyone who had been instructed in the bookkeeping of the day—were still quite plainly discernible. They were a debit to a named account (and a contra), and a credit to a named account (and its contra)—four elements.

1. "Cash" by its position first in the entry gives the name of the account which "shall give" (i.e., which is to be debited).

2. "Francisco" by its position as second in the entry gives the name of the account which "shall have" (i.e., which is to be credited).

3. "For" may be regarded as the symbol of the contra entry of cash in the credit account (Francisco).

4. "To" may be regarded as the symbol of the contra entry of Francisco in the debit account (cash).

Thus it will be seen that the journal entry in its technical abbreviation names two things in its left member: 1. the account debited (cash) and 2. the contra or explanation entry (by or for cash) belonging to the other account concerned. In its right member it names: 1. the account to be credited (Francisco) and 2. the contra or explanation entry (to Francisco) belonging to the other account concerned.

This technical form of journal entry would clearly state (to a trained bookkeeper) the whole transaction in duplicate and in terms already in use in current ledger practice. It would form a perfect bridge of the gap between the memorandum record and the ledger. But there is nothing authentic in this explanation of the origin of the form which the entry took; it is only an attempt to piece together a plausible hypothesis out of the information available. There is really nothing definite to show that journal entries were ever made in the complete-sentence form as here reconstructed. If they had been, they must have evolved into the recognized abbreviated form (By A——, to B——) within a period of about one hundred years. Double-entry ledgers are first found complete in the middle of the fourteenth century, say by 1340, the date of the accounts of the stewards of Genoa (there could have been no urge to construct journal entries of any kind before double-entry ledgers were in use) and the technical abbreviated form * of journal entry is definitely

* A people which in 1494 favored the almost excessive use of abbreviations in place of complete words, which is evident in Paciolo's *De Computis,* probably earlier than this would have been inclined to accept as reasonable, perhaps even as desirable, the outright omission of repetitive phrases in bookkeeping entries where the meaning could be imputed into the words remaining, thus producing the technicality of form here discussed.

known to have appeared by 1430. Whether or not that is a long enough period for such an evolution to take place—even assuming a great stimulus from the Renaissance background—is an unanswered question.

In regard to the later development of journal entries, much less speculation is necessary, for many examples are available and the forms in use are much less technical and therefore easier to understand.

One of the most interesting facts about the old practices of double-entry bookkeeping is the existence at the same time of two strikingly different types of journal entry, one of which has already been presented here. Yet different as they are in wording and technicalities, and different undoubtedly also as to origin, they nevertheless could serve the same function equally well without, apparently, introducing any confusion.

This other form of entry may prove to be even more interesting than the one first discussed, because in some ways it is closer to modern forms, or, perhaps it would be better to say, because the modern journal entry in English seems to evolve more naturally out of the form now to be considered than out of the "by and to" type of entry.

JOURNAL ENTRIES OF THE SECOND TYPE

(*first variation*)

ORIGINAL	TRANSLATION
(1491)	
7. *Faro debetore* Tomasone del Buono *e creditore* spese di mercanzie di s. iiij d'oro per spese fatta a un fardello di panno corsato mandato da Lucca da Bonaccorsi a Libro 203/100........ o o o	7. I *make debtor* Tomaso del Buono and *creditor* Merchandise Expenses for 4 s. in gold, for expenses incurred on a bale of cloth sent by Lucca da Bonaccorsi, in the book 203/100...... o o o
(1550)	
8. Cassa *est debiteur* adj ditto L. 987.13.4 Je Pierre du Mont ay receu	8. Cash *is debtor* on this day [for the] L. 987.13.-4 I, Pierre du Mont,

de mon maistre Nicolas de Reo en argent contant L. 987.13.4 pour luy seruir au train de marchandise dieu me donne la grace de bien servir
Nicolas de Reo *est Creditor*............ 0 0 0

have received from my master Nicholas de Reo L. 987.13.4 in ready money to be employed for him by way of business. God give me grace to serve well.
Nicholas de Reo *is Creditor*............ 0 0 0

(1559)

9. *Fa debitore* Michele Gharo Nestri a di 2 di maggio di s3 d xv posto a lui detti Contanti per sua provvigione del mese passato di aprile e *fa creditore* Cassa..... 0 0 0

9. *Make debtor* Michele Gharo Nestri on May 2nd for s3 d15 posted to his debit account for his provisions of the past month of April and *make creditor* Cash 0 0 0

(*second variation*)

(1553)

10. Devonshire Kerseys *is debitor to* Laurance Fabian, draper, and is for 10 pieces at 36 s. a piece —etc................. 0 0 0

10. (English in the original)

(1595)

11. Cassa van ghereden ghelde *is schuldich aen* Cappital van my 8000 guld. Ende is voor verscheyden penninghen van gout ende silver, so ick in mynen handen hebbe, omme daermede te dryuen den handel van coopmanchap. Godt wil my verleenen ghewin, ende behaeden voor verlies. Amen......... 0 0 0

11. Ready money *is indebted to* Capital for my 8000 guilders. And is for different coins of gold and silver that I have in hand to use in pursuing the trade of merchandise. God will grant me profit and preserve me from loss. Amen................ 0 0 0

Original	Translation
(1613)	
12. Meale in Barrels *is debitor unto* stocke for 16 tuns remaining in the house................ o o o	12. (English in the original)

(*third variation*)

Original	Translation
(1567)	
13. Caisse d'Argent comptant es mains de Pierre Savonne *doibt* 12450£ 10s 6d qu'il met pour compte de son capital, *credeteur* ledit Savonne .... o o o	13. Ready money in the hands of Pierre Savonne *owes* 12450£ 10s 6d which he places in his capital account, *Creditor* is Savonne............ o o o
(1570)	
14. Roggen *soll an* Hering, hab ich mit Audreas Klur von Thorn einen stick getroffen—etc. ... o o o	14. Rye *owes to* Herring, which I have bartered with Audreas Klus of Thorn—etc. .... o o o
(1588)	
15. Chest or money *is Debtor* or *owes to* stock belonging to me, M. N. and is for—etc. ...... o o o	15. (English in the original)
(1594)	
16. Casse *sol* m.11437.8 Per Capital. So viel befind ich bey dem Inventario an bahrschafft so ich dato zum glücklichen aufang dieser handlung in Cassa leg.......... o o o	16. Cash *owes* m.11437.8 for (to) Capital. As much as I find of ready money in the inventory I place in the cash box this day for the prosperous beginning of this business .... o o o
(1606)	
17. Cassa *is schuldig* für fl. 8560. welche ich N. N. eingelecht habe in cassa zu handeln. *Creditor* mein Capital.......... o o o	17. Cash *is indebted* (owes) for fl. 8560 which I, N. N., have invested in cash for trade. My Capital (is) *Creditor*...... o o o

(1608)

18. (original not available)	18. Trading Expenses *debit* per cash, for payments during the month as shown by the memorandum book............ 0 0 0

It will be noted in the examples of journal entries of this so-called second type that not all the cases run true to form; the wording is such as to produce three varieties of entries which, while slightly different in phrasing, are still basically related. The characteristics of these journal entries may be generalized as follows:

First variation:	A is debtor B is creditor
Second variation:	A is debtor to B
Third variation:	A owes to B

The second and third variations in form seem rather similar on the ground that, if A "is debtor," he likewise "owes," since by definition "debtor" is one who "owes." * Perhaps they are both also similar at heart to the entries of the first variation, since one might say: "A is debitor to B (who is creditor)."

But whatever virtue (or lack of it) there may be in grouping entries of the second type into three sub-classes, it is clear enough that entries in this list are radically different from those in the first list in both form and phrasing.† The first type was probably de-

* Yet one can hardly escape the feeling that this third variation is somehow related to the underlying phrasing of entries of the first, since the latter used (or implied) the technical words from the ledger ("shall give," etc.), and since the root word translated as "must" or "shall" also means "owe." The Latin *debet* from *debeo,* the Italian *deve* from *dovere,* the French *doit* from *devoir,* and the German *soll* from *sollen* all mean "he must" as well as "he owes."

† The sharp contrast in the two styles of journal entry raises the interesting question of whether or not such a difference could be the principal factor distinguishing the methods used in different localities. Paciolo says in the first chapter of *De Computis,* "This treatise will adopt the system used in Venice, which is certainly to be recommended above all others, for by means of this, one can find his way in any other." (Geijsbeek, *op. cit.,* p. 33.) Hence, one may conclude that the journal entry of the form:

By A—— to B——

was the Venetian method, and perhaps it may be that the entry in the form:

A is debtor to B

was the distinguishing characteristic of the Florentine method. Certain it is that this form was used in Florence by the Medici family in 1491.

rived from the wording of the ledger entries of the time and obviously led to the use, much later, of "to" in the debit and "by" in the credit of the English ledger entries. The second type of journal entry, on the other hand, would seem to be one to grow more naturally out of the "daybook" record of personal-account transactions, and it is quite clearly a closer antecedent of modern journal entries than the first type.

This last point is demonstrated not only by the form of the entry itself, but also by the fact that entries of the first type soon drop out of use. If some twenty-five journal entries from various sources, including those reported above, are arranged into columns according to type and in chronological sequence, it will be observed that the first type of entry predominates prior to 1550 (the entry in the Medici books of 1491 are the only example in the list of the second type to appear prior to the middle of the sixteenth century) and that after 1550, entries of the second type strongly predominate. Thus, while the real origins of the journal-entry forms are not known, the direction taken by their evolution is unmistakable. The method of which Paciolo thought so highly was proved in the sequel to be inferior, for it was driven out of use by the other form.

But the evolution of the journal entry was by no means complete at the date of the last example given above (1608). The developments of the next three hundred odd years can be traced through journal entries in English alone. Since the changes which took place can therefore be easily read from the entries themselves, the discussion accompanying the examples will be brief.

ENGLISH JOURNAL ENTRIES AFTER 1600

(1684)

19. George Pinchback Debitor to Kettles £75–8d for 5 barrels—etc. .... 75/—/8

(1717)

20. P. Q. at Gibralter my accompt current Debtor to Voyage to Gibralter, consigned to P. Q. £322.9.7½—etc. 322/ 9/7½

(1754)

21. William Wife £360 to Sherry for 10 pipes delivered to him in barter .... 360/—/-

(1788)

22. Charges merchandise Dr. to paper taken for use in shop .... —/10/6

(1841)

23.	Dr.		Cr.	
	Mdse.	1000	B/P	500
			Cash	500

(1848)

24.	Cash to Sundries	1590	
	to Bills Receivable		1500
	Profit and Loss		90

(1864)

		Dr.	Cr.
25.	Merchandise Dr.	5000	
	to James Munroe		5000

(1900)

26.	Merchandise	400	
	to Cash		400

Slight differences in the wording used by the different entries are apparent, especially in examples 19 to 22. The word "debitor" in one entry is "debtor" in another or is wholly omitted in a third (No. 21). In still other cases the abbreviation "Dr." takes the place of the word itself.* These changes, however, are of relatively little significance. But subsequently—beginning a little before the middle of the nineteenth century—a more pronounced change appears. The tendency is for the entries slowly to swing back again into a technicality of form; not the same technicality of

By A——, to B——

which had almost disappeared by 1550, but a technicality almost

* This abbreviation is found as early as 1690 in *Debtor and Creditor Made Easie* by Stephen Monteage (3d Edition). In the years around 1800 its use as in entry No. 22 was quite general; see Thomas Dilworth, *The Young Bookkeeper's Assistant,* London, 1792; William Jackson, *Practical Bookkeeping,* New York, 1816; Patrick Kelly, *The Elements of Bookkeeping,* London, 1833 (10th Edition).

altogether of position. The debits and credits are now entered in separate columns and the name of the account credited is indented below the debit item. Sometimes the abbreviation "Dr." is retained, sometimes it is omitted; the word "to" is retained, however, as the sign of the credit. But even this word "to" disappears entirely before long, and debit or credit is read into the entry purely by the position of the words and figures. Not even the columns are labeled "Dr." and "Cr."

The form of the eighteenth century—"John Doe is debtor $1000 to Stock"—was a plain statement of fact which had to be posted in two places, but these two places were not forcefully indicated. The later developments improved the mechanics of bookkeeping by stating two distinctly separate facts, each to be posted according to its name and its debit or credit characteristic. The procedure now leads one to think of *debit-entries* waiting to be posted, not *debts* or *debitors;* that is, to think of "accounting units" to be transferred or tabulated and not of personified obligations. The journalizing process under modern usage becomes a matter of sorting wholly impersonal facts in a manner designed to increase the accuracy of the sorting (posting).

Practice has passed from one definite stage to another: 1. a time of no journal entries, when the full statement of the transaction was probably entered directly in the two ledger accounts concerned; 2. a period (say 1430 to 1550) with a highly technical form of journal entry preparatory to the record in the ledger; 3. a long interval in which the journal entry expressed more or less fully a complete thought; and 4. the modern period—now quite technical in form again—when the focus is the accurate sorting of accounting units.

But the end is not yet, for evolution is carrying this bookkeeping process still deeper into technicalities. Even the journal entry itself is dispensed with for a great many transactions recorded in numerous subsidiary books of original entry. Posting is made directly to the ledger from the column totals of various special books for most of the transactions of modern American business; only a minor portion of the ledger details comes through formal debit and credit journal entries. Furthermore, some large organizations have abandoned the time-honored left and right, debit and credit, divisions of the ledger account itself; a wide sheet becomes an account, its columns are sub-accounts and entries in them are black and red instead of debit and credit.

Most of the clerks thus have no need to know bookkeeping as such. But for the persons charged with assembling the final bookkeeping data, the process is even more technical than any form of journalizing yet conceived. Only a complete knowledge of the whole ledger and of the characteristics of every book of original entry in the whole elaborate system enables one to bring the many separate debit and credit classifications and summaries together into a unified whole. As a result, the modern bookkeeper—the one who is responsible for uniting the maze of detail into a coherent whole —has a task the like of which none of his predecessors ever faced, and the very act of learning bookkeeping is harder than ever before. Bookkeeping has become a real technology instead of a simple clerical routine.

NOTE ON THE SOURCES OF THE JOURNAL-ENTRY EXAMPLES

(a) The sources of the several journal entries of the first type are as follows:

1. From the account books of Andrea Barbarigo, 1430. Entries in similar form from the books of the Barbarigo family appear for 1457, 1482, 1496, 1507, 1537. See *La Partita Doppia,* by Vittorio Affieri, p. 60.

2. From Luca Paciolo's *De Computis,* the first printed text on bookkeeping. See *Trattato de' Computi e delle Scritture,* by Prof. Vincenzo Gitti (1878).

3. From a text by Antonio Tagliente. See *La Ragioneria,* by Fabio Besta, Vol. III, p. 380.

4. From a text by Domenico Manzoni. See the photo-reproduction of a journal page in *Ancient Double Entry Bookkeeping,* by John B. Geijsbeek, p. 82.

5. From *Nieuwe Instructie* by Jan Ympyn Cristofels. See *Van Paciolo tot Stevin,* by Dr. P. G. A. DeWaal, p. 118. For other entries in English from the 1547 edition of Ympyn's book, see *The Accountant,* August 20, 1927, pp. 261-268.

6. From *Zweifach Buchhalten* by Wolffang Schweicker. See *Geschichte der Buchhaltung in Deutschland,* by Dr. Balduin Penndorf, p. 126. Other entries in similar form by Dutch writers are given in DeWaal *op. cit.;* Van Hoorebeke, 1599 (p. 253); Van Renterghem, 1592 (p. 230); Van den Dycke, 1596 (p. 242).

(b) The sources of the several journal entries of the second type are as follows:

7. From the account books of the Medici Bank in Italy. See Besta, *op. cit.,* p. 325,

there citing A. Ceccherelli, *I libri di mercatur della Banca Medici;* also see Penndorf in *The Accounting Review,* September, 1930, p. 247.

8. From *Practique brifue pour tenir liveres de compte,* by Valentin Mennher de Kempten. See Besta, *op. cit.*, p. 392. For other entries by the same author dated 1565 see DeWaal, *op. cit.*, p. 139, also *Maandblad voor het Boekhouden,* October 1, 1926, and *Der Zeitschrift für Buchhaltung,* V. 7 p. 37.

9. From the account book of Benvenuto Cellini, in Ceccherelli, *op. cit.*

10. From *The maner and fourme how to kepe a perfect reconyng*—etc., by James Peele. See *The Accountant,* January 16, 1926, p. 91 ff.

11. From *Baeckhouwen op die Italiaensche maniere*—etc., by Claes Pietersz. See DeWaal *op. cit.*, p. 164.

12. From *The Pathway to Knowledge*—etc., by John Tapp. See *Maandblad voor het Boekhouden,* March 1, 1926, p. 172.

13. From *Instruction et maniere de tenir livres*—etc., by Pierre Savonne. See DeWaal *op. cit.*, p. 147.

14. From *Buchhalten Durch Zwey Bücher*—etc., by Sebastian Gammersfelder. See Penndorf, *op. cit.*, p. 142.

15. From *Briefe Instruction*—etc., by John Mellis. See *The Accountant,* May 1, 1926, p. 64 ff.

16. From *Buchhalten fein Kurtz Zusammen Gefasst*—etc., by Passchier Goessens. See Penndorf *op. cit.*, p. 150.

17. From *Schöne Forma des Buchhaltens,* by Ambrose Lerice. See Penndorf, *op. cit.*, p. 215.

18. From *Coopmansbouckhauding op de Italiaensche wyse,* by Simon Stevin. See *The Institute of Bookkeepers Journal,* December, 1927, p. 322.

(c). The sources of the English journal entries are as follows:

19. Richard Dafforne, *The Merchant's Mirrour* (entry for January 30, 1633) reprinted in *Lex Mercatoria* by Gerard Malynes (London, 1686).

20. Thomas King, *An exact guide to Bookkeeping* (London, 1717), p. 3 of the journal.

21. William Weston, *The Complete Merchants Clerk* (London, 1754) p. 2 of Journal A.

22. Robert Hamilton, *An Introduction to Merchandise* (Edinburgh, 2d ed., 1788) p. 293.

23. Thomas Jones, *Principles and Practice of Bookkeeping* (New York, 1841) p. 58.

24. P. Duff, *Bookkeeping* (New York, 10th ed., 1st edition 1848), p. 29.

25. Bryant & Stratton, *Bookkeeping* (New York, 1861) p. 12.

26. Williams & Rogers, *Introductive Bookkeeping* (Chicago, revised edition, 1900) p. 22.

IX. DEVELOPMENT OF FINANCIAL STATEMENTS

When financial statements are mentioned today the balance-sheet and the income statement are usually meant. But strictly speaking, the term has a wider meaning. A financial statement really means any formal tabulation of the financial facts of an enterprise.

Financial statements as thus defined may be subdivided into two classes:

(a) Double-entry statements, that is, tabulations which have been 1. summarized out of double accounts and 2. separated from the ledgers.

(b) Other presentations of financial data, that is, those tabulations which either 1. derive from sources other than double-entry accounts or 2. contain the same general information as double-entry statements without being separated from the ledger.

Since statements of the second group are the more elementary and lead the way to later developments, they are considered first.

The charge-and-discharge Account (statement) is probably of very early origin. England, after the Norman conquest (1066), developed a complete feudal system wherein society was organized from the top downward into tiers of service relationships and obligations. Property was held as it were, in trust, with certain responsibilities rising to the person next higher up in the scale. To keep the individual informed of these responsibilities and of their periodic discharge was one of the principal purposes of the record keeping of the time. In royal finance this gave rise to the tally-stick method of recording part remittances from tax collections; in the management of individual manors it gave rise to the charge and discharge accounts by which stewards of the lord of the manor reported upon their activities.

[left folio]

Abstract of the accompts of John Morewood, Receiver of Rents and profits of the manor of Grub Street, and Stock there upon: viz [1]

CHARGE

		£ s d
1682 Sept. 29 to arrears then due		42.
1683 Sept. 29 to the years Rent-Roll of that Estate		592.
Casual profits	to sale of wood	87.17
	Received by A——	1. 4.11
	Received by copy-hold fines	14. 7. 6

The accompt of stock thereupon is as followeth

	given in charge £ s d		sold for £ s d	
14 oxen cost	49	14 sold	76.15.	
12 cows	36	5 "	22. 7. 6	
6 bullocks	15	6 "	21.16. 8	
20 weathers	9	20 "	14.17	
56 ewes	28	56 "	50. 4	
1 colt	1.15	1 "	3. 5	
10 piggs	6	10 "	12.15	
1 bull	3.15	8 calves sold	7.18	
1 ram	1.10	wool sold	7.10	
		Butter & cheese	22.13.10	
Sum	150.	Sum		240. 2

Valuation of stock unsold	Rest unsold, 7 cows	21.	
	1 bull	3.	
	1 ram	1. 5	
	Increased		
	10 lambs beside 30 sold	2.10	
	2 calves besides 8 sold	1.10	
			29. 5
	Total charge		£1006.16.5

[right folio]

DISCHARGE

Yearly Payments	Salary to myself	20.	
	Salary to herdsman	8.	
	A years quit rent	13. 6. 8	
	The stewards fee	2.	
	The poor rate	1.14. 8	45. 1. 4
Uncertain Payments	A levy for the church	1. 6. 8	
	Two constables levies	1.13. 4	
	Charges of keeping courts	1. 5	
	Twelve mon. tax on the rents	22. 4	
	Paid bill for hedging and ditching	8.11	
	Paid bill for repairs	5.16	52.18.4
Cattle	Paid for three loads of hay	2.10	
	Paid for 100 sheep	40.	
	Paid for 19 bullocks	57.	
	Paid charges for driving	1.15	101. 5
Ready money to my Lord and by his order	23 December 1682	50.	
	2 Mch.	50.	
	28 Feb. 1683	100.	
	26 Apl.	50.	
	23 May	43.	
	3 June	15.	
	24 June	50.	
	16 Aug.	20.	
	10 Nov.	34.19.4	412.19.4
	Thus for cash		612. 4
	Lost by Barth. Cutter's death		11. 1
	Land in hand		184.
Arrears to be charged on next accompt	of rent	106.	
	of wood	64. 6. 5	
	of cattle unsold as in the charge besides the new stock above said	29. 5	199.11. 5
	Which evens the charge		£1006.16. 5

The statement is plainly the report of an agent, not a statement of indebtedness or of ownership. In general, the agent charges himself with all financial responsibilities placed upon him (collections, natural increases in stock, loans received) and discharges himself by reporting upon the disposition (sales, expenses, losses, loans made and remainders) of those responsibilities. The foregoing example is taken from a seventeenth century textbook and illustrates particularly well the variety of details included as well as the form in which the data are arranged.

This statement, it will be noted, is not a personal account—the steward does not owe the lord of the manor; neither is it a receipt and disbursement statement nor a calculation of loss and gain. It is simply a well organized report upon an agent's responsibilities.[2] This form of presenting financial facts still has its usefulness, for it is the basis of present-day accounting for executorships and receiverships. When used under modern ledger methodology the statement becomes the agent's own account, accompanied by collateral (and opposite) accounts for the details so that dual entries can be made and a test of equilibrium taken.

Little information seems available, however, regarding the records from which the early charge-and-discharge statements were summarized. It is doubtful whether the source accounts were organized into a coherent system of records; more probable is the surmise that these statements were compiled from memoranda, warrants, vouchers, rent-rolls, etc.; in other words, from documents rather than from an organized ledger.*

Agency accounting also developed in Italy as has been explained in chapter 3. But there it was clearly associated with other accounts in a ledger and thus is more easily connected with the development of double entry than is the charge-and-discharge accounting of early England. If systematic accounts were kept, the agent's report upon his responsibility could be seen in the "master's account" kept in the ledger. A separate statement would not usually be needed. It will be recalled that Paciolo advised the use of a separate set of books for a voyage or trading journey. As an illustration of this type

* See chapter XV for a discussion of manorial accounts under audit.

of "statement," a ledger account is given below from Mennher's textbook (Antwerp, 1550):

+ LAUS DEQ. AN. 1550 ON THE FIRST OF JANUARY AT ANTWERP [3]

		Nicolas de Reo is debtor on this date per John Mas by assignation...fol.	1	326 13 4			Nicolas de Reo is creditor on this date for Cash.fol.	1	987 13 4
do	26	March per Velvet purchased from John Mas "	3	181 16 9	do	—	the same for assignation...... "	1	289 12 4
do	10	July per bankruptcy of John Mas......... "	8	50 10 –	do	17	June for pepper sold to John Mas......... "	6	112 11 4
do	31	per interest to John Fris..... "	9	1 — –	do	15	July for interest Peter Mor.... "	9	4 — –
do	—	idem per various trade expenses "	10	57 13 4	do	31	per L. Gall for balance...... "	10	103 — –
do	—	idem per myself Peter Dumont "	10	10 — –			idem per London for balance... "	10	200 — –
do	—	idem per Lyons for Balance... "	10	200 — –					
do	—	idem per Cash for Balance...... "	10	1499 6 4			&c. &c. Sum £1768.5.8		
		&c. &c. Sum £1768.5.81							

This is the ledger account of the master (Nicolas de Reo) kept by the agent (Peter Dumont). It is credited for money received from the master, or collected for him, and debited for purchases, expenses, remittances, etc. While this is still a ledger account, it nevertheless contains statement information. Formal separation (extraction) of ledger information was not yet a part of bookkeeping procedure.

The next approach to financial statements in Italian bookkeeping was through the profit-and-loss account and the balance account in the ledger. Some of the early writers like Paciolo and Manzoni did not describe the balance account but ended the closing process when the goods and expense accounts had been closed into the profit-and-loss account and the latter into the capital account. But there were other writers who did describe it. At the end of the "goods book" in the text of one of the early German authors (Gotlieb,

1546) is the following account which Jäger calls a "sort of balance account": [4]

1545	
To close this trade or account everything on hand on July 17 is found to be the following:	
to money	2,229.10.3
to debts	20.—.–
to goods	16.—.–
Together this wealth is	2,265.10.3

1545	
To close this trade or account everything that I am obligated to pay on July 17 is found to be the following:	
my capital	2,000.00.–
other creditors	44.16.–
Both together make	2,044.16.–
These deducted from the left side gives the profit gained	220.14.3
Makes together with the profit mentioned	2,265.10.3

The assets are here assembled on the left; on the right are the liabilities, the capital (presumably the amount of the previous proprietorship balance and not the original investment), and the profit. In this example assets and liabilities are used to calculate the profit. The arrangement suggests that the "balance account" was as yet not quite a formal summary of the accounts still open after the nominal accounts had been closed into capital.

In Angelo Pietra's text (1586) the ledger ends with what is in effect a balance account.

1586	
Esito generale di quest' anno, finito adi ultimo Maggio, dee dare, per li infrascritti crediti del Monastero, qui tirati da i contiloro, cioe	
Quilico Fedele, e fratelli	o o
Gordiano Lampridio affittuale	o o
Eutitio Lanciano fornasaro	o o
Henrico Lanfranco malghese	o o
Oberro Basilisco molinaro	o o
Et piu Frumento stara 10	o o

1586 [5]	
Esito generale di quest' anno finito adi ultimo Maggio, dee havere per gli infrascritti debiti del Monastero, qui tirati da i contiloro, cioe	
Bartholo Saladino in Vinegia	o o
Aquila Gradito affituale, conto di tempo	o o
Clemente Aleni nostro Curato	o o
Fabritio Gallo nostro fattore	o o
Delfino Commodo camparo	o o

Demetrio Contestabile massaro	0 0
Valerio Leoni massaro	0 0
Vittorio, e Cortese Palladini massari	0 0
Rinaldo Sansone massaro	0 0
Temistio Solimano massaro	0 0
Dante Congiurato barbero	0 0
Inessigibili & a lungo tempo	
Marco Tullio Villanuova gia affituale	0 0
Fausto Gioviale gia massaro	0 0
Innocentio Maiorano gia fattore	0 0
Leontio Manfredi gia molinaro	0 0
Somma	5940–11–3
Restanti di questo anno	
Casciaria formaggio, per uso	0 0
Cantina di Camerone, per uso	0 0
Cantina diversa, per uso	0 0
Cantina del Monastero per uso	0 0
Granaro di Camerone, per uso	0 0
da vendere	0 0
Granaro diverso, per uso	0 0
Granaro del Monastero, per uso	0 0
da vendere	0 0
Granaro di Vena, e Spelta	0 0
Cassa in contanti	0 0
Somma	8481–1–9

Annibale Germano servidore	0 0
Somma	4737–1–6
Monastero nostra resta in credito, come sivede	3744–0–3
Somma	8481–1–9

The account is named *Esito Generale* (final result). The debit list has a sub-total at the end of the personal accounts (tenants, stewards, miller, etc.). This is followed by the "remainders for this year" (cheese, wine, grain, cash), that is, the inventories. On the credit are listed the creditors ("our curator," "our agent," etc.) followed by the single item, "Balance to the Credit of our Monastery."

Since the nominal accounts had already been closed through an income-and-expense account (not profit-and-loss account) into the monastery account (corresponding to the capital account), the use of this *"Esito"* account brought all the remaining open accounts into a summary convenient for transfer to a new ledger. It is a little difficult to understand, however, why the contra to the debit in this account should be the monastery-account credit, and the contra to the credit, the monastery-account debit, instead of the contras being the real accounts themselves.

The balance account in any event became standard bookkeeping practice and was in use until quite recently.*

The following is the balance account from Dafforne, *Merchant's Mirrour*, 1635.

[left folio]			[right folio]		
	1634			1634	
20 July	to Jacob Symonson, my account by him in Company	301.—. 8	20 July	By Jacob Symonson his account by mee in Company	512. 3.8
"	to Jean du Boys, for Comp. R.R. 3/5 me 2/5 Currant	1092.17.10	"	By Randall Rice his account by me in Company	991. 7.6
"	to Hend. Van Linden & Comp. their commodities	194.12. 1	"	By Hend. Vander Lind. and Comp. their commodities	194.12.1
			"	By Hend. Vand.	

* In Postlethwate's *Universal Dictionary of Trade and Commerce* (London, 1774) the author, probably following Savary, directs the closing of all accounts in the ledger as follows (*vide Merchant Accountantship*):

"To balance an account in the ledger of profit and loss:—

if lost on the whole trade: Stock Dr. to Profit and Loss.

if gained on the whole trade: Dr. Profit and Loss to Stock."

"To balance an account in the ledger of stocks:—

Dr. stock to balance, which being credited by stock, add up the debtor side and creditor side of balance and both will be exactly equal, and a proof that every article [transaction] hath had its double entry throughout your books; which will yield an agreeable satisfaction as well as show you that this, of all methods, is the most excellent."

A balance account was used or mentioned by: T. H. Goddard, *The Merchant or Practical Accountant* (New York, 1834); Daniel Hoit, *Bookkeeping by Single and Double Entry* (Boston, 1859); J. G. Pilsen, *Complete Reform of Bookkeeping* (New York, 1877); E. G. Hall, *Business Manual* (Logansport, 1894).

20 July	to Voyage to Antw. in Comp. R.R. 3/5 and 2/5 mee.......	189.12. –		Linden Comp. their ready money.........	99. 7.7
"	to Andrew Hitchcocke due to mee by conclude..........	446.12. 9	20 July	By Hend. Vand. Lind. & Comp. their time account..........	93.19.8
"	to Arthur Mumperson my account by him in Comp..........	402.12. 1	"	By Stocke, for difference there, being my pres. estate..........	2902.12.7
"	to Tho. Trust for Comp. R.R. 3/5 me 2/5 our time acco.......	413. 6. 8		Summe	4794. 3.1
"	to Figs in Comp. Jac. Symonson 2/3 and 1/3 for mee...........	806. 6.11			
"	to Cash resting therein and brought hither..	947. 2. 1			
	Summe	4794. 3. 1			

Abraham Liset in *The Accountants Closet* (London, 1684), ends one ledger with the following:

[left folio]			[right folio]		
Balance Ledger A is Debtor			Balance Ledger A is Creditor		
1658			1658		
Dec. 31	to the Manor of Speedwell within the county of Sucesse	5000.—.–	Dec. 31	By Stock......	60928.12–
	to the Manor and Forest of Increase in Somerset............	4000.—.–			
	to Several Goods and Houses lying in and about London	15000.—.–			

to Several Ships at Sea, viz.: the *Hope* and *Good-Adventure*	9000.—.-
to Account Particular	619.16.8
to Adventure-land in Ireland.	3000.—.-
to the Farmery of Paywell	4000.—.-
to Cash, under custody of Mr. Richard Goldcoin	20308.15.4
	60928.12.-

In Liset's ledger B the first account has the same name as that quoted but the sides are reversed, with houses, ships, goods, etc. on the credit (posted to the debit of individual accounts elsewhere in the ledger) and stock on the debit (posted to the credit of stock account). The balance account in the new ledger thus took the place of the opening journal as the source of the first postings to assets, liabilities and capital accounts.

There is no indication that the balance account of these early texts was copied out of the ledger and used as a separate statement. Some of its uses (as preparation for transferring to new ledgers) would not even suggest separation. But other purposes were also served by such data, and slowly they gave rise to statements which were separated from the accounts.

One of the first indications of the use of account data outside the ledger was in the proof of completeness and equilibrium. Several examples of this are given below.

Simon Stevin, writing in 1608, summarizes the important account data better than his predecessors in this manner:

"The difference between the two totals (provided that all debts are good) is their net capital, and so much as this differs from the net capital of the previous year, so much is the profit or loss they desire to know.

"In order to effect the same in our present bookkeeping, I act as if neither the totals of debits and credits had been put in the ledger nor the balances inserted on closing the accounts, and I collect together the accounts of money, wares, debtors [and creditors?], excluding, however, the balance of the Capital account and of all other accounts that indicate increase or decrease of capital, such as Trading expenses, Household expenses, Profit and Loss, etc., so that only such things are taken of which it is usual to make up an estate on a certain day, usually on the 31st December. . . . . . Thus the Estate would appear as follows:

THE ESTATE OF DERRICK ROOSE

MADE UP ON THE LAST DAY OF DECEMBER, 1600

Estate of Capital debit	£	s	d	Estate of Capital credit	£	s	d
Per Arnold Jacobs	51	8	0	per Nuts	60	13	2
Balance debit, put here in order to close this statement	3140	9	1	per Pepper	20	0	0
				per Omar de Swarte . .	513	12	0
				per Adrian de Winter	150	6	0
				per Peter de Witte	448	0	0
				per Jack de Somer	54	18	6
				per Cash	1944	7	5
Total	3191	17	1	Total	3191	17	1

	£	s	d
The remainder at the end of the year is	3140	9	1
at the beginning of the year it was £2667 9s 8d minus 514 6 0	2153	3	8
Increase during the year	987	5	5

Proof of the Estate

"In order to make certain that the above Estate is correct I collect all remainders of accounts increasing or decreasing Capital, *i.e.,* the remainders of all accounts excluded from the above Estate, because they do not represent actual things—but accounts of profit and loss occurred since the 0th of January, 1600 . . . .

Profit and Loss debit	£	s	d	*Profit and Loss credit*	£	s	d
Per Trading Expenses.	57	7	0	Per profit on Cloves . . .	75	4	7
Per Household Expenses	107	10	0	Per profit on Nuts	109	7	2
Total	164	17	0	per profit on Pepper . .	18	19	0
				Per profit on Ginger . .	41	8	4

Remaining credit, being profit agreeing with the previous account, inserted here as balance	987 5 5	Per Account of Profit and Loss	907 3 4
Total	1152 2 5	Total	1152 2 5

"Since the profit ascertained in this way is equal to that found by means of the previous estate *viz.*, £987 5s 5d, this may be taken as the Proof of the work." [6]

The author here indicates an understanding of the heart of double-entry bookkeeping which is plainly superior to that displayed by many later writers. He also presents models for financial statements which are more in harmony with modern practice than many of those subsequently used by others. It is interesting also to note that Stevin's balance-sheet is in the form now followed in England and to speculate on the question of whether or not this Dutch author was the inspiration for the British practice.

More than two hundred years later a French author [7] presented several "tables of balances" which fell far short of Stevin's standard. The author apparently rearranged data from the works of three other writers. The statements are as follows:

1. The addition of the assets in the operations journal constructed by Garnier, edition 1815, amounts to	1,777,725
The liabilities amount to	1,540,325
difference	237,400
Capital to be deducted	198,200
His profit	39,200

Summary of profits according to the detailed columns

Profit on merchandise	24,400
on discount	65
on exchange	820
on gold bullion	4,375
on joint merchandise	4,000
on battomery	7,500
on commission	640
on freight	20,000
	61,800

Lost on insurance	18,000		
expenses	3,400		
charges	1,200		
	22,600		
		22,600	
Profits in the same sum		39,200	

2. The addition of the assets in the operations journal constructed by M. Delorme, gives me

The addition of the assets in the operations journal constructed by M. Delorme, gives me		715,038
The liabilities		696,828
Profit		18,209
The sum of the profits	21,646	
The sum of the losses	4,436	
Profit in the same sum	18,209	
The debits in the ledger amount to	700,039	
The credits	681,830	
Profit	18,209	
The balances of the asset accounts	115,136	
The balances of the liability accs.	96,927	
	18,209	

3. By the same method the accounts constructed by Desgranges give the following:

Inventory of the store at invoice prices

Cost of merchandise purchased	389,360
Expense of transportation	1,780
	391,140
Merchandise remaining	224,600
Invoice price of merchandise sold	166,540
Amount of actual sales	189,156
Profit on merchandise	22,616

These examples are indicative of an evolution toward separate financial statements, but they apparently were constructed from no stronger motive than to afford a "proof of the estate."

But real motives were not far to seek. No doubt many statements were made up for tax purposes even in the Middle Ages. Penndorf[8] states that the laws of the Italian city-states (say 1427) required a self-assessed tax upon all property and that the Medici family made up statements for that purpose. The German municipal law (Augsburg, 1516) also required such tax statements and had them sworn to before a commission. The example the author gives (from the diary of Lucas Rem) is in plain narrative rather than tabular form.

Jacques Savary[9] indicates that the ordinance of March, 1673 (Ch. 3 Sec. 8) required merchants every two years to make a statement (*Inventaire*) "of all their fixed and movable properties and of their debts receivable and payable." The purpose was to preserve this general view of their business up to the prior date if later they should fail. This, then, was more related to bankruptcy than taxation. But practically the same kind of statement would serve either purpose.

Savary, after discussing at length the process of making an inventory (very much along the lines laid down by Paciolo), concluded by giving a summary of the details or "a balance" in the following arrangement:

Balance of the present Inventory		
Debit for the sum total of merchandise, debts receivable due me and money in cash per present inventory		£35534.2.1
Personal Property		
Gold plate	280	
Household furniture, estimated	4200	4480.
Real Estate		
One house located thus and so, estimated....		15000.
Total of all my effects		£55014.2.1
Deduct debts payable due to those mentioned by name in the inventory................		10023.1
Thus all my effects amount to..........		£44991.1.1

Balance of the present Inventory	
Credit for the debts payable per inventory	£10023.1
For my capital according to the agreement of the firm....	20000.
£5511.1.1 for balance of the present Inventory, which is the profit which it has pleased God to give me from the first day of September, 1672 to the first day of September, 1673	5511.1.1
	£35534.2.1

Made and checked by my initials all the pages of the present Inventory

Paris, Sept. 1, 1673
Pierre Jacques

This lacks the clear logic and satisfying completeness of Stevin's statements, but it does show, however clumsily, the calculation of the annual gain and the present net worth, and it could be used for tax purposes (if desired) as well as to satisfy the French law.

Another strong motive for the separation of financial statements was the settlement of partnership affairs. The closing of the books would not always suffice, for then only the one having the books would preserve a record of the situation at the moment.

Penndorf[10] gives a statement prepared by the Fugger family in 1527 which seems to have had this motive behind it:

On the last of December of the year just closed, 1527		
to Real Estate		127 902
to Debts, Goods, everywhere		1 964 750
Total Capital		2 032 652
deduct donations to institutions & ch.		11 450
		2 021 202
deduct capital of 1511		196 791
Balance, profit in 17 years		1 824 411
deduct 1/8 for R. and A. Fugger		228 051
still remaining to be divided		1 596 360
Portion to Jacob Fugger, deceased	720 950	
" " Raymundus Fugger	211 953	
" " Antoni Fugger	211 953	
" " Jeronimus Fugger	451 503	
Total capital and profit	1 596 359	
Jacob Fugger, deceased		809 825
Raymundus Fugger		352 107
Antoni Fugger		352 107
Jeronimus Fugger		507 162
		2 021 201

When any fundamental change took place in a partnership, such as dissolution or the admission of a new partner, a calculation of the business capital had to be made.* If revaluation of any of the items were necessary, the capital shown by the books alone would

* Mediæval partnerships were generally for short periods and frequent, irregular closing was the general practice. See Buhl, *Die geschichtliche begründete Kontentheorie.*

[left folio]

Survey of the general balance, or Estate-reckoning Debitor	Thus ought your accounts to stand at the first view of the Bookes, when everything is transported out of the waste-booke into the Leager.	Thus ought your second, or Tryall Ballance to stand with the Losses.	Thus ought your True-balance to stand, which you transport into your new-bookes.
dito to Bancke	13688.17.8	5555. 2.–	5555. 2.–
dito to House King David	6213.15.–		
dito to Susanna Peeters Orphans	5573.16.8	713.14.8	713.14.8
dito to Jack Pudding my account currant	11328. 6.8	2648. 6.8	2648. 6.8
dito to Wines, 15 Butts unsold	1260.—.–	1260.—.–	1260.—.–
dito to French Aquae-vitae	5568.—.–		
dito to Rye, 18 Last, 7 Mudde	2877.15.8	1533.15.8	1533.15.8
dito to Couceaneille	10080.—.–	36.—.–	36.—.–
dito to Brasill	10888. 3.–	70.11.–	
dito to Interest-reckoning	44.14.–		
dito to Profit and Loss	320. 2.8		
dito to Voyage to London, consigned to Jack Pudding	7810.—.–	2600.—.–	2600.—.–
dito to Voyage to Hamberg	2353. 3.–		
dito to Voyage to Dansicke	1967. 1.–		
dito to Insurance reckoning	3463. 2.8		
dito to Cash	29561.11.–	27153. 8.–	27153. 8.–
dito to Cambrix, 11 peeces unsold	8000.—.–	440.—.–	440.—.–
dito to Ship the Rainbow	1043.12.8		
dito to Hans van Essen at Hambrough my account currant	3780.—.–	60.—.–	
dito to Peeter Brasseur at Dansicke, my account currant	3805.14.8	53.12.8	
dito to Jack Pudding at London his account currant	917.—.–		
Summe	130544.15.–	42124.10.–	41904. 6.8

be unsatisfactory. A separate statement would have to be made—the so-called "inventory" (statement of resources and liabilities).

After joint-stock companies (such as the East India Company) appeared in the seventeenth century, statements separate from the books would soon be highly advisable because of the number of

[right folio]

Survey of the general-balance, or Estate-reckoning Creditor	Thus ought your accounts to stand at the first view of the Bookes, when every-thing is transported out of the waste-booke into the Leager.	Thus ought your second, or Tryall Ballance to stand with the Gains.	Thus ought your True-balance to stand, which you transport into your new-bookes.
dito By Bancke	8133.15.8	1325.—.-	
dito By House King David	7538.15.-		
dito By Susanna Peeters Orphans	4860. 2.-		
dito By Jack Pudding, my account current	9145.—.-	465.—.-	
dito By French Aquae-vitae	6960.—.-	1392.—.-	
dito By Rye	1788.12.8	444.12.8	
dito By Couceaneille	13950.—.-	3906.—.-	
dito By Brasill	10817.12.-		
dito By Interest-reckoning	102.16.8	58. 2.8	
dito By Profit and Loss	394. 7.8	74. 5.-	
dito By Voyage to London	8350.—.-	3140.—.-	
dito By Voyage to Hambrough	3816. 6.-	1463. 3.-	
dito By Voyage to Dansicke	3805.14.8	1838.13.8	
dito By Insurance-reckoning	3576. 6.-	113. 3.8	
dito By Cash	2408. 3.-		
dito By Cambrix-cloth	8105.12.-	545.12.-	
dito By Ship the Rainbow	1432.12.8	389.—.-	
dito By Hans van Essen, my account	3720.—.-		
dito By Peeter Brasseur, my account	3752. 2.-		
dito By Jack Pudding, at London, his account current	3294.18.-	2377.18.-	2377.18.-
dito By Stocks, for my just Estate	24592.—.-	24592.—.-	39526. 8.8
Summe	130544.15.-	42124.10.-	41904. 6.8

people who had contributed capital and who would desire information about their venture. The same purpose is accomplished by the statements prepared to inform modern stockholders of the condition and progress of present day limited-liability corporations.

In addition to these reasons for separate statements, there is, under modern conditions, the necessity for carefully prepared and authenticated separate statements for credit purposes. In fact, most statements could be said to be prepared for capital purposes, since statements which are prepared for partners, shareholders or lenders all have a capital focus. Perhaps the same could be said of statements prepared for taxation purposes, at least until the advent of a tax on income.

Once statements were separated from the accounts (whatever the reason may have been) the development was in the direction of experimental arrangements of figures for the better presentation of the facts and of refinements of classification in the interest of a closer expression of actual values.

There were two ways of approaching separate statements: (1) to work from the trial balance and produce a columnar arrangement of the data and (2) to copy the key accounts much as they appeared in the ledger.

An early example of the columnar statement is given on pages 138 and 139, from Dafforne, *Merchants Mirrour,* 1635.

"When you intend generally to make a survey, or balance of your Bookes, then sheweth the first place of these three money-places, how you may fitly keep your great additions throughout your whole leager, by Ruling and Drawing them upon a Paper as the ensuing balances present unto your Eye-view":

The first column on each side is a trial balance of totals, the middle column is a trial balance of balances, the last is the balance-sheet column containing the remaining assets, liabilities and capital. It will be noted that no column is provided for the profit-and-loss calculation.*

The following examples of the account form of statement are taken from eighteenth century textbooks.

From Thomas King, *An Exact Guide to Bookkeeping by Way of Debtor and Creditor Done after the Italian Method,* 1717:

* Some of the figures in the tabulation were apparently omitted in error from the 1635 edition and are inserted here from the third edition of 1686.

[left folio]

Profit and Loss		Debtor		
1715		£		
Oct. 27	to C. S. Esq. for interest of £1000 due the 27 of April next	27	10	–
Nov. 15	to Mr. B. D.	6	17	8
23	to B. A. by Composition	15	—	–
Feb. 27	to Voyage to Gibralter consigned to P. Q.	137	12	6
1716				
Mar. 26	to P. Q. my accompt current for defect in Goods	2	10	–
Apr. 27	to C. S. Esq. for interest on £1000 due the 27 of Oct. next	27	10	–
Oct. 25	to Insurance Account, lost thereby	330	—	–
	to Charges on Merchandize	9	—	6
	to Household expenses	22	5	–
	to Stock gained by one year's trade	899	5	6¾
	to My Father's Will left me	5000	—	–
		6477	11	2¾

[right folio]

Per Contra		Creditor		
1715		£		
Oct. 27	By T. C. for Interest of £500 due 27th April next	15	—	–
28	By my Father's Will	5000	—	–
Nov. 8	By Composition with Mr. B.	9	14	8¾
1716				
Mar. 14	By Mr. G.	27	10	–
Apr. 27	By T. O. for Interest of £500 due 27th Oct. next	15	—	–
Oct. 25	By C. S. Esq. for Interest £150 due 27th inst.	5	10	3½
	By Yorkshire Cloth, gained thereby	86	6	–
	By Spanish Cloth, gained thereby	100	—	–
	By Voyage to Gibralter, gained thereby	324	14	7½
	By Norwich wares, gained thereby	23	18	–
	By Exeter wares, gained thereby	14	10	–
	By Grocery wares, gained thereby	28	11	1
	By Druggets, gained thereby	10	16	–
	By Hops, gained thereby	283	10	–
	By the Flying Eagle, gained thereby	155	—	–
	By Voyage to Salicia, gained thereby	377	10	6
		6477	11	2¾

[left folio]

Ballances	Debtor			
1716		£		
Oct. 25	to Cash resteth this day	6658	11	10
	to Yorkshire Cloth unsold	1590	—	—
	to Spanish Cloth unsold	1087	10	—
	to Voyage to Gibralter for wares unsold	77	10	—
	to Mr. G. C. due to me	20	—	—
	to Exeter wares unsold	215	—	—
	to P. Q. at Gibralter due to me	499	12	6
	to T. O. for Principal and Interest	515	—	—
	to Grocery wares unsold	404	—	—
	to Sagathee unsold	120	—	—
	to Fine Holland unsold	577	10	—
	to Mr. D. due to me	125	—	—
	to Hops unsold	76	4	9¼
	to Voyage to Galicia for wares unsold	18	10	—
	to T. K. at Galicia due to me	385	—	—
		12429	9	1¼

[right folio]

Per Contra	Creditor			
1716		£		
Oct. 25	By Stock	10337	6	¾
	By C. S. Esq. due to him	871	19	8½
	By N. S. due to him	105	3	4
	By Mr. E. due to him	315	—	-
	By Mr. G. due to him	300	—	-
	By Mr. K. due to him	500	—	-
		12429	9	1¼

While the foregoing are accounts in a textbook ledger, the next examples are stated by the author as statements outside the ledger. They are from Hamilton, *Introduction to Merchandise,* 1788:

Profit and Loss Sheet

	£	s	d		£	s	d
Salt	—	11	4	Meal	9	18	—
Charges merchandise	13	14	2	Port wine	6	15	—
Proper expenses	32	15	10	Paper	4	18	6
	47	1	4	Yarn	2	3	2
in Ledger	4	4	10	Calicoes	1	13	4
	51	6	2	Diaper	-	15	10

nett gain	16 13 8	Iron	2 7 11
	£67 19 10	Clover-seed	5 — 1
		Linseed	– 18 —
		Share of Ship Hazard	23 — —
		Train Oil	8 — —
			65 9 10
		in Ledger	2 10 —
			£67 19 10

Balance Sheet

Cash	£ 8 3 10	Meal, outcome 3B	
Meal, 124 lb. at 13/6	83 14 —	Royal Bank	201 3 2
Yarn, 474 Sp. at 2/	47 8 —	William Bruce	20 - -
House in Eden	300 — —	Tho. Sharp	8 - -
J. A. Boswell	37 11 —		229 3 2
H. Hardie	31 2 6		
D. Miller	18 — —		
J. Cuthbert	5 6 3		
Iron, 40 st. at 3/4	6 13 4		
J. Henderson	7 4 —		
W. Hunter	18 13 6		
J. A. Dalton	35 15 —		
Clover seed, 300 lb. at /6 deficiency 10 lb.	7 10 —		
J. Scott	4 7 —		
Share of ship Hazard	140 — —		
Geo. Jordon	6 3 4	Stock	528 9 1
	£757 12 3		£757 12 3

These statements approach the modern arrangement more closely than the earlier ones. The same form is found in use throughout the nineteenth century by those authors who favor the so-called "account form" of statement. Other forms favored by other authors include (1) a development of the columnar trial balance and (2) a beginning at the "report form."

The columnar arrangement, as the following examples will show, was now much improved over Dafforne's early attempt. The principal change was the inclusion of a profit-and-loss column. The tendency was to develop the columnar sheet as a calculation device in which inventories were entered to adjust the book figures and in

Balance Sheet of Hamilton & Co. 31st Dec. 1819		Face of Ledger		Face of Ledger		Profit & Loss		Hamilton's Account		Hancock's Account		State of the Concern	
		debit footing	credit footing	debit balance	credit balance	loss	gain	debit	credit	debit	credit	debtors	creditors
Folio	Account titles												
		Total loss and expenses				000							
		Total amount of gains					000						
		Balance of P&L divided				00			00				
		to partners				00					00		
				Balance due Hamilton				00					
						Balance due Hancock				00			
							Whole amount of debts due us					0000	
							Whole amount of debts we owe						0000
							Making present worth of the concern						0000

which the division of profit as between partners was clearly shown, so that the new capital accounts in the balance-sheet columns made the final equilibrium of double-entry bookkeeping plainly evident.

The illustration on the opposite page is from Thomas Goddard, *The Merchant or Practical Accountant* (New York, 1834).

From J. P. Colt, *The Science of Double Entry Bookkeeping* (Cincinnati, 2d ed., 1838) (this author uses fewer columns):

BALANCE SHEET

Name of Account	Face of Ledger		Profit and Loss Account		Stock Account		Balance Account or State of Concern preparatory to transferring or opening new books	
	Dr. Bal.	Cr. Bal.	Dr.	Cr.	Dr.	Cr.	Dr.	Cr.

Hoit (*Bookkeeping by Single and Double Entry,* Boston, 1859), Mayhew (*University Bookkeeping,* 1870), and Soule (*New Science and Practice of Accounts,* 9th ed., 1911) use an arrangement of columns similar to that of Goddard. Hoit, however, calls the last item "joint capital," while Mayhew and Soule (whose first edition appeared in 1881) introduce an inventory column following the trial-balance column. They also omit the trial balance of totals.

These statements were called "balance-sheets." The arrangement was regarded as a distinct achievement. "This form of balance-sheet is the most explicit and comprehensive that the genius of the accountant has yet devised to show, in a small space, the financial condition of a business firm." (Soule) "Such sheets exhibit the condition of one's affairs at the time and, when regularly taken and preserved, give a very concise history of his business." (Mayhew)

The account form of statement also had its advocates, and it was through this form that the evolution was continued. The columnar form gradually dropped out of use in the texts as a regularly used statement. It now finds only occasional use in auditing or in classroom problems, in which many adjustments need to be incorporated into trial balance data. It is at present called a "columnar working sheet," the term "balance-sheet" being confined to the statement of assets, liabilities and capital.

The following examples are illustrative of the account form of statement in the nineteenth century. Nicholas Harris (*Practical Bookkeeping,* 1842) presents this arrangement:

BALANCE SHEET

Dr. Cr.

1838				1838			
Jan. 31	Merchandise.......	1,000	00	Jan. 31	By Bills Payable....	12,650	00
"	Cash..............	18,853	00	"	Hampshire Monroe. Co..............	700	00
"	Bills Receivable....	11,007	50				
"	Bellnap & Hamersby	1,500	00	"	Reed & Barber.....	4,000	00
"	Spaulding & Stone..	800	00	"	Stock..............	18,900	50
"	Brown & Parsons...	1,140	00				
"	J. Burt............	190	00				
"	Andrus, Judd & Franklin.........	360	00				
		36,250	50			36,250	50

PROFIT AND LOSS SHEET

Dr. Cr.

1838				1838			
Jan. 31	to Charges.........	337	00	Jan. 31	By Real Estate.....	200	00
"	to Stock...........	1,800	50	"	By Interest.........	7	50
				"	By Ship to Orleans.	420	00
				"	By Commission....	180	00
				"	By Profit & Loss...	30	00
				"	By Merchandise....	1,300	00
		2,137	50			2,137	50

These statements are apparently made up from the information in the ledger; the author mentions the trial balance as a possible source of the data but does not stress it.

The following combined statement is labeled "balance-sheet" by the author (J. H. Palmer, *A Treatise on Practical Bookkeeping,* New York, 13th ed., 1857).

BALANCE SHEET

Estate Accounts	Res.	Liab.	Gain and Loss Accounts	Loss	Gain
Cash Dr..................00			Merchandise Cr......00		
Cr..................00	00		unsold 00 00		
			Merchandise Dr..... 00		00
Bill Rec. Dr.............00					
Cr.............00	00		Real Estate Cr.......00		
			Dr......00		00
Per a/c's Dr.............00					
Cr.............00	00		Interest Dr......... 00		
			Cr.......... 00	00	
Bills Pay. Dr.............00					
Cr.............00		00	Charges Dr................	00	
Merchandise unsold..........	00		Profit and Loss Dr..........	00	
Original Cap.............00			Net Gain (Stock)...........	00	
Net Gain................00		00			
	000	000		000	000

A slightly different arrangement is given by Lorenzo Fairbanks (*The Science and Practice of Bookkeeping by Single and Double Entry,* Philadelphia, 1866).

STATEMENT OF RESOURCES AND LIABILITIES

		Resources	Liabilities
Cash (Bank of Commerce)............................		00	
Merchandise..		00	
Bonds..		00	
Personal Accounts..................................		00	
Personal Accounts..................................			00
Bills Receivable...................................		00	
Bills Payable......................................			00
My net investment was......................	00		
My net gain is.............................	00		
			00
Showing my present capital.........................			00
		000	000

STATEMENT OF LOSSES AND GAINS

			Losses	Gains
Merchandise	as per Inventory	00		
	amount sold	00		
	Total proceeds	00		
	First cost	00		
	Gain			00
U. S. Bonds	per Inventory	00		
	First cost	00		
	Gain			00
Expense			00	
Interest Paid		00		
" Received		00		
R. R. Stock Proceeds		00		
" " Cost		00		00
Profit and Loss			00	
Net Gain			00	
			000	000

In a very similar arrangement of data by E. G. Folsom (*Logic of Accounts,* New York, 1873) the profit-and-loss tabulation is called "analysis of ideal accounts" and the balance-sheet the "analysis of commercial accounts." The same author also shows the form of a "columnar balance-sheet" with the usual headings: accounts, inventory, ideal (i.e., profit-and-loss accounts), partners, commercial (i.e., real accounts).

An early antecedent of what is now known (and widely used) as the report form of statement is found in Peter Duff's *North American Accountant,* 1848. He writes:

"I have found by experience that the most simple and rational explanation of the Balance Account will be found in the following process. Let the pupil be required to make up from his ledger, upon waste paper, a list of his effects thus:

From the Bills Receivable Account I find I have Notes in hand amounting to,	$ 500
By the Cash Account, I find cash in hand,	3,080
By W. Hayes Account, I perceive he owes me,	300
Making the total amount of my effects	3,880

By Bills Payable Account, I find I owe on my notes	300	
And to Warden and Bell, by their account, ...	600	
Amount I owe..............................		900
Leaving my present net capital.............		$2,980

"Now compare this statement with our Balance Account, and I shall be much mistaken if it does not give you a clearer insight into the nature and object of that account than all the rules that Bookkeepers have ever written about it."

By the end of the nineteenth century the development of separate financial statements was well under way. In comparison with more recent statements there were still many refinements to be added. But the pattern had been established and later developments in form made no great changes. However, the columnar statement came to be used only as a work sheet and the account form of statement, while not generally followed for the profit-and-loss, was retained for the balance-sheet.

In matters of form the greatest change which later statements showed was the grouping of the data into sub-sections. In the nineteenth century the major classifications of accounts were still being argued; some wished them called real and representative, primary and secondary; others wished accounts classified as material, property, personal, profit-and-loss; still others as real, personal and imaginary (fictitious). One writer (Pilsen, 1877) favored accounts of constant value (cash, debts, bills, etc.), accounts of changeable value (merchandise, real estate, securities) and accounts of positive profit and loss (incomes and expenses). The generally accepted classification of real and nominal accounts came later, as did the sub-division of the balance-sheet into current assets, fixed assets, intangibles, deferred charges, current liabilities, long-term debt, capital stocks, reserves and surplus.

In the matter of content the basis of financial statements was also rather well formulated; the developments to follow were generally in the direction of refinements and expansion of detail.

These changes, of course, did not occur at once; their beginnings were found in a few texts before the century ended. For example, the greatest expansion of detail since 1900 has come in the nominal accounts of the profit-and-loss statement, but J. G. Pilsen (*Complete Reform of Bookkeeping,* New York, 1877) had already increased his list of nominal accounts much beyond that of his contemporaries. Under incomes he mentions interest, commission, brokerage, guarantee, exchanges; under expenses: gas-light, fuel, stationery, rent, wages, advertisements, taxes, insurance, donations, traveling. Before that time such items were included in general terms as charges or expense.

Another refinement which is commonplace in recent statements but was not yet well developed in the nineteenth century was the use of accruals and deferred charges.

Savary (*Le Parfait Negociant,* Paris, 6th ed., 1712) approaches the matter when he recommends that the person preparing to close the books make up, among other things, "a list of what he owes to assistants for wages" and again when he advises that expense accounts should "confine themselves to the following year if the profit is not found sufficient to cover them." (p. 265). These are in the nature of accrued liability and deferred charge, respectively. Incidentally it is interesting to note that Savary recommends as the best time for closing "a month of the least activity in order to have more time to value the merchandise." Clearly he was an advocate of the natural business year.

Somewhat later the accrual methodology had become better organized. For example in Pilsen's book (1877) the author makes use of "Bookkeeper's Memoranda," * i.e., rent due or paid in advance,

* Other writers (e.g., A. L. Gilbert, *Business Bookkeeping,* 1893) used the terms "resource inventories" and "liability inventories." Of some fifty bookkeeping texts spread over the years between 1788 and 1899 only about ten per cent attempt to reflect accruals. Robert Hamilton (*An Introduction to Merchandise,* Edinburgh, 1788) makes an adjustment for interest due to the bank and for wages due a clerk; Thomas Dilworth (*The Young Book-keeper's Assistant,* London, 1792) mentions an "annuity due" on bank funds [accrued interest?]; Isaac Cory (*Mercantile, Private and Official Accounts,* London, 1840) debits merchandise account and credits bad-debts account for three per cent of the sales. Losses in collection are charged against the latter account. However, a debit balance therein is listed as an asset and a credit balance as a liability. Bryant and Stratton (*National Book-keeping,* 1861) show an item "interest payable on mortgage" as a liability on the balance-sheet after debiting interest account in red ink. The authors call this "a somewhat novel feature" and make the following observation: "Were the business to continue under the same proprietorship, this accumulating interest might be allowed to run on without mention until paid."

gas used but no bill received, fuel, stamps, stationery unconsumed. These are entered in red ink (as inventories) in the columnar balance-sheet. A. J. Cairnes (*Manual for Opening and Closing Books of Joint Stock Companies,* New York, 3d ed., 1891) shows such adjustments as full journal entries made on the columnar balance-sheet. Wages, rent, taxes, interest due by the company and not charged in the books he enters as a debit to profit-and-loss and a credit to liabilities; the same sort of items due the company but not paid he enters on the sheet as a debit to assets, and a credit to profit-and-loss. Such adjustments he says result in "nearer true gains."

A third element which has been much developed in modern statements is valuation; in fact in recent years this seems to be the major issue in financial statements. Before the present century, however, questions of valuation were less prominent, although present. Fixed assets were few and depreciation discussions were infrequent, but the problem was not ignored.* Usually such property was to be valued and entered in the account as an inventory, but nothing was said about how valuation was to be made. However, as an example of a direct statement on the matter, it may be noted that Pilsen (1877) says that for property which is for use and not for sale, such as fixtures, furniture, leases, livestock, one should make separate inventories and "take off a percentage of the total for wear and tear."

In relation to the valuation of merchandise the writers usually had more to say, although, from a modern point of view, some of the advice is not very sound. Harris (*Practical Bookkeeping,* New York, 1842) says, "Fix some definite value which should be no more or less than the property could be sold for . . ." And again, "if you value what you have unsold at a price for which you could sell it, and carry the same to the credit side of the merchandise account, the difference in the footing would be gain." John Fleming (*Bookkeeping by Double Entry,* Pittsburgh, 1854) suggests that merchandise unsold be valued in proportion to its first cost and charges; B. F. Foster (*A Concise Treatise on Commercial Bookkeeping,* Boston, 1837) merely speaks of estimating the value of

* See note chapter XIII on depreciation treatment in cost accounting.

property unsold; Thomas Jones (*Paradoxes of Debit and Credit Demolished,* New York, 1859) says the value attached to any property when varying from its cost may properly be introduced in explanations.

The most thorough consideration given to merchandise valuation in this general period is found in the work of an earlier writer, Jacques Savary (*Le Parfait Négociant,* 1712). Among about a dozen "things to observe in making a statement" (*Inventaire général*) he has a significant paragraph upon pricing the merchandise. A translation of it follows.

"The seventh thing to observe is pricing the merchandise. Take care not to estimate it at more than it is worth, for that would be endeavoring to make it valuable by imagination, but it is necessary to estimate it as if selling it afterward, so one finds the profit in the inventory taken the year following. To estimate well it is necessary to consider whether the merchandise is newly purchased or has long been in the store or shop. If it is newly purchased and, if one judges that it has not decreased in price in the factory or at the wholesalers, it should be put in at the current price.

"If this is merchandise which is commencing to deteriorate, or go out of style, or is that which one judges he could find at the factory or wholesalers at 5% less, it must be reduced to this price.

"If it is spoiled merchandise, old fashioned, beyond selling, it is necessary to reduce the price considerably for two reasons: first, because when taking inventory it is easier to reduce to the current price or take a loss than to wait until on the point of making a sale when there is no time to deliberate or reflect upon the reasons for selling without profit. . . . The second is that, however he may decrease the price of the merchandise in his inventory, that fact does not indicate he will sell it at that price; he may be able to sell it at a considerably higher price in the year following; thus he does not deceive himself at all and he has properly made a true statement of his property. . . ."

In conclusion then, it is clear that financial statements—that is to say, organized summaries of significant financial results—may be found in certain major ledger accounts or in separate tabulations. Evolution has favored the development of the latter form, and modern practice hardly considers the summary accounts in the same light as financial statements. The source of the facts in statements may be either an independent "inventory" or a re-arrangement of double-entry bookkeeping data. The modern development has been in the direction of the latter, subject to such adjustments as the auditor's judgment dictates.

From the perspective of this chapter it seems that the primary motive for separate financial statements was to obtain information regarding capital: this was the center of the interest of partners, shareholders, lenders, and the basis of the calculation of early property taxes. Thus balance-sheet data were stressed and refined in various ways, while expense and income data were incidental—in fact, the latter in the seventeenth century were presented merely as a "proof of estate"—to demonstrate by another route the correctness of the balance-sheet.

REFERENCES

1. Stephen Monteage, *Instructions for Rent-gatherer's Accompts* (London, 1683), bound with the author's *Debtor and Creditor Made Easie.*

2. Several other old financial statements may be found as indicated below:

a. Staffordshire Account of the Great Roll, 5 Henry II [1159]. The reproduction given by Hubert Hall (*The Antiquities and Curiosities of the Exchequer,* p. 132) is in bilateral form but possibly this is the arrangement of the author; certainly the heading "Balance Sheet" and the designations "Dr." and "Cr." were interpolated.

b. The Account of John, Bishop of Glasgow, as Lord Treasurer [1474] is described by Edward Boyd in Brown's, *History of Accounting and Accountants,* pp. 58-60.

c. Report of the commissioners of 37 Henry VIII [1546] as to the Gild of Palmers of Ludlow. (*English Gilds*—Early English Text Society, orig. ser. no. 40 pp. 197-99). The report appears first to state the expenses in comparison with the actual collections, leaving a remainder, and to follow this with an indication of the possessions of the guild, together with the expected income and the actual collections, the latter figure being the sum used in the first section as income.

d. A "Charge and Discharge" statement of 1624 which is in effect a cash statement is given in Edw. P. Jupp, *Historical Account of the Worshipful Company of Carpenters,* p. 445.

3. From Valentin Mennher's, *Practique brifue,* translated by P. Kats in *The Journal of Accountancy,* April, 1929.

4. Ernst Jäger, *Altes und Neues aus der Buchhaltung,* Stuttgart, 1889, p. 77.

5. Geijsbeek, *Ancient Double Entry Bookkeeping,* pp. 106-7.

6. Translation by P. Kats, *The Institute of Bookkeepers' Journal* (London), December, 1927.

7. Payen, *Essai sur la Tenue des Livres* ——, 1817.

8. *The Accounting Review,* September, 1930.

9. *Le Parfait Negociant,* Paris, 6th ed., 1712.

10. *Geschichte der Buchhaltung in Deutschland,* p. 60.

X. PROPRIETORSHIP BOOKKEEPING

THE preceding chapters have attempted to picture the expansion of account-keeping into a complete and coherent system. And now it is appropriate to summarize the first stage in the evolution of accountancy.

All the antecedents of double-entry bookkeeping were present in antiquity, but they seem to have lacked some element which was necessary to coördinate them into a completed system. Ancient wealth was not productive; it was not "capital." It originated in tribute and the spoils of war. Wealth needed the pressure of an extensive and profitable commerce to give it real productivity. Such a commerce appeared in the Middle Ages largely as a result of the crusades. Wealth now originated in active trading exchanges. The purpose of the employment of capital and credit changed from consumption and display to use in gainful enterprises in supplying newly felt wants with goods from distant sources. This was the fertile soil from which double entry grew.

But the keynote of "proprietorship" had not yet been sounded. The early records of this mediæval commerce were merely "agency bookkeeping"—the records necessary to enable an agent or the active partner of a specific venture to report intelligently upon his activities. These, together with the accounting necessitated by bankers' dealings in exchange, brought personal (debt) accounts into extensive use. Perhaps agency bookkeeping so systematized the record keeping as to make use of impersonal (goods) accounts and a "master's account."

In any event, here was a system of complementary, bi-lateral accounts in which duality of entry was a feature and equilibrium of totals was a result. But the achievement was not yet complete.

When continuing partnerships replaced single ventures and occasional agreements, the recording problem passed from that associated with an irregular reporting by an agent to that occasioned by a continuing investment of capital variously employed and periodically summarized. The new burdens expanded the account-procedure of agency bookkeeping into proprietorship bookkeeping. Not until bookkeeping was thus called upon to serve the enterprise as a unit were its full possibilities achieved.

Whereas wealth in antiquity was stagnant, wealth employed in mediæval trade became capital actively striving to reproduce itself. This was the first step toward true commercial proprietorship. The "master's account" of agency bookkeeping foreshadowed the "capital account" of the next step, but it was not thus converted until proprietorship had expanded the need for account keeping.

In transaction analysis (if the hypothesis of chapter IV be accepted) proprietorship is plainly a basic element. The well established usage of debt relationships would make it clear that a truthful record could not state that a goods account had a responsibility direct to the original seller. It would likewise be obvious that the seller would look only to the purchaser (proprietor) for payment of the debt. As a result "proprietor" would figure in every transaction. When the various ideas of bookkeeping were finally brought into a united system (as, for example, that described by Paciolo), "proprietor" again played a most prominent part, for the concentration of all operations was then in the proprietor's accounts (capital, profit-and-loss, goods, expenses). And when fifteenth-century bookkeeping procedure is compared with modern practice, it is strikingly evident that since proprietorship was added to the other elements there has been no fundamental change.

Proprietorship, then, seems to be the last important modification to be added in the expansion of account keeping into double-entry bookkeeping. And because it is so closely allied to productively employed commercial capital—that thread which runs throughout the whole story—proprietorship seems not only to furnish the most important step in the sequence of evolution but in reality to underlie the whole process by which double entry evolved.

If the first stage of the expansion of account keeping into bookkeeping was the formation of a coherent scheme of inter-related accounts which converged into proprietorship capital, the second stage may be described as the transformation of double entry into a technology.

This drift is evident in the tendency for transaction analysis to be governed more and more by rule of thumb. Bookkeeping under this development is no longer a simple, organized record clearly stating the details of what occurred; it is resolved into a formalized game of debits and credits with all possible situations worked out in advance. Analysis consists of picking out the rule which fits the circumstances; the rule will indicate how the entry is to be made.

The same trend toward technicalities is seen in the steady development toward an over-simplified ledger entry. The full-sentence type of record becomes much shortened; details of the transaction are dropped. The subject of the complete sentence of earlier usage becomes the heading (or title) of the account; the verb (debit, credit) is expressed once for all at the top of the ledger page not far from the account name with which it may still be read as if in a sentence; the contra account is briefly named; and the amount involved is written in a marginal column. Later the reference in the ledger to the contra account disappears, leaving only the page reference to the original source of the entry; then the verbs (or their abbreviations "Dr.", "Cr.") are omitted so that debit is indicated by position only—that is, on the left side of an account; credit is indicated only by position on the right.

At this point the ledger account consists of 1. title, 2. dates and posting references and 3. amounts. This display, to the uninitiated, is well-nigh incomprehensible; too much is signified by location, position or implied relationship to the whole scheme. The early ledger entries would have been understandable by any contemporary who could read what had been written, for an entry in an account was then a full grammatical sentence stating the whole essence of the transaction. But in the subsequent development an account has become merely a unit in a statistical classification; it is understandable only in its sum total (or balance) or through a laborious tabulation based upon the posting references in the books of original entry.

The development of the journal entry has also been toward simplification into technicalities. This tendency was evident in some degree in very early journal entries (1430) and became more pronounced as time went on. The typical form was:

By A——, to B——

This was quite technical; understanding depended upon a knowledge 1. of what debit and credit meant and 2. of the fact that "by" was a symbol for "debit," and "to" for "credit." The early writers did not explain either the origin or the reasonableness of these symbols; therefore, it may be inferred that the prepositions were already technicalities to be accepted and learned, not necessarily to be understood.

Another form of journal entry "A—— is debtor to B——," or "A—— owes B——," which was also in use in the fifteenth century, was perhaps more easily understandable from the words alone, a characteristic which may have caused this type to predominate after 1550 over the other wording.

By the nineteenth century a special arrangement of the facts had come into usage, and two marginal columns were provided in the journal to receive the amounts. The credit item was finally indicated by being written one line below the debit, by a slight indention and by writing the amount in the right hand column.

To the uninitiated this arrangement of data is as mystifying as the ledger account. A large part of the energy expended in teaching bookkeeping to beginners is applied to fixing in mind, somewhat mechanically it is to be feared, these and other technicalities, such as subtraction by contra position, the reversed plus and minus characteristics of certain accounts, etc.

The third stage in the expansion of account-keeping into a complete and serviceable system is found in the development of financial statements. These were needed for various purposes, especially to furnish information concerning the state of the enterprise's capital in cases in which access to the books of account would be difficult or when it was desired to present an abstract of the essential data in the books.

From what has gone before, it appears that double-entry bookkeeping is a system of recording financial changes which are of interest to proprietors according to a certain technique which results in a convenient and arithmetically accurate summary of proprietorship data. In order to compare this concept, which grows out of the view here presented of the historical evolution of the art, with the concept which prevails in modern bookkeeping literature, a large number of recent texts were surveyed for their definitions of bookkeeping.

These definitions, as might be expected, displayed a considerable variety of elements. The first of these elements is an indication of the larger category to which bookkeeping belongs: viz., a method of classifying information; a process of recording certain facts; a procedure for analyzing designated data. Evidently bookkeeping is thought of as dynamic—it refers, not to a thing, but to an act. The facts or data with which the recording procedure is concerned are likewise variously stated as elements in the definitions: business transactions, value exchanges, price events, etc. Thus the material of bookkeeping is rather definitely limited. The manner in which bookkeeping activity is carried on is usually called systematic, that is, according to a logical or preconceived plan. The word not only connotes a careful following of a prescribed methodology to obtain completeness of record, but it also implies a means of testing the accuracy of the record. These results double entry accomplishes by its completely coördinated scheme of bi-lateral accounts and by its plan of finding duality in all transactions, so that an internal equilibrium shall be present in the record at all times (to afford the test of accuracy).

These elements represent the views of various authors on the questions of what bookkeeping is, with what materials it works and how it performs its function. One other question arises: Why should bookkeeping do these things? Some authors hold that the purpose is to show the standing of the business, to furnish a view of the state of the enterprise's affairs, to exhibit the results of value exchanges. Others say bookkeeping will show the effect of operations on financial position, the extent and causes of altered financial condition, the effect of transactions upon wealth.

The variety of the ideas expressed by different authors is briefly reflected in the above paragraphs. But a composite, textbook definition of bookkeeping may be attempted. It is this: *Bookkeeping is a process of recording and classifying financial data in a systematic manner for the purpose of showing the effect of value exchanges upon wealth.*

From this survey of the concept of bookkeeping it seems that attention in modern textbooks is largely centered upon exchanges, with the consequent failure to express or forcefully to imply those many transformations and internal transfers of data within the record which make up a large part of actual bookkeeping. These last are the elements which, for example, show the movement of raw material from storeroom to shop, and indicate the union in the shop of materials with labor-energy and functional services and the subsequent transfer of the newly-priced units of product into stock, there to await a "value-exchange" when a purchaser appears. Bookkeeping, it would seem, should be as much concerned with these intermediate processes as with the value exchange occasioned by the acquisition of raw material or the disposition of the finished product.

Early bookkeeping, however, knew of practically no data unrelated to actual exchanges and therefore could quite naturally and unconsciously set up as its objective the reflection of the effect of exchanges upon wealth. But that simple condition is no longer characteristic of business; hence, the theory no longer fits the circumstances; it should be so broadened as to include the effect upon previously recorded data of non-exchange events as well.

The objection to the continued limitation to value exchanges as the material with which bookkeeping works should not obscure the fact, however, that the age-old purpose of bookkeeping, that is, the calculation of divisible profits, is still of great importance under modern conditions. But profit calculation is now no longer a simple computation based upon a comparison of the price of the thing given with the price of the thing received (a simple exchange). In modern industry the calculation of the price (cost) of the thing given is a very complicated and, for managerial purposes, a very important matter. Thus, while the determination of proprietorship and profit is still a vital point of bookkeeping, the actual process of calculation has placed a burden upon modern bookkeeping which earlier days did not know.

To conceive of bookkeeping properly, therefore, it is necessary first to perceive that business is a continuous movement of varying intensity. Bookkeeping is related to business as the strip of photographic film is to the toboggan coming down the slide—it captures and preserves the realities of the movement. However, bookkeeping has also the function of cutting and editing and reassembling various sections of its "film," and thus of producing a synthesis as well as an analysis.

In the light of these circumstances, one is tempted to recast both the historical conception and the composite textbook definition of bookkeeping and say that bookkeeping seems best described as *a quasi-statistical method of recording the sequence of conversions through which various forms of property are passed in the effort to produce a proprietary profit.*

PART TWO

THE EXPANSION OF BOOKKEEPING INTO ACCOUNTANCY

XI. PROPRIETORSHIP THEORY IN ACCOUNTING

Up to this point the theme has been the evolution through which financial recording passed while account keeping expanded into complete double-entry (proprietary) bookkeeping. Attention is now to be directed primarily to the nineteenth century—the time which marks the formative period of accountancy.* Conditions arose at that time which brought about a modification—or expansion—of double-entry bookkeeping. The century which followed the inception of the industrial revolution and witnessed an active growth of private business corporations was a period of great commercial, industrial, financial and legal progress. It was also the period in which the surrounding circumstances had the effect of transforming a mere method of systematically recording exchanges into a means of giving business management an effective control over its affairs. That is to say, the nineteenth century saw bookkeeping expanded into accounting.*

Earlier chapters have pointed toward the conclusion that the concept "proprietorship" was an element of tremendous importance in the development of double-entry bookkeeping. Early transaction analysis probably made extensive use of "proprietor" in bridging the chasm which separated the reasoning behind mere account keeping and the reasoning of the more complicated proprietary bookkeeping with its impersonal and nominal accounts. In fact, all double entry procedure was definitely directed to the computation of proprietary profits and proprietary capital. And now an examination of nineteenth-century texts affords a further indication that proprietorship is an important element of double entry.

Discussions of proprietorship which went beyond the customary explanation of entries for capital invested or withdrawn or entries for closing profit and loss to capital were, even in the nineteenth cen-

* "Accountancy" denotes a field of knowledge, while "accounting" means the processes active in that field. Compare "finance" and "financing."

tury, the exception rather than the rule. There still was a disinclination on the part of most writers to put "theory" into their books. But even though most of the bookkeeping authors were content merely to describe routine bookkeeping procedure and to depend upon familiar rules of thumb and a wealth of typical transactions for teaching purposes, yet there were a few who began to break away from the old pattern. They began to recognize the limitations of the "formalization" of bookkeeping procedure into a mere body of rules; they began to seek the logic and reasonableness which their knowledge of bookkeeping and their intuition told them were buried in it.

Their speculations concerning the fundamental nature of double-entry bookkeeping (probably the real beginning of theory) soon led them to proprietorship as the keystone of the arch. Some of the ideas of these authors are presented here. The somewhat chronological arrangement of the authors should not lead to the inference that writers of later dates drew their ideas directly from authors of earlier dates or of other countries. Such meager data as those here assembled could not alone establish a clear sequence of idea evolution and author indebtedness. Yet, in spite of the fact that it is difficult to give due credit for the actual origination of certain ideas and expressions, the evidence seems plain that there has been a development and growth in the ideas themselves, and that much of modern accounting theory has grown directly out of these and similar ideas of the past century.

Early in the eighteenth century (1718) a Scotch writer, Malcolm, emphasized the distinction between the totality of proprietor capital and its constituent parts in interesting language as follows:

> "The *Stock* you are to look upon as the Root, from which all the other Accompts in the *Book* (as far as they are for the Owner's Behoof) do flow; for whether there be Encrease or Decrease, or Equality by the various changing of some Things for others (in which trading does entirely consist) it is the *Capital Stock* that is affected, and either raised or diminished in Value; or simply changed in its constituent Parts. . . . . the State of Encrease or Loss Accompt . . . will shew . . . . . there may be a change of the State of the *Stock*, as to its constituent Parts, which is the effect of the various tossing this stock about in Trade, and the frequent Changes that are made of one Thing for another in that Course." [1]

This indicates somewhat indirectly a classification of transactions into those which constitute merely equivalent conversions and those by which "the capital stock is affected and either raised or diminished in value." There the theory of profit is definitely related to an increase of capital.* A similar indication of this distinction between the whole capital and its constituent parts is found in another book of the eighteenth century (Hustcraft, 1735) in these words:

> "That portion of Things which a Man possesses, or has otherways belonging to him, as a Security, taken all together, I call the Estate, and the Worth of a Man's Estate, consider'd abstractly from the Things which are valued, I call the computed Value or Extent of a Man's Estate. (p. 2) . . . . A general Knowledge of the computed Value of an Estate is not sufficient; but he that would act wisely must endeavour to inform himself of such computed Value, as it is divided into several Properties or Parts. (p. 3) . . . . We must arrange various Securities so that when we add to or take away from them respectively . . . . the remaining Quantity, with the alterations that produced them, may appear . . . for which Reason there must be a competent Space allow'd each Division . . . for the Recital of the Alterations of adding to, or taking from, as Occasions offer." (p. 7) . . .[2]

Shortly after the opening of the nineteenth century (1818) a text was published in London by F. W. Cronhelm[3] in which classification of accounts was so well analyzed as to present a lucid statement of the fundamental nature of double-entry bookkeeping.† The importance of this book warrants reference to a number of passages.

In this author's view the whole system of bookkeeping is conducted upon two principles: one, of secondary importance only, concerns the form of the account, and the other, of primary importance, concerns the inevitable equilibrium of the complete set of accounts. As to the account he points out (chapter IV) that changes

* The author says that profit constitutes an increase to proprietorship (capital), but it does not necessarily follow that the words also mean that every increase in capital constitutes a profit. It is unlikely that any occasion could have arisen in the eighteenth century for drawing this distinction, but in recent years the distinction has gained importance because of the debated question whether unrealized appreciation in the value of property gives rise to a distributable profit or merely to a nondistributable increment to capital.

† Other features of interest in this book are the author's attempt to keep other "day books" on a debit and credit basis similar to the cashbook and his presentation of certain "factory accounts." The latter will receive more detailed consideration in a later chapter.

in property could be recorded by adding increases and deducting decreases [as in cheque stubs]. This, however, "has great liability to error" and the method of additions alone [i.e., of dividing an account into a left and a right side for accumulating increases and decreases separately] has proved highly useful and expedient.

The principle of equilibrium is of fundamental importance and receives extended consideration. The following extracts state the author's argument concisely.

"The purpose of Book-keeping, as a record of property, is to shew the owner at all times the value of his whole capital, and of every part of it.* The component parts of property in trade are in a state of continual transformation and change; but whatever variations they undergo, and whether the whole capital increase, diminish, or remain stationary, it is evident that it must constantly be equal to the sum of all its parts. This EQUALITY is the great essential principle of book-keeping. It will at once give the Reader a clear idea of the nature of that *proof* which is so highly and so justly appreciated in Accounts. For, if the Stock Account be found equal to the collective result of all the other Accounts, the desired proof is obtained; but, if the least inequality exist between them, the Books must obviously be incorrect.

"The clear and simple principle of *the equality of the whole to the sum of its parts,* has never before been laid down as the basis of Bookkeeping. From its neglect have proceeded those vague and confused notions of Accounts, evinced in almost every treatise, by dividing them into *personal, real,* and *fictitious;* as if the whole capital and each of its parts were not equally real. In this classification, however, the Personal Accounts are treated as if neither real nor fictitious; whilst the Stock Account is actually said to be in the latter predicament; or, in equivalent words, the whole capital is pronounced an unreal and imaginary thing!" (Author's preface.)

* * * * *

"After rejecting the old classification (i.e., Personal, Real and Fictitious) a new one may be expected; and we will therefore sketch a substitute in the following tabular view of

* In another place (chapter II) the author's statement also indicates the calculation of capital (rather than profit) as the purpose of bookkeeping by distinguishing between the methods of "partial bookkeeping" and "complete bookkeeping." In the former case capital is ascertained by collecting its component parts, that is, an inventory is made to discover (reveal) the stock. In the latter case capital is obtained (computed) by two distinct processes: (1) by the stock account and (2) by the collection of the parts. The object of an inventory here is to furnish a general proof of stock and of all other accounts.

ACCOUNTS

Classes	*Divisions*	*Subdivisions*
1. Parts of Property	1. Personal	
	2. Money	1. Cash
		2. Bills Payable
		3. Bills Receivable
	3. Goods	1. Floating Merchandise
		2. Immoveables
		3. Conventional Funds
2. Whole Property	(Branches)	(Ramifications)
Stock	1. Profit	1. Commission
	2. Loss	2. Interest, etc.
	3. Private	

"It will be observed that the second class admits no divisions, but ramification only; its subordinate Accounts not exhausting the higher, as in the first class. The Accounts of Profit and Loss are simply branches of the Stock, their object being to prevent numerous petty entries in the latter, to collect together the individual augmentations and diminutions of the capital, and to transfer the general result in one entry to the Stock. In like manner, Commission, Interest, &c., are merely ramifications of the Profit and Loss Accounts, which prevent numerous petty entries in the latter, collect the aggregates of their respective departments, and transfer the results in one branch from the Stock, its use being to record all sums put into the business or withdrawn, so as to keep them entirely distinct from the Profit or Loss. The result of the Private Account is also transferred in one entry to the Stock." (p. 27).

Much of the emphasis in the above extracts and elsewhere throughout the book is placed upon the equivalence of the whole capital and its constituent parts. In chapter I the author defines bookkeeping as "the art of recording property so as to show at all times the value of the whole capital and each component part," * and in chapter III he states: "there must necessarily and inevitably be a constant equality between the stock account on the one hand

* Thus early in the nineteenth century there is definitely expressed a balance-sheet view of the purpose of accounting, although the profit-earning aim of business enterprises would seem to point toward profit calculations as the most important function of bookkeeping.

and all the remaining accounts on the other," no matter what transformations and variations may have taken place, because it is a primary axiom of the exact sciences that the whole is continually equal to the sum of its parts. In order to keep these two elements in contrast to each other it is necessary to distinguish proprietor's capital from the debts of others. This Cronhelm provides for (p. 5) by indicating that the introduction of credit into commerce produced "negative property" (e.g., bills payable) to be associated with "positive property" such as goods and bills receivable. Thus the way is opened for expressing (p. 8) the fundamental bookkeeping relation as an equation:

$$(a + b + c) - l - m - n = S$$

(positive property) — (negative property) = stock *

As a consequence of this equivalence between properties and capital, the author states that expense and income accounts (including the profit-and-loss account) are created to avoid the inconvenience of recording in stock every individual alteration in capital (p. 9). These accounts, then, are simply branches of the stock account designed to collect for periodical transfer the "individual augmentations and diminutions of the capital." From this it may be inferred that this author also thought of profit as an increase in capital.†

The three authors whose ideas have been cited were English writers. (See note concerning B. F. Foster at the end of this chapter.) The next to receive consideration is an American, Thomas Jones,[4] whose work appeared in 1841. Another book followed in 1859.

Two paragraphs from the first chapter of Jones' *Principles* admirably state the purpose of bookkeeping.

"The theory of bookkeeping teaches the simplest and most intelligible method of recording and arranging financial transactions. If we consider

* This is fundamentally different from the equation $a + b + c = l + m + n + S$, for this arrangement brings capital and debts payable into the same category and would therefore express a theory of bookkeeping which would not rest upon what might be called the "proprietorship axiom," that is, that capital (i.e., proprietorship) is the whole which is being analyzed. This axiom is the basic assumption of the first equation.

† But in this case as in that of the other author mentioned it does not follow that Cronhelm meant to imply that *every* increase in capital constitutes a profit.

the mass of occurrences that would be accumulated during a business of twelve months, the necessity of some well digested and established plan of arrangement will be obvious.

"The Method of Double Entry enables us to unravel any mass of data, and dispose of it in such a manner as to afford a clear and concise statement of the result of each or any successive step of the merchant's progress. It embraces such collections of facts only as are absolutely indispensable, in order to elicit the result contemplated as, a statement of the merchant's Resources, Liabilities, Gains, Losses, and Original Capital; but the form and position in which these collections are arranged and exhibited in the above is purely conventional."

This is far removed indeed from the clumsy personification of accounts so often followed in texts of that day. The following extracts lead still further into bookkeeping theory and away from dependence upon arbitrary rules of thumb:

"The arrangement of Double Entry is based upon the following two propositions:—

Proposition I

"If we can ascertain our Resources and Liabilities at any stated time, their comparison will determine the position of our affairs at that time. For example:—

Statement of our Resources and Liabilities
December 31st, 1840.

Cash in our possession....	15,000	Bills payable outstanding...	3,000
Bills receivable	4,000	We owe John Spring......	6,000
William James owes us...	3,000		$9,000
	$22,000		

From	$22,000
Deduct	9,000
Our present worth must, therefore, be....	$13,000

Proposition II

"If we determine the position in which our affairs stood at the commencement of any period of time, and our gains and losses during that period, we can, therefore, determine our position at the end of the period. For example:—

If on the first of January, 1840 our clear worth or net capital was..............................	$10,000
And during the year we gained..................	3,000

It follows from this, independent of any reference to

our resources and liabilities, that we must be worth, January 1st, 1841 .... $13,000

"So that by any possible way in which we may view these two distinct and independent propositions, provided we fulfill their conditions, they must necessarily lead us to the same result. Double Entry, then, embraces two distinct plans of arranging the facts that have transpired in a business, each plan involving a distinct set of accounts; the one set fulfilling the conditions of the first proposition, the other those of the second; and the agreement in the result of the two constitutes what is called the balance of books."

This is typical of Jones' clear-cut explanations of the characteristics of double-entry bookkeeping. He is here pointing to the fact that the profit-and-loss statement is coördinate with the balance-sheet rather than supplementary,* and he is indicating that as calculations both statements arrive at the same result by different paths. When the proprietor's capital is among the liabilities, the balance-sheet gives the same net gain as the profit-and-loss statement; or by another method, the addition of prior capital to the net gain shown by the profit-and-loss statement gives the same present worth as that shown by the balance-sheet.†

In the quotation given above Jones lays down the fundamental proposition that double entry "embraces two distinct plans of arranging the facts—each plan involving a distinct set of accounts." In his third chapter he reverts to this matter in more detail, as follows:

"Equality of debits and credits is the distinguishing feature of Double Entry; but instead of being, as commonly represented, a primary principle, it is a consequence of such as have been already discussed; without the help of which it necessarily cannot be established or demonstrated. We therefore proceed to

* This is a distinct improvement of explanation over Cronhelm's tendency to pass over nominal accounts almost as if they were unimportant appendages to the all-important capital account.

† An interesting antecedent of this presentation is found in Simon Stevin's book published in Holland in 1608. As was shown in chapter 9, Stevin made a sort of balance-sheet (which he called "State of my Capital") in order to compute the present proprietorship, and also a sort of profit-and-loss statement ("Proof of my Estate") apparently to serve as a test-check to the former computation. See also J. B. Geijsbeek, *Ancient Double Entry Bookkeeping*, p. 120.

show this equality as a necessary consequence of the double arrangement, or two sets of accounts."

In this paragraph Jones places the "two-sets-of-accounts" arrangement ahead of "equality of debits and credits" as the basic characteristic of double-entry bookkeeping. Indeed, in holding the latter to be the consequence of the former he implies that a "single" set of accounts could not produce equality within the entries, or that complete equality within the entries could only be reflected in two sets of accounts. This is equivalent to stating that nominal accounts, rather than duality of entry, are the basic characteristic of double entry.*

The author then proceeds to show that duality of entries is inevitable if the two sets of accounts are present. He tries to keep the situations understandable by confining them to cash transactions only.

> "The simplest exhibition of the theory of Double Entry is that afforded by the arrangement of a business transaction entirely for cash. The Cash is then the only form in which fixed property appears in the concern; and the cash account, by comparing all the sums by which it has been increased or diminished, keeps a constant measure of its amount, and is the only primary account required.

Primary Arrangement

Cash

(Debit)	(Credit)
Receipts or Increase	Payments or Decrease

Secondary Arrangement

Stock

(Debit)	(Credit)
	Capital

Merchandise

(Debit)	(Credit)
Outlay	Returns

Expenses

(Debit)	(Credit)
Outlay	Returns

Profit and Loss

(Debit)	(Credit)
Losses or Outlay	Gains or Returns

* Compare the discussion in chapter III (characteristics of double entry) on equilibrium.

"It is sufficiently obvious that in a cash business, every transaction must either increase or diminish the cash. If a transaction increases the cash, the amount of such increase must be a debit of cash; and as the same increase could only arise either from gain or some other returns of the business, the same amount must also appear in the credit columns of the secondary accounts.

"If returned by Merchandise, the whole sum would appear under that head, but if arising from several parts of the business, each portion would appear under its respective head; hence if a transaction increase the Cash, the Debits and Credits of the Ledger are equally affected.

"When in a Cash business, a transaction diminishes the Cash, it must be an equal outlay or loss in the business; and consequently, the sum entered as a credit to denote the decrease of Cash must also be entered in the debit of the secondary accounts, showing in what way it was disposed of. Hence, whether a transaction increase or diminish the cash, the debits and credits of the Ledger must be equally affected; or in other words, it follows that in a cash business the debit or debits required for any transaction must equal the credit or credits.

"When credit is introduced into a business the fixed property (sic) becomes divided into Cash, Bills Receivable, and Bills Payable and Personal Indebtedness, or book debts; and the primary accounts are required not only to keep a measure of the amount of fixed property as a whole, but to exhibit also the state of each component part.

"These additional accounts are, however, a mere extension of the principle of the Cash Account, viz., a comparison of the increase and decrease that has occurred to the fixed property, each component part being compared separately."

In another place secondary accounts are explained in an equally straightforward manner. An excerpt is placed here so as to associate it with the succinct statement about primary accounts just given.

"The Secondary Accounts constitute a method of arranging the transactions of a business, so as to fulfill the conditions of our second general proposition, viz., to represent the positions of the concern at the commencement of the period under arrangement, and its subsequent Gains or Losses.

"The position of affairs at the outset, is represented in an account called Stock, containing, in the right, or Credit column, the net capital invested. All other accounts are arranged so as to exhibit the subsequent Gains or Losses, by comparing all outlays or investments, with the proceeds or returns."

The classification of accounts here given by Jones is particularly apt and quite in harmony with his propositions I and II. On the whole, the terms "primary" and "secondary" are as likely to make the desired distinctions clear to the unbiased reader as the present terms "real" and "nominal." Probably they could as easily be used as technical terms also, if someone had not popularized the others. Jones, unquestionably, considered that a clear distinction between the two sets of accounts was indispensable to a conception of systematic bookkeeping, and thus he deliberately chose terms which were obviously opposed to each other. The modern terms suggest little more than this.

Another characteristic of Jones' discussion at this point is the recurring mention of "increase" and "decrease" in relation to entries in the accounts. These small facts are noteworthy because no one before him seems to have made such correct and effective use of them. They have since become such an integral part of our notion of bookkeeping that they are taken for granted, much as though they had been an immemorial adjunct to bookkeeping instruction. The use of these terms, with the foregoing classification of accounts, shows that Jones had a tendency to imagine bookkeeping primarily as a "sorting" (i.e., statistical) procedure, rather than as a "recording" procedure, as most of his contemporaries did. Other illustrations of Jones' use of increase and decrease are given in the following extracts.

In his introduction, in conjunction with a brief diagram of his "primary" and "secondary" arrangement of accounts, Jones states that, "the debits of one arrangement affect the merchant's financial position by indicating an increase of resources, while the debits of the other arrangement indicate outlay or decreases; in short, the debits of the one constitute the credits of the other, the order of succession only being varied."

In another place he relates these terms to profits and losses in this manner:

> "The terms Profit and Loss when applied to accounts have an extended significance and are best explained by the terms increase and decrease; for under losses are arranged expenses or outlays of various kinds; and under gains, income arising from commissions thus:—
>
> | Losses or decreases— | Gains or increase— |
> | --- | --- |
> | Clerk's hire | By Mdse. |
> | Store Expenses | Commission rec'd. |
> | Interest paid | Interest rec'd. |
>
> "When these several items are ascertained and then arranged in opposition, the difference of the two totals shows the net increase or decrease that has thereby taken place."

Again in speaking of the profit-and-loss arrangement, he says: " . . . thus our general object is to compare the decrease or outgoing with the increase or incoming; and although a sum expended is not always literally a loss, it has the same effect of decreasing our means, and vice versa with gains."

As further evidence of the author's unconscious conception of bookkeeping as a type of statistical procedure, note the following passage:

> "All debits are not sums owing to us nor are all credits sums we owe; thus, some debit items are owing to us, others (stock) are sums withdrawn by us; some (mdse.) are sums paid; others (cash) are sums received; and the credit items also stand for equally dissimilar facts; from which it must be evident that these terms are used arbitrarily and any attempt to exhibit them in one uniform relation to indebtedness must necessarily oblige us either to use language of corresponding ambiguity, or resort to the personification of things which not only have no existence, but the indebtedness of which cannot possibly have an apparent influence on the end we aim to accomplish. As names, enabling us to designate which side of any account we may refer to or speak of, they answer our purpose; and so would the blue column and red column, equally well, if custom permitted this use. In personal accounts, they bear a literal meaning, and by analogy they have been extended to all other accounts; but the relations which constitute that analogy are too obscure to be of use as a guide to the student, and are more calculated to mystify than explain the subject."

Today we accept "debit" and "credit" without question as mere indicators of "left" and "right." But in an earlier day, as has already been said, transaction analysis was taught through the personification of all the accounts, such as, the keeper of the cash owes the proprietor for the receipts; or it was taught by giving simple rules of thumb, such as "Debit the receiver, credit the giver," and then by supporting these by a multitude of subordinate rules covering various transactions and various accounts. Between these and Jones there is progress indeed.

In his later book, Thomas Jones explained the two-fold grouping of accounts by relating primary accounts to a "financial department" and secondary accounts to a "business department,"[5] and by working out an example in figures to show the exact equivalence of results. His summary will be sufficient to show his thought.

"Now taking each department as one account, we have the following—

Trial Balance

Increase	(118,254.00)	Financial Department:	98,560.00	(Decrease)
Decrease....	(30,621.06)	Business Department:	50,315.06	(Increase)
Total Debits	148,875.06	Total Credits	148,875.06	

and the following general results.

Financial Department, Increase or Drs.,.......	118,254
Decrease or Crs., ...	98,560
Dr. Balance or Capital..................	$19,694

Business Department, Increase or Crs., ...	50,315.06
Decrease or Drs., ...	30,621.06
	$19,694.00"

These extracts from Thomas Jones' books are given somewhat at length because this author represents so well the break in method of presentation which came to a head about the middle of the nineteenth century. The basic ideas behind the two "systems" of accounts and the analysis of transactions by "increases" and "decreases" had been occasionally present in the literature for some time. However, they became the main theme of Thomas Jones' book. From that time onward personification of accounts and journalization by rule steadily diminished.

This work is noteworthy also because the clarity of thought and the full expression of ideas stand out so well in contrast to the ordinary presentations of most of Jones' contemporaries. This is especially manifest in his earnest striving throughout the texts to replace rules by logic. In this effort he was primarily concerned with teaching method. Today we go far beyond this pioneer in trying to bring reasoning into play in bookkeeping instruction.

Three different German authors, who also wrote near the middle of the nineteenth century, give evidence that similar ideas in regard to the relation of proprietorship and profit were being discussed in Europe. The first work to be cited here is one [6] published in Austria in 1840.

> "The capital account is different from the accounts with things and with persons in that it has the assets in its credit side, while they have the assets in their debit side, and that it has the liabilities in its debit side, while they have them in the credit side. At the beginning of business the merchant is therefore doubly represented: (1) in the capital account by the total of his property; (2) in the several constituent parts of his property." (p. 80).
>
> * * * * *
>
> "Thus we come to a knowledge of our present net worth in two very different ways: (1) in the capital account where final gains and losses join the original assets and liabilities and (2) in the balance account where the latest assets and liabilities appear." (p. 113).

Hautschl also explains (p. 95-96) the profit-and-loss account as a temporary resting place for the increases and decreases of capital which, if entered direct in the capital account, would overburden it with detail.

The other German authors who incorporated similar ideas in their texts were G. D. Augspurg of Bremen and Georg Kurzbauer of Vienna. They come to attention through the writings of F. Hügli,[7] who quotes from the 1872 edition of Augspurg's book, *Die Kaufmännische Buchführung,* while at the same time he mentions that, according to Josef Schrott's *Lehrbuch der Verrechnungswisenschaft,* the first edition appeared in Bremen in 1852.

In his preface, Augspurg complains that most texts merely make the student familiar with the method of keeping accounts without explaining "why it is done thus"; in this text he obviously tries to explain the "whys." He says:

> "The Double Entry system of Bookkeeping consists chiefly in keeping concurrently two sets of accounts, the one for the total property and the other for the individual parts thereof, and in proving by the equality of these two sets of accounts the mathematical correctness of the financial results achieved.
>
> "The question then arises, according to what general principles are these two sets of accounts to be kept, since we already know that this must be done particularly by charges and credits to the accounts. They can be treated either as being similar or dissimilar.
>
> "If we take the first case it will follow upon a little consideration that just as it is impossible to deliver the same article to two different people at the same time, it is impossible to charge the same article at the same time to two different accounts. That is to say, in so far as they are connected they have to exercise an opposite reciprocal effect upon each other and a systematic control of the one over the other.
>
> "There remains the other treatment—to consider them as dissimilar, *i.e.,* as opposing quantities, or in other words to prove the one as creditor opposite to the other as debitor, in such a way that as soon as the one is credited, the other must be charged and vice versa.
>
> "Accordingly we establish as the basis of the whole system the principle that the account for the investment as a whole, called the capital account, stands as creditor opposite to the accounts of positive property (assets) and as debitor opposite to the negative property (liabilities), which accounts we want to designate by the collective name, Property Accounts [*Besitz-Conten*]."

In a later section Augspurg explains that "in opening the accounting one can imagine that at first the whole of the property is united in the possession of the capital account, and that the administration of the assets and liabilities is given over to the property accounts." And in a footnote to another section he says that the property accounts are in a sense stewardship or trustee accounts (*verwaltende Conten*) "since they represent only a loan from the capital account." Thus the author in some measure reverts to the old personification idea while he attempts to clarify the logic that was inherent in double entry.

In addition to Augspurg's work, Hügli mentions Kurzbauer's *Lehrbuch der einfachen und doppelten Buchhaltung* (4th edition, 1882)[8] and quotes certain significant passages.

> "In the general bookkeeping principles given in the first chapter of this work, the classification of accounts is traced back to the necessary consequences of bookkeeping. Books are kept either for the purpose of learning out of them from time to time the amounts of the different kinds of property held and to have by that means a control over the correct financial management thereof, or for the purpose of learning from the books what results (profits and losses) the several divisions of the business produced. From this came two essentially different kinds of bookkeeping. The first kind contains 'real accounts' [*Vermögensbestandteile* = constituent parts of property] in which are entered the properties acquired and given up; the second kind is related to the activity divisions [*Geschäftszweige*] of the enterprise and in the ledger accounts for these are entered in terms of money the incomes and expenditures which the activities produce.
>
> "Each of these types of bookkeeping is independent in form and content. But in order to attain both objects at the same time, both kinds are brought into close union in one system, and out of this arises both the form and content of double entry bookkeeping."

In another place Kurzbauer recurs to these fundamental classes of accounts and distinguishes them by the descriptive names of *Bestandconten* (accounts of remainders) and *Erfolgsconten* (accounts of results). We use the much less descriptive names of real accounts and nominal accounts. In chapter III he indicates the importance of the union of the two classes of accounts in these words: "double-entry bookkeeping is the combination into one system of the property-bookkeeping and the results-bookkeeping of a business enterprise."

From these examples it appears that some bookkeeping writers of the nineteenth century were not satisfied to follow the precedents of teaching by precept and example alone. They struck boldly out into new paths of inquiry. The result was that their work not only stands forth from that of their contemporaries but also marks a definite advance over the best ideas previously expressed. Their emphasis was upon logical analysis and constituted an unconscious approach to a "statistical" conception of bookkeeping processes.

This was progress, but it was only a beginning after all, for this advanced thinking was done by a few writers in widely scattered countries. The time had not yet arrived for a general acceptance of these ideas as the basis of bookkeeping instruction. The great majority of texts remained throughout the century very little changed by these few discussions in the beginning and middle of the century. A few writers in the last half of the century continued to extend these ideas, and a beginning was made by some others in another and different theory of bookkeeping. But for the most part bookkeeping texts still placed most reliance upon tried and trusty rules and numerous practical examples.

NOTE ON FOSTER'S INDEBTEDNESS TO CRONHELM AND THOMAS JONES

Reference to a book by B. F. Foster entitled *A Concise treatise on Commercial Bookkeeping* (Boston, 1836) might have been included in this chapter had not the author so clearly copied the theory sections from Cronhelm. Chapters I, II, and parts of IV, for example, are Cronhelm's chapters I, II, III, and parts of VIII.

It will be of interest to note the following letter printed in the preface to Thomas Jones' *Principles and Practices of Bookkeeping* (New York, 1841):

New York, Aug. 1—1838

Mr. Thomas Jones.

Sir: The principal features of what I understand to be your plan of teaching bookkeeping, and for which in my opinion you are entitled to the merit of having originated, are the following:

1st. Beginning your explanation of the theory with the ledger.

2nd. Explaining the scheme of each separate account, and showing its use.

3rd. Deducing from the different accounts two statements of the merchant's affairs, each showing how much he is worth.

4th. Showing that the ledger by double entry contains two sorts of accounts, which you term primary and secondary, each set producing one statement of the merchant's affairs, and showing how much he is worth. The agreement in the result of the primary accounts with the result of the secondary accounts, constitutes the balance of the books.

5th. Confirming a knowledge of this by exercising the pupil on a series of skeleton ledgers, from which he learns to deduce the results of any ledger.

6th. Requiring the pupil to fill up the columns of a blank ledger from day book transactions, by which he learns to make a ledger without a journal.

So far as my knowledge extends, this peculiar plan of teaching the science of double entry originated with you and the merit of insisting upon its utility and importance is yours.

I have availed myself of the information derived from your oral lectures in the compilation of my recent book entitled *The Merchant's Manual,* so far as relates to the explanation of the ledger in Chapter XI on the "Principles of Book-keeping," an acknowledgement of which shall be made in my next publication on this subject, and which has been inadvertently omitted in the present edition.

Very truly yours,
(signed) B. F. Foster

REFERENCES

1. Alexander Malcolm, *A New Treatise of Arithmetick and Bookkeeping, &c.,* Edinburgh, 1718, pp. 132-133.

2. Stephens Hustcraft, *Italian Book-Keeping Reduced into an Art,* London, 1735.

3. F. W. Cronhelm, *Double Entry by Single,* London, 1818.

4. Thomas Jones, *Principles and Practices of Bookkeeping,* New York, 1841; *Paradoxes of Debit and Credit Demolished,* New York, 1859.

5. For a similar and earlier division compare the French author, Payen (1817), discussed in Chapter XIX. He uses the terms *"Accompt en Argent"* and *"Accompt en Nature."*

6. Franz Hautschl, *Anfangsgründe des einfachen und doppelten kaufmännischen Buchhaltens,* Wien, 1840. The extracts are taken from the quotations in an article by Alexander Novak, *Zeitschrift für Buchhaltung,* May, 1898.

7. *Zeitschrift für Buchhaltung,* January, 1898, also in Hügli's *"Buchhaltungs-Studien,"* Bern, 1900.

8. According to Josef Schrott, *op. cit.,* Kurzbauer's explanation of double entry was also completely presented in his *Lehrbuch der kaufmännischen Buchhaltung,* 1850.

XII. THE ENTITY THEORY IN ACCOUNTING

THE views presented in the previous chapter exhibit a striking similarity in spite of their wide distribution in time and space. In general the writers adopted a "proprietorship" view of bookkeeping theory. The fundamental relationship between the accounts of double-entry bookkeeping is symbolized by Cronhelm's equation:

Positive properties—Negative properties
=Proprietor's stock

The two members of the equation represent, on the one hand, the form aspect of the proprietor's capital and, on the other hand, the totality aspect of the proprietor's capital. Kurzbauer made the same point concisely by opposing accounts of remainders (*Bestandconten*) and accounts of results (*Erfolgsconten*), or, as we would say, real accounts and nominal accounts, including capital in the latter category. Thomas Jones further clarified the relationship of these two account categories by showing that assets minus liabilities and capital plus net profit produce an identical result, i.e., net worth. According to the theory of the time "capital" meant "proprietor's investment." At the beginning of a business it consisted of the proprietor's original contribution; at any time thereafter capital might mean either original contribution, or original contribution plus and minus profits and losses realized and retained since the beginning,—that is, net worth.*

It is to be noted, too, that the concepts of "costs" and "income" had not yet formed. Capital was augmented by profits and diminished by losses. This was probably a heritage from an earlier time when the result of every transaction could be finally determined as

* The interest in this point may be greater when it is recalled that under some modern no-par stock statutes "capital" may be a designated sum even though it differs materially in amount from the stockholders' contribution.

soon as it was completed—before the day of such modern items as "overhead," "prepaid expense," "accrued liabilities" and the like. If certain expenditures occurred which could not well be associated with specific transactions, these were "losses"—technically, they were deductions from capital.

Treating losses and expenses as synonymous was bad terminology practice even then. And it still is, for most beginners in bookkeeping today who have their wits about them feel that expense partakes more of the nature of an asset, since it is an expenditure that confers a benefit on the business, than of the nature of a loss, which confers no benefit whatever in return.

The "proprietorship theory" of double-entry bookkeeping, first formulated by the writers previously mentioned, was continued and refined in the last quarter of the nineteenth century by several well known bookkeeping authors, notably Charles E. Sprague (United States), F. Hügli (Switzerland) and J. F. Schär (Germany). In the same period another view of double entry began to be discussed; the proprietorship theory, therefore, no longer stood alone as the basic explanation of the nature of double-entry bookkeeping. But more of that later.

Cronhelm had expressed the fundamental nature of double-entry accounts in a simple equation, and Thomas Jones had emphasized the purely statistical character of "debit" and "credit" (the terms could as easily have been "red" and "blue"). This use of equations and the analyzing of transactions simply as increases and decreases in accounting elements rather than as "debts" was made the central theme of Charles E. Sprague's highly interesting analysis of bookkeeping in 1880.[1] The following extracts from his articles will serve to show the author's argument:

> "The laws of debit and credit by which all book-keeping is carried on, have been stated from a different point of view by almost every writer who has treated upon them. In the practical application of these laws there is not the slightest variation in principle; but in formulating them and stating them to others, we find the utmost diversity. . . . . .
>
> "I propose, then, to work out still another way of looking at the principle of debit and credit. Treating the science of ac-

counts as a branch of mathematics (which it is), I reduce it to an algebraic notation: I constantly interpret the algebraic results into common language, and also into the technical, conventional, but often convenient, notation used by book-keepers. I show this last to be as truly algebraic as the first; and I teach that no matter what particular form is employed in the presentation of facts, if the equation is preserved, implicitly or explicitly, it is true book-keeping. . . . . .

"All the operations of double-entry bookkeeping are transformations of the following equation:

"What I *have* + what I *trust* = what I *owe* + what I am *worth*, or symbolically written:

$$H + T = O + X.$$

"The mathematical side of this history consists in certain equations, in which addition and cancellation are the only operations employed. . . . . .

"Simple Proprietorship.—If I, the subject of the history, trust no one and owe no one, then I am worth all that I have, no more, no less; or

$$\text{(Equation 1.) } H = X.$$

what I have is the measure of what I am worth; the property actually in my possession is all mine and I claim nothing more. . . . . . .

"Proprietorship with Credit.—If I trust others with part of my wealth but owe no one, Equation 1 becomes

$$(2)\ H + T = X$$

"That is, what I have, added to what is owing me, equals what I am worth; my wealth is composed of the valuables in my possession, together with what I claim and expect to receive from others, my *debtors*.

"But I may also owe other people, my *creditors*. Then H + T is not really mine; I am holding part of it as a *trustee* (in the literal sense) for those who trust me; this part must be subtracted from H + T to give the true value of X. Let O represent the amount of my debts to others; then we have

$$(4)\ H + T = X + O,$$

which is the fundamental equation,
What I *have* + what I *trust* = what I *owe* + what I am *worth*."

* * * * * *

"So much for the equation of the property *at rest;* now we must provide for recording its changes.

"There are only two kinds of change; *increase* and *decrease, more* and *less,* + and —.

More gives four modes of increase.

1. I have more
2. I trust more
3. I owe more
4. I am *worth more.*

Less gives four modes of decrease.

1. I have less.
2. I trust less.
3. I owe less.
4. I am *worth less.*

"We illustrated above the transposition of a negative term to the opposite side of the equation. The same principle is applied to the four terms in this section.

I *have more* is added to debit:

But I *have less* instead of being subtracted from the debit, is added to the credit.

I *trust more* is added to the debit:

But I *trust less* is added to the credit, not subtracted from the debit.

I *owe more* is added to the credit:

But I *owe less* instead of being subtracted from the credit, is added to the debit.

I *am worth more* is added to the credit:

But I *am worth less* is added to the debit.

"Hence the list of debits and credits, while the equation is undergoing change, is extended from 4 to 8.

(a) Elements of the Equation of Value at Rest.

Debits	*Credits*
Have	Owe
Trust	Worth

(b) Elements of the Equation of Value in Motion.

Debits	*Credits*
1. Have more.	2. Have less.
3. Trust more.	4. Trust less.
5. Owe less.	6. Owe more.
7. Worth less.	8. Worth more.

"These tables are:

(a) A complete rule for balance-sheets or statements of financial condition.

(b) A complete rule for "journalizing," that is, for ascertaining the debit and credit in any transaction or shifting of values; in other words, directions for placing the values on the left and right side of the equation respectively. As list b contains all the possible changes in the elements of the equation, it must suffice to represent any transaction or business occurrence. . . . .

"Forming Equations of Change.—Illustrations

"Let the transaction be: I buy Merchandise worth k, and pay cash, i, getting trusted by P—— for the remainder, p. Then we must ask——

Which of the 8 elements of change is true of Cash?
Which of them is true of Merchandise?
Which of them is true of indebtedness to P——?

"Answers:

I *have less* Cash, a credit:
I *have more* Merchandise, a debit;
I *owe more* to P——, a credit.

Therefore, k is a debit, i and p are credits; the equation is

$$k = i + p.$$

Assuming the numerical values,

$$k = 1{,}000,\ i = 500,\ p = 500,$$

we can put this equation into the form of a journal entry,

Merchandise Dr. to Sundries, ...	1,000	
For purchases from P——,		
To Cash, for amount paid, ...		500
To P——, for Balance unpaid, ...		500

"We give the following as results of the foregoing discussion.

I. All the statements of book-keeping are equations.

II. All *minus* (negative or subtractive) terms are transposed to the opposite side where they become *plus* (positive or additive).

III. Debit and credit mean simply 'left hand side' and 'right hand side' of the equation. To him who understands the equation, no other definition of debit and credit is necessary. To him who has never grasped the idea of the equation, no definition of debit and credit can make them clear."

These extracts from Sprague are given thus in some detail not only because the author was a pioneer in American accounting but because transaction analysis was so thoroughly systematized in his work that these methods in some degree form the basis of the explanations given in most of the subsequent American bookkeeping texts. Sprague wrote little that was not foreshadowed in earlier works (notably in Thomas Jones' books) and he lacked some of the fullness of statement and of theory found elsewhere. But he contributed such a concise description of the mental process of resolving a business occurrence into its debit and credit elements, preparatory to entering the transaction in technical bookkeeping form into the records, that he has greatly influenced the teaching of bookkeeping in this country.

In Europe the last decade of the century witnessed a lively debate about bookkeeping theory and not a little argument about priority of ideas. Among the proponents of the proprietorship view of double entry, F. Hügli (a governmental accountant of Bern, Switzerland) proved to be a leader. In a book [2] published in 1887 he discussed this characteristic formation of two opposing groups of accounts incidentally in describing various systems of bookkeeping records. In the next ten years he followed this work with numerous contributions to technical periodicals [3] explaining and advocating the proprietorship, or "two-series-of-accounts" (*Zweikontenreihentheorie*), view of bookkeeping theory. These articles were later assembled and reprinted together with others under the title: *Buchhaltungs-Studien* (Bern, 1900). They are concerned for the most part with explaining the fundamentals of double entry through the use of equations, with showing that liabilities are negative property and with arguing that "the business" owns business property and does not merely owe it to the proprietors in the sense that it owes debts to third parties.

His views in principle follow the theory already outlined by other authors. Apparently without knowledge of any predecessors to Kurzbauer and Augspurg he gave them perhaps too much credit for their accomplishment,* but he would have been first to dis-

* Hügli was evidently an admirer of Kurzbauer and Augspurg, for in his article called "Two Pathfinders," after quoting extracts from their books, he calls them

claim any originality for his own writings. His contribution seems to lie in the fact that he gave the theory sufficient body and bulk in discussion to drive its basic elements firmly home to his readers.

Hügli's contemporary, Johann Friedrich Schär,* also gave considerable attention to the basic elements of double-entry bookkeeping. He was led to do this, it seems, when he was under the necessity at one time of teaching mature engineers, lawyers and chemists the elements of bookkeeping. He tried to adapt his explanations to his audience and attacked the problem from a mathematical point of view. This was in 1889, and the next year he published his explanation in a pamphlet [4] which was soon translated into several foreign languages. Some years later this work was greatly expanded and made into a book. In 1922 the fifth edition [5] was published.

Schär's interesting analysis of the flow of value through a business enterprise is too long to present here, but, judging from the eighty-odd pages of literal symbolization of bookkeeping transactions and the extensive use made of algebraic equations in the fifth edition, there can be little doubt that he convinced his readers that equilibrium could be and actually was maintained throughout the bookkeeping record. Whether they learned by this means to keep double-entry books is perhaps not a fair question; it may not have been intended that they should. But the procedure certainly appears complicated for beginners, whatever their maturity. The example on the following page will serve to illustrate the author's method.[6]

The final equation is identical in form with the opening equation, except that the size of the basic items is different, thus demonstrating that the initial equilibrium is maintained regardless of the number of subsequent transactions to be included.

Assuming that this matter is reproduced in the fifth edition of the author's book (1922) substantially as it originally appeared in 1890, it offers an interesting comparison with Charles E. Sprague's

---

"pioneers in this field of natural theory" whose service cannot be too highly estimated.

* A professor in the Handelshochschule of Leipzig from 1899 much honored for the active part he played in the development of commercial education—see the anniversary volume in his honor: *Zur Entwicklung der Betriebswirtschaftslehre*, Berlin, 1925.

	(a) transactions in equation form		(b) transactions in account form				
			Property			*Capital*	
			Dr.	Cr.		Dr.	Cr.
			+	—		—	+
1. opening equation:	$A - P =$	K	A	P	=		K
2. equal exchanges:	$+a - a =$	O	a	a			
	$+b - b =$	O	b	b			
3. gain or loss transaction:	$+g \quad =$	$+g$	g		=		g
	$-l =$	$-l$		l	=	l	
4. combined transaction:							
	$+q \quad +r - q =$	$+r$	$q + r$	q	=		r
	$+m - (m + t) =$	$-t$	m	$m - t$	=	t	

summing the equations above:

a, b, q, and m cancel out:

$A + g + r$ are new assets........................call them A_1

$P + l + t$ are new liabilities........................call them P_1

$K + g + r - (l + t)$ is the new net worth.............call it K_1

5. final equation ....$A_1 - P_1 = K_1$

summation[7] in 1880 of a series of transaction equations expressed in literal symbols:

* $(I + i_2 + i_3)$		$(i + i_4 + i_5 + I_1)$ *
$+ I_1$		
* $+ (K + K + x_3)$		$+ (k_1 + K_1)$ *
$+ K_1$		
* $+ L$		$+ L$ *
* $+ U$		$+ U$ *
* $+ (V + v)$		$+ V$ *
$+ V_1$		
$+ W$	=	$+ P$ *
* $+ P$		
		$+ Q$
		$+ R$
* $+ (x_2 + X_1)$		$+ (x + X_3)$ *
* $+ Y$		$+ (Y + y_1)$ *
		$+ Y_1$
* $+ Z$		$+ (Z + z)$ *
		$+ Z_1$

Canceling the lines marked * we have

$$I_1 + K_1 + V_1 + W = Q + R + Y_1 + Z_1$$

This is an equation balance-sheet with the elements indicated by letters; V and W represent debtors, Q is a creditor, R is bills payable, Y_1 and Z_1 are partners' capital, I_1 is cash, and K is merchandise. The resulting equation (cash + merchandise + debtors = creditor + bills payable + capital), the author points out, is still in the original form: What I have + what I trust = What I owe + What I am worth, in spite of all the transactions which have altered the original situation. This is the same theory as that later expressed by the German author, Schär, no doubt without a prior knowledge of Sprague's work. These two authors, working along similar basic lines regarding the fundamental nature of double entry, thus apparently arrived at similar explanations quite independently.*

These writers of the last quarter of the century added little that was really new—no matter how original either writer's ideas may have seemed to him. Either they independently arrived at explanations of their own which were similar to others' views, or, like Hügli, they enriched previous explanations with further arguments and better illustrations. The characteristic of the "proprietorship theory" as formulated in the middle of the century was therefore unchanged by the writings of the last part of the century.

But these explanations of the fundamental nature of double-entry bookkeeping did not go unchallenged. At about the same time that Hügli and Schär in Europe and Sprague in America were presenting the "proprietorship theory" of bookkeeping certain other writers were explaining double entry by what may be called the "entity theory" (*Geschäfts-theorie*).

The entity theory, as the name suggests, stresses the separateness of "the business" and the proprietor. Bookkeeping, under this view, is primarily concerned with accounting to "outsiders" for all property *entrusted* from without to "the business" and dedicated to its purposes. This is quite opposite to the proprietorship theory, in which bookkeeping is viewed as an accounting by the proprietor for his own property in detail and in total.

* J. G. Ch. Volmer (*Zeitschrift für Buchhaltung*, Vol. III, 1894, p. 25) calls attention to the work of a Dutch author (F. W. Balabrega, *De leer van het boekhauden volgens wiskundige grondeginselen*, 1890) in which appears algebraic explanation of bookkeeping very similar to Schär's. Volmer says that this author told him that he had not known of the work done by either Hügli or Schär when he wrote.

So fundamental a difference in point of view as this must be indicative of an underlying difference in the concepts of the real function of bookkeeping and of capital and income. Capital, according to the proprietorship view, is the proprietor's contribution; liabilities are merely negative assets. But in the entity theory, capital is the sum total of property active in the business from whatever source derived; liabilities (loans) here are considered to be "capital sources" as much as proprietary investments can be. Profit, according to the proprietorship theory, is an increase in the net figure of positive and negative property (i.e., in net assets); in the equity theory, profit is the excess of proceeds recovered over the outlays advanced during the business process. In the first view, profit is any increment to proprietorship however obtained; in the other, it is the reward for managerial skill in advancing such outlays as will produce an excess when recovered. In the first theory the concept of capital produces a balance-sheet equation of: assets — liabilities = proprietorship. In the second theory the concept of capital produces a balance-sheet equation of: assets = investments.

The full consequences of such differences of theory can not be given much consideration in an historical discussion. But it will be evident to anyone acquainted with the trends of recent discussions in accounting, that modern theory must be based upon such fundamentals as the purpose of business enterprise, the functions of proprietor and creditor, the nature of capital and profit and the like. These are the elements which these writers of an earlier generation were beginning to discuss without intending to consider theory as such.

The manner of classifying financial facts and the method of analyzing business transactions are merely the outward expressions of an inward purpose, namely, to distinguish clearly between capital and profit so that the objective of the business enterprise may be most directly effected—that is to say, accounting is the inward purpose of which bookkeeping is the outward expression.

The recognition of this deeper significance of basic concepts is largely a contemporary development; discussions before the twentieth century did not probe deeply into consequences. The supporters of one type of theory were mainly intent upon raising the analysis of transactions above the level of the axiom, "debit the receiver; credit the giver," and the advocates of the other were bent upon clarifying the concept of "the enterprise." Much of the discussion of these matters in the literature of the late nineteenth century was so concerned with explaining both the equilibrium of the trial balance and those phenomena of double-entry bookkeeping which place increasing items on the left side of some accounts but on the right side of others, that points of deeper significance to theory were passed with slight attention.

But since the perspective of later knowledge shows the present to be rooted in the past, it may be worth while briefly to outline the chronology of the ideas which are reflected in the entity theory of double-entry bookkeeping. It is to be noted again, however, that mere chronological sequence does not necessarily indicate any indebtedness of a particular author to his immediate predecessors; the material is in most instances too meager to permit an attempt to trace the source of a writer's ideas. The outline will serve, however, to indicate the persistence of certain ideas throughout a period of years.

Continental writers of the last decade of the nineteenth century labored under the impression that the origin of the entity theory reached back only into the eighties. But later researches [8] tend to show that the basis at least extends much further back than that period. It is shown, for example, that calculations of proprietorship were not always the aim of mediæval bookkeeping, and that much early bookkeeping of that time was an "agency" accounting for ventures, consignments and the like. It is shown also that nobles would "lend" to business ventures, but in reality share in the profit to avoid the charge of usury, and that the so-called "capital account" was in fact often treated as any other debt having a credit balance.[9]

The fact must be evident in such situations as are here suggested that even at an early date the actual proprietor (principal investor and risk bearer) was a person quite distinctly separate from the unit which was called upon to render an accounting. The accounting required by these situations would naturally be different from that demanded by a strictly proprietorship theory of bookkeeping.

These situations, best described perhaps as agency or accountability operations, would require a reporting upon property entrusted, not property owned. Thus to the reporting (record-keeping) person the account with a "proprietor" was not different in principle from an account with a lender; in fact, a lender often took the form of a proprietor to avoid the appearance of being a lender. To the active manager (in contrast to the silent partner) of the trading ventures so common in the fifteenth century, there were two elements present: (a) kinds of property for which he was accountable and (b) sources of property to which he was accountable; profit was but an additional "indebtedness" to the sources of the property in use.

This, it will be noted, is exactly the view of the subsequent entity theory. Much later references (yet earlier than the eighties or nineties when the theory was first thought to have originated) are given by Leon Gomberg,[10] which show that the idea that capital and loan accounts were similar in nature existed in the second and third quarters of the nineteenth century. Lodovico Crippa (*La Scienza dei Conti,* Milan, 1838) and an unknown author (*Thoughts on double entry and balance sheets,* London, 1869) are cited as holding that the capital account is essentially the trader's own personal account with the business. J. G. Courcelles-Seneuil (*Cours de Comptabilite,* 2d edition, Paris, 1870) is quoted in the following words:

> "The principle of double-entry bookkeeping is that all commercial capital is a capital entrusted to a firm to manage, which must be able at any time to say where it is, in whose hands and in what forms it is to be found, and how and when it has been increased or decreased. . . . .
>
> "The firm has an account with the merchant as if he were a stranger. . . ."

Gomberg notes that the French author does not commit the error, into which some others fell, of calling the merchant (proprietor) a real creditor. He then goes on to say that the separation of proprietor and firm is not a fiction; the two are really separate in fact, but it is a fiction to call the proprietorship items in the accounts by the name "debts," for "proprietor" is not identical with "creditor" in rights and privileges. Bookkeeping, in Gomberg's opinion, is concerned with the movement of values within a business enterprise, not with the affairs of a proprietor as such. The latter may have many financial activities outside the firm's affairs and hence outside its bookkeeping.

Before continuing the sequence of European writers who discussed the entity theory, it will be necessary to interpose at this point brief comments upon an American writer who presented some of the same basic concepts which, a decade or more later, found such ardent advocates as Brenkman of Holland and Berliner of Germany.

In many ways E. G. Folsom's book (1873) is unusual.[11] The author was a man of some education (he signs as a master of arts) who was not unacquainted with the political economy of his day, for he mentions Mill and Carey specifically. His book contains much more discussion (about one-fifth of the total number of pages) than other texts on bookkeeping. This discussion is found mainly in the early part of the work and deals with labor, expense, money, exchange value and the like from the economic side. In this manner he definitely attempts to lay a theory foundation for bookkeeping by definitions, concepts and classifications drawn from economics; later he tries to organize all business transactions into a systematic scheme. His principal aim, therefore (like that of Thomas Jones before him and Charles Sprague after him), is to reduce to a logical system the procedure of analyzing business transactions into debits and credits for entry into bookkeeping records. But in the process of explaining to the reader how to analyze transactions and make bookkeeping records, he expresses a number of ideas which tend to relate his book to the so-called entity theory of bookkeeping, although the author is not apparently conscious of following any particular "theory," to say nothing of constructing one.

The basis of his presentation of transaction analysis is his subclassification of value which is here given in outline form:

Value consists of—
- 1. Commercial value, subdivided as
  - (a) Actual (cash, merchandise, securities, real estate)
  - (b) Evidential (personal accounts, bills receivable, bills payable)

2. Ideal value, subdivided as
   (a) Labor and service
      (I) direct (expense, interest, discount, commissions)
      (II) Loss and gain (service received is loss, service given is gain)
   (b) Ownership in individuality (i.e., self)
      in property
      in proprietor or stock
      in partners or capital stock

He follows this outline by resolving all exchanges of values into nine equations, in sub-groups of three.

	Illustrations
1. *Equations of the 1st order—*	
(a) Commercial value = Commercial value	(Mdse. to Cash)
(b) Commercial value = Ideal value	(Cash to Rent)
(c) Commercial value = Ideal and Com'l. value	(Cash to Mdse. and Profit)
2. *Equations of the 2nd order—*	
(a) Ideal value = Commercial value	(Rent to Cash)
(b) Ideal value = Ideal value	(Labor to Labor)
(c) Ideal value = Ideal and Com'l. value	(Labor to Labor and Cash)
3. *Equations of the 3rd order—*	
(a) Com'l. and ideal value = Com'l. value	(Cash and Loss to Mdse.)
(b) Com'l. and ideal value = Ideal value	(Labor and Cash to Labor)
(c) Com'l. and ideal value = Ideal and Com'l. value	(Note Payable and Disc. to Note Receivable and Disc.)

This is an excellent framework based upon the propositions that "all transactions have their origin in an exchange of values" and that "in all business transactions there is a co-equal receiving and giving of values." (p. 16). But the author fails to follow up this beginning by a clear-cut application of the equations to transactions (such as Thomas Jones employed so well). Folsom goes astray after the old gods: a debit is something received and a credit is something given. He also becomes confused by trying to associate *debit* with "owes" and *credit* with "is owed." This is not surprising, for the attempt to analyze impersonal elements (which can not owe in a strict sense) by the same rules which seem proper for personal elements (which, representing persons, can be said to owe) has always been a stumbling block to good reasoning in bookkeeping. The literal translation of "debit" as "owes" is probably responsible for the difficulty, together with the astonishingly tenacious persistence of prior influences, such as, for example, early association of bookkeeping with purely personal records.

The principal interest at the moment, however, is not so much in Folsom's methods of transaction analysis as in those ideas of his which seem to connect his work with the entity theory. For example, he stresses service throughout when explaining profit—and this is significant. Most other authors have nothing to say in so direct a manner about the nature of profit and capital.

"How can increase and decrease in capital take place?" (p. 38). Not by the exchange of commercial values as such for they are completely equivalent, but through ideal values since these complete the equation of exchange and measure the increase and decrease of property. The receiving of more commercial value than is given plainly indicates an increase of wealth because some service has been given for the excess. Thus the author associates his concept of profit with a service rendered. The accounts which show loss and gain are labeled "received service" on the debit (expense) side and "gave service" on the credit (income) side. (pp. 44–46). In another place (p. 54) Folsom says that the proprietor can only serve and be served. Because the ideal values (services) have their source and termination in the proprietor, an account is kept with him to record these services. Thus the "service rendered," which the author has already linked with profit, is also associated with the proprietor. The author conceives of profit, therefore, as due to a proprietor-rendered-service.*

A few years later [12] Folsom revised some parts of the theory sections of his book, apparently in the hope of clarifying and extending the discussion. Some of the items in this revision approach the doctrines of the entity theory. In his introduction, for example, he analyzes transactions into three forms—

* This concept, it will be noted, would hardly seem to include the result of fluctuating prices as a source of true profit. Whether or not the author would have labeled the result of price changes as "capital increment" in contra-distinction to "profit" one has, of course, no means of knowing.

1. *Service,* which is incorporeal and unembodied (i.e., present service)
2. *Commodity,* which is stored service of the past (i.e., past service)
3. *Claim,* which is promissory service still to be rendered (i.e., future service)

All business transactions, he holds, are composed of exchanges of these three classes. All exchanges are based on the principle of equality which is the foundation of all equitable commerce. Therefore, all business transactions are equations of values exchanged and are reducible to six in number:

1. Service = Service,
2. Service = Commodity,
3. Service = Claim,
4. Commodity = Commodity,
5. Commodity = Claim,
6. Claim = Claim.

This is an advance over his earlier classification of transactions and, it will be noted, effects a reduction of all elements to some aspect or other of "service." *

Folsom continues to relate "service" to other matters in bookkeeping. For example, loss, he says, is paying for a service which is not exchangeable (p. 10); and in this category he includes a sale at less than cost, interest, rent, commissions, and "the consumptive use of materials, as fixtures and other incidentals . . . unless services of this kind are also treated as embodied in the merchandise and are charged in with it as enhancing its value." (p. 11).

In spite of his failure to distinguish clearly between "loss" and "expense," Folsom has here grasped a fundamental quite in advance of his contemporaries. He says that these services are losses (i.e., decreases of proprietorship) but from the last sentences it is clear that he means that these services are "expenses" when they are not "costs" attached to the product. This is a fundamental proposition of cost accounting which in 1881 would hardly have been of much practical use, for cost accounting was not yet ready for this idea.

On the same page Folsom speaks of gain as "receiving pay for our services." We gain, he says, because we bring new-born value

* A similar emphasis upon service is found in later German writers who espouse the entity theory, especially in twentieth century authors such as Berliner, Nicklish, *et al.*

to the sphere of exchange, as all human effort put forth in view of a return is the source of the production of all financial wealth. Here again the author relates profit to proprietor-service and omits to mention speculative increments.

Capital, he writes, must be re-exchangeable; that is, it must be a commodity or claim (a present service such as labor not being exchangeable). But not all property is capital; to be capital, he points out, property must be devoted exclusively to some business enterprise with a view of realizing profit. Capital thus set apart constitutes a business which from the beginning establishes relations between itself and all parties dealing with it. (p. 12).

In this last section the separateness of the enterprise and of the proprietor is plainly indicated; in other places, as shown already, stress is laid upon the service characteristic of the elements of business property. A relationship is also established between the conception of profit and proprietor-service. These, it may be noted, are also the essentials of the entity theory of bookkeeping which received its name (*Geschäfts-theorie*) and most of its codification at other hands.

Attention is now directed to the last quarter of the nineteenth century, and to Europe, in order to continue the thread of the continental development of this body of theory.

The details of the European controversy over priority in statement of the essentials of the entity theory are of little concern here. It will be sufficient to indicate the two writers involved, and to say that, judging from their articles, they were both apparently unconscious of having had any European, to say nothing of American, predecessors (e.g., Folsom).

In the early eighties a Dutch writer, I. N. Brenkman, published a book [13] later regarded by a countryman of his, J. G. Ch. Volmer,[14] as containing expressions of bookkeeping theory which constituted a bridge uniting the old doctrines of bookkeeping with the science of accounting. By "old doctrines" was meant the "personification" view of accounts, which attempted to explain all transactions as personal debts and leaned heavily upon a "debit the receiver, credit the giver" type of analysis. Later it became evident, Volmer points out, that the mechanism of double-entry bookkeeping, i.e., the reversal of the + and — sides in different accounts, the necessary equilibrium of the trial balance, etc., was a matter of secondary importance, and that the substance and mission of accounting science (*Verrechnungswissenschaft*) lay in keeping a statistical-economic record so that proper supervision over certain properties might be maintained. Brenkman is described as recognizing this view of accounting, for he is said to have designated the appearance and expiration of assets and liabilities as the occasions for debiting and crediting.

At about the same time, a German writer, Manfred Berliner, without knowledge of Brenkman's work, wrote an article which advanced many of the same basic views.[15] He stressed the separateness of the merchant's private life and activities and correspondingly his separate private property and business capital, and he held that commercial bookkeeping was only a mirror of this separately dedicated capital. Business assets, therefore, were debts of the firm to the proprietor and business liabilities were claims of the firm upon the proprietor. In discussing profit, Berliner said that "profit" or "loss" was only an indication of the value of services (of the proprietor). Expenses were not to be considered as "losses"; they must be accounted for as part of the production costs of the goods concerned. "Profit and loss," he writes, "exists for bookkeeping first at the time of settlement between the business and the principal when it is determined whether the items of property put into the business are still present or have been increased or decreased as a result of the activity and service of the principal." Later Berliner reiterated these essential items of his theory and disavowed any prior knowledge that anyone had held similar views. He intimated that he had taught these views to students as early as 1870 but was deterred from publishing them by the lack of a suitable medium.

It can hardly be said that the entity theory had achieved its full stature as an organized exposition of the nature of double-entry bookkeeping prior to 1900. Much that was necessary to round out the early notions was added after the turn of the century. For example, a clear exposition of all assets as "latent services" and of expenses as "active services," together with the consequent interrelations between accounts, is well presented in the later German periodical literature, especially that of 1912.[16]

Without attempting to follow the course of the development of German accounting theory in detail, it may be of assistance in making more intelligible the somewhat unfamiliar entity theory, which has been discussed, to restate briefly its essential assumptions.

Assets and expenses are all included in one category, that is profit-making media, which are expressed either as active services (if contributing directly and immediately to the economic process) or as latent services (if direct contribution to the economic process is deferred for some time). These potential services are obtained from various sources such as proprietorship investments, retained profits and loans of various types. Consequently a balance-sheet is essentially an equation wherein the equivalence may be variously expressed as

(a) *Kinds of profit-making-media* = *Sources of profit-making-media*
(b) *Unrecovered outlays* = *Invested sums*
(c) *Properties* = *Equities.*

In a sense, this conception tends to place "assets" upon the plane of "expenses," by regarding the former as productive outlays awaiting appropriation rather than as objects intended for liquidation sale to satisfy creditors. The only difference between asset and expense is one of time of appropriation or association with specific units of income. Therefore, asset and expense accounts may all be generalized in the form of a single account:

Unrecovered Outlays Account

Dr: Recoverable outlays made in advance.	*Cr:* Outlays actually recovered through a sale transaction. (*Contra Dr:* "recovery account") *Bal:* Outlays still to be recovered (= assets, deferred charges, etc.)

According to this theory, every sale (income) is considered as the compensation paid by consumers for the economic services received by them. This service is resolved into two parts: 1. a portion of each specific service-form originally acquired by the seller (asset or expense) and now passed on to the buyer; 2. a compensation (profit or loss) for the service rendered by the business itself (or proprietor).

This doctrine may be expressed in account form as follows:

Recovery Account

Dr: A portion of every asset and expense contributing to the sale. (*Contra Cr:* Each specific asset and expense account concerned.) *Bal:* Compensation for the service of the enterprise. (*Contra Cr:* In closing, transfer to one of the "sources of profit-making-media" accounts—e.g., retained profits.)	*Cr:* Amount of compensation received for economic services rendered to consumers. (*Contra Dr:* The form of property given by the consumer for the service he gets.

This view of the essentials of double entry is evidently an economic one, since it obviously considers the entrepreneur's activity as that of making advances and recouping them when his specific, particular service is performed, and since it regards profit as the compensation for the entrepreneur's service in making the advances,* etc. This theory also definitely gives a greater emphasis to "costing" than to balance-sheets; the intention is to associate cost and return, effort and effect. The so-called "recovery account" supplies evidence that analysis of transactions, according to this theory, consists in large measure of apportioning various costs (i.e., outlay advances) so as to associate them properly with specific units of return.

The center of attention in the proprietorship theory, however, is somewhat different. There interest is mainly in the more or less

* It is not certain what is the explanation of speculative or fluctuation profits. Judging by later writers (e.g., Schmidt, *Die Organische Tageswert Bilanz,* 1929) fluctuation changes would not be profits but increments to capital. This too, in all probability, would be the nature of all gifts, natural increase (as animal progeny), capital gains, etc.

legal relationships, that is, in ownership and debts. Capital is equivalent to proprietor's investment plus his net gains and losses not withdrawn (i.e., his net worth); loans are only negative properties; profits are the increments to proprietorship; expenses are "losses" (deductions from proprietorship).

The proprietorship theory can best be associated with the proprietorship form of enterprise, in which proprietor (including partners) and business are so inseparable (legally) that an accounting for the one is for all practical purposes an accounting for the other also. The entity theory is well presented in the corporate form of enterprise, for in this the contributors of capital are (legally) so distinct from the business that the term "ownership" loses its force; claims against the assets are so various in degree that the many forms of "indebtedness" shade off into one another without sharply defining the "owners."

Both these opinions are rooted deeply in the past; both have much logic to support them and have given rise to considerable discussion in literature. But it would be difficult to say which view prevailed in fact and which most deserved to prevail. General impressions, however, suggest that the proprietorship theory strongly influenced American writers and that the entity theory greatly affected German writers on accounting.

In any event, however, there has been progress in matters of theory. It is a long way from the (presumable) transaction analysis of Paciolo's time and earlier to the late nineteenth-century arguments about the nature of capital and profit and discussions of proprietorship and debt. This progress in theory is one of the principal factors which indicate the expansion of bookkeeping into accounting.

REFERENCES

1. A series of articles contributed to the periodical, *The Bookkeeper* (New York) during July and August, 1880, under the title "Algebra of Accounts." Over twenty-five years later the same material, much revised and elaborated, appeared as Charles E. Sprague's *"Philosophy of Accounts"* (New York, 1907).

2. F. Hügli, *Buchhaltungs-systeme und Buchhaltungs-forme,* Bern, 1887.

3. Especially in *Zeitschrift für Buchhaltung* for 1894, 1896, 1897, 1898.

4. J. F. Schär, *Versuch einer wissenchaftlichen Behandlung der Buchhaltung,* Basel, 1890.

5. J. F. Schär, *Buchhaltung und Bilanz,* 5th ed., Berlin, 1922.

6. Schär, *Buchhaltung und Bilanz,* 5th ed., p. 32. For a recent statement of the "algebra of double-entry" see Prof. Theodor Forjancic's article "Die rechnerischen Grundlagen im Aufbau der Vermögensverrechnung" in *Zeitschrift für Betriebswirtschaft,* April, 1933.

7. *The Bookkeeper,* August 31, 1880, p. 53.

8. e.g., Herbert Buhl, *Die geschichtlich begrundete Kontentheorie,* Stuttgart, 1929; Leon Gomberg, *Histoire Critique de la Theorie des Comptes,* Geneva, 1929.

9. Buhl, *op. cit.,* especially pp. 36-49.

10. Gomberg, *op. cit.,* pp. 68-71.

11. E. G. Folsom, *The Logic of Accounts,* New York, 1873.

12. E. G. Folsom, *Logic of Accounts,* Albany, 1881.

13. I. N. Brenkman, *Nieuwe Theorie van het dubbel boekhouden,* Gravenhage, 1882.

14. *Zeitschrift für Buchhaltung,* Vol. 3, pp. 6-73 (1894).

15. *Allgemeine Lehrsatze der Kaufmännischen Buchhaltung,* published in *"Kaufmännischen Blättern"* in 1887. Later the material was expanded in Berliner's *Schwierige Fälle der kaufmännischen Buchhaltung,* Leipzig, 1893.

16. H. Nichlish in *Zeitschrift für Buchhaltung,* V. 21, p. 63, and H. Biedermann in *Zeitschrift für Handelswissenschaft und Handelspraxis,* V. 5, p. 99.

XIII. INFLUENCE OF THE CORPORATION

No list of the factors which contributed to the expansion of bookkeeping into accounting would be complete without including the influence of the corporation. This form of business organization has become so predominant that it is taken very much for granted, at least in the United States. But it is a patent fact that the corporation modifies its environment even while it is itself being changed by economic evolution within that environment. Bookkeeping is one element of environment which has thus been influenced by the growth of business corporations. It could hardly have escaped being affected; the very factors which made the corporation superior for the conduct of business also laid additional burdens upon the record aspect of the transaction of business.

The corporation, as a method of assembling far-flung capital and of effectively administering it for absent owners offered advantages which greatly stimulated the growth of business. This created many recording problems related to size and complexity; but at the same time it also gave rise to certain peculiar relationships which created their own problems. The corporate form of organization was particularly favorable for the development of business enterprises of great size; size brought greater volume of transactions and with it the urgent need for economy in the labor of recording and for an increased assurance of accuracy in the recorded results. These conditions are reflected in the choice and design of bookkeeping records and in the procedures set up for the accurate and expeditious handling of the data. In this way the corporation probably influenced bookkeeping considerably. But a study of accounting history is not the place in which to enter into a consideration of the bookkeeping mechanics involved in large-scale enterprises, so this subject must be passed over with the mere mention of its existence.

The corporation possessed characteristics which tended not only to stimulate the formation of larger enterprises but also to create an increasing preference for this type of business unit. Therefore, number of corporations as well as size was a factor. A corollary to this was that many persons rather than a few were associated with a given enterprise; most of them would have less personal contact with business operations within the enterprise than would have been the case in a partnership. They were therefore dependent upon figures and reports for their knowledge of details. This situation would quite naturally increase the responsibilities of bookkeeping. The lack of personal contact of stockholders furthermore meant delegated management, which in turn implied or made necessary a means of control from outside. Here is another area in which the corporation influenced accounting: this "outside control" is auditing—a subject which is given attention in another chapter.

But the influence of the corporation's underlying characteristics upon bookkeeping was not confined to these points of contact. Deeper impressions lie elsewhere. Among these is the theory that a corporation is a continuing enterprise, and that money invested in the corporation's stock is not a "venture" from which a profit or loss will materialize, when a "division" is made, but is rather a long-lived "investment" from which periodic returns will flow. If the corporation lives up to this expectation it must constantly and carefully distinguish between that which is capital and that which is income. The power of expressing the difference between these two elements is one of the basic characteristics of double-entry bookkeeping, and the accurate computation of the actual periodic income is one of the chief functions of accounting. Therefore, so far as the corporation made such a distinction in elements increasingly important, just so far it stimulated the expansion of bookkeeping into accounting.

The central accounting issue in a corporation concerns the amount of profit available for dividends. This in turn is primarily a matter of preserving the proper distinctions between capital and income. It is at this point that the corporation influences accounting most. The historical foundations of this influence are examined in some detail in this and immediately following chapters. The matter is approached, first, by a consideration of the view that a business is a permanent, continuing activity, which yields an income instead of a series of separate speculative profits and losses, and followed by a consideration of the development of depreciation and the cause and effect of the idea of limited liability.

While feudalism was slowly giving way before the strengthening of national governments and the rising influence of free cities, the economic circumstances of the people of England were changing with it. The agricultural life which prevailed in the mediæval manor became in a large measure the industrial and trading life of the town. It was thus an approach to "business," yet not quite business in the modern sense. Production was still handicraft operated in "lots"; when one lot of articles was finished, a buyer was sought. Production was probably halted until a purchaser was found and a bargain made which released the meager capital for another turnover. Thus production itself was not continuous, that is, "for stock," but was rather a series of separate speculations.

Trading at the time was largely conducted upon a similar plane. Traders bought anything they thought they could later sell at a profit, and each transaction was thought of as a unit. They bought and sold whatever was at hand; they did not "merchandise a stock," as we would say now. Business in the early days was "venturing" for profits—a series of speculations; modern business is more stabilized and has in general a continuity of transactions which places it on an "income basis," so to speak,—that is, makes it a producer of a steady, regular return upon a permanent capital, in contrast to irregular, sporadic profits upon separately ventured capital.

But this was not the only point at which the spirit of "venturing" touched the people. When the routine life of artisans in free towns and of overland traders moving between the great market fairs felt the influence of disrupted trade routes (1453), the effect was to increase the spirit of speculation as well as the urge toward exploration. As a result, before 1500 the Portuguese had opened the west coast of Africa to previously unknown trade and the Spanish had discovered the New World. By 1532 silver was discovered in Mexico, and images of vast metallic wealth at once took their place in men's minds beside dreams of a great and profitable trade with the Orient like that which had made the Italian city-states so prosperous in the period of the Renaissance.

These attractions furnished additional motives for leaving the routine of life in towns and going a-venturing on the sea. Fame and fortune awaited him who found a sea route to the East; untold wealth would be the share of those who opened up another Mexico with its hoard of precious metals.

These were attractive prospects, but they were not business prospects; they offered a chance for speculation and possible profits, but not an opportunity for investment for income. The results were bound to be a gamble, hence only a few hardy men were ready to sail in person upon such hazardous enterprises, and there were few who cared to venture their whole fortunes upon such a risk. Yet so tempting were the rewards of success that a way was found which afforded safety of person and adventure of some capital at the same time—this was through the joint-stock company, a type of organization related both to the ordinary partnership and to the "regulated company" of trading associates of that day.

The adventurers were all partners, but not all were active in carrying forward the project. There was a "joint stock," but not "joint management." Had the enterprises included both these features, they would have been plain partnerships; had they included joint management but not the joint-stock feature, they would have been "regulated companies"—that is, associations of separate members, each trading with his own capital under jointly prescribed rules of trade conduct.

The ventures were speculations; some of them seem almost like military enterprises. Frobisher's voyages and Drake's expeditions in the last quarter of the sixteenth century were all risky enterprises, which sought gain at the expense of the Spanish and took the hazard of death in battle in addition to the chance of failure to return a profit. Such buccaneering expeditions were, as a matter of course, separate ventures and not a continuous business. This was also true of the trading and exploring voyages of the adventurers to Africa in the reign of Elizabeth, and of the Russia Company begun by Sebastian Cabot and a few others in their attempt to discover a northwest passage to China. The East India Company also embodied the same characteristics; that is, capital was employed which was not only a joint stock but a terminable stock as well; all the proceeds were divided at the end of each expedition and each subsequent voyage was supplied with newly subscribed capital.

The transformation of speculative ventures having terminable stocks into continuing businesses with permanently invested capital is the development of most interest here. This change will be briefly traced through the rise of the East India Company, for that vast enterprise, part trader for profit and part a long arm of the government, had an extended and varied experience under both types of management.[1]

For more than half a century (1600–1657) the East India Company operated under a system of terminable joint stocks. It was natural that it should. Many of the early contributors to the joint stock were men who had made great profits from Drake's privateering voyage around the world. They would be inclined to look upon the proposed trading expeditions to India as just another speculation in which they might risk a few hundred pounds with a chance for enormous gain.* Others of the early members in the venture were Levant merchants, who were inclined to regard their association with the India enterprise as merely a temporary stopgap while their regular business with Turkey was poor.

These influences were no doubt strong enough to determine the early policies of the company; and such a policy as terminable stocks, once formed, would be likely to continue for some time

* John Maynard Keynes has expressed the opinion that the modern age began with the sixteenth century accumulation of capital and that British capital for foreign investment began with the Spanish treasures brought back by Drake. "Queen Elizabeth was a considerable shareholder in the syndicate which had financed (his) expedition: Out of her share she paid off the whole of England's foreign debt, balanced her budget, and found herself with about £40,000 in hand. This she invested in the Levant Company which prospered. Out of the profits of the Levant Company, the East India Company was founded: and the profits of this great enterprise were the foundation of England's subsequent foreign investment." (*Saturday Evening Post,* October 11, 1930, p. 160, "Economic Possibilities for our Grandchildren.")

even after the original influence had been withdrawn. Other factors arose later which also made terminable stocks seem advisable. For example, there was some apprehension of interference by the crown,* and so men were not inclined to put in money for long periods. The procedure of withdrawing an individual investment, it must be understood, was not well developed, and liquidation of the capital at the end of each voyage was regarded as necessary so that those adventurers who desired might drop out and new ones might be admitted. Outsiders were also inclined at times to feel that even this arrangement was too limited to include all who wished to venture in the trade.

From 1600, when the long series of East Indian voyages began, to 1617 there were 113 distinct voyages, each with a separately subscribed capital. In each case all the assets were to be divided when the voyage terminated. Yet it is evident that what was chosen in theory could not be fully accomplished in practice because of unliquidated "balances." For example, the "rests" or "remains" of the first voyage finally had to be merged with those of the second, and the third with the fifth, and so on.

In 1613 the capital called up was subscribed for four years; that is, one-fourth was to be paid each year for fitting out ships for that year. This was the first avowedly continuous capital of the East India Company, and marked a definite step in the direction of passing from the "share-in-the-goods" idea of membership in a joint-stock company toward the idea of capital as an invested sum consisting of transferable units of specific amount. Here was the beginning of a change from a limited number of shareholders contributing, or ready to contribute, an undesignated amount of capital (if it should be called up), to an organization with a limited or designated amount of capital to come from an indeterminate number of contributors. This 1613 enterprise also took over the balance of the unrealized property from the ninth, tenth, eleventh, twelfth and thirteenth voyages.

The India trading continued, but all the while the pressure toward a permanent capital became greater. Dutch competition was

* James I had granted some licences which seemed to threaten the companies' monopolistic privileges; Wm. R. Scott, *op. cit.*, Vol. I, p. 197.

severely felt, because the Dutch East India Company operated under better protection from its well fortified trading posts. Clearly the British East India Company needed similar long-term investments in continuing properties. Furthermore, the numerous incompletely wound-up voyages, each with its separate "remains" and differing lists of shareholders, resulted in continual embarrassment and confusion. The bookkeeping skill of the day was unequal to the task of successfully juggling the assets and the profits of a dozen distinct trading ventures in various stages of completion. The need for a policy of long-time investments was thus indicated as a prerequisite to intelligent current management.

Under these conditions it is not surprising that at last the company finally came to accept the principle of a non-terminable stock or, as it would now be called, a permanently invested capital. In 1657 the company secured a new charter, in which provision was made that the stock was to be valued, first at the end of seven years and at the end of each three years thereafter. On the basis of that valuation, any shareholder was entitled to have his place taken by another who wished to join the company. Prior to this, in order to get an interest in the undertaking one had to subscribe to new stock—if he could manage to get in—or to buy a fraction of a share in a voyage from a present member. Under this new charter, therefore, it would be simpler to withdraw or to become a member. Such a provision also opened the way for trading in the shares of the company and thus made it easier to attract the necessary capital.

It is significant, too, that within four years after this charter went into operation (by 1661) the governor of the company stated that future distributions would consist of the profits earned (dividends) and not "divisions," as in the past. In other words, it was then possible—even necessary—to distinguish carefully between "capital" and "income." Thus another great forward step was taken in arranging the conditions under which modern corporations operate and modern accounting assumes some of its greatest responsibilities.*

* The separation of profit and capital and the annual closing of profit-and-loss accounts into a capital account were a definite part of double-entry-bookkeeping pro-

It must not be assumed from what has been said that non-terminable stocks were unknown until used by the East India Company in the middle of the seventeenth century. In fact, permanency of investment was the natural consequence of the nature of some enterprises, such as the Mines Royal (chartered in 1568), and the Mineral and Battery Works (chartered in 1568), which were engaged in mining, and the New River Company (chartered in 1609), which brought spring water to London by conduit. Furthermore, the capital invested in the Russia Company was little changed in the

---

cedure long before periodicity of return replaced terminable stocks in the British trading companies. This "periodicity" is explained in the early bookkeeping texts. Cotrugli (1458) gave directions for checking the ledger and journal each year and for carrying all profits and losses into the capital account, and Manzoni (1534) said that in many places bookkeepers ruled up the accounts and began new books at the end of the year. (Otto Bauer, *Monuments of Bookkeeping History,* Moscow, 1911, pp. 47, 111.) Paciolo (1494) stated that in some localities it was customary to balance the books annually even though they are not filled; and Pietra (1588) described accounts suitable for a monastery and indicated that a report was rendered to church authorities at the end of a fiscal year. (J. B. Geijsbeek, *Ancient Double Entry Bookkeeping,* pp. 39, 90.) Systematic double-entry bookkeeping antedated the English trading companies by some time, but England was not then able to make very extended use of it, for the Italian methods spread abroad slowly. The dates of the appearance of the principal early bookkeeping texts are as follows: Cotrugli (Italy, 1458 in MSS), Paciolo (Italy, 1494), Manzoni (Italy, 1534), Oldcastle (England, 1543?), Ympyn (Holland, 1543), Mennher (Holland, 1550), Peele (England, 1553), Pietra (Italy, 1586), Mellis (England, 1588), Stevin (Holland, 1602), Dafforne (England, 1636, 1651, 1660, 1684). In view of the few texts in England in the sixteenth century, it is doubtful whether a knowledge of Italian double entry was very wide spread before Dafforne, whose book went through a number of editions. The English development of fixed capital investment (and periodicity) instead of terminable stocks was probably more influenced by the conditions which have been described than by Italian bookkeeping.

The possible influence of the early bookkeeping practices in instituting annual periodicity should not be too much stressed, for the writers often qualify their statements about periodical closing of the accounts by indicating that an annual closing was customary only in some localities, or that it was optional with the merchant, or by implying in the context that the accounts were closed when the books were full. Personal accounts went unbalanced for long periods, as in the books of the Freres Bonis, where an account ran without intermission from 1345 to 1358, and in the books of Andrea Barbarigo who kept a ledger between 1440 and 1449 without a single attempt at balancing. The latter's son Nicola kept another ledger from 1456 to 1482, and did not balance the books until they were full in 1482, although he made an annual calculation of profits. (Richard Brown, *History of Accounting and Accountants,* pp. 98, 107.) Brown's comment at this point that "the practice of not making a general balance till the ledger was completed continued to be wide-spread until the seventeenth century," is an indication that interest centered upon the calculation of profits, and that it was not until later that much usefulness was attached to a summary of the real accounts (balance account or balance-sheet).

sixty-seven years prior to 1620. Each voyage was considered a separate undertaking yet there was evidently a distinct sense of the continuity of the whole enterprise, for debts which had been carried forward from voyage "H" as far as voyage "N" were carried back in the accounts when ultimately found to be uncollectible.

Nor is evidence of the existence of non-terminable stocks found only in England, for the Dutch East India Company was chartered in 1602 for twenty-one years, but actually continued the original stock up to 1630.[2] The permanent investment of considerable sums by the Dutch in fortifying their trading posts has already been mentioned.

Although terminable stocks were not fully typical of British business in the sixteenth and early seventeenth centuries, they were more frequently used at that time than later. In other words, permanency of investment was beginning to force terminable stocks out of use. Although one can not say that the appearance of the idea of permanent investment (and with it, of course, the idea of severable income) was an advanced stage of business theory growing directly out of the use of terminable stocks, yet it is noticeable that terminable stocks finally disappeared, after existing side by side with permanent investments up to the middle of the seventeenth century. The one practice may not have been rooted solely in the earlier one, but there was nevertheless an apparent evolution —a survival of the more serviceable form.

The importance of the distinction between capital and income has been approached so far from the economic side. The economic necessity for using long-lived capital assets made a relatively permanent investment of funds necessary. This "permanent" investment, together with the transferability of shares, made the separation of income an economic necessity. Italian double-entry bookkeeping, already well developed and in a sense awaiting its destiny, afforded the organic mechanism for accomplishing the careful separation of these two elements, capital and income, under most diverse and, as future centuries were to demonstrate, unexpected circumstances. The joint stock companies (corporations) were the catalyst in whose presence the permanent investment of capital assets was united with the mechanism for measuring income.

The existence of the business corporation had a positive effect upon accounting, as it provided definite reasons for careful efforts to preserve the investment intact. But the corporation's influence extended beyond the seventeenth-century emphasis upon the distinction between capital and income, and even beyond the nineteenth-century statutory prescriptions regarding the limitations of dividends to income.* These statutes did not define income, and it was to be expected that controversies would arise as to whether or not given situations revealed profits available for dividends. The calculation of profit or income was, of course, an accounting problem; but, until the principles guiding that calculation had been established, differences of opinion would arise which would be taken to the courts. The courts were thus called upon to consider issues which were of importance to accounting before accounting literature (as contrasted with *bookkeeping* texts) began to appear.† For this reason some attention is here devoted to nineteenth century law cases which touched upon matters related to profits available for dividends.‡

A survey of the *Revised Reports* (English) 1785–1866 and John Mew's *Digest of English Case Law* fails to reveal much of interest during this time concerning profits and dividends. The corporation cases brought before the courts dealt mostly with questions of corporate powers to contract and to borrow, or with the powers and liabilities of directors, actions brought by or against shareholders in allotment of shares, calls upon subscription contracts, and so on. But in the '60's and '70's numerous cases were adjudicated which

* "The Company shall not make any dividend whereby their capital stock will be in any degree reduced." 8 and 9 Vict. c. 16, Sec. 121 (1845).

"No dividend shall be payable except out of the profits arising from the business of the Company." 25 and 26 Vict. c. 86, Table A, Sec. 73 (1862).

The letters-patent acts of 1834 and 1837 make no mention of dividends.

† The British periodical *The Accountant* began publication in November, 1874, and was for some time more concerned with professional news and legal notes than with auditing procedure and accounting principles. In 1881 Francis W. Pixley published his *Auditors: their duties and responsibilities,* which drew heavily upon court cases in many chapters, as most British auditing texts have continued to do.

‡ It is unnecessary to attempt any extensive examination of the available cases relative to the legal responsibilities of auditors or those turning upon the question of restoring losses of capital before declaring dividends. That material has been well presented in other places, especially in the later British texts on auditing and in Prosper Reiter, *Profits, Dividends and the Law,* New York, 1926.

dealt with questions of profits or dividends. These are discussed so far as they relate to accounting principles.

The statutes of 1845 and 1862 seem reasonable in placing a responsibility upon directors of trying to preserve the capital of their corporation intact by drawing dividends from profits alone. At present this requirement is accepted as almost axiomatic and needing no further justification, for it is known now that just as a corporation legally has perpetual succession, so financially it should have maintenance of capital in order to assure real continuity of existence as well as a merely legal continuity. But this has not always been equally obvious; in the earlier days the reasons for this restriction of dividends were being formulated and the principles by which the available profit should be calculated were being determined.

In one case,[3] in which an insurance company was held out to the public as having certain capital, it was stated that it would be fraud to declare a dividend out of that capital since such action would decrease the security of the creditors—in this case the policy-holders. In an attempt to pay "interest" on capital, when there was no profit, another company met opposition by the courts on the ground that such action was against public policy, since the proposal "is not in accordance with the contract entered into with the legislature on behalf of the public."[4] In a later case[5] much the same explanation of the grounds for denying a dividend, construed as being out of capital, is given. Here the proposal was held to be *ultra vires,* since it would be equivalent to diverting capital from the objects of the business, and to reducing, by a part return to members, the fund which the creditors had a right to look to for payment.

The decisions in these cases gave expression to the reasons against allowing dividends out of capital. Other cases are mentioned which are of even more interest since they dealt with specific situations in which the ascertainment of profits available for dividends was an issue.

Several cases are to be found in which more or less general statements were made concerning the method of ascertaining net profit. In one of these[6] an article is quoted from the memorandum of association [by-laws] of the company, dated 1864. It stated that for the purpose of semi-annual meetings of shareholders the balance-sheet "shall contain a true account of the capital, credits and properties belonging to the company, and the debts, gains and losses of the company, which may have arisen in the course of the preceding half year, and shall show the balance remaining after payment of all expenses of maintenance and working of the railway, which balance shall be designated the 'net revenue'."

In two other cases the courts stated this matter much as the by-laws of this company did two years before. "The first step would be to make good the capital by taking stock and putting a value upon all the assets of the company of whatever nature and of deducting therefrom all the liabilities (including amongst those liabilities the amount of contributed capital), and the surplus, if any, remaining of the gross receipts would be net profit." [7] In the other case, in holding that directors' "reports" were not a substitute for balance-sheets, the court said, "The object [of the clause in the by-laws] was that the directors should produce a balance-sheet in order to show the assets of the company and their value and on the other hand the liabilities of the company; because it is only on that sort of statement that you can draw any rational conclusion as to whether there is a profit." [8]

These views, expressed about the middle of the nineteenth century, touch upon an interesting accounting matter. The first thing which attracts attention is the use of the balance-sheet to calculate the "net revenue" or "net profit." This indicates a conception of profit which is associated with the final liquidation and winding-up of a company: the profit consisting of whatever property was left after using the assets to discharge the liabilities and reimburse the shareholders for their capital contributions.* But as a concept it is deficient in some respects, for it fails to meet satisfactorily the burdens placed upon it by later conditions. As a statement of how to ascertain profit under liquidation it is perhaps adequate, but it does not establish nearly so satisfactory a method of ascertaining the periodic profit of a going concern. For an enterprise in liquidation,

* This concept still underlies much of the modern accounting literature and may well be associated with the proprietorship theory of accounting outlined in a previous chapter.

the facts in the case are all in hand and the values ascertained by completed and closed transactions; profit under those conditions is realized profit. But for a going concern the final facts are not yet available; it does not suffice to consider values (assets and liabilities) as if in liquidation, nor to use current values, for in both cases there is a lack of reality in the resulting calculation of profit because of the lack of actuality of the values used. The modern problem has come to be viewed as the problem of ascertaining income rather than profit; * that is to say, the need at present is to distinguish between operating income and capital increments.

It is no fault of nineteenth-century theories, however, that they do not fully meet twentieth-century needs: a better criticism would be that twentieth-century needs are so poorly comprehended that we still try to make nineteenth-century notions suffice.

In trying to understand the accounting ideas of the past century, the balance-sheet theory of profit which was expressed in the cases cited may be further examined in its relation to the type of business enterprise concerned. The words of the courts' definitions of profits are better suited to the calculation of partnership than of corporation profit. Usually, in a partnership or single proprietorship, any undivided profits remaining at the end of the fiscal period are transferred to the capital accounts of the persons concerned. Thereafter, when another period has elapsed, the "balance" of the balance-sheet measures current profit, because past profit has previously been merged with contributed capital.

In the case of a corporation, however, the situation is different, for undivided profit is not plainly merged with contributed capital; it stands in a "surplus" account or perhaps in reserve accounts of one kind or another. Since "surplus" is not dedicated capital, it must consist of retained profit or income; consequently, the balance of the corporate balance-sheets (assets minus liabilities and capital stock) can not represent profit of the period. If the balance-sheet of a corporation is a means of calculating profit, then surplus

* "Income" is conceived in relation to a continuing periodicity. (An example is rent earned monthly by leasing a house.) "Profit," in contrast, has much less connection with definite periods of time; it is more comparable to the gain from the resale of a house.

from retained past profits would need to be considered as capital without being dedicated as such by stock dividend or otherwise.

What the balance of a corporate balance-sheet really shows is the accumulation of profits to date, including those retained from past periods. It is true that the entire amount is available for dividends, but this sum can hardly be described by the terms "net revenue" or "net income," as used by the courts in the cases cited. If the terms meant then what they mean now, they do not accurately designate the element to which they were attached. The usage perhaps fitted the case of partnerships, in which the undivided profits remaining were usually absorbed (dedicated) into the capital accounts; but it would not be expedient in corporations, for there are definite reasons for keeping the capital-stock account unchanged at its legally authorized amount.

It is not necessary to raise the question at this time as to whether corporation surplus partakes more of the character of capital or of profit, or whether surplus should be subdivided (without prior appropriation as a reserve), a part being considered as an adjunct or increment to capital and a part as profits available for dividends. The point emphasized here is merely that the advent of the corporation brought about certain additional accounting problems, and that the early attempts at solutions drew heavily upon logic better suited to partnerships or proprietorships than to the real nature of the new type of business organization.

When now we more or less unconsciously attempt to follow the older concepts into new situations we come upon previously unsuspected difficulties, as for example when the balance-sheet definition of profit leads us, if strictly followed, to the undesirable position of counting as "profit" or ordinary surplus the credit item which accompanies an upward revaluation of fixed assets.

There were other issues before the courts in the nineteenth century which are recognized as relating to matters of accounting principle. For example, the English courts decided the question of whether or not it was proper to charge as a part of the assets the interest paid during construction. This was held correct,[9] but it was later pointed out that dividends on new securities were not properly chargeable to capital.[10] These were questions which required discrimination between assets and expenses, or, as usually worded, between capital charges and revenue charges.

Another indication of the application of sound principles is seen in cases in which there had been resort to borrowing in order to pay dividends. Here it was clearly laid down[11] that if revenue had been absorbed in paying for items properly chargeable to capital there was no objection to borrowing to pay a dividend; the borrowing was in effect to obtain the item chargeable as a capital asset even though the loan was entered into somewhat after the fact. The courts were equally certain that a proper expense item charged as an asset produces a fictitious profit "deceiving both the company and the public."

Uncollectible accounts came in for their share of scrutiny by the courts. A balance-sheet for a trading company of February, 1864, contained debts due from the American Confederate States as well as cotton owned but still in America; according to the statement there was at that time ample profit to cover the dividend proposed for May. When the issue reached the court[12] the ruling was that there was no fraud against the public or the shareholders; because there was no attempt to conceal the nature of the assets, the court was disinclined "to search out minute errors in the calculations of an account honestly made and openly declared." In other words, the court was unwilling to question the judgment of the directors of 1864 in the light of the situation of 1869, or to question the judgment of business men when made in good faith. When, however, directors of another corporation declared a dividend on the basis of a balance-sheet containing debts known by them to be bad, the courts held the action *ultra vires* for the corporation and the directors liable for the whole amount of the dividend.[13] It is easy to see now that prudence would suggest that reserves be set up to afford protection against unexpected losses from uncollectible debts; auditors did in fact dwell on this need[14] as their experience dictated, but directors have power of final judgment, whereas auditors have only the power of criticism.

While the courts did not suggest a reserve for bad debts, such as has become a customary practice of modern accounting, they did find occasion to indicate the need for reserves. When dividends were paid by the directors of an insurance company without proper provision for meeting the probable claims against it, the court said (in 1870): "To consider money received for premiums as money capable of being divided as profit without making any estimate of what the risks were in respect of which the money was paid, seems to me to be the most extravagant proceeding that I ever heard of." [15] A somewhat later case [16] held that the directors were liable upon a dividend out of capital as a breach of trust even though no element of fraud was present. Their practice, in this case, had been to state the value of the principal assets (instalment contracts on house-building loans) at their present value, using a 5 per cent annuity table; this showed a much larger book value than actually existed—this without producing any compensating reserve for possible shrinkages due to property taken over when instalment payments lapsed.

Allowance for depreciation in calculating profits available for dividends was also given support at this time by the courts,[17] although there was a tendency to treat it somewhat in the nature of a reserve. That is, depreciation was regarded more as replacing the exhausted asset than as spreading the cost over the periods in which the asset was active. And depletion was recognized as something to be considered in calculating net profit "the same as a man would deduct the cost value of inherited property later sold." [18]

These illustrations, drawn from English court cases of the last half of the nineteenth century, throw additional light upon the manner in which the corporation exerted its influence toward expanding bookkeeping into accounting. The cases examined were concerned for the most part with questions relative to profits available for dividends; since the statutes restricted dividends to profits without attempting further definitions, it was the province of the courts to determine whether or not, under the conditions described, capital had in fact been reduced by the dividend. Usually the issue turned upon the questions of whether certain expenditures were in the nature of assets or of expense, or whether proper provision had been made for future operations, as depreciation, bad debts, insurance reserves, etc. These questions were matters of accounting principle, and undoubtedly contending parties frequently had advice from experienced accountants.*

It is not suggested, therefore, that the courts were formulating entirely new principles; it is more probable that principles which it was customary for auditors to apply in their professional engagements were here being given public and legal sanction. In fact, interest centers less in the fact that these matters were dealt with by law courts than in the implication that the cases probably reflected current professional accounting opinion. It is possible to observe directly from accounting textbooks, after they began to appear, the expression of professional opinion upon accounting principles. There we find for the most part a general agreement with the enunciations of the courts, and this of itself helps to confirm the impression that the earlier court decisions reflected quite well the professional accounting views of the time.

REFERENCES

1. Wm. R. Scott, *Joint Stock Companies before 1720*, is the principal source of the facts stated.

2. Wm. C. Webster, *General History of Commerce*, p. 155.

COURT CITATIONS

3. *Evans v. Coventry*, 25 L. J. Ch. 489 (1856), see also *Rances Case* discussed later in the chapter.

4. *MacDougal v. Jersey Imperial Hotel Company, Ltd.*, 2 H and M 528 (1864).

5. *Ginnes v. Land Corporation*, 22 Ch. D. 349 (1882).

6. *Bishop v. Smyrna and Cassaba Railway Co.*, 2 Ch. 265 (1895).

7. *Binney v. Ince Hall Coal and Cannell Co.*, 35 L.J. Ch. 363 (1866).

8. *Helby's Case*, 14 L.T. (N.S.) 47; 2 Eq. 175.

9. *Bardwell v. Sheffield Waterworks Co.*, 14 Eq. 517 (1872).

10. *re Alexander Palace Co.*, 21 Ch. D. 149 (1882).

11. *Hoole v. Great Western Railway Co.*, 3 Ch. App. 262 (1867). *Mills v. Northern Railway of Buenos Aires Co.*, 5 Ch. App. 621 (1870).

12. *Stringers Case*, 4 Ch. App. 475 (1869); *City of Glasgow Bank v. Mackinnon*, 9 Ct. Sess. 535 (1882); *re Peruvian Guano Co.*, 3 Ch. 690 (1894).

* For example, both sides in the Oxford Benefit Building and Investment Society case (1886) employed accountants to report upon the calculation of the net profit.

13. *Flitcrofts Case*, 21 Ch. D. 519 (1882).

14. *re National Bank of Wales, Ltd.*, 2 Ch. D. 674 (1899).

15. *Rances Case*, 6 Ch., App. 117 (1870).

16. *re Oxford Benefit Building and Investment Society*, 35 Ch. D. 502 (1886).

17. *Davidson v. Gilles*, 16 Ch. D. 347 (1879); *Dent v. London Tramways Co.*, 16 Ch. D. 244 (1880).

18. *Knowles v. McAdam*, 3 Ex. D. 23 (1877).

XIV. DEPRECIATION

THE issue which the development of corporations made plain, that is, what should constitute a proper charge against revenue, gave rise presently to discussions of depreciation and renewals. A search for early mention of depreciation reveals that there were two ways of looking at the matter. One was to consider depreciating property as if it were the unsold merchandise of a simple proprietorship; the other was to relate depreciation to the maintenance of long-lived corporate assets. The second point of view is plainly reflected in nineteenth century discussions of railroad problems and in many railroad corporations' reports of that day. What may be called the proprietor's view of depreciation is found scattered through a few bookkeeping texts over a long period and omitted entirely from very many. It will be discussed first.

One of the earliest bookkeeping texts in English, John Mellis, *A Briefe Instruction* ... (1588), shows the following entry on the credit side of the ledger account "Implements of householde":

> Implements of householde here against is due to have x*l*. x*s*. and is for so much as I doe finde at this day to be consumed and worn, which said x*l*. x*s*. for the decay of the said household stuffe is borne to profit and losse in Debitor (15) 10 10 0

In the debit side of the profit-and-loss account appears the following:

> More x*l*. x*s*. for so much lost by decay householde stuff as in Creditor (06) 10 10 0

Examples taken from Stephen Monteage will illustrate the seventeenth century practices. In the second edition (1683) of his *Debtor and Creditor Made Easie,* there is a charge and discharge account.* One section of this is "The Accompt of Stock" wherein are set forth

* Reproduced in chapter IX.

the details of certain transactions in live stock. The section closes with "valuation of the stock unsold": seven cows are valued there at the same price at which they were charged, one bull is valued at 15 shillings less than charged at the beginning of the account, and one ram at 5 shillings less. This same example does not appear in the third edition (1690), but in ledger A of the bookkeeping set the author shows an account for "Horses" which is equally apropos:

Horses Debtor				Horses Creditor			
1675 Apr. 10, to Stock 6 Horses Val. at 8 £ pc........	48	-	-	1676 Apr. 9, By Loss and Gain, lost by their use....	6	-	-
				By Balance resting, Val. at 7 £ pc	42	-	-

The journal entry from which the posting came was:

Ballance is Dr. to Account of Horses for 6 resting, valued at 7 £ apiece, ...	£42	-	-
Loss and Gain is Debtor to the said, for their use and impairing, ...	£ 6	-	-

On the debit side of the loss-and-gain account is the entry: "To Horses impaired by a year's use—6:—:—". On another page the account for cows shows an opening price of £4 each, a later purchase at 5s. 11d. each and a balance remaining which is priced at 4s. 5d. each. This inventory price is slightly above the price at the opening but below an average price. So it would seem that the closing price was probably made somewhat higher by reason of the most recent purchase and yet low enough to represent a reduction in value for the animals owned throughout the year. In the sheep account, however, the balance (inventory) was priced at the same figure as at the opening of the account. Perhaps sheep, not being service animals, were not considered as having any "loss by use."

The eighteenth century may be represented by John Mair's *Book-*

keeping Methodiz'd (5th ed. 1757) where the method of treating long-lived assets is stated as follows:

> "Accompts of ships, houses, or other possessions . . contain, upon the Dr. side, what they cost at first, or are valued at, with all charges, such as repairs, or other expenses laid out upon them. The Cr. side contains, (if any thing be writ upon it), either what they are sold or exchanged for, or the profits arising from them; such as, freight, rent, etc. Here there are three cases. *1st,* If nothing be written upon the Cr. side, it is closed, by being credited by *Balance. 2dly,* If the Cr. side be filled up, with the price of the ship, house, etc. sold, or otherwise disposed of, then the difference of the sides is the gain or loss made upon the sale; and the accompt is closed, by being debited or credited to or by *Profit and Loss. 3dly,* If the Cr. side contain only the freight or rent; in this case first charge the ship, house, etc. Dr. to *Profit and Loss,* for the freight or rent; and then close the accompt with *Balance.*"

The fixed assets according to this plan, were to be treated as mixed accounts much like a merchandise account; the inventory portion was carried forward and the remainder transferred to loss-and-gain. It is not certain from Mair's statement whether the ship or the house was to be shown in the credit side in closing the account at its then value or at its original cost; he only mentions "the price of the ship, house, etc." In a later text bearing the title *Book-Keeping Modernized* (2d ed. 1768), he uses the term "value": ". . . . first give the account credit by *Balance,* for the value of the ship or house, and then close the account with Profit and Loss." If "value" was used then in the modern sense, any shrinkage or depreciation would be transmitted to profit-and-loss by carrying forward a decreased amount as inventory or balance.

In the nineteenth century the recognition of depreciation by the inventory method becomes unmistakable.*

* From France about this time comes an example of depreciation directly related to production: Payen, in a book entitled *Essai sur la tenue des Livres d'un Manufacturies* (1817), has a discussion of costing for a glue factory. He there shows a boilers account as follows:

Boilers

2 boilers	4500	as valued for inventory	4100
Repairs	400	carried to cost	800

The 800 covered 400 repairs, and 400, depreciation. A similar treatment was accorded utensils and furnaces.

William Jackson, in *Book-Keeping in the True Italian Form* (1801), uses the same formula as Mair's: credit the account by balance for the value of the ship; close the account with profit-and-loss for the remaining difference. In an illustrated ship account, the credit entry carries the explanation, "by profit and loss for wearing, age, etc." The balance is called "present value."

By the middle of the century the treatment of fixed assets in the manner of a merchandise account was extended to a variety of accounts. Real-estate account, for example, was debited with "its cost—as purchase money, repairs, taxes, etc.," and credited with "rent, sales and the value of what remains unsold"; the remainder is loss or gain on real estate. (Fulton and Eastman, *A Practical System of Book-keeping,* 1853). John Fleming (*Bookkeeping by Double Entry,* Pittsburgh, 1854) mentions a steamboat account which is to be debited with "her cost and charges" and credited with "what she produces either by sale, freight or passage." Another writer (Thomas Jones, *Paradoxes of Debit and Credit Demolished,* N. Y. 1859) includes cotton, real estate and railroad stock in his "secondary accounts . . . wherein it is desired to see the outlay and returns so as to find the profit and loss thereon." John Q. Pilsen, *Complete Reform in Bookkeeping* (N. Y. 1877), includes in his "accounts of Changeable Values": merchandise, real estate, ships, securities. In regard to properties not for sale but for business use (he mentions fixtures, furniture, equipment, livestock, leases), he advises separate inventories for each and suggests that one "take off a percentage rate of total cost for wear and tear." Bryant, Stratton and Packard (*Counting House Bookkeeping,* N. Y. 1863), charged taxes to real-estate account and credited rent received. In set II of the practice, real-estate inventory is entered in the accounts at more than cost. Appreciation of real-estate inventory is also found in S. W. Crittenden, *An Inductive and Practical Treatise on Bookkeeping* (1853).

Soon depreciation receives mention as such. In discussing "taking stock," W. Inglish, *Bookkeeping,* 1861, says of buildings and machinery, "In such accounts, a yearly deduction of 5 and 10 per cent requires to be made from original cost, to allow for deterioration, or wear and tear." In the illustrative furniture account the explanation of the entry is: "By depreciation, 5% carried to Trade Expenses."

These examples show that depreciation had been recognized very early and that a method had been developed for giving some effect to it in the accounts. But in all probability the methods described represent only the best practice of the time rather than the general practice, for a great deal of business has always been transacted without the benefit of double-entry bookkeeping and much more without the use of the best bookkeeping methods. Yet even the best bookkeeping practice reflected a very simple concept of depreciation. The treatment accorded a depreciating property in the accounts was to enter it at the end of a period on the credit side "as if sold." The method was a strict analogy to the goods account of the oldest texts. Depreciation apparently was not regarded as expense or cost but as loss, as "decay from use." The depreciation of a ship was therefore no different in principle from the loss of a ship in a storm.

Although it was more correct to look at depreciation in this light than to ignore it completely, this simple concept was nevertheless an inadequate view of the real nature of depreciation. But there is little evidence of fresh ideas regarding depreciation until the middle of the nineteenth century. The appearance of steam railroads at that time directed attention as never before to fixed assets and their associated problems of maintenance, renewal and improvement. Out of the discussion and experience which followed, new ideas about depreciation took form and the ground was prepared for a better comprehension of the real nature of depreciation itself.

As early in the development of railroads as 1841 it is evident that at least a few people had a very good conception of the relationship between depreciation and net income. For example, *The American Railroad Journal* for that year reproduced an article "from the English Railway Magazine" in which emphasis is given to the necessity for carefully and periodically ascertaining "the precise comparative degree of wear and tear" so that only bona-fide net income would be apportioned to the shareholders. In calculating the profit really available for distribution, it was stated that current expense should include "the whole actual expenditure in every shape and not merely expenses paid . . . so that future proprietors are not left responsible for any portion of the expenditure which has been in fact incurred and exhausted in earning the present apparent dividend." And again: "the object should be to avoid heaping an unusually large expenditure on particular periods for wear and tear going on gradually during a whole series of years."

This is indeed a greatly improved view of the nature of depreciation, but it is still somewhat indefinite. And it is not unexpected, therefore, to find the practice varied. The Liverpool and Manchester railroad, as the same article indicates, followed the practice of charging new engines to current expenditures, while the Grand Junction railroad adopted the method of an annual valuation. The London and Birmingham, however, formed a depreciation [replacement] fund by setting aside for repairs an annual percentage above the ordinary charges. Each of these ways of treating depreciation seemed to meet the necessities of the case; that is, they all were ways of reducing the net distributable profit in order to prevent unwise dividends. But we in later years can see from our point of vantage that these methods were not all equally desirable and we are not surprised that much confusion and controversy should follow.*

An early American writer, Dionysius Lardner, indicates in his book *Railway Economics* (1850) that he is opposed to the "annual valuation of stock." "If time has deteriorated some portions," he writes, "new portions have been infused so that on the whole the value in use remains the same." (p. 117). An annual valuation therefore would reflect only "marketable depreciation," that is, a fall in price not caused by any deterioration in the real value of the rolling stock. If revenue must make up to capital any diminution of marketable value such as this, then capital should supply to revenue "the augmentation" which rising prices would bring. But such principles, he thinks, can not be maintained since market values are determined by causes over which the company has no control and causes which are quite independent of the "use or abuse of their property." †

* Indeed the end of controversy is not yet at hand although the cost view of depreciation has now come to be generally accepted. For example there was not a little urging during the late 1920's that depreciation should be increased in order to accumulate a replacement fund against prospective higher prices, and during the early 1930's that existing high depreciation charges were impeding recovery from the depression.

† That these were also British views is indicated by the author's statement that similar questions were discussed with much ability in two reports to the directors by Captain Huish, manager of the Northwestern Railway.

At the same time Lardner takes a stand (p. 115) against charging to revenue new rolling stock which was required by increase in trade. This would be to "debit revenue with capital" and would be unjust to the temporary shareholder who stresses the importance of current dividends. On the other hand, failing to burden revenue with a charge for the maintenance and depreciation of existing rolling stock would favor the speculative holder at the expense of the permanent holder.

While thus opposing the annual valuation of equipment the author accepts both the other two methods as suitable to corporation purposes. Rolling stock ("moving capital") he considers in a state of "continual reproduction" or "constant rejuvenescence." A practical inquiry, he says (p. 114), has demonstrated that the natural progress of repairs and renewals is such that no gradual deterioration exists which is not made good. Nothing is lost; even old material is worked up into other equipment, and "never totally disappears from the road." Under this plan, outright replacements would be charged as current expense.

In the case of rails, however, renewals would be so long deferred as to make a different treatment necessary. Lardner pointed out that since a study by English and Belgian railroad managers had shown seventy-pound rails to have a probable life of twenty years, "it is evident that if from its nature the amount of wear which thus gradually takes place upon the rails from year to year could be included in the annual repairs, it ought to be comprised in them; but from the nature of the case it must be allowed to accumulate, so that at the end of a period of twenty years the entire expense of relaying the line would have to be incurred." (p. 64). He then describes the way to calculate an annuity "to find the reserve which ought to be reinvested . . . so that the rails could be replaced from the accumulated annual reserve fund."

Similar questions were mentioned in numerous railroad reports. In the course of his extended study of depreciation Professor Perry Mason examined a large number of early railroad reports and found a diversity of depreciation practice, which is reflected in the section to follow.

Even before the middle of the century railroad managers had

faced the depreciation question in several ways. The Baltimore and Ohio report (1833) for example, estimated the necessary annual provision for tie renewals by calculating an annuity for twelve years which would accumulate to the necessary total of $3,342. An analysis of operating costs on the Reading Railroad (1839) included depreciation and repairs of engines together at an estimated 25 per cent. In another case (the Columbia and Philadelphia) an item was included in the estimated expenses for "wear and tear" in addition to an annuity to pay interest on first cost of certain baggage cars and to replace the principal at the end of five years.

The interweaving of repairs, replacements and depreciation is well illustrated in the following paragraph from the 15th annual report of the Boston and Worcester (1846):

> "In the returns . . . of current expenses, a slight departure from the form prescribed in the printed schedule has been rendered necessary, from the manner in which these expenditures are charged in the books. Under the several heads of repairs, . . . are entered all expenditures not only for repairs strictly speaking, but for new constructions, improvements, or additions; unless the additions so made exceed in value the deterioration of the property . . . beyond the amount which represents it in the general stock; in which case, the excess is charged to the appropriate head of the general account, and the residue to repairs. For this purpose, an estimate is made, as nearly as is practicable, before the closing of each year's accounts, of the property under each head of account, and of the amount of depreciation beyond the repairs in comparison with the additions. . . ."

The section headed "estimated depreciation beyond repairs" simply reported "none."

In 1844 the Boston and Providence made an estimate of the present value of the cars, engines, etc., and "charged . . . to income account the sum of forty thousand dollars and deducted the same from the cost of construction"; this was the accumulated depreciation for the prior ten years. The Nashville and Chattanooga report for 1855 includes this apt paragraph:

> "Another strong reason for appropriating a sufficient sum to cover every description of loss by deterioration, is to enable the

> officers and directors to know the actual cost of the moveage of tonnage, and thereby prevent them from falling into the popular error of railroad companies in fixing the tariff of charges too low . . ."

In another place the report also says, "It is far better for the future prosperity of the company, to place it conspicuously in the items of current expenses."

Yet for all of this apparent understanding of the relation of depreciation to net income, the thought also finds expression that depreciation could best be "stored away in times of prosperity" or that in lieu of depreciating entries, capital expenditures could be charged to expense. For example, Charles Elliot, Jr. wrote in the *American Railroad Journal* (1843):

> "To those companies whose works are now new, and who seem to be making money, I would suggest the timely formation of a contingent fund, to prepare them for a contingency which will as surely reach them as the next new year. It is bad policy to divide the annual expenses [sic] as if they were real profits; the money that is earned at the expense of the rails, cars and machinery, should be hoarded to replace those things, and not distributed, as if they were to last forever. It can be shown that every company should annually store away, in times of prosperity, while their work is new, at least 6 cents for every mile travelled by their engines, 1 cent for every ton conveyed one mile, and 200 dollars for every mile of road, to replace decayed materials, and injured iron and machinery. If their profits will not permit that reservation, then the prudent man will avoid their stock. . . ."

From the 13th annual report of the Boston and Worcester (1844) comes the following:

> ". . . . it is obvious that the actual expenditure in any single year is no criterion of the actual decay. The only mode of arriving at a satisfactory result, is to be guided by the experience of successive years, and to apportion upon each year an amount equal to the average cost of making good the value of each description of value at the expiration of each year, before making the dividend of the year. In conformity with this principle, it was the early practice of the directors to make an annual allowance for the deterioration when the expenditures for repairs were not deemed equivalent to the waste from wear and decay;

whereby a fund was created to meet expenditures of succeeding years, whenever they should exceed the average cost of the necessary repairs. This fund is now exhausted, and it is the intention of the directors, in lieu of such a fund hereafter, to make an annual expenditure in repairs, and in the supply of new machinery in place of old, or new rails in place of those which are broken or injured, to an amount which will keep the property as nearly equal, as is practicable, to the original cost, and in this manner to avoid the error of confounding with net profits, such portion of the income as is required for preserving the capital entire. . . . In estimating the net annual income of the road, a proper caution has been used, before declaring dividends or profits, to allow an amount which shall be sufficient, and no more than sufficient, to preserve the capital stock entire."

The report of the same road for the next year included this paragraph:

> "It was deemed proper to make the whole amount a charge on the income of the year as a part of the current expenses, instead of charging it to the construction account, representing capital, inasmuch as the expenditure charged within the year to the account of repairs of engines and cars is inadequate to meet the heavy depreciation from wear and damage to the very large number of engines, tenders and passenger and freight cars required for the business of the road. It would be difficult, were it desirable, so to apportion the current expenditures of every year in each separate branch of account as to preserve an exact equilibrium between the wear and the renewal on each division of property, but the object of determining the net divisible income of the year is sufficiently attained if the aggregate of the expenditures for repairs is sufficient to maintain the value of the whole property against wear, decay, damage and depreciation from every cause."

In 1846, after writing off $76,000 for depreciation in 1844 and 1845, the Boston and Providence reported: "The stock of cars and engines has not depreciated this year, the additions having much exceeded in value the deterioration of the old stock."

Various phrases suggest a reserve for depreciation, sometimes derived from a charge to expense, sometimes from net income. For example, "If their profits will not permit that reservation . . ." ". . . .

the annual appropriation of £15,000 for the purpose of forming a fund to meet that contingency [rail replacement]." ". . . . the propriety and indeed the absolute necessity of creating an adequate sinking fund to provide for this large item of depreciation." ". . . . reserved from income and carried to reserved funds on account of decay and wear . . . beyond what is replaced by repairs and new work." But the accounting technique of reserves is not described, and we are left to surmise that it was not yet developed.

In the last quarter of the nineteenth century the consideration given depreciation was broadened somewhat. The discussion of railroad renewals continued, but it was soon associated with the problems of uniform accounts and commission regulation. At the same time a beginning was made, in a few books and student lectures, in relating depreciation to factory production.

There was a certain logic in the contention of railroad men that adequate renewal of parts would keep the equipment up to standard operating efficiency.* The locomotive, for example, consisted of a multitude of renewable parts of greatly varying service life. Brass tubing would need replacement every few months; frame and axles, however, would probably last thirty years. Similarly the roadway consisted of a multitude of separate units (rails, ties, ballast) which were naturally retired from service piecemeal since all did not expire at the same time. On the surface it seemed a simple matter therefore to charge renewals as expense and still to leave the original capital asset intact.

But although this procedure might seem logical it was not always accepted without question. The Boston and Worcester reports which have been quoted indicated quite early the possibility that renewal expenditures might fail to agree with the "waste from wear and decay." And twenty-five years later a thorough analysis of the service life of locomotive parts was reported in 1870 in the *Proceedings of the Institution of Civil Engineers* (England), which pointed in a similar direction. The conclusion of the investigators at that time was that even full renewal of parts did not prevent final deprecia-

* Obsolescence could have seriously disturbed this conviction had it been more in evidence at that time.

tion, because a day would come when the timing of the expiration of parts having differing lengths of service life would so coincide as to leave the locomotive practically beyond repair.

A few years later another railroad report appeared (Louisville and Nashville, 1874) in which these matters were further discussed. In this report Albert Fink, vice president and general superintendent, advocated the use of a "renewal account" as a means of reconciling current expenditure with current expirations.

> "To make the annual report of a railroad company valuable, the accounts of the company should be so kept as to show the expense due to that year's operations. For that purpose an account should be opened which might be called 'renewal account' and to which should be credited or charged the difference between the estimated cost of operating expense due to the year's work and the operating expense actually incurred during that year. . . . The balance of this account at the end of the year will be a proper charge against the revenue account. . . . There will always be a certain amount to be charged to this renewal account which will represent the depreciation of the property and the owner will have a clearer idea of its value than if no such account had been kept although it may not be entirely correct." [Because of being based on estimates.]

The "estimated cost of operating expense" was, however, a rather elastic element varying somewhat according to the winds that blew. In the figures accompanying the report, Fink takes pains to indicate that the current expenditures for repairs and renewals of bridges, ties, rails, etc., were above the average of the past eight years and to suggest that the condition of the equipment therefore was such that repairs thereafter would be less than average. Thus is the way prepared for meeting the lighter traffic and other after-effects of the panic of 1873.

Several correspondents of the *Railroad Gazette* in 1879 described a renewal account as a renewal fund. They were opposed to the practice of varying the maintenance expenditure according to good and poor current earnings, of "skinning the maintenance," as they said, to reduce operating costs. They favored the use of an account called "renewal fund" which would be debited for all repair and renewal disbursements as made. Monthly there would then be a debit to operating expense and a credit to renewal fund. The sum thus transferred is to be "the proper amount" to cover depreciation and repairs, or, according to the other correspondent, to cover the average depreciation and natural decay caused by the action of the weather and the movement of trains. How this sum was to be determined was not indicated.

There is no need to discuss either the conditions which ultimately led to the regulation of railroads by state or federal commissions or the means by which that control was exercised. But it is worthy of note here that the commissions from their beginning prescribed uniform accounting reports and that renewals came in for a share of consideration.

Under the laws of Massachusetts of 1846 the railroads were required to submit annual reports which included analyses of expenses. In one section were to be stated the amounts spent "for repair of locomotives, for new locomotives to cover depreciation [as replacements?], for repair of passenger cars, for new passenger cars to cover depreciation."

In a later section was to be reported:

> "Estimated depreciation beyond the renewals, viz:—
> Road and bridges
> Buildings
> Engines and cars."

Thirty years later the Massachusetts railway commissioners' instructions regarding railway accounts called for the separate reporting of "new locomotives charged to operating expense to make good original numbers." This was in addition to repairs; no mention was made of depreciation as such.

In June, 1879, the third national convention of railroad commissioners, meeting at Saratoga Springs, New York, adopted a committee report on uniform accounts which included the following rules:

"1. All liabilities are to be entered in the month incurred without reference to the date of payment.

"2. Expenses are to be charged each month as used, without reference to the time purchased or paid for.

"3. No expenditure is chargeable to the property accounts ex-

> cept for an actual increase thereof unless it is made on old work in such a way as to clearly increase the value of the property over and above the cost of renewing the original structures."

The report also included a typical analysis of expenses which specifically mentioned repairs to various structures and renewals of rails and ties, but gave no place to depreciation as such.

The precedents thus established were followed later by the Interstate Commerce Commission when railroad regulation became national in scope. In the commission's second annual report (1888) a form of company report was outlined which placed repairs or renewals of ties, rails, roadway, locomotives and cars under the classification "operating expenses" but did not mention depreciation.

From this brief survey it is evident that some of the methods suggested for reflecting depreciation in the accounts seemed to receive little support in railroad circles. An annual revaluation of properties was one of these; setting aside an annuity which would accumulate to the desired sum by the time replacement became necessary was another. Preference was given to the renewal method of making good depreciation. Under this plan repairs and renewals could be charged to expense (either directly or through an intermediate "renewal fund account") unless the expenditures were obviously for an expansion of the total property. In that case a new charge to an asset account resulted.

It will be noted that this preferred treatment centered attention at the time when the expenditures were made upon preserving the distinction between capital and revenue charges. Apparently the nature of depreciation was not yet sufficiently understood to bring forth the suggestion that all expenditures for long-lived assets be charged to asset accounts, and that this cost be gradually amortized into operating expenses either by direct credits or by the use of a valuation reserve.

In England some further progress had been made. The discussion of depreciation in the 80's began to expand beyond railroad circles and to be spoken of in factories as well. For example, Edwin Guthrie, in lecturing to the Manchester Students Society in 1883 on manufacturing accounts, said among other things, "Because the profit of manufacturing is the difference in value of that which is consumed and the value of that which is produced, it is important to ascertain accurately the value or cost of that which is consumed." The values consumable within the period, he indicated, are raw materials, stores, direct labor and outside services, and those consumable over a number of years are machinery and buildings. The object of this accounting for values consumed is stated as "the recoupment of capital outlay."

Here was a better recognition of the cost-of-production aspect of depreciation than was evident in the railroads' treatment. This was to be expected as soon as attention was directed to the accounting side of factory production.

The application of depreciation to industry received further impetus the next year from a book by Ewing Matheson entitled *The Depreciation of Factories* (London, 1884). This work, the first on the subject, was developed out of a series of articles contributed to *The Engineer* a year earlier and formed, with Pixley's *Auditors: their duties and responsibilities,* the foundation of the technical literature of professional accounting.

Matheson recognized the possibilities in railroad work that depreciation would be made good by regular renewal of separate units; he says that, in theory, maintenance may be considered to balance depreciation. But he also sees certain inconsistencies in the practice and much room for error in particular years. The early years, for example, will not usually have sufficient renewal expenditures to balance the depreciation, and the temptation to treat "the surplus of receipts over expenditures" as profit will arise, especially if first earnings are small at best. Only when the undertaking is so large that it affords "a wide average of deterioration and renewal," or when many years of operations have indicated a fair average rate of expenditures, can renewals be trusted to balance depreciation. And, in addition, it is often difficult to disentangle maintenance expenditures from capital expenditures even when the transaction occurs. Yet a proper separation is important. If an expenditure properly belongs against future revenue it is unfair to the present stockholders to charge it against present revenue and thus to show earnings reduced. And if expenditures, properly chargeable against current revenue, are carried to asset accounts, the stockholders will be deceived as to the real earnings available for dividends.

Some American railroad companies, Matheson points out, build new lines with the least possible capital and as soon as earnings appear they use the revenue to finish the road. He then adds, "In Great Britain the opposite extreme is to be guarded against." Careful accounting is needed in both cases to constitute a trustworthy record.

Turning from railroads with their emphasis on renewals, the author outlines a variety of methods for systematically recognizing depreciation in factories.

The most effectual method, in Matheson's opinion, for recording alterations in value would be to revalue everything at stated intervals. But this is hardly feasible, because of the time and trouble involved and the faulty valuations due to the absence in the early years of unmistakable signs of deterioration. The next best plan is to establish a rate which can "without much trouble" be written off every year and then to check the result with part valuations at longer intervals.

Sometimes a method which applies a fixed proportion of profits to make good the depreciation is used. This, Matheson thinks, is unsound, since "deterioration goes on even if no profits are being earned." The best method is to use a percentage of the capital value "as it was left at the previous review" besides charging expenditures for maintenance to revenue.

The essential thought in Matheson's presentation was to preserve the distinction between capital and revenue charges, to the end that current revenue as the basis of dividends and withdrawals should be correctly stated. His theory included recognition of the relation of depreciation to the calculation of divisible net profits and of the persistence of depreciation in spite of a lack of profits. Yet elsewhere he stated that fluctuations often rendered plant idle and that therefore, high rates of depreciation should be charged in years of full operation "to make up for idle years where little or no profits are earned." He also indicated the possibility of establishing "a separate fund entitled Depreciation and Reserve" by the application of a part of the profits where this plan was preferred to the actual writing down of the value of the plant in the account; and he saw that the value of plant might be affected by various circumstances beside physical condition. Ample reductions should be made in the early years, he said, because new inventions might supersede the machines; increased rate of charge-off should prevail for a plant which was producing for uncertain demands.

Yet with all of his excellent grasp of much of the problem, he does not fully associate depreciation with factory cost of production. This, however, does not detract from the importance of Matheson's book, because the factory system had not then developed to a point where overhead costs were either much in mind or systematically transferred into production cost.

Later writers treated depreciation even less thoroughly, although avowedly writing on cost accounting. For example, J. S. Lewis, in *The Commercial Organization of Factories* (3d edition 1896), says that the sound way to deal with depreciation is to keep all plants in thorough repair and in addition to set aside out of revenue a sum of money which in a given number of years will purchase an entirely new series of machines. Garcke and Fells (*Factory Accounts,* 4th ed., 1893) go so far as to say that the amount of depreciation is varied in practice according to the condition of the firm's business in all but a comparatively few establishments and that only rarely is an attempt made to allocate depreciation to departments or operations.

One's first thought at the end of a brief survey of the development of depreciation accounting is that the essential problem of depreciation was not recognized until quite late. Prior to the middle of the nineteenth century depreciation appeared, if mentioned at all, simply as a variation in an inventoriable item, not unlike the familiar treatment of merchandise inventory. But upon second thought its slowness to develop seems only natural because there was little occasion for a long time to raise the question of depreciation. Business units were small, and there was no deep interest on the part of proprietors in refining the calculation of net profit. In addition, relatively little use was made of long-lived assets.

But the growth of the corporation changed many of these conditions. Corporations meant limited liability and the protection of capital stock against impairment from dividends; correct dividends, therefore, necessitated new niceties in the calculation of net profit. The experience of the trading companies with their ships and forts made it evident that the advantages of the corporate form of organization extended beyond the increased facility with which capital could be assembled. Business men soon perceived that the corporation was also admirably adapted for ensuring continuity of business operations to parallel the long life of some of the important assets.

The simultaneous appearance of these two elements—active, long-lived assets and a special need for the careful calculation of net profit—seems to be essential to the recognition of the importance of depreciation. Before these two are joined depreciation is incidental to the profit calculation; afterward it becomes indispensable. First in the trading companies, later in the railroads, these two elements were united and the foundations for depreciation accounting were laid. But, so far as could be learned, the depreciation of ships and forts did not receive consideration in the trading companies' bookkeeping, while the railroads, as has been seen, did give considerable attention to the problem of wear and tear of roadway and equipment. Apparently some third element was also needed, which was present in the case of the railroads but not earlier.

The profits of the early trading companies were so ample, men were so occupied in the new pastime of trading in company shares and company creditors were so few, that there was less real incentive to the careful calculation of correct net profit than now seems inherent in even the oldest of limited-liability corporations. The long-lived assets were there, but the need for correct net profits, although also present to a degree, was not recognized as such and so was sterile so far as depreciation accounting was concerned. The business corporation probably was still too new for its full significance to be appreciated.

Another two hundred years and the nature of the corporation was better known. Especially was there a clearer perception of the necessity for careful distinction between capital and revenue in relation to correct net profit. This, no doubt, was attributable largely to a greatly improved knowledge of bookkeeping by the middle of the nineteenth century. Therefore when railroad corporations were put in operation, the principles of good accounting having been considerably developed in the meantime, it was natural that more attention should be given to the problem of depreciation than had been the practice in the early trading companies.

It was expenditure for maintaining existing structures and equipment which placed depreciation questions before the railroad men. Maintenance as a physical act consisted of pulling out a worn part and substituting a good one. The locomotives, cars, and roadway were simply a multiplicity of separable units; hence the accounting problem was visualized as a simple one of charging expenditures as expense, if they represented renewal of worn parts, and of charging asset accounts if the expenditures were for entirely new and additional units. There was therefore no "reserve" for depreciation and no uniform allocation of first cost over the asset's service life. The treatment arose from a belief that the assets were wholly permanent if kept in good repair; it also had the effects of varying the charge to expense according to conditions and of ignoring the factor of obsolescence. But with all its imperfections seen from the twentieth-century point of view, depreciation in the nineteenth century made more progress than all of the centuries before had known.

XV. LIMITED LIABILITY

LIMITATIONS of shareholders' liability for corporate debts is another characteristic of the corporation which has an important effect upon accounting, for it involves the legal obligation to preserve the invested capital intact against diminution by dividends. Economic pressure which made for long-term investment of capital may be said also to have made a careful distinction between capital and income an economic necessity. But it is the limited-liability characteristic of the corporation which makes this distinction a legal necessity. A brief glance at the background of the concept of "corporateness" will serve to show that limited liability is an inevitable feature of a business corporation and that, because this is the case, corporate income must be carefully separated from corporate capital.

One of the most indispensable elements of the corporation is its separateness from its stockholding members. In the eyes of the law it is itself an entity with many of the attributes and powers of a human person and some additional ones. But a corporation was not simply endowed with this characteristic by statute or by sovereign will; the law merely perceived and acknowledged, and later prescribed, what was essentially inherent in this socially-created institution.

Several factors contributed to the appearance and acceptance of a separate entity which was without human personality or soul. For example, the Christian church from a very early day was a potent factor; "one-ness" was an inseparable part of its doctrines. The singleness of its headship and the unity of spirit of its members, the submergence of the monk's personality in the composite of the monastery, the permanency of the office of bishop despite the passing of individual bishops (and later the necessity of vesting title to property in the office of bishop to give continuity regardless of personal incumbency)—all these showed men that there could be a one-ness outside of that which each one knew in his own person.

As men drawn together by a common religious creed felt a unity which was more than the sum of the persons, so, too, those drawn together into trade fields for mutual protection in their occupations felt themselves united in an organization which was an entity of itself. This was the craft guild. And when mediæval municipalities began to appear, the people felt similarly that there was a "town" in addition to the individual inhabitants. Indeed, as soon as those organized bodies of burghers were strong enough, they won or bought a definite recognition of their "one-ness," in the form of a franchise from the crown.

Not only was there within these social institutions a sense of "corporateness" and "one-ness," but there was separately held private property as well. Personal wealth was dedicated to religion through the founding of monasteries by persons of means. These institutions were later taken over by the church itself, and, as time went on, were expanded by vast wealth in a variety of forms which none considered as the property of individual persons, whether monks, abbots or bishops. The town also held property which was often used to produce earnings with which to defray the tax money due by the burghers to the crown in consideration of certain grants and liberties of self-government. The guilds too had common funds to be used for charities, and somewhat later they even owned hospitals and meeting halls. Always it was recognized that ownership vested in the "entity" which could enjoy perpetual succession, and not in persons.[1]

Thus the three greatest institutions of the Middle Ages exhibited the same characteristic: the church, the guild, the town, each was a separate entity. Obviously none of these sprang into existence fully endowed, nor were they at a given moment invested from without with this essential element; it was social evolution which made an "entity" concept inevitable.* Since this characteristic was present

* It is not practicable to attempt here a justification of the entity theory of the corporation as against other explanations of its peculiar characteristics. The subject is somewhat controversial. It is felt, however, that this view is probably the most logical and useful, especially in seeking an understanding of the limited liability enjoyed by shareholders. At the same time it is recognized that an "entity" characteristic is not essential to every limitation of liability—as is exemplified by the limited partner-

in the principal institutions of the day, it was, of course, only a matter of time until it would be recognized in corporations. Lawyers had discerning eyes for such distinctions even in the Middle Ages, and we are told that they had attributed a separateness of entity to these three types of social organizations from the thirteenth century onward and that by the reign of Edward IV (1461–1483) they were discussing the nature and types of "corporations."[2] The attributes of the corporation were further discussed (1612) in the *Case of Sutton's Hospital* (V *Coke's Reports* p. 285), and the separateness of the members and the corporation was recognized. Hall and Blackstone followed Coke and carried forward the early precedents.

It was certain that sooner or later the relation of creditors to the corporation and to the shareholders would come into question. When this issue arose the way was found prepared, for as soon as the separateness of corporation and member is accepted, it must follow as a matter of logic and justice that corporate property could not be made available to the creditors of members, because the members had now no more direct property rights in the assets of the active corporation than they would have had if the originally owned goods had been sold to another human being. In like manner creditors could not in logic and justice expect to reach the private property of members for debts of the corporation. A lawyer's argument in explanation of the logic inherent in the common-law imputation of limited liability to shareholders would be somewhat as follows:

Inter-relations between shareholder, corporation and creditor are matters of contract between separate entities. If C (the corporation) owes $1,000 to CR (the corporation's creditor), there is no point of contact between CR and S (the shareholder), for there has been no meeting of their minds in agreement. One can not go out in the highways and attach any random passerby to an obligation to which he was not a party. Of course, if S owes $50 to C on an unpaid balance of a stock subscription or if S has borrowed from

ship wherein the qualification is secured by simple agreement. Cf. Frederick Hallis, *Corporate Personality*, London, 1930, and Stanley E. Howard, "Business Partnerships in France before 1807," *The Accounting Review*, December, 1932.

C, CR could, if necessary, follow those debts to the one who owes them and thus reach so much of the private property of S as S owed C, but no more. There is no way, however, under the long settled law of contract, of establishing any debt obligation running between S and CR because of their separate relation to the corporation. Hence there is no escaping the conclusion that the shareholder in a corporation can not be liable (unless by specific agreement to the contrary) for corporate debts beyond his investment or unpaid subscriptions, so long as the corporation is regarded as a separate entity with its own power to contract, hold property, etc.

This characteristic of "separateness" is not, it will be observed, an emanation from the law; in a real sense it antedates firmly established governments and modern law; it is "natural," that is, it arises out of surrounding conditions without premeditation or deliberate intent. The law, which is merely a statement of man-made and man-accepted rules, can be made to recognize or ignore the existence of the "entity," but it can not of itself produce an entity.[3]

Limited liability is now so fixed in both statutes and common law, and is so indispensable to modern corporations, that it is easy for the layman to accept it as a matter of course, or at best, to attribute it directly to some vague and unnamed legislator of rather recent date. But, like most of our business institutions, this one is also a product of economic evolution, and consequently it is difficult to cite chapter and verse concerning its origin. In fact, one can say it had no "origin," if the word signifies a point of beginning. Limited liability did not begin at any specific point of time; it is rooted in ideas and relationships which for centuries were as nebulous as a summer's mist and achieved form and consistency almost as imperceptibly as mists become clouds.

The same consequence follows the recognition of limited liability as was shown to follow the establishment of permanently invested capital: namely, the necessity for a careful separation of enterprise capital and enterprise income. A permanent capital made separation an economic necessity; limited liability made separation a legal necessity. From both points of view business is conceived as a continuing activity, and it is essential for both that the capital fund be most carefully preserved intact. On the one hand, economic capital must be maintained in order that the economic power of the business unit may be unimpaired; on the other, legal capital must be preserved in order that the rights of outside parties—shareholders and creditors—may be duly protected.

The economic power of an enterprise needs to be maintained in order that individual persons and society as a whole may not suffer a loss in productivity and a shrinkage in wealth. All parties concerned feel the effect: price disturbances affect the consumer, low net earnings jeopardize the security of the investor, shrinkages in working capital retard the liquidation of the debts which are due short-term creditors, the state loses tax revenue, the management operates under an unhealthy strain. The failure to preserve economic capital leaves a trail of disastrous consequences the prevention of which is worth a great deal of effort.

A failure to maintain legal capital intact likewise entails undesirable consequences, but in this case the burden of loss usually falls upon innocent third parties. Whereas the economic view is chiefly concerned with avoiding unforeseen losses or making them good for the sake of continued productivity, the legal view looks rather toward directors' conscious acts in disbursing property to the impairment of the "protective margin" of contributed capital which should be maintained for the security of the creditors.

While the idea of limited liability was no doubt inherent in the corporation entity from the beginning, it seems probable that the principal root-stock which led to freedom of incorporation and statutory limitation of liability was the mediæval partnership *en commendite*. This type of organization found considerable favor in the great Italian city-states of the twelfth and thirteenth centuries * because the church frowned upon the taking of interest and wealthy nobles felt it beneath them to engage in trade directly.[4] Since the church offered no protest to taking profit, nobles were able to satisfy their conscience—and at the same time save their dignity while reaping the reward—by entrusting sums of money

* *Commenda* contracts are cited as having existed in Italy in 1155 and in Marcelles in 1210; and it is to be noted that "*Commendatores*" in Florence were freed from all liability beyond their capital quota by statute in 1408—*Select Essays in Legal History*, Vol. III, pp. 183, 185. See also M. B. Beglie, *Partnerships in Commendite*.

to trustworthy merchants for a share in the profits of their ventures, but with the collateral understanding that the noble was not liable beyond the amount of his contribution. There were maritime partnerships (*societas navalis*) also at this time in which the investor's liability, as against third parties, was limited to the interest he had in the ship; the shareholder could escape assessment by abandoning his share. The captain was fully liable while the "silent" partners were not. After each voyage a certain division of the profits was made to the captain, crew and shipowners, and the remainder went to the *commendatores* who had ventured money or goods on speculation.[5]

These practices were reflected in the codes of sea laws of the Middle Ages. There were three of these codes which constituted a base for subsequent legislation: first, the *Consolato del Mare,* which was the sea law of Pisa, Venice and Genoa and is thought to antedate the First Crusade (1096); second, the Laws of Oleron (about 1150), which were brought to northern Europe by the wife of Louis VII of France upon their return from the Second Crusade; and, third, the Laws of Wisby (1240), which constituted the maritime code of the Hanseatic League.[6]

In 1673, Louis XIV of France obtained some codification of the then existing commercial law. These ordinances (often referred to as the "Savary Code") * embodied the substance of older codes and led directly to the French Commercial Code of 1807. Here specific provision was made for limited partnerships (*Societe en commendite*) which were practically identical with the mediæval type of organization.

The laws of Scotland also reach back to a similar base through the close contact which that country long maintained with the Continent. The Scottish court of sessions, established in 1532 by James V, was modeled upon the law courts of Paris, and Scotch lawyers were trained in continental law. It is not astonishing, therefore, to find that in the eighteenth century there developed in Scotland a doctrine which held that a partnership itself was primarily liable for debts and that the partner was liable only if necessary,

* Portions of the code are discussed by Stanley E. Howard in *The Accounting Review* for June, 1932.

i.e., after recourse to the partnership had failed. When care was taken to keep the names of certain partners out of the firm name, the creditors were held to have extended credit to the entity created by the joint capital and not to the individual (silent) partners.[7]

In Ireland also some progress was made toward limited liability by the adoption in 1782 of the continental practice of permitting silent partners. The active partners alone were responsible for the firm's debts, shares were transferable, and the firm was not dissolved by the death of a partner.[8]

England was therefore surrounded by countries in which limitation of liability was possible through the formation of limited partnerships based upon the old *Commenda* idea; yet England herself for a long time lagged behind. Why that should have been the case is not easy to see. Perhaps the English, having developed the joint-stock company under a charter by the crown, were satisfied with this form of business organization. It is certain that it was widely employed, and that the so-called Bubble legislation was not intended to suppress chartered companies.* Or perhaps there was in English common law a concept of partnerships different from that prevailing on the continent. This would seem to be implied at least in a case in 1788 in which Lord Laughborough said: "In many parts of Europe, limited partnerships are admitted, provided they be entered on a register; but the law of England is otherwise, the rule being that if a partner shares in the advantages, he also shares in all disadvantages." (*Coope v. Eyre,* 1 H. Bl. 48).

A similar implication lies in Simeon E. Baldwin's brief contrast of English and French law.[9] Under continental civil law, associations were at base matters of contract and, unless expressly declared otherwise, each of the associated parties was held to contract only for his share of the obligation. Consequently commercial associations (partnerships), because of their need for a firm basis for business credit, were made by law an exception to the basic type by

* The Bubble act (6 Geo. I c. 18) was aimed at three supposed evils, (1) unwarranted presumption of corporate existence by unincorporated bodies, (2) excessive, even fraudulent, speculations in the issue and sale of transferable shares, and (3) unwarranted use of existing charters for business to which they were never meant to apply, and one real evil, (4) the formation of fraudulent or stock-selling companies. E. T. Powell, *Evolution of the Money Market,* p. 176.

laying upon all partners a joint responsibility to creditors. The English conception of partnership, however, was one of agency. This meant that each partner had the power to bind the others, and that all were, by the underlying nature of the association itself, jointly and severally responsible for the debts. In England, then, no change of basic concept was necessary to give partners the joint liability necessary for commercial purposes. In other words, basic law on the continent involved limited liability of associates, and basic law in England involved unlimited liability of associates. Consequently it was easy for Continental jurists to accept the idea and use of limited partnerships, for this was merely a reversion to their basic principle, but it was difficult in England, for to adopt the same plan there meant a complete reversal of the English theory of partnerships.

Attempts to impute a recognized limitation of shareholders' liability for the debts of the early English joint-stock companies were not altogether successful. The prospectus of the Million Bank, it is said, promised limited liability in that no subscriber should be further answerable than for the amount of his stock, and again a point is made of the fact that the Fisheries Company (1633), having experienced a loss, resolved that further capital subscriptions should be held exempt from liability for this deficit.[10] These conditions do not attempt to inform possible creditors that they can not look to the shareholders, but rather seem to express a desire to assure subscribers that it will not be the policy of the company to call up additional capital from time to time as was generally customary then. In the Mosquito Island Company this was evidently the case, for any member who had paid in one hundred pounds a share might elect to "go no further," that is, to be free from further calls. This, however, is not the same thing as denying creditors any right of recourse against the shareholders' private property.

These instances are more in the nature of illustrations of the early development of a "par value" doctrine—a fully paid share—than examples of limited liability as the term is usually understood. The Million Bank's prospectus promised nothing more than that the subscriber would not be called upon for additional capital. This may be equivalent to saying that capital for further enlargement of the enterprise, or for covering losses, would be obtained in some other way than by making calls upon the prior shareholders. But it can hardly be equivalent to saying that creditors could have no recourse to the shareholders' property if the assets of the company in liquidation would not suffice. In fact, creditors of joint-stock enterprises were so infrequent that they could hardly have entered into the promoters' calculation.

Another instance which is relied upon as evidence of the existence of a species of limited liability in the English trading company of the seventeenth century is an act passed in 1662 (14 Charles II c. 24) which removed members of the East India Company, the Africa Company and the Fisheries Company from the classification of "traders" under the bankruptcy laws. [11]

The bankruptcy law then in effect was expressed in a statute of Henry VIII (1542) and supplemented by a statute of Elizabeth (1570). The earlier law stated:

> "Where persons craftily obtain other men's goods and do so suddenly flee to parts unknown or keep their houses, not minding to pay . . . then the Lord Chancellor may seize and sell any property found and divide ratably among the creditors . . . But the creditors still had a right against the debtor for any unsettled portion of the debt." (34 Henry VIII c. 4).

The Elizabethan statute amplified the earlier law in this manner:

> "If any merchant exercising the trade of merchandise shall keep his house, or depart the realm, or take sanctuary, or suffer himself to be arrested for lawful cause, or suffer himself to be outlawed, to the intent and purpose to defraud or hinder his creditors, he shall be reputed and taken for a bankrupt." (13 Elizabeth c. 7).

By these laws the government made the private property of a defrauding merchant available to his creditors; by the act of 1662, members of the three large joint-stock companies were placed outside the earlier statutes:

> " . . . no person who has adventerred any sum of money in the East India Company or the Guiney Company, or the new trade called the Royal Fisheries, shall be adjudged, taken, esteemed or reputed a merchant or trader within any statute for bankrupts . . . "

From these statutes it would seem that a shareholder was not to be held a "merchant," that he (being a private person) could not be adjudged a bankrupt and that therefore his property could not be seized as the older statutes provided. Since the act of 1662 was passed to set aside a verdict of bankruptcy rendered in 1653 against one Sir John Walstenholme, who held stock in the East India Company, it seems probable (a report of the case itself being unavailable) that an attempt had been made to reach Sir John's stock by having him adjudged bankrupt, or to reach the assets of the company through action against a shareholder, as though the latter were individually an owner of the specific assets held by the company. More information, were it obtainable, would possibly clarify the matter; but in any event, it is unlikely that the East India Company was bankrupt and that the plaintiffs in the case were creditors of the company attempting to have recourse to the private estate of a shareholder. Since this would have to be the situation if this act of 1662 actually created a species of limited liability for joint-stock company members, it must be concluded that the act did not accomplish that end.

The term "limited liability" should be restricted to the condition under which the shareholder's private property can not be reached (after he has fully paid his subscriptions) by creditors who find the assets of the company insufficient to protect them from loss. It is doubtful if the question of shareholders' responsibility to the creditors was raised as early as this. The relationship is a purely legal conception. The concept may have been inherent in any "body corporate and politic," but it is probable that this legal aspect was not fully disclosed until the spread of limited partnerships brought "limitations" under closer scrutiny. The statutes which then followed became merely the open recognition of a state of affairs which was inherent in every artificial or corporate being.

The existence of a pressure which was striving to liberalize the English law is evident in some of the litigation of the earlier years of the nineteenth century.* In 1808 the court expressed the dictum (*The King v. Dodd,* 9 East 516) that making a pretense of non-

* See also: "The Coming of General Limited Liability" by H. A. Shannon in *Economic History,* Vol. 2, No. 6 (January, 1931).

liability on a share of stock was a "mischievous delusion," but the court declined on other grounds to bring the case under the Bubble act. A few years later (1811) there appears to have been a weakening of the resistance to the formation of joint-stock companies when it was decided (*The King v. Webb et al,* 14 East 406) that the mere transferability of shares in a certain bread company did not bring the company within the prohibitions of the Bubble act, there being no showing of anything dangerous or mischievous in the undertaking in the sense implied in the act. In 1832 the court refused to hold a joint-stock company illegal even though the directors engaged to prevent any shareholder from having additional liability by making the fact public in all contracts and outside dealings. (*Walburn v. Ingilby,* 1 M and K 61, 76). This may be construed as a test of the statute of 1825 which repealed the prohibition on joint-stock companies and opened the way for such declarations in the charter as this case presents. Two cases in 1843 indicate that the struggle to attain full corporate powers was continuing. One of these cases (*Garrard v. Hardy,* 15 Man. and Gr. 471) held that the mere raising a stock of capital and creating transferable shares was not of itself an offense at common law; some showing of injury or fraud upon the public was necessary. A similar holding appeared in the other case. (*Harrison v. Heathorn,* 6 Man. and Gr. 81). The company here concerned had placed a section in its articles of association which provided for issuing to any person ceasing to be a member of the company a certificate declaring him discharged of all liability. Of this the court said there was no evidence that these shares had produced any injury or inconvenience to the public and hence the clause was not reprehensible.

In 1825 the crown was given the power to grant charters having specific provisions regarding liability or non-liability of members, but such charters were still authorized by separate acts of parliament. It was not until 1844 that incorporation could be accomplished by registration, and not until 1855 that such companies as were registered could obtain certificates of limited liability. The brief survey which follows presents the steps taken in England to make limited liability freely available.

1825—A statute at this time repealed the "Bubble act" of 1719 which had prohibited joint-stock companies. Besides other provisions the act (Sec. 2) gave the crown the power to declare in future charters that "the members of such corporation shall be individually liable in their persons and property for the debts, contracts, and engagements of such corporations to such an extent as His Majesty may deem fit and proper and such as shall be declared and limited in and by such charter and the members shall be rendered so liable accordingly." (George IV c. 91).

The act can hardly be said to have *created* limited liability. What the statute did was to require the extent and conditions of shareholders' liability to be stated in the charter, thus in a legal sense putting the world on notice. If the incorporators and the king agreed, a charter could provide unlimited or partly limited liability by the inclusion of a proper clause.

1837—An act of this year made it possible for the crown to authorize chartered companies by letters patent with the same rights and the same stated limitations as under a formal charter. This operated to make the process of company formation somewhat less expensive and burdensome. (7 Wm. IV and 1 Vict. c. 73).

1844—The joint-stock companies registration act "in order to prevent the establishment of fraudulent companies and to protect the interests of shareholders and the public—" permitted the easy formation of joint-stock companies under specific regulations, especially registration, which was designed to make public the underlying facts about the companies. (7 & 8 Vict. c. 110).

It is to be noted, however, that registration did not place the company concerned on the same plane as the chartered company, for until the transfer of a share to another holder had been reported as provided in the act, the one transferring continued his liability as a stockholder. (Sec. 13). It is further specifically provided that when the prescribed details had been carried out the company would be considered incorporated, but not so as to restrict in any way the liability of any of the shareholders under any judgment against the company; every shareholder was to be liable as he would have been if the company had not been incorporated. (Sec. 25). Another section is still plainer in providing that a judgment against the company shall run first against the property of the company, but if due diligence fails to give satisfaction, then against the property of any shareholder. (Sec. 66).

1855—After much public discussion and much investigation by parliamentary committees,[12] a statute of this year enabled companies registered under the registration act of 1844 to obtain certificates of limited liability. (18 & 19 Vict. c. 133). Subsequent acts in 1856, 1857 and 1858 removed the exception which had previously existed with respect to insurance and banking companies. (19 & 20 Vict. c. 47; 20 & 21 Vict. c. 78; 22 Vict. c. 91).

1862—The companies act of this year consolidated the British law on the subject and included (Secs. 7, 8) due provision for limited liability; the liability of shareholders could be limited according to the statement in the original memorandum of association either to the amount unpaid on shares, or to such an amount as the shareholders agreed to contribute if the company dissolved.
The company must use the word "limited" or (Ltd.) as the last word in its corporate name. (25 & 26 Vict. c. 9).

Freedom of incorporation by general statute spread with some rapidity after this time: France had such a statute by 1867; Germany, 1870; Hungary, 1875; Italy, 1882; Switzerland, 1883; Spain, 1885.[13]

In America this development took place much earlier than in Europe. Almost as soon as the Revolution freed the colonies from the control of the laws of England, statutes relating to corporations were passed. The English tradition that corporate power was granted only in rare instances was never firmly established here. A strong prejudice in favor of open equality of opportunity in the colonies led to the early enactment of general incorporation laws. The first of these were for ecclesiastical, educational or literary associations—South Carolina, 1778; New York, 1784; New Jersey, 1786; Delaware, 1787; Pennsylvania, 1791.[14] The earliest statute for freely incorporating business enterprise was passed in 1795 in North Carolina.* In 1811 a New York statute permitted the incorporation

* Of this law it was said: "Here for the first time since the beginning of the Roman Empire, a sovereign state offered incorporation for business purposes to any who desired it, freely and on equal terms"—S. E. Baldwin, "American Business Corporations Before 1789"—*Report of the American Historical Association,* Vol. I, 1902. This statute, however, was confined to a single class of enterprise—canal construction.

of various types of manufacturing companies, and in Michigan in 1837 the principle was extended to banking. Before long many states had definitely excluded the formation of corporations by special legislation and had substituted general statutes: Louisiana, 1845; Iowa and New York, 1846; Wisconsin, 1848; Ohio and Indiana, 1851.

This early and energetic encouragement of the corporation in America is especially noteworthy in comparison with the much slower acceptance of the principle in England. But the differences between the two countries must not be overlooked. America had not yet experienced a "Bubble period" of insane speculation which in the early eighteenth century made such an indelible impression upon English thought and policy. In England a corporation was considered a political body practically endowed with perpetuity and possessed of obligations distinctly separate from those of its members, and therefore it was of too grave import to be left free to all. In America there was no opposition from tradition or from vested interests to the extension of incorporation; here the principle of governmental action was democracy and the public good; consequently, the opportunity to incorporate was not to be considered a special favor of the sovereign to a limited few but a privilege to be dealt out with an equal hand. Furthermore, the legal view of the powers of a corporation was different in the two countries. In England the courts held to the doctrine that a corporation could do anything not forbidden in its charter. This gave corporations an element of danger. The American judges, on the other hand, held to the theory that a corporation had no power not granted expressly or by fair implication. This made the corporation much less an object of fearsome possibilities. As a result of these quite different doctrines the corporate franchise could safely be given with much freer hand in America and the advantages of the attendant limitations of stockholders' liability could be more widespread.

It must be evident from the discussion in the last few chapters that the influence of the business corporation upon the formation of accounting has been very important indeed. Since one of the two basic functions of present-day accounting is to apply the established principles which properly differentiate assets and expenses,* the indebtedness to the corporation is quite plain. It is here more than in any other element that the importance of maintaining a sharp distinction between capital and income is emphasized. The corporate form of business organization was of such a nature as to give great prominence to this distinction both as an economic and as a legal necessity. It is also noteworthy that delegated management, with its greater dependence upon carefully analyzed income data as a basis for formulating sound managerial policies, is so characteristic of the corporate form that it constitutes another reason why accounting flourished where bookkeeping alone would hardly suffice.

From an economic point of view it appears that the corporation, through its continuity of existence and other characteristics, has made it possible to assemble large amounts of capital; this fact of itself would lead to an emphasis upon a relative permanency of the capital investment. But in combination with the factory system of machine production and the increased use of long-lived capital assets, the corporation form of organization made still more necessary a permanent, not to say fixed, amount of capitalization. With capital investment a continuing element, the use of "dividends" rather than "divisions" was inescapable, and attention to the preservation intact of the economic capital was inevitable.† The very existence of the business enterprise, and perhaps the welfare of the creditors as well, required that the power of the enterprise to continue to perform its economic purpose be preserved as far as it was possible to do so. If accounting, through depreciation or otherwise, could contribute to that end, it had a useful service to perform, and the expansion of its use is understandable.

The separation of capital and income for the better preservation of capital is likewise a legal necessity. In this case, however, it is legal, or contributed, capital rather than economic capital which is considered to be in need of safeguarding. The peculiar right of

* The other basic function is to effect the association of units of income and units of the cost which produced that income.

† Cf. Adam Smith, *Wealth of Nations,* Vol. I, p. 124, regarding the necessity of seeing that fixed and circulating capital are maintained before withdrawing anything as profit.

creditors to special protection in the face of shareholders' limited liability is the foundation of this legal concern about the capital stock, and back of that is the doctrine of corporate entity which makes limited liability of shareholders logical if not inevitable. The protection of the capital fund is sought in statutes which limit dividends to profits and in principles which indicate what is and what is not profit available for dividends. But that these protective measures may be applied, it is necessary for the directors to ascertain correctly the amount of the available profit. Since the measurement of profits is the province of accounting, it is at this point that accounting makes one of its principal contacts with corporation law.

Put concisely, the matter may be stated thus: the separateness of the corporate entity provides the logic behind limited liability in corporations; limited liability brings about the positive legal and equitable obligation to preserve invested capital intact from the encroachments of dividends; restriction of dividends in turn makes necessary the careful calculation of profit, including allowance for depreciation; and in accounting (bookkeeping expanded under the pressure of new responsibilities) is found the instrument par excellence for analyzing and recording the occurrences of business in such a manner as to make possible a fair computation of available profit.

The influence of the corporation upon accounting ideas is thus a direct one; it lays the direct burden upon accounting to go far beyond the confines of simple double-entry bookkeeping in distinguishing properly between capital and income.

REFERENCES

1. John P. Davis, *Corporations*, Vol. I, pp. 99, 232.

2. Pollack and Maitland, *History of English Law*, Vol. I, pp. 489, 491.

3. Floyd R. Mechem, 24 *Harvard Law Review*; J. T. Carter, *The Nature of the Corporation as a Legal Entity*, pp. 52, 57.

4. Paul Pic, *Des Societes Commerciales*, Paris, 1925, p. 108.

5. A. K. Kuhn, *A Comparative Study of the Law of Corporations*, pp. 34, 35.

6. C. P. Sherman, *Roman Law in the Middle Ages*, pp. 207, 226, 306.

7. George J. Bell, *Principles of the Laws of Scotland*, cites: *Sevenson and Company v. M'Nair* (*or Arron Fishing Co.*) 1757, 3 Ross, *Leading Cases on Scotch Law*, 580.

8. S. E. Baldwin, *Modern Political Institutions*, p. 201.

9. *Ibid.*, p. 181; Pothier, *Traite du contrat de Societe,* Sec. 96 et seq.

10. Wm. R. Scott, *Joint Stock Companies Before 1720,* Vol. I, pp. 228, 344.

11. Wm. R. Scott, *ibid.,* Vol. I, p. 270.

12. George Dodd, *British Almanac and Companion,* 1865, p. 101; Leon Levi, *Journal of the Royal Statistical Society,* xxxiii (1870).

13. S. E. Baldwin, *op. cit.* p. 208.

14. J. S. Davis, *Essays in the Earlier History of American Corporations,* pp. 7, 16.

XVI. BACKGROUND OF BRITISH AUDITING

One of the elements of accounting which definitely distinguishes it from bookkeeping is auditing. Ever since double entry has been in use textbook instructions have been given for checking the recorded data for error; and some of the earliest advice in this respect is still sound as far as it goes.* But professional auditing is more than a search for errors in footings and omitted or incorrect postings from journal to ledger. According to modern practice auditing is a critical examination of the records undertaken by the auditor to enable him to pass judgment upon the truth or falsity of the picture which the figures display. The procedures usually followed in verifying the truth of the facts presented reflect the accumulated experiences of several generations of men skilled in the varied technicalities of bookkeeping and business and carry the auditor at many points outside the account books themselves to complete his investigations.

But the present resourcefulness in financial investigation and the independence of mind which is now expected of every public practitioner were not quickly achieved, nor was a really professional status easily established. Yet resourcefulness has grown and a professional standing has been achieved. The circumstances in which this development occurred are, therefore, a part of the background of modern accountancy, and as such deserve consideration.

Attention must be turned to Great Britain, for it was there that auditing made an early appearance, and public accounting, about

* Chapter 32 of Paciolo's *De Computis* has already been mentioned. It gives careful consideration to checking the book entries as a preliminary to closing an old ledger and opening a new one. He requires that the journal be given to an assistant while the proprietor takes the ledger; the former reads the journal entries aloud one by one and the latter finds the corresponding items in the ledger. If all is correct both persons make a dot or tick-mark at the entry so that a scrutiny of the books when the calling back is completed will reveal any items which may be in one book but not in the other.

the middle of the nineteenth century, began the movement for a professional status which still continues to grow.

In order to give a little more perspective, the discussion of nineteenth-century developments may be prefaced by a brief review of such auditing as was probably practised as early as the fourteenth century. Although the background period is a long one—including the fourteenth, fifteenth and sixteenth centuries—the subject matter is quite homogeneous because the same characteristics are exhibited throughout.

In general, such auditing as then existed was designed to verify the honesty of persons charged with fiscal, rather than managerial, responsibilities. Government officers naturally were prominent in that category. The records of the chamberlains of the City of London as early as 1311 were subject to audit. Town treasurers in Ireland, 1456, and government officers (provost, bailies and aldermen) under a statute of James I in Scotland, 1535 had to submit their accounts to audit.[1] Nor were public officers subject to audit to the exclusion of officers in private enterprise; the financial officers of the Worshipful Company of Pewterers of the City of London kept records which were periodically audited. So also were the records of the "receivors-general" in some of the larger manors of the sixteenth century. These various officers collected funds as governmental officers did, and their accountability was subjected to much the same sort of tests or audits.

Those who conducted the audits were generally other officers, who had been given that particular function, or groups of responsible persons acting as representatives of a larger body of interested parties. The City of Dublin in 1316 required the collectors of taxes to render account of receipts and payments "before the commonalty or their auditors."

The chamberlain of the City of London was at first (1298) audited by a committee consisting of the mayor, aldermen, sheriffs and certain others, but later (1310) by "six good men of the city, elected in the presence of the whole commonalty." In some towns of fifteenth-century Scotland the audit was held before the provost, council and inhabitants. In the craft guilds, auditors were chosen every year. The transfer of money and valuables to newly elected wardens of the Worshipful Company of Grocers of the City of London (1346) was carefully and formally executed in the presence of four members chosen by all the members for that specific purpose, and the book of ordinances of the Worshipful Company of Pewterers (1564) provided:

> "Also it is agreed that there shalbe foure Awdytours chosen every yeare to awdit the crafts accompts and they to paruse it and search it that it be parfect."

What is perhaps the best picture of organized accounting practice in sixteenth-century England (excepting the accounting of the English exchequer) is to be read out of the household books and accounts of the manors of the period, such as those of Sir John Howard and Sir William Howard.[2]

The manor of that day was a large establishment and needed several officers to manage its financial affairs and practical business operations. Three officers in particular were charged with weighty responsibilities. The "surveyor" must know in detail the character and location of the lord's lands and tenants. From this knowledge he assembled a book of rentals, tolls and fees—an accounting, in fact, of the sources of revenue. This rental book was passed to the "receivor-general," who collected the revenue, recorded it by sources, and made payments therefrom upon signed warrants from his lordship. The "auditor" * examined in detail the accounts of receipts and expenses prepared by the receivor-general and summarized them, after giving close consideration, no doubt, to supporting documents such as the rental book prepared by the surveyor and to his lordship's warrants.

The importance of the auditor in the economy of the manor is shown, in an unsigned breviate of 1605, by the following statement of his function:

> "The auditor being the laste of all officers, is to bee judge

* A correspondent in *The Accountant,* January 1, 1884, contributes an interesting epitaph, from a mural slab in the chancel of St. Mary's Church, Chesham, Buckinghamshire, England: "Here lyeth part of Richard Bowle, who faithfully served diverse great lords as auditor on earth, but also prepared himself to give up his account to the Lord in heaven . . . He died on 16th December 1626, and of his age, 77."

If Richard Bowle had served in this capacity for forty years of his life, he must have been auditing accounts by 1586.

> betwixte the lorde and his accomptants, and to deale trulie for and beetween all parties, and upon the determination of his audite, to presente to his lorde by booke or breviate, all his receiptes, expenses, imprestes; whatsoever, with the remaines of monye, if any bee. . . ."

The seriousness of the business with which he was concerned is shown by the fact that, once he was engaged in his work with the records, the auditor often remained steadfastly in his room, even his food being brought to him.[3]

The next consideration to arise in a review of early auditing is the manner in which an audit was accomplished. Since the issue was usually one of honest discharge of fiscal responsibility, the purpose of these audits would be to test the proper administration of that responsibility. To accomplish this purpose, the facts in the case would need to be laid before persons who would recognize error or omission when present. In the early days this usually involved "hearing the accounts" for few could read and very few could write; the word "audit" itself means to hear.*

The practice of hearing the accounts is old and it was continued for a long time. Early in the fourteenth century Walter of Henley's book on estate management called *Husbandry* gave this advice to auditors of manorial accounts:

> "The auditors ought to be faithful and prudent . . . and the accounts ought to be heard at each manor, and then one can know the profit and loss, the doings and approvements of seneschal, bailiff, provost, and others. . . ." [4]

That the auditor at the nobleman's manor was endowed with adequate authority is demonstrated by a statute [5] of Edward I in 1285 which provided that servants found "in arrearages upon the account could be sent to prison by the testimony of the auditor." And the auditors of the Pewterers' Company (ordinance of 1581) were empowered to fine the highest officers if necessary. In the fifteenth century (1456) the city of Dublin passed a law, "that ther

* An "old Encyclopaedia," referred to in a lecture reprinted in *The Accountant* of December 9, 1882, said: "to audit is to hear whatever may be said on the subject in hand with a view of passing a judgment, generally applied to the examination and passing of accounts by persons denominated auditors, but who are, perhaps, in these transactions more properly inspectors." Cf. the German term *Revisionswesen.*

schold be from that tym forward two Audytores assignet upon the tresowrerys [of] saud cytee, to hyr har acownt yerly . . . ," thus plainly delegating two persons to audit the treasury accounts by hearing them read. At about the same time the audit of city accounts in Scotland was held before the provost, council and inhabitants of the town, after the latter had been warned by proclamation to come and hear their treasurer "to mak his comt as use is."

In the sixteenth century the practice of hearing the accounts was continued, although the ordinance of the Pewterers' Company (1564) may seem to imply an audit by scrutiny in the phrase "paruse it and search it." It is probable that this is not evidence enough to constitute an exception, for "searching it" was no doubt preliminary to a later reading of the account, together with the auditor's comments, before the assembled members. Certain it is that the auditor of the manorial accounts of this time most carefully examined the details of the records by scrutiny, and then later held a "declaration of audit," that is, an oral reporting upon the accounts, in the presence of the lord of the manor and the various officers who sat in the domestic council.[6]

Reports of city audits in the middle of the sixteenth century indicate in such phrases as "heard by their auditors undersigned," "The auditors heard the footing of Robert Youngis count," and "The charge and discharge being seen, heard and understood" that hearing the accounts was still customary. Other phrases of similar import could almost be considered as audit certificates, as for example (City of Aberdeen audits, 1586–1587): "Heard, seen, considerit, calculat, and allowit by the auditors," and "futit, calculat and endit by Auditors." The "footings" probably called for specific mention in the report because not everyone was equal to the task of correctly adding the Roman numerals which were still in use in the accounts; consequently such adding constituted one of the important tests of correctness.

Early audits, therefore, are seen to follow one of two types. In the first, the audit consisted of a more or less public hearing of the results of the fiscal activities of governmental officers by delegated representatives of the citizens. The second type called for a careful scrutiny by a trusted officer of the manor of the "charge and discharge" accounts of those household officers who had fiscal responsibilities. In the first instance the necessities of the case seemed satisfied when the details of receipts were tested against common or public knowledge of what should have been collected and when the details of payments reported against the receipts were made sufficiently public to reduce the temptation to fraud. In the audit of the second type the auditor apparently made up a combined statement of account from all other officers' books, making sure of the correctness of addition, examining warrants for reasonableness of expenditure in the meantime, and finally attesting to the subamounts and totals presented in a "charge and discharge" form.

Both types of audit were designated to afford a check upon "accountability" and nothing more. It was in effect a case of examining and testing an account of stewardship. There was, of course, no question at issue of net ownership of property or of financial condition as a basis of credit; and obviously neither the record nor the audit attempted to reveal "profitableness" in a commercial or business sense.

During the seventeenth and eighteenth centuries the center of economic life shifted from the self-sufficient manors where responsibilities were highly centralized in one man—the lord of the manor—and where "accountabilities" were separately delegated to numerous persons of lower rank. The new centers of economic life were still widely dispersed as feudalism passed away, but the allocation now was vastly different. Towns took the place of manors as the important centers, and independent "masters" (small manufacturers employing hand workers for wages in "factories") took the place of closely regulated guild craftsmen.

In place of community isolation, a sea-borne trade, following hard upon explorations which opened new lands, had brought unparalleled expansion of contact with new markets and new sources of supply. With these beginnings of centralized manufacturing and far-flung commerce, banking and insurance rapidly developed to keep pace with new conditions. It was the beginning of "business."

With the advent of business, there came, instead of "accountability," the accounting problems attendant upon the ownership of property and the calculation of profits or losses. Auditing, no longer an auditory process of checking another's stewardship, now began to lay increasing emphasis upon the visual scrutiny of written records and the testing of entries by documentary evidence.

In contrast with the manorial practice, in which, as already shown, there was an officer called an auditor, the development of business in the seventeenth and eighteenth centuries only slowly gave rise to a definite occupation worthy of the designation, "auditing." Bookkeeping there was, of course, and men especially skilled in this field were called upon not infrequently to give aid in their leisure time to merchants and others who could not themselves keep their records satisfactorily. But such men were doing bookkeeping work for hire in addition to their regular employments rather than practising professionally.*

Certain types of law practice of the time necessitated more or less contact with financial facts, and this factor, too, had its effect. It is likely that prior to the middle of the eighteenth century the reports and statements of account which were required by bankruptcies, executorships or other law court practices were prepared by lawyers for the most part, and it is not improbable that the difficulties which they experienced in dealing with intricate accounts and financial transactions led them to employ persons skilled in double-entry bookkeeping whenever possible.[7] It is logical also to assume that lawyers whose practice brought them frequently into contact with financial affairs would acquire for themselves such a knowledge of bookkeeping technique as would enable them to discharge their duties.

These conditions appeared fairly early in the period, especially in Scotland. Until comparatively recently, much of the accounting work in that country was done from solicitors' offices, and later, after professional accountants had organized their own society (1854 in Scotland), practicing accountants were in some cases also members of the solicitors' society.[8]

Many of the men listed by Brown as early professional account-

* Bailey's Dictionary, under the date of 1770, is cited as defining an accountant as one well versed in adding up accounts (A. Murray, *The Accountant,* December 24, 1881). Another writer is of the opinion that until about 1790 an accountant was considered merely an expert at figures in the sense of the French term "expert comptable." (George Yard, *The Accountant Students Journal,* May 1, 1883.)

ants in Scotland had definite accounting responsibilities in governmental affairs. George Watson (1645–1723), whom Brown calls the first professional accountant in Scotland, was treasurer for Edinburgh's ale tax for many years while acting as cashier to a great merchant of the city; later he was accountant for the Bank of Scotland. Alexander Chalmers was accountant general to the board of excise and accountant to the City of Edinburgh, 1717–59; John Buchan (died 1808) was accountant to the General Post Office of Scotland; James Bruce was accountant to the City of Edinburgh, 1796–1825. There is little doubt that these men, because of their places of trust and their skill in accounts, often served others in a professional capacity, even as more humble bookkeepers and teachers used their leisure in the wider application of their special skill.*

Men of integrity and business experience were also in demand as executors of estates and trustees in bankruptcies. Alexander Farquharson (died 1788) was one of these. He made reports on forfeited estates and acted as trustee for creditors. David Russell, who died late in the eighteenth century, was both accountant and solicitor. Charles Selkrig (1760–1837) had a large practice (once having received a fee of £20,000), and was trustee to many large estates. In the field of bankruptcy expert assistance was also needed. For example, Walter Ewing Maclae, "merchant and accountant," was employed to wind up some of the largest failures which in 1777 followed upon the disruption of trade with the American colonies. In 1793 Maclae was again trustee, this time for one of the three banks which failed with many other enterprises at that time.

These men were not auditors in a strictly modern sense, but they did engage in various semi-professional activities, and in a sense they do link the past to the present, connecting the mediæval "audi-

* David Murray in *Chapters in the History of Bookkeeping and Accountancy*, Glasgow, 1930, quotes (pp. 60-66) the language by which persons in the seventeenth century held themselves out for professional engagements. Robert Hartwell (1623) advertises the "perfecting of accompts in controuversie"; Richard Dafforne (1670) writes that he "Rectifieth Books of Accompts abroad or at home whether in Proper, Factorage or Company"; John Collins (1675) states that he "has been much lately concerned in great and public accompts . . ."; Thomas Brown (1670) gave notice that he was ready to serve any who apply in "auditing, stating or drawing up any reports of accompts . . ."

tor" in a single nobleman's household with the present day "chartered accountant," who holds himself out to the general public for whatever expert services may be required within his field.

Some glimpses of the status of accounting in England toward the end of the eighteenth century and onward into the early nineteenth century are to be had from the studies which have been made of the old directories.[9] The title "accomptant" or the like is not met in the directories of 1766,[10] but from 1773 onward the title either alone or in combination with others is met with increasing frequency. More often than not the entry appears as "accomptant and agent," * "accomptant and broker," "writing master and accomptant," "auctineer, appraiser and accomptant," or some such combination of occupations. Once in 1790 one man was listed in Liverpool as "mercantile accomptant and dealer in tin plate." [11]

The number of entries under these titles in the eighteenth-century directories is indicative of the slow growth of "public practice." In the notations which follow the figures in parentheses indicate the number of accountants listed in the directory for that city and year: Edinburgh in 1773 (7), 1774 (14); Glasgow in 1783 (6); London in 1776 (1), 1790 (1), 1799 (11); Liverpool in 1783 (1), 1790 (5), 1796 (10); Bristol in 1783 (2); Manchester in 1794 (2). Assuming that this list is complete and without duplications (a matter much in doubt) it contains only 60 entries for all the directories named prior to the year 1800—not a very important professional representation as compared with a population (for Great Britain) of 12,560,000 in 1780 and 15,717,000 in 1800.

Even in the early part of the nineteenth century the growth was still slow. Referring again to items in the directories: Edinburgh, 1821 (58), 1834 (80); Glasgow, 1807 (10), 1821 (16); London 1811 (24), 1820 (44), 1840 (107), 1843 (160),† 1845 (210), 1847 (186); Liverpool, 1832 (37), 1849 (69); Bristol, 1824 (20), 1830 (28); Man-

* It is thought that the word agent may have broadly denoted the practice of effecting arrangements between debtors and creditors—a procedure of very early origin. Cf. B. Worthington, *Professional Accountants,* p. 10.

† Ernest Cooper in *The Accountants Journal,* December 1, 1886, cites this figure from the post-office directory as "a remarkable increase possibly attributed to the Bankruptcy Act of 1825."

chester, 1815 (14), 1829 (24), 1831 (32), 1840 (52); Birmingham, 1808 (2); Leicester, 1831 (5).

A few similar figures for typical years in the second half of the century will be sufficient to indicate the trend: Liverpool, 1860 (91), 1870 (139); London, 1860 (310), 1870 (464);* Birmingham, 1861 (45); Manchester, 1861 (84), 1871 (159); Bristol, 1861 (74); Leicester, 1863 (13).

With the exception of London (with 210 accountants in 1845) none of the cities prior to 1850 had as many as one hundred men publicly listing themselves as accountants; in fact, only London, Edinburgh, Liverpool and Manchester passed the fifty mark by mid-century, and it was not until the seventies that the last two named passed a hundred.

For convenience in comparison and reference the directory figures, shown on the opposite page, are summarized in order of date.

From the facts thus presented it is obvious that up to the beginning of the nineteenth century there was as yet in England no accountancy profession, no body of skilled experts holding themselves out to the public as open to technical engagements in matters of accounts. But evidence of budding and growth increases as the nineteenth century progresses. In the single generation between 1811 and 1847 the number of firms listed in the directories of London as accountants increased almost eightfold, that is, from 24 to 186; the total population did not quite double in this time. This is indeed a rapid increase in numbers of accountants, but the total number is still rather insignificant, and there were even fewer practitioners outside London. In another generation—up to 1883—the number of London accountants listed in the occupational directories increased four and one-half times. Now the rate is less rapid, but the total has reached the imposing figure of 840. More important than this matter of mere numbers, the Scottish accountants by 1854 had organized a professional society to foster the members' interest and regulate their professional conduct; and between 1870 and 1877 several similar professional societies had sprung up in important English cities and had begun to admit members by general and technical examinations only.

* At the time of the formation of the Institute of Accountants of London.

TABLE 1

NUMBER OF ACCOUNTANTS LISTED IN THE OLD DIRECTORIES

Year	City							
	Edinburgh	Glasgow	London	Liverpool	Bristol	Manchester	Birmingham	Leicester
1773	7 *							
1774	14							
1776	— *		1					
1783	—	6 *	—	1	2			
1790	—	—	1	5	—			
1794	—	—	—	—	—	2		
1796	—	—	—	10	—	—		
1799	—	—	11	—	—	—		
1807	—	10	—	—	—	—		
1808	—	—	—	—	—	—	2	
1811	—	—	24	—	—	—	—	
1815	—	—	—	—	—	14	—	
1820	—	—	44	—	—	—	—	
1821	58	16	—	—	—	—	—	
1824	—	—	—	—	20	—	—	
1829	—	—	—	—	—	24	—	
1830	—	—	—	—	28	—	—	
1831	—	—	—	—	—	32	5	
1832	—	—	—	37	—	—	—	
1834	80	—	—	—	—	—	—	
1840	—	—	107	—	—	52	—	
1843	—	—	160	—	—	—	—	
1845	—	—	210	—	—	—	—	
1847	—	—	186	—	—	—	—	
1849	—	—	—	69	—	—	—	
1860	—	—	310	91	—	—	—	
1861	—	—	—	—	74	84	45	
1863	—	—	—	—	—	—	—	13
1870	—	—	464	139	—	—	—	—
1871	—	—	—	—	—	159	—	—

* Murray, (*op. cit.*, pp. 101, 106, 116) gives 6 for the Edinburgh directory in 1773, 15 in 1775 and 14 in 1778; 5 for the Glasgow directory in 1783 and 6 (plus 3 other names gleaned from newspaper notices) in 1801.

Thus in a period measured by little more than two generations, or within the span of a single lifetime of three score and ten, there had developed a body of independent practitioners offering skilled services to the public.

The next chapters undertake to survey some of the social and economic forces which conspired to the same end—to note how, out of the germ of scientific method which lay in double-entry bookkeeping, out of the needs arising in a rapid industrialization of society, and out of the parliamentary action of the day, a profession took root and grew.

REFERENCES

1. Richard Brown, *History of Accounting and Accountants,* Edinburgh, 1905, pp. 77-91, furnishes many of the facts stated in this section of the chapter.

2. See *The Household of a Tudor Nobleman,* by Paul V. B. Jones, University of Illinois, Studies in Social Science, Vol. VI, No. 4, December, 1917, Chapter IV, "Financial Management in the Household."

3. P. V. B. Jones, *op. cit.,* pp. 143, 144.

4. A. H. Woolf, *A Short History of Accountants and Accountancy,* p. 86.

5. 13 Edward I, c. 2.

6. P. V. B. Jones, *op. cit.,* p. 144.

7. A. W. Chalmers, *The Accountant Students' Journal,* June 11, 1883.

8. Brown, *op. cit.,* pp. 182, 193.

9. Especially Brown, pp. 183, 202, 234, Woolf, pp. 31, 171, Appendix II, and Murray, pp. 90-111.

10. A. W. Chalmers, *The Accountant Students' Journal,* June 1, 1883.

11. A. W. Chalmers, *op. cit.*

XVII. DEVELOPMENT OF EXPERTS IN ACCOUNTS

IT IS now necessary to note the ebb and flow of business during the nineteenth century: the succession of prosperity, crisis, depression; to scrutinize bankruptcy statutes and failure statistics of that time; to observe (in the chapter to follow) the growth of social control through statutory regulation of public works and joint stock companies generally. The reason for looking into these matters is that the expanding scope of the accountant's work is rooted in these conditions. This period gave rise to certain activities which slowly created a class of specialists in accounts. When these specialists organized to educate themselves and their successors the better to serve the general public in matters related to accounts, then modern professional accounting began.

In the half century between the close of the Napoleonic War and the end of the American Civil War, England experienced a number of significant financial crises and industrial depressions which, with the accompanying commercial failures, created a demand for men who were experienced in accounts. The years which stand out most strikingly are 1815, 1836, 1857, and 1866. Obviously no exhaustive inquiry into the intricate causes of the crises at these times is needed in this place. Consequently, the circumstances surrounding the depressions will be outlined only so far as is necessary to relate the economic conditions of the period to the development of accountancy.

The Napoleonic War led to England's crisis of 1815. During the long years of continental warfare, her territory was isolated from actual conflict and her supremacy on the sea unquestioned. She was, therefore, free to build up her industry and commerce. This opportunity, with the fact that the industrial revolution had its beginnings in England, resulted in a rapid expansion of her productive capacity and her manufactured products during the war.

The prospect of peace seemed to many to promise a greater demand for goods when the continental blockade should be lifted, and production was accordingly further increased. However, peace had quite different consequences: continental countries were now able in some measure to compete with England in offering supplies to the market, and general buying power was very much weakened throughout Europe. Consequently, England could not sell her accumulated goods and depression inevitably resulted.

When ten years had elapsed, England was again undergoing a depression following the panic of 1825. Powell [1] describes it as terrible in scope and intensity, the country at one time being practically "within twenty-four hours of barter." Losses were estimated at £45,000,000.

According to some opinions, the difficulties of 1820–40 arose out of the deadly competition of the putting-out system of textile manufacturing and the increasing adoption of the power loom; the *laissez-faire* economic philosophy was leading to overproduction. But others seek the explanation of the crisis in the reckless extension of bank-note issues following the abundant harvests of 1822, and in the speculation which accompanied the easy credit of that time. Commodities (cotton, sugar, rice) were rashly bought and held for a rise in price; the repeal of the Bubble act greatly encouraged the formation of joint-stock companies; public men and periodicals waxed eloquent about the wide-spread prosperity; the entrance to the stock exchange was daily choked with men eager to speculate.[2] In November a bank in Plymouth failed, in December one in London closed; in three weeks seventy banks had stopped payment; gold held by the Bank of England fell from 11¾ million pounds to 3¾ millions.

After another decade still another panic convulsed the country. Three explanations of the troubles of 1836 are advanced by an early writer:[3] (a) continued speculations in joint-stock companies, including joint-stock banks, of which about two hundred appeared between 1826 and 1836; (b) an over-extension of joint-stock banks in the United States (private banks increased from 329 in 1830 to 700 in 1836), and land speculation in the West, all of which led to over-trading in America; and (c) the development of credit on open account in America (abandonment of draft with bill-of-lading attached), which was accompanied by competition for American business and led to excessive trading on this sort of credit.

The depression which followed was long and severe. In the worst of the period practically every third man, it is said, had defaulted in some of his debts, and many closed their books and waited in abject despair for the end. But by 1844 the condition had virtually worked itself out; good harvests matured, surplus savings appeared, and railway construction in England was expanding at a rapid rate.* By the next year speculation was rampant again. Prices collapsed in the autumn, and in the next year there were continued demands for the payment of unpaid calls on stocks. A series of business failures soon swept the country into a panic in the autumn of 1847.

The periodic disturbances continued. In 1857 another crisis caused by British investments in America spread to England and resulted in the closing of many factories in the textile trades and the extinguishing of many blast furnaces. Again in 1866, when business had barely recovered from the preceding blow, it was once more reduced to desperate straits. This situation was partly the result of further speculation, and partly the effect of the Civil War in the United States. Locker, writing immediately after the events, considered that the crisis resulted from the erroneous ideas regarding the lack of risk attached to joint-stock companies with limited liability under the companies act of 1862, which led to the formation of new joint-stock banks and to their subsequently partaking in various hazardous ventures to make profits for their stockholders. A later writer,[4] however, attributed the crisis of 1866 to the fact that the close of the Civil War threw American cotton on the English market just when blockade prices had trebled the Indian and Egyptian production. But whatever combination of circumstances may have been the precise cause, the effect of the disaster itself was all too evident in such a gigantic failure as that of Overend, Guerney & Co., with liabilities of £19,000,000.

The inevitable consequences of these recurring periods of depression were heavy financial losses and the failure of many business

* 2264 miles (1845), 6621 miles (1850), 10,433 miles (1860).

Table 2

BRITISH BANKRUPTCY STATISTICS, 1817–1890

(Compiled from the British Almanac and Whitaker's Almanac)

Year	Bankruptcy commissions sealed
1817	2311
1818	1248
1819	*
1820	1784
1821	1665
1822	1419
1823	1250
1824	1244
(new law)	
1825	1475
1826	3307
1827	1688
1828	1519
1829	2150
1830	1720
(new law)	
1831	1886
1832	1519
1833	1150
1834	1013
1835	959
1836	890
1837	1462
1838	956
1839	930
1840	1516
1841	1330
1842	1373
1843	1169
1844	1064
1845	1028
1846	1326
1847	1373
1848	1907
1849	1298
(new law)	
1850	*
1851	*
1852	*
1853	*
1854	*

Year	Bankruptcy petitions
1855	*
1856	*
1857	*
1858	*
1859	2765
1860	2820
1861	3129
(new law)	

Year	Bankruptcy "adjudications"
1862	9663
1863	8470
1864	7224
1865	8305
1866	8126
1867	8994
1868	9195
1869	10396
(new law)	

Year	Bankruptcy cases	Liquidation by arrangement	Composition	Total
1870	1351	2035	1616	5002
1871	1238	2872	2170	6280
1872	933	3694	2208	6835
1873	915	4152	2422	7489
1874	930	4440	2549	7919
1875	965	4233	2691	7889
1876	976	4986	3287	9249
1877	967	5239	3327	9533
1878	1084	6356	4010	11450
1879	1156	7167	4809	13132
1880	995	5546	3757	10298
1881	1005	5216	3506	9727
1882	995	4679	3567	9241
1883	1646	4011	2938	8595
	(new law)			
1884	2998	485	687	
1885	4566	61	189	
1886	4816			
1887	4839			
1888	4826			
1889	4520			
1890	4011			

firms. Unsatisfactory as the available bankruptcy statistics are because of a lack of continuity or the frequent changes in statute law, they nevertheless plainly show that not only were there definite years of crisis, as previously mentioned, but that bankruptcy was an ever-present phenomenon as well.

The table on the opposite page is compiled from successive numbers of the British Almanac from 1817 to 1867, and from Whitaker's Almanac from 1868 to 1890, the original data having been gathered from parliamentary documents and official judicial statistics for use in the almanacs.

No sufficiently early figures were found to portray directly the crisis of 1815, but in 1817, 2,311 bankruptcy commissions were sealed. This figure represented conditions two years after the crisis, and yet it probably reflected the influence of the panic, for the number of bankruptcies in each of the next three years was noticeably less than in 1817. The disturbance in 1825 is reflected in the number of bankruptcies in 1826, namely, 3307 cases, or considerably more than twice the number for the year next preceding. Bankruptcy cases in 1836 totaled 890, but in 1837 they reached 1,462, plainly reflecting the financial difficulties of the crisis of 1836. The period of railroad speculation reveals equally significant figures: 1847, 1,373 bankruptcies; 1848, 1,907 bankruptcies; 1849, 1,298 bankruptcies. The crisis of 1857 was followed by 2,765 failures in 1859 and 2,820 in 1860. The financial troubles of 1866 seem to have extended with cumulative effect into the next few years: 1866 (8,126 bankruptcies); 1867 (8,994) 1868 (9,195), 1869 (10,396). Evidently this was no mere stock-exchange panic or speculative crisis, but a severe industrial depression.

These were the conditions which periodically brought bankruptcy regulations before parliament for revision. These statutes, with their background of economic causation, will repay consideration because certain sections in them made work for men who were offering themselves to the public as expert accountants.

The English statutes prior to 1800 are of little present interest: they merely laid the foundations of bankruptcy procedure and may therefore be passed by with the briefest mention.

The earliest statute[5] was enacted in 1542 and simply gave the

Lord Chancellor the power to seize and sell the property of "persons who obtained other men's goods—not minding to pay." The property so seized was to be divided ratably among the creditors, but they still had a right against the debtor for any unsettled portion of the debt. Under Queen Elizabeth (1570) parliament extended the act specifically to any merchant who committed various specified acts "to the intent and purpose to defraud or hinder any of his creditors." [6] In 1604, under James I, another statute extended the description of a bankrupt by including anyone who made a fraudulent conveyance of lands, goods or chattels with intent to defeat or delay the creditors' recovery of their debts. At this time also power was given to commissioners of the courts to call witnesses, examine the bankrupt's goods and assign his debts if necessary. A few years later (1623) the bankrupt, under certain conditions, was made subject to the punishment of being pilloried for two hours and having one ear cut off.[7] In 1662 Parliament ruled that no stockholder of a joint-stock company should be deemed a merchant exercising the trade of merchandise within the meaning of any statute of bankruptcy,[8] and the statute [9] of 1705 gave full discharge of the debt when the law had been complied with and made felons of bankrupts who did not render themselves within thirty days.

No other English statutes on bankruptcy appeared until more than one hundred years later. But during that interval tremendous social and industrial changes had taken place, and when attention was again directed to the laws of bankruptcy several new statutes followed one another in rapid succession. In a little more than half a century seven important bankruptcy statutes were passed by parliament—those of 1825, 1831, 1833, 1849, 1861, 1869, 1883. It is these later statutes which deserve particular notice here, especially for their provisions regarding the persons who were to handle the bankrupt's affairs, and in relation to the background of business crises.

It is probably not without significance that these bankruptcy statutes were spaced somewhat regularly between crises. The following tabulation places both items in chronological sequence.

Crisis — 1815	
	1825 — Bankruptcy statute
Crisis — 1825	
	1831 — Bankruptcy statute
	1833 — Bankruptcy statute
Crisis — 1836	
Crisis — 1847	
	1849 — Bankruptcy statute
Crisis — 1857	
	1861 — Bankruptcy statute
Crisis — 1866	
	1869 — Bankruptcy statute
	1883 — Bankruptcy statute

In most cases the statute followed the crisis so closely as to indicate a probable relationship of cause and effect. Statutes were enacted within two years after the crisis of 1847, within three years after the crisis of 1866, within four years after that of 1857, within six years after that of 1825, and within ten years after that of 1815. It has already been shown (page 275) how the numbers of bankruptcies quickly reflected the years of crisis. Comparison of the dates of the largest number of failures with the sequence presented here will show that, as a rule, in some year between a crisis and a new bankruptcy statute there occurred a large increase in the number of failures. The sequence of events, therefore, seems to have been: a financial crisis, extensive business failures, a new bankruptcy statute.

Bankruptcy undoubtedly occupied the public mind a great deal. For two generations constructive legislation attempted to secure better protection for creditors (who here represent the general public) and to decrease the losses attendant upon business failures. The devices for control which were written into the statutes were various, but throughout a responsibility was laid upon some person or persons for administering the bankrupt's estate to the best interests of all concerned. Naturally persons who were found to be particularly capable of meeting the requirements of the law and the circumstances with honesty and good judgment were in repeated demand; their growth in technical knowledge naturally increased with experience.

The specific provisions found in the statutes next deserve attention and are briefly outlined. In the statute of 1825 [10] the lord chancellor was given power to appoint "such persons as to him seem fit" to act as commissioners in bankruptcy to direct the handling of the bankrupt's property in satisfaction of his debts (Sec. XII). The major part in number and value of the creditors might elect assignees to receive and distribute the bankrupt's property (Sec. LXI) or the commissioners might appoint assignees if the creditors did not. (Sec. XLV.) The assignees were required to keep accounts of all the bankrupt's property received and all payments made for his estate (Sec. CI), and the commissioners were to audit (inspect and question?) the accounts of the assignees in a public meeting. (Sec. CVI.)

The act [11] of 1831 made an important change by creating a court of bankruptcy and "official assignees." The latter consisted of not more than thirty persons, "being merchants, bankers, accountants or traders," chosen by the lord chancellor. One official assignee was to have charge of each bankrupt's estate, together with the assignee chosen by the creditors, but the property was to be received and possessed by the official assignee only. (Secs. XXII, XXV, XXVI.) The appointment of commissioners under the previous act had often been made for political reasons, and the men chosen rarely had any knowledge of the special duties required. The act of 1831 attempted to remedy this defect by limiting appointment to those with business experience of the various types mentioned. In 1842 this bankruptcy court was extended beyond London and the number of official assignees correspondingly increased. The act of 1833 merely elaborated details unimportant for the present purposes.

In 1849 all the bankruptcy laws were consolidated and amended to such an extent that the new act [12] fills a hundred pages in the *Statutes at Large*. Much of the material is repeated from the earlier statutes, including the organization of bankruptcy courts in London and the country districts and the appointment of official assignees, as previously mentioned. In regard to settlements outside public bankruptcy the statute provides (Sec. CCXVI) that three-fifths in number and value of the creditors can accept a proposal of the bankrupt to make a deed of arrangement, and the court may approve it against all creditors as of the date of the petition in bankruptcy.

All the matters of composition, of course, require more or less work with accounting statements, but more to the point for the present purpose are the several sections which deal directly with accounting. The bankrupt is required to deliver his records and books of account to the official assignee and to assist the latter in making out the statement of his estate. (Sec. CV.) Since the official assignee supervised many bankruptcy cases at the same time the need for expert assistance in the bankrupt's presentation of his affairs is obvious. It is further required (Sec. CLX) that the bankrupt must file such balance-sheets and accounts as the court shall direct and make oath of their truth. Upon application of the assignees, allowances for the preparation of balance-sheets and accounts may be made out of the estate to persons whom the court shall think fit. It is further provided (Sec. CLXXXV) that a public hearing of the bankrupt's affairs shall be held by the court, including the examination of sworn statements of the assignee's receipts and disbursements, before concluding the case.

Most of the provisions just mentioned are new to the bankruptcy statutes, but it seems likely that this statute of 1849 is, to some extent at least, a codification of previous "good practice." A correspondent in *The Accountant*[13] in 1877 testifies to the fact that accountants were largely engaged in bankruptcy cases long before the acts of 1831 and 1849. He submits an advertisement from the *Liverpool Mercury* of June 20, 1817, to the effect that creditors who have proved their debts against one Jonathan Barker might receive their dividends in liquidation by applying to Joseph King & Son, accountants, at Temple Place.

Whatever the practice may have been prior to 1849, the Bankruptcy Act of that year clearly provided for a considerable amount of accounting work. Passing the last hearing in court was contingent upon a favorable report by the official assignee as to the accuracy of the accounts. As a consequence it was the regular practice to employ an accountant to insure correctness of the statements. Correct and convincing statements were not easy to prepare for courts and officers who were inclined to view the bankrupt as practically a criminal. It was the rule, however, to carry the statements back to a time when the bankrupt could show he had been solvent.[14] In other words, it was necessary to show the court by means of the statements the reasons for insolvency. Not only was the bankrupt interested in presenting to the court a well-prepared statement of affairs and deficiency account to help his case toward discharge or compromise, but the creditors would often oppose a compromise and would have the filed statements thoroughly investigated in their own behalf.

The need for the services of men equipped with an expert knowledge of bookkeeping is evident. Contemporary opinion was even stronger. Worthington reports having interviewed a chartered accountant who began practice near the middle of the century. This man said that after due consideration he had reached the confirmed conclusion that the disastrous period of 1847–48 "did more than anything else to place professional accountancy on a solid and substantial basis." The same author, writing in 1895, goes on to say that there are some accountants whose practice is almost entirely made up of work arising from failures of persons in particular trades. Brown[15] says that the requirements of the act of 1849 relative to the preparation of bankrupts' statements "brought many well known accountants into prominence and repute." *

Even though it was an improvement, the act of 1849 was not without its defects, as experience revealed. Since the details of it are of no present concern, it will suffice to point out that the bankruptcy act[16] of 1861 undertook to remedy these defects, with the result, in part, that official assignees were abolished and the estate was vested completely in the creditors' assignees. (Secs. 117, 127). Whereas creditors formerly complained of lacking sufficient voice

* The researches of Professor Penndorf of the University of Leipzig suggest that the profession of auditing in Germany could be traced back to the use of experienced bookkeepers to review the reports rendered by agents and branches to the great trading firms of the sixteenth century, such as the Fugger family, and to examine records and statements submitted in connection with the composition or liquidation of enterprises in financial difficulty.—Voss, *Handbuch für das Revisions—und Treuhandwesen*, p. 8.

in the bankrupt's affairs, they were now in full control. This facilitated settlement by composition outside the court, and thereby made more business for accountants both in preparing statements and in serving as trustees in bankruptcy and as creditors' assignees.*

Schedule 16 of the act prescribed a form of a statement of accounts, and a contemporary writer[17] gives an "illustration taken from practice." It presents on the left side lists of the creditors, secured and unsecured, the creditors to be paid in full, and any contingent liabilities or discounted bills; on the right side, the debtors classified as good, doubtful and bad, the property given up to the assignees or in the hands of creditors and the amount of the deficiency. This is a "statement of affairs" practically as it is shown in the textbooks today. It was even then supplemented with a "deficiency account" in quite modern form, with the various losses detailed on one side and the firm's capital on the other. The balance was the deficiency of the capital for covering the losses. This final figure, "deficiency," was in agreement with the balancing figure of the statement of affairs.

Within a few years (in 1869) the several acts then in effect were combined[18] in a form much like the act of 1861. The creditors were given full power to agree as seemed best without intervention of the courts. (Sec. 13). Composition was made easy. An agreement to this effect was made binding by resolution of a majority in number and three-fourths in value of the creditors; liquidation and release of the debtor could also be effected by resolution of the creditors. (Secs. 125, 126). Voting in this case could be by proxy as well as in person (Sec. 16)—a fact which will call for further comment presently.

Several consequences of the new laws were soon evident. While the total cases of financial difficulties increased slowly compared with their tendency in the years immediately prior to the act (1862–1869 in the table on page 274), a sharp classification of cases was now made. In 1870, for example, there were 5,002 cases, but 3,651

* Cf. Secs. 129, 130: assignees' statement of account to be furnished the creditors every three months; and Sec. 141: bankrupt must file complete statement of account before final discharge.

of these were settled by composition agreement or liquidated by arrangement (i.e., with a minimum of recourse to the courts) as compared with 1,351 cases which went through formal bankruptcy. Thus a contemporary could well report that, after the law of 1869, the creditors generally preferred liquidation to bankruptcy.[19] One might add that of the large number of cases coming under the act (84,778), in the ten years from 1870 to 1879, inclusive, only about one-eighth (10,515 cases) chose the path of full bankruptcy. Here is an indication of a tremendous number of insolvencies, a large proportion of which made necessary an agreement among the creditors as to the facts in the case and as to the best way out of the difficulty.

It is evident from this that men already well acquainted with bookkeeping would be serviceable as trustees under the deeds of arrangement by which informal liquidation proceded. That such men were available has already been shown in the directory statistics: Liverpool, 1860 (91), 1870 (139); London, 1860 (310), 1870 (464). But it fell to a contemporary [20] to write that "within a few years after the act accountants doubled in numbers and we find accountants, whilst practising in their profession, were also agents of various sorts—auctioneers, bailiffs, brokers, debt collectors, clerks to law solicitors, law stationers, hatters, tailors, publicans, keepers of refreshment rooms, wine merchants and so on—can you wonder why skilled accountants applied for a charter so that distinction might be made between skilled accountants and others?"

Now the significance of creditors' proxies becomes evident. Add to wide-spread insolvency the power to control the appointment of receivers (and set their fees) through holding enough creditor proxies, and the way is open to manipulation, if not at times to down-right misrepresentation and fraud. Large numbers of poorly trained and rapacious persons began to call themselves accountants and to canvass scattered creditors for proxies, or to urge them to agree to terms of settlement which, varying with the circumstances of the individual persons, might be turned to the advantage of the self-styled "accountant" who sought to represent them at the creditors' meetings or even to gain the appointment as trustee of the insolvent estate.

This solicitation for creditors' proxies and the insinuation of "brokers, hatters and publicans" into a field which had slowly been developing as a sphere of professional activities naturally incensed those who really had special qualifications for trustee work. So obvious was the incompetence of many of those who fastened themselves upon the bankrupts that it attracted outside attention. The skilled accountants had not yet achieved any large degree of professional standing generally, and they accordingly suffered in reputation not a little when, through the mere similarity of a self-assumed title, they were classed in the public mind with the "touts" who preyed upon the unwary. The law journals, as often quoted in the early numbers of *The Accountant,* not infrequently charged accountants as a class with incompetence and greed, which closer attention would have attributed to only the spurious element. Even the courts were unable to distinguish between the two types which, under the same name, were serving bankrupts or creditors in executing the provisions of the act of 1869. As late as 1875 a judge said from the bench: "The whole affairs in bankruptcy have been handed over to an ignorant set of men called accountants, which was one of the greatest abuses ever introduced into the law."[21]

It is not at all surprising, therefore, that the conditions of the times should have introduced a hitherto unknown element of solidarity among the skilled and experienced accountants, or that they should have banded together into professional associations which were to teach the public to discriminate between the qualified and the unqualified.

The subject of English bankruptcy and accounting needs only one other brief comment. The evils of unchecked creditor control over the debtors' affairs finally (1883) brought a reaction in Parliament and with it one more bankruptcy statute.[22] As can be easily read from the table given of bankruptcy statistics, the new law soon put an end to settlements by unrestricted creditor agreements of composition or liquidation; debtors' affairs were once more placed under the eyes of the courts. This situation did not mean the disappearance of composition agreements, although it did cause a great diminution of liquidation of insolvent estates by accountants.* It did, however, place such agreements upon a safer footing than they had occupied under the use of proxies. In fact the new law reinforced the use of fair and reasonable compositions by strengthening in its details the prescribed report, "statement of affairs." † The statement was a definite part of the accounting practice of the day and the statute was in all probability only recognizing this custom. In a memorial addressed to the president of the Board of Trade by the council of the Institute of Accountants regarding the working of the act of 1883, the accountants pointed out that it was their practice to lay before the creditors more information than section 16 required, especially in respect to the probable realizable value of the assets. The memorial goes on to say:

> "The statement of affairs, therefore, becomes a very important document, in as much as it is a guide to creditors as to whether or not they should accept a composition offered by the debtor or a scheme of arrangement. Up to the present time the creditors have been accustomed to rely upon it as presenting accurately the debtor's position, because, although the latter is responsible for it, it has generally been prepared and presented by an accountant." [23]

It is unnecessary to trace the development of bankruptcy statutes any further; the discussion has already shown that commercial crises led to bankruptcy laws and that the latter made work for men skilled in bookkeeping. And finally it has been demonstrated how the attempts to reduce the evils of "officialism" ‡ in English bankruptcy procedure so loosened the restraint of the courts that new evils developed. Out of the latter came the conflict of interest which led men of recognized skill in accounting matters to band themselves together for their mutual good and for the better protection of the public against the activities of men technically less qualified.

* A contemporary writer sees the accountants' services likely to be in more frequent demand in other directions; so (the implication is) there is less need to be concerned about the prospective decrease in insolvency business for the accountants. C. R. Trevor, F.C.A., in *The Accountant*, November 1, 1884.

† See Baldwin, *Law of Bankruptcy*, 10th edition, pp. 866, 872, for reproductions of the statements.

‡ See note on Scottish bankruptcy statutes at the end of this chapter.

NOTE ON SCOTTISH BANKRUPTCY STATUTES

The tendency of the early English bankruptcy statutes to produce "officialism" was probably the law's greatest weakness and the cause of much experimental legislation. The soundness of the early Scottish legislation on bankruptcy shows a marked contrast. That the basic procedure established in Scotland in 1772 (12 Geo. III c. 3) proved a satisfactory foundation for bankruptcy procedure is made evident by the fact that its essential features are also found in the statute of 1856, which still forms the Scottish law on the subject.*

The statute of 1772 was passed, as the preamble recites, to protect the personal effects of insolvent debtors from being carried off by a few creditors of earliest notice, to the prejudice and inequality of remote creditors. The court was to sequester the debtor's whole estate and appoint a temporary factor to take charge of it for the benefit of the creditors (Sec. 1), and was to prefer for that office the person presented by a majority of the creditors who concurred in the application for sequestration. (Sec. 2). The factor (after nine months) was to lodge with the court "a state of the debtor's funds then come to his knowledge," the creditors were to have twenty days to examine the "state of accounts" in the court, and thereafter the court was to order a ratable distribution among the creditors of the estate recovered. (Sec. 7). Two-thirds of the creditors could choose trustees to manage the estate rather than a factor to liquidate the claims (Sec. 30), and the trustees could choose a factor (manager) to act for them. (Sec. 31).

The act of 1793 (23 Geo. III c. 18) expanded the details of the procedure of citing a debtor before the courts and of examining the bankrupt. The act also contained the same general procedure with added provisions operating to round out certain details, such as requiring the bankrupt to exhibit "a state of his affairs," specifying his whole estate and effects, etc. (Sec. 21); requiring a majority of the creditors to name three of their number as commissioners to audit the trustee's accounts, settle the commission, etc. (Sec. 28); and establishing the procedure by which nine-tenths of the creditors could approve an offer of compromise from the bankrupt and by which the court, after hearing objections, could put the compromise into effect.

The act of 1814 (54 Geo. III c. 137) repealed the prior acts and codified them into one comprehensive statute of great clearness of statement and logic of organization. The majority of the general creditors controlled all meetings; they elected three of their members as com-

* "The rules for ranking creditors and the adjusting of preferences as interpreted by Voet and other exponents of the [Roman] civil law are the foundation of the present bankruptcy practice of Scotland." Murray, *Chapters in the History of Bookkeeping and Accountancy*, p. 133.

missioners to represent the general body of creditors; they elected one person as trustee, who became the active agent. The relationships provided for were almost as if there were to be shareholders (the general creditors), directors (the commissioners) and manager (the trustee). Thus it was logical for the trustee to be an expert under the supervision of three representative creditors (who audited his accounts, decided questions of liquidating dividends, commissions, etc.), and were responsible to the general body of creditors. The statute also provided for frequent accounting statements (Secs. 33, 36, 37, 45) and for considering any offer of composition the debtor might make.

In 1839 an act (2 & 3 Vict. c. 41) was passed amending in some particulars the existing bankruptcy law (e.g., giving a majority in number and value of the creditors the power to accept an offer of compromise), but introducing no important modification of the long established procedure and control.

Another thorough-going recodification of the bankruptcy laws was completed in 1856 (19 & 20 Vict. c. 79) after much deliberation, in which the professional accountants of Scotland played no small part. The net result, as already suggested, was to preserve in the latest statute and to improve where needed the basic procedure established eighty-four years before in 1772. If the bankruptcy laws of 1856 were affected by the opinions of the Scottish accountants of the day, the profession in Scotland was undoubtedly much influenced by the existence of the sound and orderly statutes of earlier days. The Scottish laws, by providing so clearly a place for skilled technicians in law and accounts (factors, trustees), undoubtedly fostered the growth of a body of men relying upon their own merits for success. The early English laws, while in a sense they opened the way for skilled services, at the same time placed much responsibility in the hands of officers poorly qualified for the exacting work. Many questions which in Scotland would be submitted to accountants were in England dealt with by the masters in chancery.

It is perhaps not far from the truth to say that in this difference in the bankruptcy laws of the two countries lies some of the explanation of the reason why professional accounting was firmly established to the extent of justifying professional societies in Scotland almost a generation before it was in England (1854 compared with 1870). While the English laws undoubtedly occasioned a good deal of work for accountants, the statutes required a large amount of "tinkering" to make them equitable and to give them the sound stability so necessary to secure full public confidence and honest use.

REFERENCES

1. E. T. Powell, *Evolution of the Money Market,* p. 330.

2. Locker, in *The British Almanac,* 1867, p. 5.

3. Locker, *op. cit.,* p. 12.

4. O. C. Lightner, *History of Business Depressions,* p. 65.

5. 34 & 35 Henry VIII, c. 4.

6. 13 Elizabeth c. 7.

7. 23 James I, c. 19.

8. 14 Charles II, c. 24.

9. 4 Anne c. 1.

10. 6 Geo. IV, c. 16.

11. 1 & 2 Wm. IV, c. 56.

12. 12 & 13 Vict. c. 106.

13. *The Accountant,* June 16, 1877.

14. George Yard, speaking before the London Accountant Students Society, reported in *The Accountant Student's Journal,* May 1, 1883.

15. B. Worthington, *Professional Accountants,* pp. 47, 69; Brown, *History of Accounting and Accountants,* p. 324.

16. 24 & 25 Vict. c. 134.

17. *Deacon on Bankruptcy*—3d ed. pp. 699, 702.

18. 33 Vict. c. 71.

19. *Whitaker's Almanac,* 1873, p. 303.

20. Edward Carter in the presidential address at the inaugural meeting of the Birmingham Accounting Students Society reported in *The Accountant Student's Journal,* May 1, 1883.

21. Mr. Justice Quain, quoted by Worthington, *op. cit.,* p. 72.

22. 46 & 47 Vict. c. 52.

23. *The Accountants' Journal,* April 2, 1885, p. 460.

XVIII. THE BRITISH STATUTORY AUDIT

A VIEW of industrial crises and bankruptcy statutes alone is not sufficient to present the nineteenth-century environment in which English professional auditing arose. The development of joint-stock companies also placed a premium upon technical knowledge and accounting skill. The general contributions of limited-liability corporations to the expansion of bookkeeping into accountancy have been considered in a previous chapter, and reference has already been made to the principal statutes concerned. At this point, therefore, attention need be directed only to specific sections of the several important companies acts in which accounting or auditing work is required or mentioned.

British experience with joint-stock companies in the past had not been a happy one. The extensive frauds in early eighteenth-century speculation in shares brought so severe a reaction as to place company formation practically under a ban for a hundred years. Slowly, in the first half of the nineteenth century, the advantages of joint-stock companies were impressed upon parliament, with the result that after preliminary legislation in 1825 and 1837, a new act was passed in 1844,[1] setting up the conditions under which companies with a joint stock might be legally formed by complying with certain rules concerning public registration. Particular care was taken to establish safeguards against uncontrolled actions of promoters and directors such as had contributed so much to earlier disasters.

The act required (Sec. 1) the registration of all joint-stock companies and prohibited the formation of any without registration. Registration made necessary a certain amount of publicity and official scrutiny of the contemplated project between the first provisional registration and the completed registration. That this formality had some effect is shown by the large number of companies which were proposed but never completely registered.*

With a like intention of establishing a check or control over directors, the act contained certain sections providing for the keeping of accounts by the directors and for the audit of the accounts by persons other than the directors (or their clerks). No certificate of complete registration was to be granted unless the stockholders in their original agreement appointed one or more auditors (Sec. 7); subsequent auditors were to be appointed at the annual shareholders' meeting (Sec. 38). Account books were to be kept (Sec. 34), and the directors were also required to make up a "full and fair balance-sheet," sign it and deliver it to the auditors. (Sec. 35). The directors were also required to send a printed copy of the balance-sheet and the auditors' report on it to the shareholders ten days before the general meeting and also to the registrar of joint-stock companies.

Within a few months this statute was revised and repassed as the "companies clauses consolidation act" of 1845.[2] It provided in more detail for the keeping of accounts (Secs. 115–119) and the preparation of statements by the directors, and added the specific qualification (probably thought to have been implied in the former act) that "every auditor shall have at least one share in the undertaking, and he shall not hold any office in the company, nor be in any other manner interested in its concerns, except as a shareholder." (Sec. 102). In another section (Sec. 108) the statute opened the way for the outside expert in these words:

> "It shall be lawful for the auditors to employ such accountants and other persons as they may think proper, at the expense of the company, and they shall either make a special report on the said accounts, or simply confirm the same; and such report or confirmation shall be read together with the report of the directors at the ordinary meeting."

Parliament's distrust of directors is evident in the care taken in these two statutes to ensure that the auditors should be representatives of the stockholders and subject to their control alone, and also in

* For statistics of new incorporations, etc., see the note on company registrations at the end of the chapter.

the precaution of requiring financial statements to be filed with the registrar. By these provisions, fraudulent promotion and operation of companies was to be made more difficult. The action of parliament thus required a separate check or control of another's stewardship. In principle this control is derived from similar practices of a much earlier day, when the lord of a manor himself inspected and tested the accounts of his stewards and bailiffs,[3] or specifically delegated that duty to a skilled and trusted personal representative, his auditor, as described in a previous chapter. In the nineteenth-century stock company the shareholders stood in the place of the lord of the manor, the directors represented the bailiffs or stewards of the estate, and the auditor, under the statute, still retained his place as the personal representative of the proprietary interest appointed to inspect the record of stewardship.

The auditors contemplated in the statute, however, were "amateurs," so to speak, not professionals; they were to be shareholders, although permission is specifically granted in the statute to employ accountants (i.e., professionals) to assist them. If such skilled assistance was not used, the audits were no doubt merely perfunctory and often quite inadequate because of lack of technical knowledge on the part of the auditors. This rudimentary audit was a simple process, consisting even in 1875 * in ascertaining that some sort of voucher could be produced for every payment and that the printed balance-sheet corresponded with the balances in the ledger. A writer in 1861, in a pamphlet[4] urging that accounts be examined by public (i.e., governmental) auditors, considered the audit under the statute of 1845 a "complete farce." The directors, he says, called a meeting of the shareholders and gave the auditor only ten or fourteen days' notice. The so-called audit then consisted of ticking off the balances in the books against the statement and marking the vouchers produced to cover the payments.

Inadequate and amateurish as shareholders' audits must neces-

* In *The Accountant* of January 1, 1886, Ernest Cooper, said that conditions were still unsatisfactory. The audit of the accounts of companies and charities, he wrote, was already to a large extent intrusted to chartered accountants, but general auditing was still in a great part and probably in a large majority of instances in the hands of unskilled, or at least incompletely qualified, persons. (p. 139). Also see editorials in *The Accountant,* January 30, 1875, and June 12, 1875.

sarily have been, they were far better than no check at all upon the directors' stewardship; and because the necessity for some such check was early recognized and provision made for employing skilled accountants if desired, the statutes of 1844 and 1845 laid a solid foundation for the development of a class of professional accountants.*

The manner in which this foundation was supplemented by the companies act[5] of 1862 is the next subject of immediate interest. The statute proper concerned itself mainly with the formation of companies and their winding-up, with the legal relationships which arose among the various parties concerned. Matters associated with the management and operation of a company were regulated by a long supplementary schedule called "Table A.—Regulations of management of a company limited by shares."

These regulations constituted what might be termed a recommended set of by-laws, and set forth the minimum requirements as conceived by parliament for a well managed company. By section 15 of the act these regulations were to be considered as applying to any company under the act "if the Memorandum of Association is not accompanied by Articles of Association, or in so far as the articles do not exclude or modify the regulations contained in table A. . . ." In other words, companies without their own by-laws or with by-laws in conflict with the specific regulations of table A were considered as operating under table A requirements. For present purposes, interest centers in the provisions of table A because the accounting clauses of the act of 1862 were found therein.

Briefly summarized the accounting clauses of the table were as follows: No dividends should be payable except out of the profits arising from the business of the company. (Sec. 73). The directors should cause true accounts to be kept of the goods, of money received and expended, and of creditors and liabilities (Sec. 78) and once a year should make out a balance-sheet and statement of income and expenditures and lay them before the general meeting

* A number of other statutes passed in the generation to follow also provided possibilities for professional accounting engagements, yet without specifically requiring outside experts. Some of these are briefly mentioned in the note on miscellaneous statutes at the end of the chapter.

of the shareholders. (Secs. 79, 81). Once a year, at least, the accounts of the company should be examined and the correctness of the balance-sheet ascertained by one or more auditors (Sec. 83) who might be members of the company (Sec. 86) and, after the first appointment by the directors, should be appointed by the company in general meeting. (Sec. 84).

Every auditor was to be supplied with a copy of the balance-sheet, and it should be his duty to examine it, with the accounts and vouchers relating to it (Sec. 92). These auditors were to report to the members "whether in their opinion the balance-sheet is a full and fair balance-sheet containing the particulars required by these regulations and properly drawn up so as to exhibit a true and correct view of the state of the company's affairs." (Sec. 94). To accomplish this the auditors might employ accountants or other persons at the expense of the company to assist in investigating the accounts. (Sec. 93).

From these provisions it is evident that the main accounting features established in the laws of 1844–45 were retained and, in some particulars, strengthened. The same sort of clauses were met in the new law concerning the appointment of the auditor by the shareholders in general meeting and the option of employing accountants to assist the auditors. The same responsibility was placed upon the directors to keep accounts and prepare financial statements, and it continued to be the duty of the auditors to examine the books and statements and report to the shareholders.

As indicating a tendency to strengthen the company laws in regard to accounting particulars, the following modifications may be pointed out. No dividends, according to the later law, should be paid except out of profits. This was a more positive and definite statement than the provision in the earlier law that no dividend could be paid which would reduce the company's capital. It is to be noted also that the earlier requirement of shareholding no longer applied to the auditor, though he *might be* a member.* The re-

* An evolution may be noted here. Under the act of 1845 every auditor "*shall have* at least one share" and may employ an accountant to assist (Sec. 102); under the act of 1862 the auditors "*may be* members of the company" and may employ

sponsibilities and duties attached to the auditor's examination and report were, under the newer law, much more precisely set forth. This marked a definite advance.

In addition to these modifications, the act of 1862 set forth a carefully detailed form of balance-sheet which was to be used by companies. Examination of details of the copy of the statement given on the following pages as table 3 will suffice without further comment to indicate the growth which had taken place in making over a mere list of debit and credit balances, as earlier balance-sheets usually were, into an analytical and classified presentation of assets, liabilities and capital.

It must be evident from this consideration of British company law in the nineteenth century that parliament was deeply concerned with securing adequate protection for the stockholders in joint-stock enterprises—and not without reason. The unrestricted flotation of joint-stock companies with transferable shares in the early eighteenth century had brought forth such a carnival of greedy speculation and shallow fraud that the public badly needed the protection of a "Bubble act." Not for a hundred years, and then very slowly, did it become apparent that fraud upon shareholders was not inherent in the joint-stock system and that regulation (in place of restriction) could reduce the evils while still permitting the good to result from the aggregation of small capitals.

The main purpose of the companies acts was to establish some degree of public control (that is, the necessary knowledge of the conditions attending company formation) and some counter-check upon the directors' responsibilities in managing the companies' affairs. The first was accomplished by requiring registration, scrutiny and related formalities; the second, by requiring the shareholders for their own protection to audit (inspect) the records and financial statements of the directors. The registrar of companies, therefore, had the power to deny registration to unfit projects, and the shareholders had the power, through the knowledge of conditions obtained from their representatives (auditors), to follow up

accountants to assist (table A, Sec. 86); under the companies act of 1908 no qualification in regard to stock holding by the auditor was mentioned and the item about employing an accountant to assist was omitted. (Sec. 112).

Table 3

BALANCE-SHEET PRESCRIBED BY COMPANIES ACT, 1862.—TABLE A.

BALANCE-SHEET OF THE CO. MADE UP TO 18 .

Dr. **Cr.**

Capital and Liabilities					Property and Assets.				
			£ s. d.	£ s. d.				£ s. d.	£ s. d.
I. Capital		Shewing:			III. Property held by the Company		Shewing:		
	1	The Number of Shares				7	Immovable Property, distinguishing:—		
	2	The Amount paid per Share					(a) Freehold Land		
	3	If any arrears of Calls, the Nature of the Arrear, and the Names of the Defaulters					(b) Freehold Buildings		
	4	The Particulars of any forfeited Shares					(c) Leasehold Buildings		
II. Debts and Liabilities of the Company		Shewing:				8	Movable Property, distinguishing:—		
	5	The Amount of Loans on Mortgages or Debenture Bonds					(d) Stock in Trade		
	6	The Amount of Debts owing by the Company, distinguishing:—					(e) Plant		
		(a) Debts for which acceptances have been given.					The cost to be stated with deductions for deterioration in value as charged to the Reserve Fund or Profit and Loss.		
		(b) Debts to Tradesmen for supplies of Stock in Trade or other Articles.			IV. Debts owing to the Company		Shewing:		
		(c) Debts for Law Expenses.				9	Debts considered good, for which the Company hold Bills or other Securities.		

TABLE 3

BALANCE-SHEET PRESCRIBED BY COMPANIES ACT, 1862.—TABLE A.

BALANCE-SHEET OF THE CO. MADE UP TO 18 .

Dr. | Cr.

Capital and Liabilities			£ s. d.	£ s. d.	Property and Assets			£ s. d.	£ s. d,
		(d) Debts for Interest on Debentures or other Loans.				10	Debts considered good, for which the Company hold no Security.		
		(e) Unclaimed Dividends.					Debts considered doubtful and bad.		
		(f) Debts not enumerated above.				11	Any Debt due from a Director or other Officer of the Company to be separately stated.		
VI. Reserve Fund.		Shewing: The Amount set aside from Profits to meet Contingencies.			V. Cash and Investments				
VII. Profit and Loss		Shewing: The Disposable Balance for Payment of Dividends, &c.				12	The Nature of Investment and Rate of Interest.		
						13	The Amount of Cash, where lodged, and if bearing Interest.		
Contingent Liabilities		Claims against the Company not acknowledged as Debts.							
		Moneys for which the Company is contingently liable.							

the directors' responsibility and to control their subsequent acts intelligently.*

It was quite incidental that these statutes, among many other results, should contribute to the formation of a definite profession of accounting whose practitioners were independent experts. The original intent was that a few shareholders would check the records of the directors and report to their colleagues. But here and there a few men, who had gained considerable experience with accounts, were already making themselves available for special services in this field as needed. Some of these, no doubt, had already been helpful to shareholders in companies organized under letters patent and were recognized as likely to be even more helpful to the shareholders who were selected as auditing committees under the companies act of 1844. Some such idea must have been present for, as has been indicated, the act was elaborated in certain particulars within a few months; it was especially made permissible for shareholder-auditors to employ "accountants" as outside assistants having more specialized knowledge than the general shareholders.

This was meager statutory recognition of the existence of men with special knowledge; but it opened the way. What was to follow would depend, of course, upon the manner in which the men concerned increased their capacity for service and their ability to secure more and more recognition for that capacity.

These nineteenth-century developments in extending the sphere and importance of bookkeeping were not in the least inconsistent with England's past; in fact, in the light of the surrounding conditions, the professionalization of auditing seems a most natural consequence. The need for independent check or control (inspection or audit) lies deep in human nature. When persons were given certain designated fiscal responsibilities in relation to governmental

* It is to be observed that audits under these conditions were not particularly related to the problem of granting credit, which receives so much attention under modern conditions in America. The issue under these statutes was not one of a company's financial condition in the sense of ability to repay loans, but rather its ability to repay (if necessary) the shareholders' contributions. Hence both at this time and under modern conditions (though for different reasons), the balance-sheet received more consideration at the hands of auditors than the income statement, although the primary service of accounting to the entrepreneur is in the means it affords for carefully calculating the net income of the enterprise.

revenue, manorial management or craft guild operation, some type of "audit" would suggest itself. The form which these conditions produced has been discussed in an earlier chapter.

When industrial society and a town economy had evolved far enough out of feudalism to produce business corporations and to give rise to industrial crises, the same needs for inspection and check were met in new situations and the same device for outside control was called into play. The financial responsibilities placed upon the directors of joint-stock business enterprises were not unlike those delegated to the officers in the feudal lord's household. And in the joint-stock company the need for an independent check upon the officers' activities was even more plainly evident, for England had had sad experience with uncontrolled stock promotions—experience which left responsible legislators and officers with no taste for stock speculation by which the welfare of the public might be threatened.

In framing the companies acts, parliament undoubtedly had in mind the need to protect shareholders and prospective shareholders against fraudulent promotions and directors' mismanagement. To ensure such protection would be good public policy. With a sense of the need shown by bitter experience and an historical knowledge of methods which had served an earlier day, it would indeed have been surprising if an audit provision had been omitted from the companies acts.

An indication of the same governmental policy of trying to protect the public against fraud is to be seen in the British bankruptcy statutes. However various the conditions may have been which brought about industrial crises, the fact remains that creditors (i.e., the public) suffered severely in losses from insolvent debtors and that there was ample opportunity for waste and fraud. In its bankruptcy laws parliament was trying to create an independent and disinterested control over the liquidation of the debtor's property. All this was as much in the public interest as was the joint-stock legislation.

A knowledge of accounts made men good trustees, other things being equal, for a correct presentation of the real situation must aid in the formation of good judgments by the creditors. These conditions naturally attracted men having such knowledge, and the possibilities of this kind of work would lead others to acquire the necessary skill. This was also true in regard to joint-stock companies, for a knowledge of accounts was quite necessary to testing adequately the directors' discharge of their financial responsibilities. Men with a knowledge of accounts were called in to assist the shareholder-auditors, and so well was their task done that finally the whole audit was placed in their hands.

If British audit procedures are compared with American audits, this background may take on an additional significance. The British auditing practice, as it developed during the nineteenth century, had nothing to do with a proposed request by the company for the extension of credit. No particular emphasis, therefore, had to be placed upon the liquidity of the firm's financial condition. It is significant also that the audit was not particularly directed toward an examination of the internal control of operations for the better guidance of managerial efficiency. The management was itself under financial scrutiny; the audit was an instrument for the shareholders' control over the discharge of the responsibilities which they had delegated.

The whole discussion of the development of British auditing stresses the subject of outside control and the ever-present background of governmental interest in the reduction of fraud in promotion, management and liquidation of business enterprises. It is not difficult to understand, therefore, why public accounting became a profession; there was little of competitive trade about its activities and there was more than a touch of public service. Its practitioners could be justly proud of their independence and could properly take a quasi-judicial attitude toward their duties.

NOTE ON COMPANY REGISTRATIONS

The figures which follow are arranged from data compiled from parliamentary documents by Leone Levi and reported in *The Journal of the Royal Statistical Society,* Vol. xxxiii, pp. 1-40 (March, 1870).

The companies act of 1844, providing for the formation of companies by registration, was passed in the midst of extensive railway developments and speculation. In the twelve years after the act (1844–1855

TABLE 1

NUMBER OF COMPANIES REGISTERED
1844–1855 INCLUSIVE

Year	No. companies provisionally registered	No. companies not completing registration	No. companies completing registration
Total	4 049	3 084	965
1844	119	119	—
1845	1 520	1 463	57
1846	292	180	112
1847	215	117	98
1848	123	60	63
1849	165	97	68
1850	159	102	57
1851	211	148	63
1852	414	304	110
1853	339	215	124
1854	239	107	132
1855	253	172	.81

TABLE 2

CLASSIFICATION OF COMPANIES
PROVISIONALLY REGISTERED
1844–1855 INCLUSIVE

Type of company	No. provisionally registered	No. completing registration
Total	4 049	965
Railroad	1 605	32
Insurance	411	203
Gas	361	253
Public Buildings	305	43
Mining	235	98
Manufacturing	209	81
Various	923	255

TABLE 3

NUMBER OF COMPANIES REGISTERED
1856–1868 INCLUSIVE

Year	No. companies provisionally registered	No. companies not completing registration	No. companies completing registration
Total	7 056	1 245	5 811
1856	227	61	166
1857	392	123	269
1858	301	111	190
1859	326	108	218
1860	409	104	305
1861	479	135	344
1862	502	112	390
1863	760	190	570
1864	975	193	782
1865	1 014	77	937
1866	754	28	726
1867	469	1	468
1868	448	2	446

TABLE 4

CLASSIFICATION OF COMPANIES
REGISTERED 1856–1868 INCLUSIVE

Type of company	No. provisionally registered	No. abandoned	No. wound up	No. remaining active
Total	7 056	1 245	2 837	2 974
Mining	1 419	259	721	439
Manufacturing	1 016	214	450	352
Gas	678	41	102	535
Trading	539	90	256	193
Public buildings	364	33	98	233
	4 016	637	1 627	1 752
Various	3 040	608	1 210	1 222

TABLE 5

NUMBER OF JOINT-STOCK COMPANIES
REGISTERED IN ENGLAND
1844–1884

Year	No. companies completing registration	
	1844–1869	1863–1885
Companies act 1844	—	
1845	57	
1846	112	
Crisis 1847	98	
1848	63	
Bankruptcy act 1849	68	
1850	57	
1851	63	
1852	110	
1853	124	
1854	132	
Companies act 1855	81	
1856	166	
Crisis 1857	269	
1858	190	
1859	218	
1860	305	
Bankruptcy act 1861	344	
Companies act 1862	390	
1863	570	790
1864	782	997
1865	937	1034
Crisis 1866	726	762
1867	468	479
1868	446	461
1869		475
Bankruptcy act 1870		595
1871		821
1872		1116
1873		1234
1874		1241
1875		1172
1876		1066

TABLE 5—CONTINUED

NUMBER OF JOINT-STOCK COMPANIES
REGISTERED IN ENGLAND
1844–1884

Year	No. companies completing registration	
	1844–1869	1863–1885
1877		990
1878		886
1879		1034
1880		1302
1881		1581
1882		1632
1883		1766
1884		1541

incl.) 4,049 companies were provisionally registered (i.e., projected), of which 1,520 were announced in the single year of 1845 immediately after the act was passed. There were 1,605 proposed railway companies in the total number. With the bursting of the bubble of railway speculation most of these projects were abandoned without having completed incorporation. In the one year 1845, alone 1,463 were abandoned.

The appearance of registered joint-stock companies of course follows the act of 1844; the speculative tendencies of 1846 are reflected in the large increase in the number of companies formed, and the next few years indicate the effects of the panic of 1847 in the smaller number of companies formed. The bankruptcy act of 1849 soon followed. A new companies act in 1855 introduced limited liability and this, together with the current monetary and industrial conditions, laid the foundation for the crisis of 1857, which in turn was soon followed (1861) by another bankruptcy statute. In the next year the whole of the company law of England was consolidated and amended. Then, in 1866 came another crisis followed by a new bankruptcy law in 1869.

It is not intended in table 5 to imply that a chain of perfect cause and effect existed which connected corporations, crises and bankruptcy. However, the implication would seem to be that changes in these three elements accompanied the gradual evolution of business out of the soil of national aspirations and general economic conditions.

NOTE ON MISCELLANEOUS STATUTES

1847, The gas-works clauses act (10 & 11 Vict. Ch. 15) *Sec. 38:* Undertakers must report yearly to the county officers on the receipts and expenditures duly audited and certified by the chairman of the undertakers and also by the auditors thereof, if any.

1847, The water-works clauses act of 1847 (10 & 11 Vict. Ch. 17) *Sec. 83:* (same requirements as above).

1852, The Metropolis water act (15 & 16 Vict. Ch. 84) *Sec. 19:* (same requirements as above).

1867, The railway companies act (30 & 31 Vict. Ch. 127) *Sec. 30:* No dividend shall be declared until the auditors have certified that the half-yearly accounts contain a full and true statement of the financial condition of the company and that the dividend proposed is bona fide, after charging revenue with all expenses which in the judgment of the auditors ought to be paid out of it.

1868, The regulation of railways act (31 & 32 Vict. Ch. 119) *Sec. 3:* Financial statements to be prepared and submitted to the auditors. *Secs. 4, 5:* Penalties for default in submitting statements to the board of trade and shareholders and for falsifying the accounts. *Sec. 11:* Auditor need not be a shareholder. *Sec. 12:* Board of trade may appoint an additional auditor. The act also prescribes in general terms the forms of the revenue statement and general balance-sheet.

1870, The life-assurance companies act (33 & 34 Vict. Ch. 61) *Secs. 5, 6:* Annual statements of revenue and a balance-sheet to be made in prescribed manner. *Sec. 10:* Statements to be sent to the board of trade and to every shareholder and policy holder. *Secs. 18, 19:* Penalties for defaults under the act or for false statements.

1871, The metropolis water company act (34 & 35 Vict. Ch. 113) *Sec. 38:* There shall be an auditor of the accounts of the company, being a competent and impartial person, from time to time appointed by and removable by the board of trade. *Sec. 40:* The auditor is to make half-yearly audits.

1874, The building societies act (37 & 38 Vict. Ch. 42) *Sec. 40:* Officers shall prepare annual accounts of receipts and disbursements and statements of its liabilities and assets. Every such statement is to be attested by the company's auditors and copies are to be sent to the registrar of joint-stock companies and posted in the society's office.

1875, The friendly societies act (38 & 39 Vict. Ch. 60) *Sec. 14:* Each year the society shall submit its account for audit either to one of the public (governmental) auditors or to two or more persons appointed by the society's rules. The auditors shall examine the general statements of receipts and expenditures, funds and effects, and verify them with the accounts and vouchers relating thereto and shall sign them as found correct, duly vouched and in accordance with the law.

REFERENCES

1. 7 & 8 Vict. c. 110.

2. 8 Vict. c. 16.

3. See the extract from the rules drawn up for the guidance of Margaret, Countess of Lincoln, 1240, Cunningham, *Growth of English Industry and Commerce*, Vol. I, p. 240, cited by Woolf, *A Short History of Accountants and Accountancy*, p. 87.

4. James Hutton, "Suggestions as to the Appointment of Public Accountants," *Hazlett Tracts*, Vol. 30, No. 6, London, 1861.

5. 25 & 26 Vict. c. 89.

XIX. AUDITING PROCEDURE

No material is available to indicate the character of the auditing procedure of the first half of the nineteenth century. In fact, certain contemporary statements concerning the scope of the accountant's work give the impression that auditing engagements were relatively infrequent.

Judging from the circular announcing James McClelland's entry upon public practice on his own account (1824) and from the petitions to the crown asking for a charter for a society of accountants in Edinburgh (1854) and in Glasgow (1855),[1] little emphasis was given at that time to auditing in the modern sense. The kind of work the professional accountants of that day felt themselves qualified to do include the following:

Bankruptcy and liquidation—
- Winding up dissolved partnerships.
- Acting as trustee for creditors of a bankrupt.
- Acting as agent for distant firms interested in local bankruptcies.
- Recovering old debts and dividends from bankrupt estates.
- Making up statements for laying before arbiters, courts or council.

Fiduciary—
- Acting as trustees of sequestered estates.
- Acting as managers of rentable property.

Insurance—
- Making actuarial computations.

Accounting—
- Keeping or balancing account books for business firms.
- Examining and adjusting disputed accounts.

The close relationship which the professional accountant had with certain fields of law is apparent in this classification of his services. The petitions plainly stress this fact. The Edinburgh petition is almost wholly given over to indicating accountants' intimate acquaintance with the law and to urging their ability properly to serve the courts as disinterested experts in many matters under investigation. The Glasgow petition says that the business of the accountant "comprehends all matters connected with arithmetical calculations or involving investigation into figures; it also ranges over a much wider field in which considerable acquaintance with the general principles of law is quite indispensable." In a letter quoted by Brown (p. 197), Sir Walter Scott, writing under date of July 23, 1820, about the qualities which a young man should possess to succeed in accounting, goes on to say "... the harvest is small and the labourers numerous in this as in other branches of our legal profession." The last phrase directly associates accounting practice with law practice.

In the last quarter of the century, however, and coincident with the beginnings of an accounting literature,* indications appeared that an expansion had taken place in the accounting side of professional activities. In the British accounting periodical literature of the 'eighties such writers as F. W. Pixley, F. R. Goddard, Joseph Slocombe, David Chadwick and Ernest Cooper referred to the accounting service which the chartered accountant was prepared to render. Such items as the following occur:

Give advice in regard to the forms and modes of bookkeeping.
Prepare accounts for litigation (as statement of affairs).
Make up income-tax returns.
Unravel confused accounts.
Detect details of frauds and defalcations.
Certify profits at the introduction of new partners or in seeking financial assistance.

It is evident that a period of about a generation near the middle of the nineteenth century witnessed an expansion in the scope of the services offered by professional accountants. While not forgetting the legal aspects of their work, accountants extended the accounting aspects. More emphasis was now placed upon auditing than had been the case in the first half of the century. It is to the

* See note on early professional literature at the end of the chapter.

details of these audits that attention will be directed in this chapter. Special consideration will be given to the objects of auditing as they were conceived at that time and to a brief outline of the items which constituted the program for conducting an audit.

As explained in a previous chapter, the statutory requirements of an audit for joint-stock companies were instituted for the protection of the stockholders. It was the British belief that the stockholders, because of their numbers, could not themselves operate the company, and that this duty was delegated to certain members as directors. Neither could the stockholders examine the records and accounts of the company, and therefore this duty was delegated to certain other members as auditors. Thus the stockholders had two groups of representatives: administrative (i.e., directors) and critical (i.e., auditors). The statutes plainly required the directors to keep accounts and to prepare accounting reports to be submitted to the stockholders; they likewise prescribed that these statements should be examined critically by auditors and supplemented by a report showing whether the funds placed in the care of the directors had been properly spent, as indicated by the books of account, or were still unexpended, as indicated by the balance-sheet submitted.*

As to the procedure of making an audit, we know that, from Paciolo's time down to the present, it has been an almost unvaried plan to call back the entries between books of original entry and ledgers—"the way to prick a pair of books over," as Richard Hayes (1739) called it. But this is not auditing; it is a part of bookkeeping methodology designed to attain an arithmetically accurate trial balance. A most natural addition to this simple checking for correctly transcribed figures was "vouching," which may be described as an examination of the circumstances and documents of the original entries.

That this item of audit procedure received attention even in the

* John Stuart Mill considered the joint-stock-company law of 1844 fully warranted by conditions, but felt that the capital should be required to be fully paid up and that such accounts should be kept (and made public if necessary) as to show "whether the capital which is the sole security for the engagements into which they [the company] enter, still subsists unimpaired." *Principles of Political Economy,* Vol. II, p. 402.

Middle Ages has already been indicated in chapter XVI relative to the affairs of the manorial steward of that time. The details of the procedures then followed in vouching the steward's accounts are unknown; but a document from the end of the eighteenth century gives us a glimpse of the practice at a somewhat later date. The following is a letter of instruction (with some parts missing in the original) to the factor of James Boswell's estate at Auchinleck, Scotland, dated 1792.

"Sum up the debit & credit sides of the cash book & see if the ballance corresponds with what

Examin every article of money received; if the article is rent, see if it corresponds with the rental Book; if the amount or part of the amount of a Bill or part of a Bill &c. compair it with the register or list of Bills which ought to be keept very accurately. enquire if any meal, oats, or wood have been sold and if there are separate books for any of these article see if the entrys in them correspond with the

I mention wood because some trees may have been blown since last year & the wood sold: enquire also if any fruite has been sold and if the amount is brought into the cash book see if it appears to be just.

In examining the side of the Cash book which contains money laid out, graet care must be taken; every article ought to be examined one by one, to see if it is such as should be allowed as far as relates to the quantity, price &c. & the vouchers must be compaired to see if they agree with what is charged in the cash book when the vouchers is an acct. not only the sum total is to be looked to but also the various articles of which it may be composed & the calculations checked or proved. The same operation must be done when in the cash book any sum is met with susceptable of calculation, as for instance paid to three men for such or such work at so much per day; received for so much meal at so much pr. peck &c. &c. The rental Book ought also to be carfully examined in order to see if the different sums in each acct. are properly stated according to the rent, and if the addition is just this will require to be done not in a cursory but deliberate manner and great advantages will be derived from it more than one point of view & not only by correcting or having the satisfaction so that there are none but also by this means the names of the various Farms, the rent of them, and their possessors will become more and more familiar to you." [2]

But auditing involves more than assuring oneself that the actual transactions are truly reflected in the original entries (vouching), that the original entries are correctly posted to the ledger, and that the balance-sheet agrees with the ledger. And the balance-sheet is more than a "detailed statement of the ledger account which is the culmination of the double-entry system of bookkeeping"; it is, in reality, a statement of the composition of the capital account of the enterprise concerned.[3]

If the balance-sheet were merely to conform to the books, it might be misleading because of the erroneous omission of elements needed to reflect the concern's true capital, or the inclusion of elements which, though arising in actual business transactions, might in some particular be incorrectly stated. The balance-sheet also has as a part of its purpose the presentation of the profit or loss [available surplus] of a fiscal period.* The statement therefore might be deceptive to the reader if its compilers made it a merely mechanically revised list of book balances and if they failed to give due consideration to any element which was essential to the calculation of the true profit and the true capital.

The balance-sheet is of great importance to the stockholders, both because it exhibits the composition of the concern's capital and because it indicates the profits available for dividends. Verifying such a statement must soon pass beyond the mere checking of arithmetical details and the simple examination of vouchers. Thus, it is quite understandable that the experience of accountants would sooner or later lead them to select a number of matters to which special attention was to be given that the statements finally presented to stockholders should not only reflect the recorded facts but also state the full truth as well.

For example, by the latter part of the nineteenth century it was held to be the duty of the auditors to see that the stock in trade was properly valued. A few writers were more specific and indicated that inventories (manufactured goods) should be valued at prime cost of raw material (plus freight and duties if any) plus the cost

* "What a company has beyond its stock or capital (*capitale salvum*) is profit (*lucrum*)"—*Socini Consilia,* 24, Col. 12 (1544), cited by Murray, p. 145. "The balance-sheet is an account of balances made for the purpose of showing whether there has been an increase or diminution of the capital of the proprietor. It is an account made for the purpose of answering the question: What has the business made or lost?" Wm. Sandeman, *The Accountant,* August 18, 1883. See also *The Accountant,* December 19, 1885, *The Accountants' Journal,* January 1, and February 1, 1886.

of direct labor,[4] or that cost price should be used if market price exceeded, but market price should be used if cost price exceeded.[5] In regard to receivables, the auditor was to see that provision was made for bad debts, but it is not certain whether a direct writing-off or the setting-up of a reserve was favored. Depreciation was another important element in regard to which the auditor's duty might frequently carry him outside the books of account. F. W. Pixley [6] calls the omission of provision for bad debts and depreciation "the most frequent error in the accounts of public companies," and further points out that the neglect of periodical depreciation entries allows a large loss to be shown when an item of equipment must finally be replaced, and that this may seriously interfere with the current dividend. The subject was important enough to be the occasion of a book in October, 1884: Matheson, *Depreciation of Factories*. Contemporary articles indicate that matters under discussion in this field included the questions of whether repairs should be charged against depreciation or against profit-and-loss, and whether or not valuations by experts should be made occasionally to test the book entries for depreciation.

The accountant was also to see that leaseholds and patents were properly amortized. That this was a matter needing expert advice is shown by the statement in *The Accountant* (October 15, 1881), "from our contemporary of the 17th ultimo," that it was a common weakness in hard times to increase by revaluation the amount at which freeholds and leases stood in the ledger. The comment is added, apparently by a professional correspondent, that, if properly audited, such a revaluation would only serve to create a reserve "specially guarded against dividends" and would not be permitted to influence the amount available for dividends. Accountants are of the same opinion today and still have to oppose the same proposals, although, to be sure, most "appreciation" projects now appear in good times when prices are rising instead of in hard times as appears to have been the case formerly.

Another element which would not usually come to light in a merely arithmetical testing of the accounts was the omission of one or more liabilities, either direct liabilities or contingent liabilities on notes receivable discounted or on insurance agreements. The professional auditor was expected to make these matters the subject of careful inquiry, as well as to see that the firm's borrowing power was not exceeded.*

It may be of interest to examine further the opinions of the auditor's duty and to present in more detail the items which were expected to be included in the usual audit program. The following summary is based upon several lectures given in the 'eighties before student societies and published in professional periodicals.[7] No one of these several lectures contained all the items in this audit program; the suggestions of the authors are here assembled into one program and organized somewhat differently from the order in the original presentations.

A RECONSTRUCTED AUDIT PROGRAM

In beginning an audit: Get a list of the books kept and the names of the persons authorized to receive and pay money; note the details of the bookkeeping system and plan the checking of the accounts; examine the articles of incorporation and the board minutes in regard to drawing cheques, signing notes, etc.

General instructions, cashbook: Examine the cashbook exhaustively as it is the root and foundation of all; report if the fair cashbook is punctually made from the rough cashbook; note any unusual receipt or payment; see that no additional expenditures are made on capital account except as authorized by the board of directors.

Vouching cashbook: Scrutinize every cash payment and require a satisfactory voucher for every item, compare cash receipts with the counterfoil receipt books; report if accounts and vouchers are submitted to the directors and whether they are systematically certified; initial or stamp all vouchers and tick all entries; list the missing vouchers and obtain the missing documents before the accounts are certified, unless the accuracy of the unvouched items can be tested in some other way. Check all additions and postings.

Day-books and journals: See that day-books contain only proper entries and that they agree with the quantities and prices on the invoices; ex-

* Borrowing seems to have been rather frowned upon in the 'eighties, one writer urging for the protection of stockholders that a limit be set upon credit, because companies saddled with debt in bad times and having no profits with which to pay were often wrecked. He further maintained that, should credit be extended to a company, it should rest upon the value of property and not upon the assurance of large amounts of un-called capital subscriptions, as the company could sell out and "have only men of straw to answer the calls." G. Auldjo Jamison, *The Accountants' Journal,* August, 1888.

amine all entries and transfers in the journal, and note any items of revenue charged as capital or vice versa. Check all additions and postings.

Ledgers: Check all postings of nominal and personal ledgers and scrutinize the nature of the entries; check all additions and balances; check balances to the trial balance and add the trial balance; look for erasures in the accounts and investigate alterations.

These instructions cover the so-called mechanical work of the audit. Several features may be noted: 1. that vouching is stressed, while the modern account analysis is not mentioned; 2. that there is no instruction for reconciling cashbook and bank-book (one writer in 1887 merely mentioned it); 3. that nothing is said regarding "tests" in place of a complete checking of details. This last possibility was not wholly overlooked, however. In the early eighties one writer in *The Accountant* (April 23, 1881) stated that complete verification was often impossible because the client declined to pay for more than a comparatively brief and superficial investigation. Consequently it was necessary to study how to make tests so that the verification made should be "practically sufficient." But so little is said regarding the way to test-check that the conclusion is inescapable that very little of it was done.

That part of the audit program related to the verification of balance-sheet items rather than to the mechanical work on the accounts also received some attention. But one emerges from a review of these instructions with the feeling that audit technique was weaker at this point than in the examination of bookkeeping details.

Securities and cash: Check all securities and examine all bills as to *bona fides;* test the reality of the assets and the existence of alleged money, securities and book debts; examine the bill books for past due, renewed or dishonored bills.

Debtors' accounts: Age the debtors' accounts and form your own opinion regarding their value; write off all dead accounts and make ample provision for a debt-reserve fund for the doubtful debts; allow a percentage for discount and allowances likely to be deducted; send every debtor a circular showing his balance to be deducted; and ask a reply regarding its accuracy.*

* The author says, "This gives a check on a great bulk but not all of the [cash] receipts." Apparently this procedure was not so much used for testing the accounts receivable balances as for vouching cash receipts.

Inventories: Study the mode of taking and valuing the stock on hand; see that obsolete patterns and tarnished goods are not included at the price of better goods; compare quantities and prices with those of previous inventories; see that all stock sheets are signed by the department heads and correctly carried to the general stock accounts; ask assurance that the stock has been taken at cost prices and allowance made for any depreciation; require the manager to sign the stock-book as a guarantee of its accuracy.

Fixed assets and depreciation: See that freehold land and buildings are stated at cost; note the distinction between new works and mere replacements; establish sinking funds at compound interest to extinguish leasehold properties; note if the usual and proper deductions are made in the profit-and-loss account for wear and tear and depreciation and for recouping capital expended on premises held on lease.*

Liabilities: Examine the mortgage register and check receipts and payments into the bank pass-book; see that the directors have not exceeded their power to borrow as stated in the articles of incorporation; include unpaid interest on mortgage and unpaid dividends among the liabilities; in cases of insolvency include liability for endorsements of discounted bills; obtain a declaration that all sundry creditors and other liabilities have been provided for, but in case of doubt add a round sum to total creditors by way of provision against unstated debts.

Capital shares: Compare share allotments with applications for shares and with memorandum of association; check the register of members for correct holdings, deposits and calls made, and reconcile with entries in the private ledger.

This is a summary of the audit procedure. A further word is necessary concerning certificates.

The statutes which required joint-stock companies to be audited did not at first prescribe an audit certificate. The companies act of 1862 and the banking and joint-stock companies act of 1879, however, required the auditors to report to the shareholders whether or not in their opinion the balance-sheet was a full and fair balance-sheet, properly drawn up so as to exhibit a true and correct view of the state of the company's affairs as shown by the books of the company. This in effect constituted a certificate. But it did not pass without criticism, for the last clause seemed to some people to

* Little is said regarding the method of calculating depreciation. One author, however, points out that the general practice is "to write off out of profit lump sums from time to time," but goes on to express his own preference for establishing a fund by a yearly percentage.

imply that little need be done by the auditor except a formal examination of vouchers and a comparison of the items in the statement with the ledger. Such a perfunctory examination would of course leave the possibilities of irregularities very largely uninvestigated and the "audit" would therefore be of little value.

Such a criticism is even more understandable when some of the contemporary (1883) certificates are read. "Examined the securities and found them to be in accord with the books and accounts of the bank"; "We have compared the balances set forth in this balance-sheet with the books and found the same correct"; "We compared the above statement with the books and vouchers and found the cash, bills and loans of the balance-sheet to be in accord therewith." [8]

These are indeed little better than the "futit, calculat and endit" certificates of the sixteenth century. They suggest the amateur, shareholder-committee type of audit. In cases in which professional auditors of the last quarter of the nineteenth century furnished such statements they had probably worked under severe limitations as to time available and fees allowed. They could therefore hardly be expected to take as much responsibility as the full certificate would indicate.

Nor should the last clause, "as shown by the books of the company," be construed as a substantial limitation behind which the auditor would choose to hide. The clause was written into the statute "to relieve the auditors from any responsibility as to the affairs of the company kept out of the books and concealed from them, but not to confine it to a mere statement of the correspondence with the entries in the books." [9] Usually auditors did much more than was implied in the wording of the certificate.

From even this brief consideration it must be evident that auditing procedure had become fairly well organized by the last quarter of the nineteenth century. Most of the outline represents good practice today, although modern conditions have made it necessary for the auditor to offer a variety of services in order to extend the scope of his examination or reduce the amount of detail as the engagement might require.

NOTE ON EARLY PROFESSIONAL LITERATURE

Although there were societies of professional accountants in some Scots cities in 1854 and in England in 1870, a professional literature—especially that dealing with auditing—was very slow to develop until after the societies of accountants in the English cities united (1880) in the formation of the Institute of Chartered Accountants of England and Wales.

The principal source of information concerning the opinions and activities of accountants prior to the organization of the institute is *The Accountant*, a periodical established late in 1874. There is little material available concerning the period before this time, except some general statutes and a small number of court cases dealing with matters of interest in accounting. These include a few cases in which the nature of net profit was mentioned and a few others about auditors' duties.*

During the first five years of its existence, that is up to 1880, *The Accountant* contained little material about auditing. Instead a great deal of space was given to bankruptcy statutes and court cases, to disputes and counter-arguments regarding the conflicting fields of work of attorneys and accountants, and to the discussion of the need for professional accountants rather than "amateur auditors" to carry out the provisions of the companies acts. The periodical, therefore, is not very helpful in disclosing the details of what auditors actually did when they were examining the accounts of an enterprise.

This deficiency of information about these early years might be made good, however, if two other publications could be found

* See the cases cited in chapter XIII on the subject of profits and the following in regard to auditors' duties:

Nichols Case, 3 De G. & J. 387, 441 (1858)
Spockman vs. Evans, 3 H.L. 236 (1864)
Mattock Old Bath H. Co., 29 L.T.R. 324 (1873)

Other cases in this last category for the next twenty years are:

Steel vs. Sutton Gas Co. 12 QBD 68 (1883)
Leeds Estate vs. Sheppard, 36 ch. D 787 (1887)
London and General Bank, 2 ch. 166, 682 (1895)
re Kingston Cotton Mill, 1 ch. 6; A. Mausen 631 (1896)
re Western Counties Baking Co., 1 ch. 617 (1897)

which are mentioned in the pages of *The Accountant*. The first of these is—

> *An Essay in the Qualifications and Duties of Accountants and Auditors,* by John Caldcott, London, Letts Son & co., [c1875].

The Accountant refers to this work (January 6, 1877) as useful, but remarks that there is no single work which explains completely "the multifarious duties" of accountants. A letter from a correspondent (January 20, 1877), in referring to this comment by the editor, says that such a complete work will be sought in vain, as "the only way to acquire a thorough knowledge of the business is by close application in a good office."

Apparently this discussion stimulated interest in writing about auditing procedure, for soon mention was made of the following:

> *Prize Essays on Auditing,* by Chas. H. Galand, Chas. J. Recton and John J. Dunn, published by the Society of Accountants in England, September, 1876.

But unfortunately the book itself does not seem to be available.

The year 1880 saw the formation of the Institute from the following societies:

Society	Date founded	Membership May, 1880
Incorporated Society of Liverpool Accountants	January, 1870	29
Institute of Accountants (London)	November, 1870	188
Manchester Institute of Accountants	February, 1871	103
Society of Accountants in England	January, 1873	286
Sheffield Institute of Accountants	March, 1877	32

In March, 1880, a royal charter incorporating these societies into one body was granted to "The Institute of Chartered Accountants in England and Wales." The membership of the new institute stood at 527, 224 fellows, 241 associates and 62 miscellaneous members. Before February, 1881, the membership (on applications received during 1880) had increased to 1025.

The influence of the institute was at once apparent. Admission by examination only was begun in July, 1882. The scope of these examinations is indicated by the following outline of subjects (*The Accountant Student's Journal,* August 1, 1884):

Preliminary examination—

Writing from dictation, writing a short English composition, arithmetic, algebra, Euclid, geography, history of England, elementary Latin, *options:* two of the following—Latin, Greek, French, German, physics, chemistry, animal physiology, electricity, magnetism, light, geology, higher mathematics.

Intermediate examination—

Bookkeeping, accounting, auditing, adjustment of partnership and executorship accounts, rights and duties of trustees, liquidations and receivers.

Final examination—

In addition to further questions on the topics in the intermediate examination: principles of the law of bankruptcy, joint-stock companies, mercantile practices, arbitration and award.

A syllabus for the Scottish examinations (*The Accountants' Journal,* September 1, 1886) shows an even wider range of subjects, especially in law:

Preliminary examination—

Writing from dictation, English grammar, arithmetic, English history, geography.

Intermediate examination—

Arithmetic, algebra, logarithms, English composition.

Final examination—

Laws of Scotland, bankruptcy, bills of exchange, partnerships, joint-stock companies, receivership and arbitration, succession [inheritance], life insurance, actuarial science, probabilities, life annuities, theory and practice of bookkeeping, trust and bankrupt accounts, auditing, procedure under judicial references.

With such examinations required, the need was increasingly evident for an accounting literature which would go beyond bookkeeping and special topics in law. As a result the 'eighties witnessed an expansion of material which had a truly professional nature. Some of this was expressed in a new text, *Auditors, Their Duties and Responsibilities,* by F. W. Pixley (London, 1881), which was destined to go through many editions and established the pattern for many later works. The table of contents of the first edition, taken from *The Accountant* of February 19, 1881, is as follows:

1. History of the law of companies.
2. Mode of appointing auditors.
3. Sections of the statutes regarding accounts and audits.
4. Principles of bookkeeping and audits (including the books prescribed by statute).
5. Nature and principles of an audit.
6. Forms of accounts published by companies.
7, 8. Important items in the balance-sheet and revenue account.
9. Duties and responsibilities of auditors.

Pixley's seventh edition (1896) followed the same outline somewhat expanded and with additional chapters on "the position of the auditor," "profits available for dividends," "certificates and reports."

The stimulus of the institute was also reflected in the periodical literature of the 'eighties. A change came over the nature of the contributed articles. Beginning with the autumn of 1882 much more space in *The Accountant* was given to auditors, auditors' duties, balance-sheet form, etc. In May, 1883, *The Accountant Student's Journal* made its appearance. Student societies were rapidly formed at different centers to prepare men for the examinations, and both journals began to print the lectures which were delivered at these meetings. Some idea of the scope of these discussions is indicated by the following summary of topics of the lectures in 1883–1885:

Law: Receivers and bankruptcy, estates and trusteeship, partnerships, companies acts, arbitration and awards, income tax, insurance, building societies.

Accountancy: Bookkeeping (railways, brewers, collieries, cities, etc.), auditors' duties and procedure, balance-sheet form and content, company accounts, depreciation, goodwill.

By this time (1885) the method of giving intstructions preparatory to the professional examinations had been worked out and the pattern of the professional literature established. From that time the development was chiefly one of filling in details of the outline.

REFERENCES

1. Brown, *History of Accounting and Accountants,* pp. 201, 207, 210.

2. Reprinted in *The Journal of Accountancy,* October, 1923.

3. Correspondence in *The Accountant,* November 11, 1882.

4. Lisle, *Accounting in Theory and Practice,* Edinburgh, 1903, p. 53.

5. J. W. Best, *The Accountants' Journal,* January 1, 1886. In 1857 the draft for a proposed uniform commercial code for the independent German states contained a provision regarding valuing inventories at cost or market. J. L. Weiner, *The Journal of Accountancy,* New York, V. 48, p. 195.

6. *The Accountant,* February 25, 1882. For further references to accruals and bad debts see chapter 9.

7. *The Accountant,* May 13, 1876, April 23, 1881, September 29, 1882, December 9, 1882; *The Accountants' Journal,* March 1, 1887. A first or second edition of Pixley, *Auditors, Their Duties and Responsibilities* (1881, 1882) would have been an excellent source had either been available.

8. *The Accountants,* October 13, 1883.

9. *re London and General Bank* (1895) 2 Ch. 692.

XX. GENESIS OF COST ACCOUNTING

COST ACCOUNTING is not as old by several hundred years as is mercantile bookkeeping by double entry. It is, in fact, of quite recent origin, essentially a product of the nineteenth century, which has been greatly extended and developed in the twentieth.

In a sense cost accounting introduced a new element into bookkeeping—one which it may not be amiss to designate as the only new feature of large importance appearing in bookkeeping between the formulation of double entry itself in the fifteenth century and the introduction of financial budgeting in the twentieth. Here for the first time the acquisition prices of goods were resolved into their constituent parts. There had been no earlier need for a synthesis of production cost prices. Production had been by the domestic handicraft system in which few worked for wages and no one was interested in calculating the profit which might result from such productive activities. Production for sales was like production for consumption—an occupation largely within the family. Trade, moreover, dealt with articles of handicraft production or with raw materials themselves, and the trader's acquisition prices were therefore known directly from his bargains—he would have no interest in thinking of his goods in terms of subdivided costs.

But when the factory system began to displace the domestic system, production fell under the direction of enterprisers who paid wages, bought materials and supervised the process of producing goods for the profit they could obtain by selling the goods created at prices above the costs. They had a motive for records, therefore, which the family or the solitary producer had not had. The latter, making no money outlay for wages, counted his return (above materials) as his own wage; the former could not gauge his degree of success or intelligently set his prices without some more or less systematic apposition of his returns and his several outlays.

Cost accounting, therefore, is one of the many consequences of the industrial revolution. The factory system, one element of that period of transition, raised new bookkeeping problems as well as problems following upon the use of machinery and power. The reason was that the factory system was a movement away from production which was for the most part for direct consumption, in which the articles constituted their own reward, and toward centralized production for commerce, in which the worker's reward was in his wage and the master's compensation was in his profit. The resulting cost problem was in reality a price problem related to calculating the profit and to bidding for work in competition. What the master must know was the acquisition price of what he produced, first so that he might judge what price to ask in bidding, second, so that he could value his inventory of finished goods when necessary and, third, so that he would be able to learn the cost to him of the goods he had already sold, and thus calculate his profit and put to a test his pricing policies. For the merchant who bought completed articles outright the amount of the acquisition outlay would be known directly and would be readily available for pricing both the inventory and the cost of goods sold in making the calculation of profit. In the case of the producer, however, these elements could be known only from a prior record and a synthetic computation.

The factory system thus raised new bookkeeping problems. When the productivity of the factory system was greatly increased by the use of power machinery, additional burdens were laid upon bookkeeping. Fixed-asset accounting was very greatly expanded, for much greater sums were invested in plant and equipment; indeed, fixed-property accounting (including an adequate conception of depreciation) was in most respects a late development. It had received relatively little attention in the trader's bookkeeping from the fifteenth to the nineteenth century.

Increased capital investment in fixed plant made necessary additional attention to adequate plant-expense analyses; there were maintenance charges, running expenses for light, heat and power, several varieties of superintendence and the like, in ever-expanding detail as production became departmentalized and integrated. In a word, "overhead" was born; and as power was utilized more and more the ratio of overhead to wages constantly increased. These conditions created their own problems.

Additional accounting responsibilities grew out of the intense competition which followed this finding of the key to large production. As competition grew keener, the interest of management in the analysis of costs and expenses increased. The search for indications of waste and of unprofitable products, for the means of increasing unit productivity and so on is still unceasing. This is the field of cost accounting, that field in which greatest stress is laid upon refinements in the classification of expenses and allocation of costs to units of products. It is here that attention is centered upon the correct association of units of income with units of the cost-outlays made to produce that income.

But most of these refinements came in the twentieth century, since they were associated with mass production by the use of large investments in power machinery—a condition not characteristic of the nineteenth century. The use of the inventions of the late eighteenth century was very slow to spread in appreciable degrees. In 1833, for example, there were still 200,000 hand weavers in Yorkshire, and many technical difficulties rendered it undesirable to use the power loom in the woolen industry until about 1850. Even though American interchangeability of parts (the basis of present-day mass production) appeared in the first quarter of the nineteenth century,[1] it was a long time before the principle received extended adoption, for a great deal of skill in machine design had to be developed before the modern miracles of production could be achieved.

The developments which are more directly associated with the factory system than with mass production were, however, as characteristic of the nineteenth century as mass production is of the twentieth. In fact, it might be proper to designate the matter discussed in this chapter as "factory bookkeeping," in order to distinguish the later refinements in cost allocation ("cost accounting") from the simpler problems of labor and materials accounting which characterized the years of transition from mercantile bookkeeping practice to factory cost finding.

The earliest examples * obtained of cost bookkeeping in the nineteenth century are drawn from two books, one French (1817), and the other English (1818). Since the French book by Payen is the more thorough of the two, as well as the earlier in date of publication, it will be discussed first.

The first illustration in this book [2] concerns a carriage manufacturer's production of three vehicles. To record the necessary facts two sets of records are used: a journal and ledger "in money" (*en argent*), and a journal and ledger "in kind" (*en nature*).†

JOURNAL IN KIND

FOR THE PRODUCTION OF THREE CARRIAGES

ABSTRACT OF MEMORANDA

Carriage (1)	305	carpenter's	407
Carriage (2)	102	memo	
Carriage (1)	475	smith's	
Carriage (2)	400	memo	875
Carriage (1)	440	lumber	
Carriage (2)	310	merchant's	
Carriage (3)	222	memo	972
Carriage (1)	340	wheelwright's	
Carriage (2)	100	memo	645
Carriage (3)	205		
Carriage (1)	70	saddler's	
Carriage (2)	65	memo	190
Carriage (3)	55		
Carriage (1)	345	painter's	
Carriage (2)	200	memo	575
Carriage (3)	30		
	3 664		3 664

* Stanley E. Howard (*The Accounting Review* for June, 1932) indicates that Savary (*Le Parfait Négociant,* 1675) suggested the use of a *livre de teintare* or book of dyeing since the man in his illustration was running a dyeing business in connection with his mercantile enterprise.

† It has elsewhere been pointed out that under the Roman empire "accounts of commodities like natural produce were kept separate from others in which the movements of money values such as cash, debts receivable and debts payable were recorded; in the accounts of produce and the like no commutation of the various commodities to money values took place." P. Kats in *The Accounting Review,* December, 1930.

Factory Ware-house	Carriage (1) amounting to	1 975	enterprise is discharged of accountability by the transfer to warehouse	3 664
	Carriage (2) amounting to	1 177		
	Carriage (3) amounting to	512		
		7 328		7 328

This "journal" is a simple analysis of labor distributed over three units of product and leads to the summary figures shown at the end where the cost of each carriage is assembled and the productive side of the business is shown "discharged" of the total amount. It is noteworthy that great care was taken by the author to obtain an equality of figures throughout and to subject the whole to the test of equality of totals.

The journal in money carries the record somewhat further; it is concerned with debts incurred and payments made rather than with the elements "in kind" (which we should probably call "production data") shown in the preceding journal.

JOURNAL IN MONEY

	Dr.			*Cr.*	*Profit*	*Loss*
The business is accountable for	3 664	Carpenter		407		
		Smith		875		
		Lumber merchant		972		
		Wheelwright		645		
		Saddler		190		
		Painter		575		
				3664		
The warehouse receives 3 carriages	3 664	The business is discharged of		3 664		
A buys carriage No. 1,	2 045	Warehouse is discharged by carriage No. 1,	1 975		70	
B buys carriage No. 2,	1 095	Warehouse is discharged by carriage No. 2,	1 177	3 664		82
C buys carriage No. 3,	637	Warehouse is discharged by carriage No. 3,	512		125	

Cash	3 777	Buyers A, B, C.	3 777		
Paid the above mechanics	3 664	Cash	3 664	195	82
	18 546		18 433	195	82

This reflects with unusual clearness the movement of values which took place in converting labor and materials into a new product and that product into cash to be used for paying those who contributed to the act of production. The sequence is as follows: The business receives (and owes for) the services of several persons; the warehouse receives (and owes for) the finished carriages produced by the workmen; the carriages then pass to the three buyers, who finally pay their debt in cash; and this cash is used to pay the mechanics. In the words of the author, "thus the business is the first debtor, the warehouse the second, the purchasers the third, cash the fourth and the mechanics the fifth debtors" (p. 12).

In this pleasingly direct way the duty of manufacturers' bookkeeping to record those conversions of service and transfers of values which inevitably occur during the manufacture and sale of articles is set forth with a clarity and simplicity of style which might easily be the envy of modern writers.

A second illustration drawn from the same source, this time of a glue factory, is also presented because its greater detail throws further light upon the cost-finding methods of the day. The entries are made in the author's journal without explanations and are reproduced here as given. Brief explanations (keyed by the figures in parentheses) are appended in the footnote, however, so that the specific transactions may be understood without the reproduction of the "day-book" used by the author.

JOURNAL OF ACCOUNTS IN MONEY

		Dr.			*Cr.*
(1)	The business (of manufacturing)	14 200	(1)	Roger, tanner	12 900
			(1)	Roussel, leather dresser	1 300
(2)	Cash	2 800	(2)	Leroy, agent	2 800
(3)	The business	1 000	(3)	Houel, proprietor	1 000
(4)	The business	300	(4)	Manager, expense	300
(5)	Manager has received	300	(5)	Cash, Sundry expense	300
(6)	Roger	7 000	(6)	Letters and bills	7 000
(7)	Roussel, money	700	(7)	Cash to Roussel	700
(8)	Mistral, coppersmith	3 000	(8)	Cash, coppersmith	3 000

(9)	The business	3 000	(9)	Desvignes	3 000
(10)	The business debit ac-		(10)	Workers	2 000
	count	2 000	(11)	Cash	2 000
(11)	Workers have received	2 000	(12)	Mistral, coppersmith	5 000
(12)	The business debit ac-		(13)	Mistral, for repairs	500
	count	5 000	(14)	Landlord (rent) credit	500
(13)	The business	500	(15)	Creditors for interest def.	300
(14)	The business	500	(16)	The business 6 barrels	
(15)	The business	300		The business 10 barrels	
(16)	Leroy, agent, 6 barrels			The business 3 barrels	
	Leroy, agent, 10 barrels			The business 5 barrels	
	Leroy, agent, 3 barrels		(17)	Payer of bill	3 000
	Guerin, agent, 5 barrels		(18)	Leroy, his notes	8 000
(17)	Desvignes	3 000	(19)	Bill-box	2 000
(18)	Bill-box	8 000	(20)	Storeroom of manufac-	
(19)	Mistral, note	2 000		tured merchandise	457
(20)	Guerin, agent	457		Storeroom of manufac-	
	Guerin, agent	294		tured merchandise	294
(21)	Jean-Jacquet, accepts 2		(21)	Guerin, 2 drafts	457
	drafts	457		Guerin, 2 drafts	294
	Jean-Jacquet, accepts 2		(22)	Jean-Jacquet	294
	drafts	294	(23)	Cash paid to H——	100
(22)	Cash received from J. J.	294	(24)	Storeroom of manufac-	
(23)	Houel debit	100		tured merchandise	18 948
(24)	Leroy, sale 19 barrels	18 948	(25)	Leroy remits in cash	8 148
(25)	Cash, from Leroy	8 148			84 592
		84 592			

(1) Tanning materials furnished on account.
(2) Cash advanced (loaned).
(3) Construction of furnaces.
(4) Due manager for expenses he had paid.
(5) Reimburse manager.
(6) Executed note payable.
(7) Paid part of debt.
(8) Cash advanced in part.
(9) Due for coal on account.
(10) Wages paid in the current quarter.
(11) Cash for wages.
(12)–(13) Copper boiler 3,000, several turn-cocks 2,000, repairs.
(14) Six months rent on lease of house at 1,000 liv. per yr. (500).
(15) Creditors agree to wait for payment until sales have been made.
(16) Sent to agents at different times, invoice after sales.
(17) Gave D—— a note on his open account.
(18) L—— has remitted two notes, 2,000 and 6,000.
(19) One of L——'s notes sent to M——.
(20) An account sales rendered by agent.
(21) Draw on buyer for merchandise.
(22) Cash remittance received.
(23) Paid on account.
(24) Leroy's account sales for 19 barrels of glue.
(25) L—— pays balance in cash.

This journal is posted to its own ledger, but the accounts need not be reproduced here. They are for the most part simple personal accounts or note accounts; there is no "capital account" and no "profit-and-loss account." One account (from p. 18), however, is given below to illustrate the form and to show the grouping of the cost elements in this "financial" ledger. The marginal numbers are inserted to refer to the transaction in the journal and do not appear in the original.

The business of manufacturing:

(3)	Proprietor for construction work ..	1 000
(1)	Materials	14 200
(12)	Utensils	5 000
(9)	Coal	3 000
(15)	Interest	300
(10)	Workers	2 000
(4)	Minor utensils	300
(14)	Rent	500
(13)	Repair boilers	400
(13)	Repair utensils	100
		26 800

to be used in the discharge of the account:		
Product sold by Leroy....		18 948
Product sold by Guerin	(457)	
	(294)	751
Proceeds from the 24 barrels of glue............		19 699
[Balance, 7 101]		

The reader is impressed by the incompleteness of the account from the modern point of view; we might expect it to be brought to a balance with the profit plainly shown. If this account were to be credited with an inventory of manufactured goods unsold and raw material unconsumed and with the value of the fixed assets which are in the account, the account would then be brought to a balance which would indicate the profit. But it should be remembered that this account was concerned only with the financial side (*en argent*) of the business; the operating side was the concern of the records *"en nature."*

The journal *"en nature,"* of this illustration is omitted since the details which it shows are unnecessary to the present purpose; the "ledger in kind" includes all the data needed to understand the presentation of costs and profits. (Payen, pp. 23-26).

These are "operating" accounts used to calculate the cost of goods manufactured and sold.* It is evident that careful and systematic attention was given to entering the inventories so that the remaining balances of the respective accounts would reveal the value consumed in manufacturing. It is especially noteworthy that a portion of the value of furnaces, boilers and utensils (all representing fixed assets) is transferred to the cost of the manufactured product. This sum was not called depreciation but was derived from the asset account after a figure for the (reduced) inventory value had been entered in it. No indication is given, however, of the basis for the inventory valuation.

LEDGER IN KIND

	Dr.		*Cr.*
Storeroom:			
Raw materials	14,200	Consumed	12,000
		Inventory	2,200
Shop:			
Raw materials	12,000	24 barrels of glue manufactured	12,000
Storeroom:			
Manufactured merchandise 24 barrels	——	Sent to Leroy 6 barrels	
		Sent to Leroy 13 barrels	
		Sent to Guerin 5 barrels	
		24 barrels	
Furnaces:			
Mason's work	300	As valued for the inventory	900
Iron	200		
Locksmith	150		
Bricks	200		
Plaster	50	Carried forward to the cost of manufactured glue	100
Lead	75		
Rough stone	25		
	1,000		
Workers:			
Wages in manufacturing of glue	2,000	As used in cost	2,000

* One of the accomplishments of modern accountancy has been the knitting together of these two sets of accounts into one coherent system and the reduction of internal transfers between accounts in the ledger to a routine.

Boilers:			
2 boilers	4,500	As valued for the invent.	4,100
Repair costing	400	Carried to cost	800
Utensils:			
2 skimmers	225	As valued for the invent.	400
4 funnels	275		
Repairs	100	Transferred to cost	200
Coal:			
25 loads	3,000	Consumed	1,000
		Balance, valued at	2,000
Sundry expenses:			
(1) Interest paid		Transferred to cost	300
creditors	300	Those remaining valued at	200
(2) Sundry utensils	300	Transferred to cost	100
(3) Rent	500	Transferred to cost	500

Again the records seem incomplete, because they lack a ledger account to summarize or assemble the various costs (credits) marked "carried to cost." This is one of the items needed to knit the two sets of accounts together which apparently had not yet been devised. But the approach to this was very close; most of the author's objectives were accomplished by an "abstract" of the ledger such as the following:

ABSTRACT OF THE LEDGER IN KIND

Asset inventory, or balance of which the business is charged on new account:		Costs of glue:	
		Materials	12,000
		Use of utensils (boilers)	800
Materials	2,200	Use of utensils	200
Furnaces	900	Coal	1,000
Boilers	2,100	Interest	300
Utensils	400	Sundry expense	100
Coal	2,000	Rent	500
Sundry utensils	200	Use of furnaces	100
		Wages	2,000
		The business has expended	17,000
Total to be charged to the business	17,000	There remains in kind	9,800
	26,800	Similar total	26,800

If one cares to check the items in this "abstract" with the credits in the journal, it will be found that the abstract allocates each credit into one of two classes, inventory or costs. The abstract is almost a manufacturing account in a modern sense.

By the use of later knowledge of cost accounts, it is easy to see how close this "abstract" comes to duplicating the account presented previously from the "ledger in money," that is, "the business of manufacturing" account. The abstract gives the inventory of equipment, etc. (i.e., 9,800); this deducted (i.e., credited) from the 26,800 total debits in the "business of manufacturing" account gives 17,000 as the cost of manufactured goods to be opposed to the 19,699 proceeds from sales and finished-goods inventory.

This shows how nearly the practice of 1817 approached interrelated cost accounts; the key to the union of the two sets of accounts lay in the entry necessary to bring together the inventories from the "ledger in kind" and the business of manufacturing account from the "ledger in money." But this key was not used. The practice of the time was content if the abstract at this point came into agreement with the business-of-manufacturing account through the equivalence of the two separately derived totals. By adding the costs (17,000 credits in the abstract) to the inventories (9,800 debits in the abstract), a total (26,800) was produced, which was in exact agreement with the total charged to the business in the financial records.

The "abstract" was therefore in reality an analysis of the financial charges to manufacturing and was made in order to separate the consumed and the unconsumed portions of the purchases. In the language of the author:

> "The task which the business has to accomplish by its accounts is to distinguish between those expenditures applicable to the cost of the product made and those which remain as inventoriable value. There then only remains to deduct the sum of the costs from the amount received from the sale of the merchandise to calculate the profit." (p. 27).

There is little to criticise in such a conception of the purpose of cost accounts; it is a well-stated objective. But the practical expedients necessary to work out that objective consistently and smoothly had not been developed. Yet one must marvel at the ingenuity with which the data were manipulated into these fairly satisfactory results. The wonder is, not that the methodology should seem clumsy and indirect, but rather that a way had been found so early which was so direct and so lacking in the complicated and voluminous "paper work" which was to characterize cost finding two generations or more later (discussed in the next chapter).

A few other items from this system of manufacturing accounts remain to be presented. They show still more plainly than the previous examples that the French author grasped the problem of cost finding as a whole. What follows is concerned mainly with showing the profits made and with "tying-in" the two sets of accounts through similarity of results.

ABSTRACT OF THE LEDGER IN KIND

The business has at its credit the proceeds of sales	19,699
There are to be added the articles not sold	312
Total product	20,011
The merchandise manufactured has cost	17,000
Profit produced	3,011

This second portion * of the "abstract" brings together the cost of manufacture (17,000 from the first section of the "abstract") and the proceeds from sales plus the inventory (20,011 from the financial account "the business of manufacturing"). The result is the profit from operations. This calculation, it will be noted, is from the comparison of sales proceeds and costs; the calculation which follows is from the comparison of assets and liabilities (Payen, p. 20).

* The author's "abstract" is here shown in two sections to simplify the explanations; in the original there is no such separation.

BALANCE OF BALANCES OF THE LEDGER ACCOUNTS

	Dr.	Cr.
Leroy		5,900
Roussel		600
Workers		—
Mistral		500
Creditors		300
Landlord		500
Manager		—
Notes Payable		10,000
Cash	5,142	
Note-box	6,000	
Jean-Jacquet	457	
Houel, proprietor		900
	11,599	18,700
Addition to balance after calculating the accounts in kind. Debit the business on new account:		
Storeroom	312	
Furnaces	900	
Utensils	4,500	
Coal	2,000	
Petty articles	200	
Materials	2,200	
Assets	21,711	
Liabilities	18,700	
Profit	3,011	3,011
		21,711

(resulting from the balance of the ledger. It is the same as that found by the account rendered by the business of the raw materials manufactured.)

Before deriving this "balance of balances," the author shows a trial balance of totals from the "financial" ledger. The first section of the tabulation is an incomplete trial balance of balances and compares in detail with the other trial balance except that "the business of manufacturing" account is omitted.* This omission is made good by the inclusion of the second section of the "balance of balances" as shown, the so-called "addition to the balance after calculating the accounts in kind." These "debits on new account," as the author also calls them, are the inventories; these and the 11,599 of other assets constitute the total of assets (21,711). This total less the liabilities (18,700) shows the amount of profit (the illustration had no initial capital investment).

This second computation of profit, it will be observed, was by the use of assets and liability figures. The first calculation was by the use of cost and sales figures. Both computations bring the same result, thus affording the equality test which has for so many centuries been characteristic of double-entry bookkeeping.

From this it is quite evident that the French methods, as described by this author, had succeeded in bringing manufacturing accounts under the control of double-entry bookkeeping in a rather complete manner in spite of many obvious defects from the modern cost-accounting point of view. How generally these methods were used is unknown.

Another glimpse of bookkeeping for manufacturing enterprises in the early nineteenth century may be derived from a few chapters of an English work[3] dated 1818 and already cited in the previous discussion of bookkeeping theory. Cronhelm, the author, had an excellent grasp of mercantile bookkeeping by double entry and in much of his theoretical discussion was outstanding among

	Dr.	Cr.
* Trial balance sub-totals as above	11,599	18,700
Debit balance of the "manufacturing" account (see p. 395)	7,101	
	18,700	18,700

This balance could be analyzed as follows:

Inventory of equipment	9,800
Inventory of merchandise	312
	10,112
Less profits	3,011
	7,101

Therefore, "the business of manufacturing" account could have been made to show the profit if the inventories had been entered.

his contemporaries, in spite of certain unorthodox bookkeeping practices which he used. But his is a very much less clearly organized exposition of manufacturing bookkeeping than Payen's.

Cronhelm's understanding of the essential nature of double entry as shown by his other chapters was so good that it is surprising to find his illustration of manufacturers' accounts so deficient. No doubt in writing his book he was so obsessed by his "invention" as to overlook the opportunity to explain clearly the use of bookkeeping in manufacturing. Cronhelm's attention was centered upon saving half the bookkeeping work of posting journal entries in equal debits and credits. His proposal (his "invention") was that all books of original entry be modeled upon the cashbook, which, as we know, is at once ledger account for cash and posting medium for the accounts which are contra to cash in the transactions. The center of his system is the "merchandise book," in which purchases and charges are entered on the debit side (and posted contra to the credit of the cashbook or to personal accounts of creditors), and in which sales are entered on the credit side (and posted contra to the debit of the cashbook or personal accounts of debtors). Such a book, completed at the end of a period by the entry on the credit side of an inventory of the goods and materials unsold, would furnish a remainder which was the profit or loss figure ready to be posted to its final resting place in the proprietor's capital account.*

This glimpse of Cronhelm's general methodology is a necessary introduction to a statement of the treatment he accorded the transactions peculiar to manufacturing. All costs (purchased materials, expenses, wages and salaries) are debited to merchandise in this "merchandise book," with voluminous details written into the entry, as was usual at that time. Besides the purchase of various grades of wool (his illustration was a textile factory), other expenses are found charged to merchandise, such as stamps and stationery, bankers' charges, taxes, carriage, dyeing for the month, millwright's work, coal and freight, "healds and slays." In the category "wages and

* Savary, in *Le Parfait Négociant* (1675), recommended a book for petty trade in which the left hand pages were used as *livre d'achat* [purchases] and the right hand pages as *livre journal de vente à credit* [sales on credit]. See, Stanley E. Howard, *The Accounting Review*, June, 1932. It does not appear however that any attempt was made to bring the two pages to a balance.

salary" are found entries for the salaries of "overlookers" (foremen) and clerks, and the wages of the textile workers themselves. This last item of wages deserves a separate word.

Apparently a large amount of responsibility devolved upon the "overlookers" in relation to labor costs, for these foremen kept the payroll records from which the wage entries were made.* These records must have been kept in considerable detail, for an entry in the merchandise book (and cashbook) showed the following facts:

March 8 *to cash*—for wages and petty expenses this week.

Sorting, carding, spinning as per book A	178	15	9
Weaving, milling, etc. as per book B	193	15	10
Dressing, pressing, packing, etc. as per book C ..	181	4	8

Thus there was in existence in the original memorandum books a rough classification of labor costs corresponding to the three textile processes of spinning, weaving and finishing; and no doubt these details, with information regarding the quantity of work produced, gave the proprietor such unit cost figures as he needed. But the double-entry records provided no separation and analysis of costs by processes or by lots of goods.

In some respects the records of materials and manufactured cloth were in better form than the labor records; yet here, too, the final touch was lacking to unite the material records consistently with the financial records of purchases, payments, etc. The author lays stress upon the observation that comparatively little attention has been given to accounting for materials, and holds that there is no difference between losses by fraudulent entry and by embezzlement of goods in a warehouse. (p. 44). With this logic as a basis he presents a well worked-out system of material records, and sounds a very modern note when he states that three accounts are needed, one each for raw materials, goods in the process of manufacture

* "In large manufactories, the unlimited detail of expenditure requires a number of subordinate Books in order to disburthen the cash and merchandise accounts [book?] from minute entries and accordingly in this concern the overlookers of the woolshop, the factory, and the warehouse, keep distinct Books for the wages and petty expenses in their respective departments. The overlooker frequently requires several Day Books and a ledger, comprehending a little system of accounts within themselves; but in subordination to the Principal Books, they are mere memoranda which transmit their periodical additions." (Cronhelm, p. 127).

and manufactured goods. But his "invention" to save posting leads him to keep each of these accounts in a separate book.*

These three materials books are excellent models for later day "stores ledgers," and, in view of their early date, may deserve some further description. The wool book is debited, in quantities and by grades, for the wool bought and credited for "all applications to manufacture." The balance is the quantity unapplied. The manufactory book is debited with the applications of the raw material, not in pounds of wool, but in the quantity of manufactures [pieces of cloth] it ought to produce "according to the rules and proportions which are established in all regular and well managed concerns." It is credited with all manufactured goods, and the balance represents the goods in the process of manufacture. The finished-goods book is debited with all manufactures completed and credited for all sales or consignments. The balance shows the manufactured goods on hand unsold. (p. 45).

These records, it is to be noted, were kept in quantities only. Wool was recorded by weight and grade in separate columns on both debit and credit sides. The last column on the right side of the credit page showed the number of pieces of cloth which the quantity of wool transferred should produce. In the other books the unit of record is not pounds (quantity) but pieces [bolts?] of cloth. Here, too, the record is subdivided into types of cloth ("Casimires," etc.) and into four grades under each type. Money values were not shown in these three material-record books.

It seems that it would have been easy to carry money values with quantities and to add a suitable classification of labor costs to these books, thus securing a really systematic accounting for prime cost. But the step was too great to be taken at that time. Many of these data must have impressed the authors of that day as not quite proper bookkeeping material; bookkeeping was still under the spell of its original association with debts and trading exchanges. Both Payen and Cronhelm, as has been seen, were unable to bring themselves to go so far as to incorporate purely manipulative transac-

* What he saved in posting, however, was more than offset by missing the unity which would come from having a clear separation of his chronological record and his classified record. Clarity of record, we now believe, is more important than saving some of a bookkeeper's time.

tions (i.e., transactions not involving persons or payments) as an integral part of the traditional financial bookkeeping. Payen preserved the separation of operations and exchanges by using two distinct sets of records; Cronhelm kept the basic operating data in memoranda poorly coördinated at best with the financial records.

Apparently bookkeeping was then only beginning to be dimly perceived as something which could be more than a financial record of buying and selling, of owing and being owed, of paying and collecting debts. Non-financial transactions, such as adding the cost of labor acquired and material bought or transferring the cost of material from storehouse account to factory account and thence to warehouse account, were strangers among the kinds of transactions which had been familiar for perhaps three hundred years or more. To fit such newcomers into the long established scheme was no easy task; it necessitated a new view of the purposes and possibilities of bookkeeping.*

One further detail in the presentation of manufacturing accounts by Cronhelm remains to be discussed. This is the matter of inventories. As has been explained, the material-record books showed plainly the quantities of goods on hand. These inventory figures did not rest there, however, but were made use of to bring the merchandise book to a stage of completeness which permitted the calculation of the total net profit.

The author presents an inventory sheet which draws its quantities from the materials books and shows them extended into money values. Goods in process are noted as "averaged at the middle stage." Unit prices are not stated, and the data given are insufficient to enable the reader to calculate from the record what the prices were. Thus the author either overlooked one of the main functions of cost records (pricing inventories) or he inadvertently omitted to explain the matter. The grand total of those inventory figures, however, is properly placed in the credit side of the merchandise book and the excess of the two sides thereafter is labeled "to profit."

* The elasticity of bookkeeping as an instrumentality of record still astonishes us a hundred and thirty years later, for it is still able to shoulder added responsibilities, such as standard costs.

Few bookkeeping texts of the nineteenth century included a consideration of manufacturing accounting. The chapters in Payen and in Cronhelm, with all their incompleteness from the modern point of view, are none the less exceptional and superior to the meager presentations of other writers in the first three quarters of the century. A few examples will serve to indicate the contrast.

One writer before 1800 (Robert Hamilton) [4] gives a few pages to the books and accounts of "artificers and manufacturers." He mentions a book of materials in which quantities purchased and consumed are entered; a book of wages with names of workers, number of days, rates of pay; and a book of work "where the quantities of material delivered to journeymen, the quantities of wrought goods received in return, ... the value of the material and wages and the value of the wrought goods are entered in separate columns."

Because values as well as quantities are systematically entered in the book of work, this record is superior in this respect to the material records described by Cronhelm thirty years later. Hamilton differs from Cronhelm also in another particular, namely, in attempting more explanations of the important ledger accounts. The ledger, he states, besides containing accounts for persons, profit and loss, stock, cash, etc., should also have accounts "for the different branches under which the expense of the business may be distributed, as materials, wages, upholding of machinery [maintenance?], rents, excise, incident charges, etc." He also briefly describes "a general accompt of the trade or manufacture," which is debited at the end of the year "for the balances of the accompts of materials and other expenses" and credited for "the value of the goods manufactured." The balance, after allowing for the value of the goods not completely manufactured, is said to show loss or gain. His account for manufactured goods is described as being debited monthly for the quantity made and credited for sales. The account will balance, the author says, by the value of goods on hand "if the prices be constant." But if the prices vary, the balance compared with the value on hand per inventory will show the gain or loss by the alteration.

While this author is obviously trying to unite all of the costing elements and the inventory in certain ledger accounts (a thing which Cronhelm and Payen did not attempt), he comes perilously near to making a sad mess of the explanations. The subdivision of expenses is an excellent suggestion for so early a period, but the use of his "general accompt of the trade" and his account for manufactured goods is by no means satisfactory. Perhaps he was striving to make a "goods in process" account of the one and a "finished goods" account of the other. If this was his object, it is an error to say that the balance of the former would show loss or gain; since it is debited for costs and credited for goods manufactured (at cost prices), the account should balance except for any partly finished inventory. His manufactured-goods account is better, for naturally the account will balance to the amount of unsold goods if both the debits (goods produced) and the credits (goods sold) are priced at cost ("if the prices be constant"); and likewise it is correct to say that the account will show gain or loss "if the prices vary," that is, if debits are at cost and credits are at selling prices.

Hamilton wrote a generation before Cronhelm; a generation after Cronhelm the textbooks, if they mentioned the subject at all, generally failed to do as well as he did in explaining manufacturing accounts. F. C. Krepp's book in 1858 is an example.[5] He makes a show at writing about "manufacturers' system" (p. 151) but gets little beyond a raw-materials book and a goods-produced book in quantities and kinds. These are apparently used to calculate quantity inventories. The multiplication of these quantities "with the respective average prices" produces "an exact estimate of the actual value of the stock." The author, however, says nothing about how to determine "average prices." Neither Hamilton nor Krepp succeeded in describing a comprehensive system of keeping factory accounts, although they gave attention to some phases which Payen and Cronhelm did not. But cost accounting had come into existence.

REFERENCES

1. Alford, L. P., *Laws of Management,* New York, 1928, p. 53.

2. Payen, Anselme, *Essai sur la tenue des Livres d'un Manufacturies,* Paris, 1817, pp. 8–12.

3. Cronhelm, F. W., *Double Entry by Single,* London, 1818.

4. Hamilton, Robert, *Introduction to Merchandise,* Edinburgh, 1788.

5. Krepp, Frederick C., *Statistical Bookkeeping,* London, 1858.

XXI. COST DEVELOPMENTS IN THE LATE NINETEENTH CENTURY

MANUFACTURING, during most of the nineteenth century, was itself very much in process of development; hence it is not surprising that the bookkeeping textbooks of the first three quarters of the century for the most part failed to present adequate methods for keeping manufacturers' accounts. The account-problems of the factory had to make their appearance before ways of solving them would be sought. Payen and Cronhelm may therefore be thought of as pioneers who sensed the recording problems of the factory while it was as yet a relatively young institution.

But judging from the available books, the last quarter of the century, particularly the last fifteen years, saw manufacturers' accounts well organized and explained, although, of course, not with twentieth-century completeness. Three notable English books of this short period deserve extended consideration at this point.[1] Since the authors (Garcke and Fells, Geo. P. Norton and J. S. Lewis) were experienced men (factory managers, chartered accountants, etc.) their books may be accepted as representing the best thought and practice of their day.

There is no necessity to describe at length the ramifications of the system of records advocated by the respective authors. It is desirable only to give a picture of English cost accounting in the 'eighties and 'nineties. In order to do this, at least two different aspects of the subject require examination: (a) the coördination or absence of coördination between cost records as such and commercial bookkeeping by double entry and (b) the treatment accorded to the charges for overhead expenses.

In Norton's exposition the separation of commercial accounts and manufacturing records is quite distinct. In fact the author takes a definite stand in favor of such a separation. "Accounts of manufacturing departments," he writes, "should be entirely *supplemental* to the trading account,* and they should neither interfere with nor form a part of the ordinary bookkeeping. . . . The intention of including everything in one comprehensive system of double-entry is perfectly right, but the method is altogether injudicious." (Norton p. 219).

Norton's explanations of cost accounting methods center about the trading account and the manufacturing account, the former, a careful classification in statement form of the details of that important account, and the latter, a statement made up from data for the most part accumulated outside the account books. The trading account (or statement) is reproduced on pages 342 to 344.

Section I of this enlarged trading account sets in contrast the total prime costs (materials and wages) and the income from sales; and, after making allowances for the inventory of goods in process and in warehouse,† carries the balance [prime cost] forward to section II. Section II shows discount on purchases as an income item and sub-divides the expenses into three divisions, namely, standing expenses (mill), standing expenses (warehouse and office) and general charges. The balance of this section is labeled "profit" and carried forward to section III where interest on loans and capital and income tax are deducted, and the remainder is then divided between the two partners and transferred to their respective capital accounts.

The feature of this account which probably impresses the reader most is the division into sections separating the manufacturing

* At the end of a paper on "Defalcations and How to Prevent Them" (*The Accountants' Journal*, London, March 1, 1887) F. R. Goddard said: "Cost books, being supplemental to, and outside of, the commercial books can not be used for the purpose of embezzling."

† Inventories, according to Norton (p. 259), should be priced as follows:

Raw materials, at cost price plus carriage, brokerage, and less vendors' discount.

Goods in process, at cost of material (as above) plus the usual trade price for the processes through which the goods have passed.

Piece goods, finished and on order, at selling price less an estimate for commissions, carriage, returns, damage, discounts, etc.

Piece goods, not on order, at selling price less an allowance as above and also for possible depreciation, for warehouse expense, selling expense, selling profit.

"If preferred," the author continues, "salable goods may be priced at cost price, calculated at the cost of the year plus the usual trade charges for the processes of manufacture, but the selling price is usually a more reliable basis."

NORTON'S TRADING ACCOUNT

[left folio]

Dr.	Trading Account,	
To *Stock on hand,* viz.:—		
Material in process	xxx	
Finished pieces	xxx	xx
" Material consumed		xxx
" Dyewares consumed		xxx
" Chemicals, Soap, Size, Oil &c., consumed		xxx
" Outwork		xxx
" Packing Materials consumed		xxx
" Carriage		xxx
" Wages		xxx
		xxx
" Balance to Section II		xxx
		xxx

	Trading Account,	
To *Standing Expenses (Mill)*:—		
Mill Managers' Salaries	xxx	
Mechanics, Joiners, and Plumbers' Wages	xxx	
Watchmen and Timekeepers' Wages	xxx	
Motive Power Account	xxx	
Rent, Rates, Taxes, Gas and Insurance	xxx	
Mill Furnishings, Repairs and Renewals to machinery	xxx	
Stables	xxx	
Mill Building Repairs	xxx	
Incidentals	xxx	
Depreciation, Plant and Machinery	xxx	
Cards	xxx	
		xxx
To *Standing Expenses (Warehouse and Office)*—		
Stables	xxx	
Rents, Rates, Taxes, Gas and Insurance	xxx	
Incidentals	xxx	
Warehouse and Office Salaries	xxx	
Travellers' Salaries and Expenses	xxx	
Commission	xxx	
Depreciation, Warehouse & Office Fittings	xxx	
		xxx
To *General Charges*:—		
Bank Charges	xxx	
Discount on Sales	xxx	
Bad Debts	xxx	
		xxx
Balance Profit		xxx
		xxx

	Trading Account,	
To Interest on Loans and Capital	xxx	
" Income Tax	xxx	
		xxx
" Summers, Benjamin, two-thirds	xxx	
" Blackburn, William, one-third	xxx	
		xxx
		xxx

NORTON'S TRADING ACCOUNT

[right folio]

Section I		Cr.
By Sales	xxx	
Less Returns and Allowances	xxx	
" Commission Work		xxx
" *Stock on hand:—*		
Material in process	xxx	
Finished pieces in Warehouse	xxx	
		xxx
		xxx

Section II	
By Surplus from Section I	xxx
" Discount on Purchases	xxx
	xxx

Section III	
By Balance down	xxx
	xxx

overhead expenses (standing expenses, mill) from the prime cost for materials and wages. The author explains this subdivision (p. 217) as being desirable, because any change in the percentage relationship between the balance of section I and the sales figures will be the result of altered prices (for materials, wages or sales). Any variation in the standing expenses under section II (unless accounted for by a large increase or decrease of production) is held to indicate economy or extravagance in the working expenses, for "any reasonable addition to sales . . . will increase the surplus of section I without appreciably adding to the expenses under section II," (p. 218).

This subdivision seems strange since the modern reader is inclined to expect the account to show the calculation of the cost of goods manufactured and to furnish the basis for unit cost prices to be used in computing inventory valuations. But it is to be observed that the trading account presented by Norton had no such purpose; it is not analogous to a present-day manufacturing account, which is part of a system of records in which the commercial and the factory bookkeeping are coördinated in one system. But these accounts are from the commercial ledger of the textile factory; the cost records proper are separate and independent. This means that the trading accounts are designed to deal with expenditures rather than costs and to show a calculation of final profit rather than the cost of manufactured goods.*

* Several subordinate accounts in the commercial ledger, however, show certain characteristics now associated with cost accounting. The stable account is one. On the debit side appear: horses, supplies, blacksmiths' wages, teamsters' wages (the latter transferred from the wages account); on the credit side are: balance carried forward (as an asset), an amount transferred to mill account, and another sum transferred to warehouse account. This account-type is now well recognized and extensively used in redistributing the charges for service departments.

Other modern elements also appear. Accrued expense unpaid and expense paid in advance were recognized in the subordinate accounts by an entry "to reserve." In the rent and power, gas and insurance account (p. 46), for example, the following inserted entry appears on the debit side:

June 30, to reserve viz:—		
Rent to June 30	xx	
Gas do	xx	
		xx
less fire insurance paid in advance		x
		£ 144 4 0

This "reserve" of £ 144 4 0 was then carried forward below the ruling as a balance on the credit side for the next period.

Norton's cost records are separate from the commercial accounts and are designed to allocate costs to departments and processes. This would make it possible for the manufacturer to compare his figures with the usual trade charges at which he could have had his goods processed elsewhere. The focus of these separate records was the so-called "manufacturing account," which was an independent statement and not a true ledger account, as will be shown presently after the sources of its data have been mentioned.

The foremen of the several process departments keep records of the quantity of work done each week under their supervision; these quantity-data are assembled in the central office and priced, according to the manufacturing departments or processes, at the trade (or outside) price for similar work. Another preliminary to constructing the manufacturing account is an analysis by manufacturing processes of the expenditures shown in the trading account in the commercial books. This analysis sheet (Norton, p. 196) has column headings for goods, woolen carding and spinning, worsted combing and spinning, weaving, dyeing, finishing and pattern making. In addition to this there is a storekeeper's report of the quantities of materials supplied to the separate processes and a pay-ticket analysis of wages by processes. Standing expenses, mill (that is, manufacturing overhead), are distributed throughout the process columns of this master analysis according to proportions which will be discussed presently in a separate section. With these data assembled, it is possible to construct a manufacturing account like the example below.

The first section of this manufacturing statement sets in contrast the cost of the materials consumed and the trade-price cost for processing on the one hand with the sales prices and stock unsold on the other. The process cost data are those obtained from the foremen's reports of work done. The "gross selling profit" which brings the section to a balance therefore represents the profit which would have appeared had the manufacturing been "put out" to specialists in each process at the current prices for such work.

In the second section of the statement the warehouse and office standing expenses and the general charges are entered on the debit side at the same amounts as in the trading account. On the credit

MANUFACTURING ACCOUNT

[left folio]

Dr.	Manufacturing Account,		
To Stock on hand		xxx	
" Material		xxx	
" Outwork		xxx	
" Packing Materials		xxx	
" Carriage		xxx	
			xxx
" Pattern Making (cost exclusive of Material)			xxx
" PROCESSES OF MANUFACTURE, at Trade Prices viz.:—			
Woolen Spinning Department			
Condensing and Spinning	xx		
Twisting	xx		
Winding	xx		
		xxx	
Worsted Combing & Spinning Dept.			
Combing	xx		
Spinning	xx		
		xxx	
Weaving Department			
Warping and Winding	xx		
Weaving	xx		
		xxx	
Dyeing Department			
Dyeing Woolen Materials	xx		
" Tops	xx		
" Yarns	xx		
" Pieces	xx		
Extracting	xx		
		xxx	
Finishing Department			
Scouring	xx		
Mending	xx		
Finishing	xx	xxx	xxx
			xxx
" Balance—Gross Selling to Section II			xxx

Manufacturing Account,	Section II	
To *Warehouse & Office Standing Expenses, viz.:—*		
Stables	xxx	
Rent	xxx	
Incidentals	xxx	
Warehouse and Office Salaries	xxx	
Travellers' Salaries and Expenses	xxx	
Commission	xxx	
Depreciation of fittings	xxx	xxx
" *General charges, viz.:—*		
Bank Charges	xxx	
Discount on Sales	xxx	
Bad Debts	xxx	xxx
" Net Profit as per Trading Account		xxx

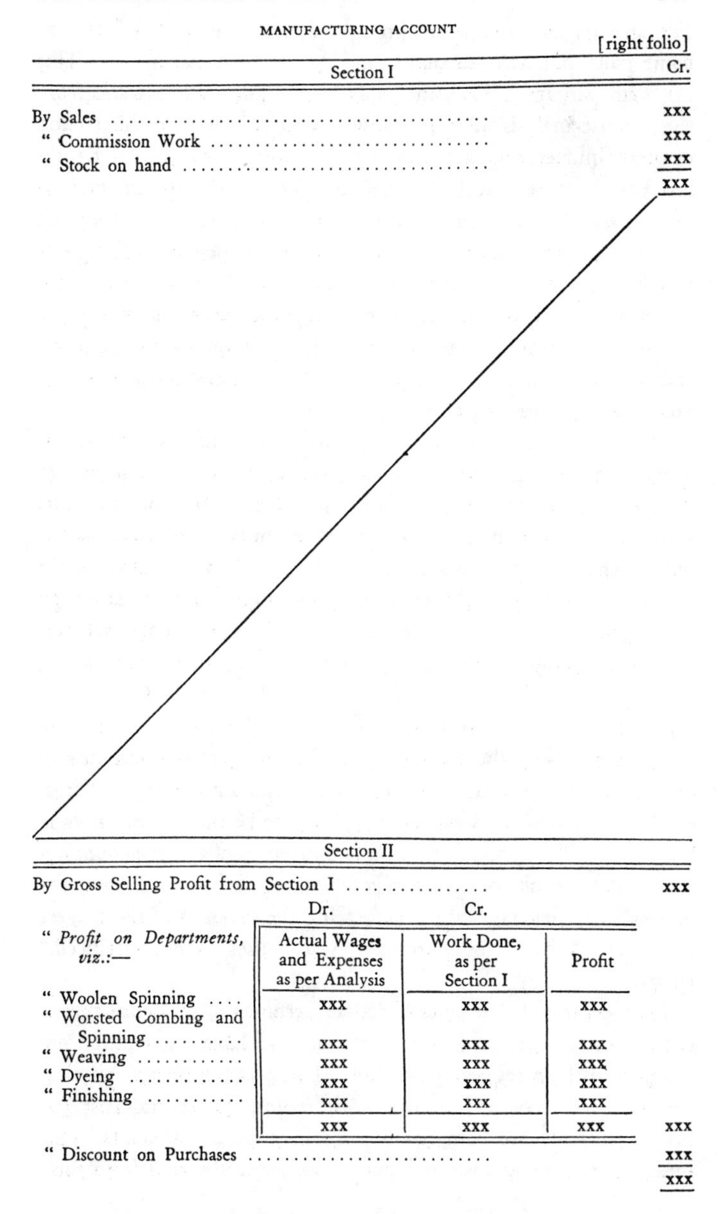

MANUFACTURING ACCOUNT

[right folio]

Section I	Cr.
By Sales	xxx
" Commission Work	xxx
" Stock on hand	xxx
	xxx

Section II				
By Gross Selling Profit from Section I				xxx
	Dr.	Cr.		
" *Profit on Departments, viz.:—*	Actual Wages and Expenses as per Analysis	Work Done, as per Section I	Profit	
" Woolen Spinning	xxx	xxx	xxx	
" Worsted Combing and Spinning	xxx	xxx	xxx	
" Weaving	xxx	xxx	xxx	
" Dyeing	xxx	xxx	xxx	
" Finishing	xxx	xxx	xxx	
	xxx	xxx	xxx	xxx
" Discount on Purchases				xxx
				xxx

side appears the gross profit brought down from section I, the income from purchase discounts, and "profit on departments." This last item perhaps needs some explanation. The column totals from the expense-analysis sheet are shown by departments in this section of the manufacturing statement beside similar departmental figures brought from section I. In this manner actual departmental or process costs are compared with the current trade price or outside cost of a similar quantity of work. The departmental profit figures which result show the profitableness of doing the work in the proprietor's own factory rather than letting the work out, while the "gross selling profit" figure from the first section shows the profit (before deducting selling and general expenses) attributable to non-manufacturing activities.

This arrangement of data is very ingenious and gives the management more information of managerial value in the circumstances than would be true of a statement in which actual process costs alone were presented. Even though this manufacturing statement is outside the double-entry system, it is nevertheless carefully tied in by finally resulting in the same net profit figure as that shown by the trading account, which was a part of the double-entry records, and by checking at other points with totals from the commercial accounts.

In contrast to Norton, Garcke and Fells take a definite stand in favor of including the commercial and manufacturing accounts in one coördinated system. "Factory books," the authors write, "must not be considered, as is generally the case, to be merely memoranda books. . . . They should so assimilate to the books of the counting-house that the obvious advantage of having a balance-sheet made up from the General Ledger, embracing the balances of the ledgers and books kept in the stores and warehouses, is not sacrificed." (p. 7).

Their coördinated scheme of ledger accounts is so logical that it can be readily described. Raw materials and labor as acquired are charged to their respective accounts. Then, as the several physical elements are combined in the work rooms, the several cost (or price) elements are comparably combined in the accounts. This means that material costs and labor costs are transferred from their respective accounts to a summary manufacturing account. The manufacturing account also receives debits from the cashbook for sundry expenditures applicable directly to manufacturing processes.* Periodically the (prime) cost of the goods completed is transferred from the manufacturing account to the stock account, leaving in the former as a balance the cost value of goods partly completed. The amount standing changed in the stock account represents the cost-price value of the goods manufactured and not yet sold. At the time a sale is made two adjustments of the accounts are necessary. One of these charges the customer for the selling price and credits trading account; the other transfers the cost-price value of the goods sold from the stock account to the debit of the trading account. In this way there are placed in opposition in one account the production cost of all goods sold and the selling price, so that the gross profit may be correctly calculated in the ledger itself as a part of the double-entry system.† These interrelations may be presented in the form of a diagram which follows.

The principal fact which this presentation shows is that there is

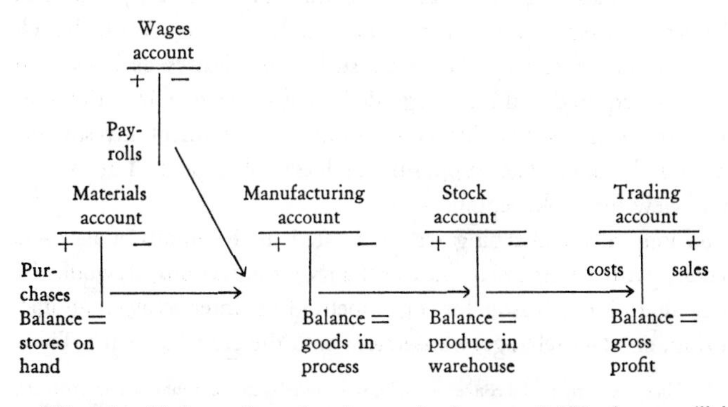

* Note that this is not "manufacturing overhead expense." This element will be discussed in another section. The manufacturing account is itself not described by Garcke and Fells, but the context (e.g., pp. 67, 69, 235) seems to suggest that it was used.

† Garcke and Fells state in the preface to the second edition (1887) that they believe their book to be the first attempt to place before English readers "a systematized statement of the principles regulating factory accounts." But they probably would have hesitated even to think that the basic accounts for a manufacturing concern which they described would remain, as they have practically unaltered as to content and interrelations for the next forty years or more.

a flow of price-data through a sequence of ledger accounts which is concurrent with the corresponding flow of work through the processes of manufacture which are converting raw materials and labor into commodities.* And this it seems, is the new concept which manufacturers' accounting brought to bookkeeping. Garcke and Fells did not discuss it in this sense—they probably philosophized little in conceiving and outlining their book—but no one can thoughtfully compare this arrangement with the usual commercial scheme of accounts without realizing that something new was entering double-entry bookkeeping. In other words, double-entry bookkeeping was found to be adaptable to new and unprecedented uses.†

In manufacturing, the center of thought is converting materials and labor: in commercial undertakings the center of thought is exchanging existing goods. Double-entry bookkeeping developed as a complete system in an era of exchange transactions and until the nineteenth century remained in an atmosphere of exchange. So long as exchange was its purpose and its environment, bookkeeping expressed many expenditures for services as temporarily withheld deductions from capital—that is, practically as losses. With the advent of manufacturing, however, such expenditures as labor and services acquired must be regarded (with concrete materials) as property-elements awaiting conversion; they represent investments of capital rather than suppositional losses of capital. This was a new view for bookkeeping.

So long as bookkeeping was associated in the minds of its users wholly with commercial (i.e., exchange) transactions, it would be difficult to see a reason for, or a method of, interjecting manufacturing, or non-exchange, transactions into the closed system.‡ These

* "When we come to the conversion of raw material and labor into salable products, there is, in addition to the complicated transactions of an extensive trade, a series of operations to be watched, the supervision of which demands a rigorous method of accurately and swiftly realizing the progress made." J. S. Lewis, *The Commercial Organization of Factories.*, p. xxxv.

† It is regrettable that more material is not at hand to permit the further study of the attempts between 1818 and 1887 to use double-entry bookkeeping in the treatment of manufacturing records.

‡ This may, perhaps, explain in some measure the lack of coördination between manufacturing and commercial transactions in the methods described by Payen and by Norton. Yet Norton must have known Garcke and Fells' work, for his book is

non-commercial transactions would, in these circumstances, most naturally be dealt with in independent and separate analyses of the total commercial expenditures and would be put to the test of agreement in total with the key figures from the double-entry records. This is just what Payen and Norton both describe. The later appearance of a complete coördination of commercial and manufacturing elements, such as Garcke and Fells wrote about, must therefore be taken as evidence of the growth at about this time of a broader conception of the possibilities of double-entry bookkeeping as an administrative instrument.*

The second feature of particular interest in these three books is the treatment of manufacturing overhead. It is here that the great-

---

dated two years after theirs, and he may, therefore, be presumed deliberately to have chosen to keep the commercial and the manufacturing elements separate for some special reason. He may have recognized the possibilities of a coördinated system for textile manufacturers but felt that the incorporation in the computations of information regarding "putting-out" costs would be the more valuable to textile manufacturers who had continually to choose the more profitable of the two new ways of getting their work done. On the other hand, Norton's illustrations are dated 1884; this fact, therefore, offers the suggestion that the manuscript may have been completed some time prior to its publication date of 1889 and that it may really picture conditions existing in practice before those described by Garcke and Fells' book, dated 1887.

* A complete system of reports, abstracts, and record books is provided by Garcke and Fells to furnish the mechanism for passing the cost figures from account to account. Employees' time tickets furnish the original data for the wages book from which pay-rolls are made up (Dr. wages, Cr. cash) and for the wages-allocation book wherein labor is analyzed according to job orders or processes for entry in the prime-cost ledger (Dr. manufacturing, Cr. wages). Purchase invoices pass through a stores-received book into the stores ledger and through an invoice-allocation book into the commercial ledger (Dr. stores, Cr. vendors). Stores warrants (we say requisitions) come to the stores ledger through a stores-issued book and are also entered by jobs in the prime-cost ledger (Dr. manufacturing, Cr. stores). A periodic abstract of the prime-cost book gives the data regarding goods completed and passed to the warehouse (Dr. stock, Cr. manufacturing). Upon sale the cost value of goods is transferred through a sales-analysis book (Dr. trading, Cr. stock) and the selling price is entered through the day-book and journal (Dr. customer, Cr. trading). The balances in the stores ledger will agree in total with the stores account, the balances in the prime-cost ledger with the manufacturing account, and the stock ledger with the stock, or warehouse, account. With the exception of the names of some of the books and the failure adequately to provide for charging overhead expenses, this procedure is still good practice, today.

Of late years, overhead has received much attention; but the early writers seem to have considered it as a minor matter in comparison with labor and material costing. Perhaps the large increase in the relative proportion of overhead expense in recent years may in part account for the shift that has taken place.

est difference exists between nineteenth and twentieth-century practices. In the earlier period there seems to have been an understanding of the nature of this type of expenditure but some difficulty in disposing of it without undue complications.

Mention has already been made of the analysis sheet used by Norton in getting expenditures broken down by departments or processes. Material and supply costs are distributed according to a storekeepers' report, and wages according to the jobs or processes, but standing expenses for the mill are variously apportioned. (pp. 196, 222). Motive power cost is allocated "according to the machinery turned in each department," gas, according to the relative number of lights or by separate departmental meters; floor area is the basis for subdividing "rent, rates and taxes," while insurance "is apportioned in the policy"; repairs and maintenance costs may be analyzed from the expenditure records and time reports of the workmen. Depreciation on plant and machinery is, by preference, figured as a percentage of the diminishing value of the respective groups of fixed assets, although periodic revaluation and fixed annual deductions according to the estimated working life of the asset and its residual value, are also mentioned as possible alternative methods. (p. 235). The treatment of expense is quite satisfactory as far as it goes; but like all of Norton's costing, the allocation of overhead to departments is outside the double-entry books.

Garcke and Fells introduce the costing elements into the double-entry system, but do not make clear the ledger procedure of handling overhead, or "establishment charges," as they were called. Some of this failure is no doubt due to inadequately differentiated terminology, such as indirect expenses, establishment charges, standing charges, factory charges, indirect factory expenses, factory general charges, general charges, shop expenses, etc. It seems probable, however, that the distinction is best made by the terms factory charges (foremen's wages, rent, fuel, lighting, heating, cleaning, etc.) and establishment charges (clerks' salaries, office rent, stationery, etc.). In any event, the authors evidently have the necessary distinction in mind, for they state (p. 122) that the best manufacturing firms price their manufactured inventory at cost of production (labor, material and factory charges) "without any addition for profit or for standing charges as distinguished from factory charges." The practice of including a percentage for establishment charges "can not be too strongly condemned."

Yet, in spite of this seemingly sound understanding of those expenses which are costs of production and those which are costs of administration, these authors do not present a clear-cut method for manipulating the expenses in the accounts. They point out (p. 71-74) that, although some firms make no attempt to allocate indirect expenses, a more efficient control over these items would result from distributing them over the various jobs as a percentage either of the wages expended on them or of the cost of wages and materials. Little direction is given, however, for the actual incorporation of these data in the cost records. It is intimated that a column could be added in the prime-cost ledger (the modern job-cost ledger) for these expenses, or a percentage for indirect expenses and depreciation could be added at the end of each job recorded in the cost ledger; yet the procedure of passing this "overhead" from the expense accounts through the manufacturing account to the stock account and finally to the trading account with the labor and material costs is not explained. Presumably expense would follow the same course as labor and materials, and thus three cost elements instead of two would follow the sequence described. In this case the whole procedure would be quite modern in outline. But from general impressions of the entire book it seems improbable that the cost accounting in actual use in business carried overhead expenses through the ledger accounts in this systematic way. This conclusion is strengthened by the description which Lewis gives of costing methods.

There is much in Lewis' book to indicate that factory overhead was reduced to rates (percentages of wages) only for job estimating purposes, (see his Chap. XXII), and that the actual expenditures as recorded in the establishment-charges account were closed directly to profit-and-loss account after the manner of the expense accounts of a mercantile business. In support of the latter statement it may be pointed out that Lewis says that all establishment charges, depreciations, up-keep of plant and buildings, rents, rates, taxes, trade expenses, etc. "are abstracted to the debit of Profit and Loss" (pp. 221, 386) and that upon delivery to the warehouse finished goods are debited to stock account at prime cost (pp. 210, 353). Yet, tucked away in a "miscellaneous" chapter at the end of the book, as if the practice were not a part of current usage, is a statement that the charges (for heavy machine tools) should be so arranged that the debits to job-order numbers will as nearly as possible absorb the shop-establishment-charges account when credited to it. (p. 475). This seems to suggest ledger transfers of shop expenses to the manufacturing account. But elsewhere (as on p. 176) even this association of expense with prime cost is found in estimating for bidding on new work and for stock-taking rather than direct ledger transfers.

The authors of this period were not unconscious of the possibilities of spreading overhead to the work in process through ledger entries but they preferred other methods. Lewis states that in some classes of business it is highly desirable to allocate the overhead to the work in progress but that this practice is at the same time open to serious objections. The most important bad effect of the practice would be that the "arbitrary" [estimated in advance] establishment charges percentage might bring to the credit of the expense account much more than the actual amount paid. This, through the accompanying debit to goods in process, would "create a fictitious asset." *

A preference is therefore expressed for bringing the overhead expense into contact with prime cost only at the end of a period when an inventory was taken. This permitted not only handling overhead expense *en bloc,* but also made certain that the adjustment would be in terms of actual expenditures and not arbitrary or fictitious estimates. By means of an intermediate "suspense account," which it is unnecessary here to describe, a proper portion of the paid-out expenses was temporarily attached to the inventory of manufactured goods unsold and thus withheld from the profit-and-loss account. After the accounts were closed the suspense item was reversed, thus restoring the inventory (stock account) to its original

* It may be noted, however, that this fear of arbitrary percentage rates was not felt by all writers. John Mann, writing in *The Accountant* for August 29, and September 5, 1891, had no hesitancy in advocating periodical credits to the direct-expenses account (as a percentage of wages) and debits to cost-ledger account with wages and materials.

prime cost valuation and deferring to a later date the transfer of the remaining overhead expense to profit-and-loss account.*

The meager information on nineteenth-century accounting in the United States indicates that in general views similar to the British were held but were expressed much less completely and systematically. The subject was quite inadequately treated in short sections of a few texts on general bookkeeping and in a few periodical contributions. The only work of any weight to come to attention was a book [2] by Henry Metcalfe (New York, 1885). Even this excellent book must be regarded as insufficient from an accounting point of view, for the author in the end (p. 289) confesses his inability to present a method for proving the cost sheets by the cash accounts (i.e., of "tying-in" the cost records and the general records). Another explanation of its inadequacy is the fact that the book is concerned mostly with shop management in a government arsenal where there are no problems of capital or entrepreneur's profit. It describes, therefore, not a system of accounts, but the "paper work" of army accountability, so arranged as to enable the officers in charge to compare their results with the prices of similar work in the open market. Captain Metcalfe strongly advocates the use of cards for all original records. This practice speeds up recording procedure by permitting varied sortings of data before tabulation and summarization and is, therefore, greatly superior to books for original records. The idea is much in favor in modern systems and, apparently, was here applied to factory records for the first time.

In America, as in England, the early practice was to broaden somewhat the concept of the customary merchandise account and to make it suffice for simple factory bookkeeping. An excellent and early example is found in John Fleming's text [3] which appeared in 1854. In a small practice set he made use of a Factory Account

* This treatment, it will be observed, would imply that "shop establishment charges" were fundamentally "expense" in nature, whereas the modern treatment, by which overhead is associated in the accounts from the beginning with labor and material, implies a theory of value which gives overhead an "asset" characteristic. The distinction is similar to the familiar alternative treatment of the insurance account: if conceived as an asset account, the consumed portion is calculated and transferred, leaving the unconsumed (asset) portion in the account; if it is considered an expense account, the asset portion is calculated and transferred, leaving the consumed (expense) portion as the balance.

which was manipulated to produce a balance which represented the profit.

FACTORY ACCOUNT

Cost of building	Cloth etc. sold
Cotton purchased	Cloth etc. shipped on consignment
Wages of hands	
Purchase of coal	Balance [inventory].
Clerk and expenses	
Profit or Loss [remainder]	

The inclusion of the cost of the building on the debit side and periodically, in the inventory, on the credit side was quite in harmony with the long established usage which brought an earning asset into account with its own expenses and incomes. The most common example in the older textbooks was the real-estate account which received not only the cost of the property but the expense of maintenance and the rental income as well. After having had the property entered as an inventory (slightly depreciated) at the end of the year, the account would show the net profit or loss from that source.

In the 'eighties a similar idea is occasionally found. Dwight S. Dow,[4] in describing the procedure of working out one of his practice sets, says that the "bookkeeper opens an account which he calls the manufacturing account and treats it exactly as he has the merchandise account . . . that is, he debits it with all it receives (the cost of material, labor, etc.) and credits it with all it gives (the proceeds of the sale of the manufactured articles)." He does not explain manufacturing expense. A. O. Kittridge[5] mentions a manufacturers' account which is credited when the customer is debited. Preceding this account is one called "cost items," compiled mainly, it appears, from a special column in the cashbook. The balance of this account represents "the total cost to date of the manufactured product," but no explanation is given of the relation to manufacturers' account. The author's view of expense is confused; he does not separate factory and general expenses.

But the use of an account on the pattern of a merchandise account did not escape criticism. For example, the editors of *The*

Bookkeeper[6] object to the lack of elucidating details and hold that "systematic accountantship" in a factory calls for three divisions of information: 1. for representing the cost of raw material, 2. for arriving at the cost of converting raw material into manufactured products [labor?], and 3. for ascertaining the returns for productions manufactured.

Overhead expense evidently received little consideration. James Howard[7] gives a list of accounts concerned in costing, and says that these should be grouped under three heads to show the purchase of all articles used in manufacturing, to show the articles produced and the cost prices of them, and to show the costs and charges incidental to the sale of goods manufactured. But he does not indicate how to classify the accounts he names into these three groups.

Henry Ellis of the Institute of Accountants in Ontario, Canada,[8] apparently lumps all expenses together (he mentions traveling expense, freight and delivery charges) and says that it is necessary to know the percentage represented by those items of expenditure "which must be added to the cost to arrive at the price at which sales can be effected at a profit." This might be interpreted as referring to general management overhead were it not for the fact that the author a little further on says that "prime cost is the proper criterion of value" for inventory purposes. There is no evidence to lead one to think that he might be using the term "prime cost" in any other than the present sense of material and labor cost. Captain Metcalfe[9] favored dividing the total shop expenses for the prior year (or the average for the past two years) by the total hours of shop work done, thus to "obtain a load by which to increase the charge for each hour's labor for the present year." But this spreading of the estimated expense over the work is not correlated with actual expenditures.

Readers today may wish that some of these writers had elaborated their theme and presented a better picture of the thought of the time. Especially do we miss the discussion of the incidence and application of factory-overhead expense to product. This, however, is merely another way of saying that present-day interests are directed toward a better analysis of overhead, or that recent developments, such as increased competition, increased use of large investments in capital equipment, and increased managerial supervision of operations, have necessitated a closer control, and therefore a refinement of the analysis, of overhead costs.

It is natural that the nineteenth century should be deficient in some particulars in even its best cost-accounting practice, for at that time costing was new, as factory management was new. This was a transition or growing period for bookkeeping; traditionally connected for so long with the recording of mercantile exchanges, it was now called upon to answer new needs which must have seemed rather foreign to its very nature. But there was progress. It was a great step toward the ultimate accomplishment of bookkeeping's destiny when it became necessary for accountants to follow the conversion of value through the various manufacturing processes into stock and thence into the customer's hands (by exchange) at the end of the sequence. Like the conception of debits and credits as mere increases of properties, the perception of the possibilities of representing a flow of value through ledger accounts advanced bookkeeping still further as a quasi-statistical procedure for treating certain data scientifically.

It is easy to see deficiencies—now. It is always much easier after the foundations have been laid to add to the superstructure than it is to make the original departure from the accepted plan. It is quite understandable, therefore, why cost records in the nineteenth century were so often not coördinated with commercial bookkeeping. The possibilities of coördinating the two were recognized and in some cases strongly advocated, but after a survey of a large number of texts, one is left with the feeling that coördination was more honored in the breach than in the observance.

In this period considerable emphasis was placed upon the records of prime costs and only incidental attention was given to overhead costs. The correct allocation of materials and wages to specific products or jobs and the maintenance of running balances for separate material accounts required a great many records and much reclassification of data—requirements which mercantile bookkeeping did not know. To develop this "bookkeeping machinery" was of itself no small achievement; and to "tie-in" these records with ledger accounts so as to prove the stores account by a stores ledger and the prime-cost account by a prime-cost ledger, and at the same time to coördinate stores and prime costs with cash disbursements, was an enviable and original accomplishment. Indeed, it is not too much to say that the formulation of cost-accounting procedure can be ranked as an achievement second only to the original development of bookkeeping according to double-entry principles.

So great a change as this could not be completed in the generation or two which witnessed the laying of the foundation. In the circumstances the lack of attention to overhead expense is quite understandable; it has already been suggested that neither the intense modern industrial competition nor the great expansion of industrial fixed capital had taken place when these foundations of cost accounting were being laid. The necessity for taking thought regarding expense was not overlooked, for it was to be specifically allowed for in estimating contract prices or in fixing selling prices. But expense did not receive the same careful and detailed treatment in the commercial records or the cost records that was accorded to goods, materials or wages. The best practice of the time knew how to allocate expense to jobs by adding it as a percentage of labor cost (or of labor and material cost together), but this knowledge was not consistently used to show that expense could "flow" through the accounts and attach to the product as labor cost could.

"Expense" was apparently still thought of as "loss"; it was too early to realize that expense was an acquired service-cost which could and should move through the accounts as if it had physical characteristics capable of manipulation in the shop. Expense was perceived as an element which should be deferred as a part of the inventory of unsold goods—as an unrecovered investment like the raw material embodied in the inventoried product. But the procedure was not as well organized for attaching expenses to the product currently during manufacture as it was for labor costs.

On the whole the contribution of the nineteenth century to accountancy through cost accounting was a notable one. It was a basic one also, for little more has been done since that time than to adapt the established procedure to current conditions and to refine the allocation of cost details to units of product. Cost accounting appeared in response to needs growing out of the industrialization of business. It undertook to place such detailed information regarding labor and material cost in the hands of the manager as would enable him to compare his production costs with outside prices for similar work or to estimate on the basis of past records at what price he could afford to contract in undertaking specific production. Cost accounting, therefore, in the last analysis, represents the influence of the industrial revolution upon double-entry bookkeeping; it is an important element in marking the expansion of bookkeeping (a record) into accounting (a managerial instrument of precision).

REFERENCES

1. These books are: Emil Garcke and J. M. Fells, *Factory Accounts,* London, 1887; Geo. P. Norton, *Textile Manufacturers Bookkeeping,* London, 1889; and J. S. Lewis, *The Commercial Organization of Factories,* London, 1896.

The original editions of the first two of these books are not at hand; the fourth edition (1893) of Garcke and Fells was examined and the fourth edition (1900) of Norton. It seems probable, however, that these later editions still represent quite closely the best practices of the 'eighties. For example, a recent writer (John Whitmore, *Journal of Accountancy,* September, 1930, p. 200) says "I think I can say from memory that the 1902 edition [of Garcke and Fells] is substantially the same as the original edition of 1887." Norton writes in the preface to the third edition of his book (1894) that the previous editions had been revised in minor matters but the book was substantially unchanged.

2. Henry Metcalfe, *The Cost of Manufactures,* New York, 1885.
3. John Fleming, *Bookkeeping by Double Entry,* Pittsburgh, 1854, p. 115.
4. Dwight S. Dow, *Keeping Books,* New York, 1882, p. 80.
5. *The Bookkeeper,* New York, October 26, 1880, Vol. I, p. 131.
6. *Ibid.,* Vol. IV (1882), p. 157.
7. *Ibid.,* Vol. II (1881), p. 33.
8. *Ibid.,* Vol. II (1881), p. 146.
9. Metcalfe, *op. cit.,* p. 166.

XXII. ACCOUNTING EVOLUTION

The preceding chapters have given some indications of the evolution through which bookkeeping and accounting passed prior to the beginning of the twentieth century. They have told another section of the familiar story of all history: the story of interacting events.

Accounting is relative and progressive. The phenomena which form its subject matter are constantly changing. Older methods become less effective under altered conditions; earlier ideas become irrelevant in the face of new problems. Thus surrounding conditions generate fresh ideas and stimulate the ingenious to advise new methods. And as such ideas and methods prove successful they in turn begin to modify the surrounding conditions. The result we call progress.*

There are two kinds of relativity in accounting. The first of these is the relativity of accounting to present-day problems, the power of accounting to contribute to current solutions. Merely to maintain itself in the midst of the complexities of modern organization and the intricacies of present-day finance, accounting must continue to make a real contribution. But it has succeeded in the past in doing more than merely maintaining a status quo. This is shown by the increased utilization of professional audits and the great expansion in the field of cost accounting. Such devices as standard costs, interpretive ratios and financial budgets are concrete examples of recent accounting contributions to the solution of modern business problems. But consideration of the contribution which accounting is

* "Progress in the science and technique of accounting has made possible an increase in the size, complexity, and territorial scope of business operations. Conversely, these changes have spurred the advance in accounting knowledge and technique. The kind of records that are needed depends upon the business, but the kind of business that is possible depends upon the records that have been kept."—John Bauer in *Encyclopaedia of the Social Sciences,* V. I, p. 404.

prepared to make is clearly outside the scope of the present work, however fascinating the subject may be.*

The second kind of relativity associates the past development of accounting with its historical surroundings in an attempt to explain its origins. This has been the real theme of this book. Accounting originated in known circumstances in response to known needs; it has evolved and grown in harmony with its surroundings; its changes can be explained in terms of forces current at the time. Truly, then, accounting is progressive and relative. It came from definite causes; it moves toward a definite destiny.

The relation of surrounding conditions to the origins of double-entry bookkeeping need to be only briefly restated here in view of the consideration given to these matters in part I. It is quite significant, however, that double entry was a product of the Middle Ages rather than of classical antiquity, that its development coincided with the extensive commerce which followed the crusades, and that its formulation seemed to require a proprietary commerce rather than an aristocrat-slave commerce. When these conditions were fulfilled, the details of financial record-making were quickly coördinated into the complete and unified methodology of double-entry bookkeeping. For centuries thereafter there was little change in the type of enterprise (proprietorship and partnership) or in the basic character of commerce. Nor was there any fundamental development in bookkeeping during this time. There was no pressure which could produce anything more than certain refinements in technique in the interest of increased accuracy and economy of recording effort.

However, when the relativity of later developments is considered there is more to be said. The evolution of bookkeeping into accounting is closer to the present, and less surmise is necessary as to the facts. It is easier, therefore, to understand the interaction of forces and to describe the changes which have taken place.

The nineteenth-century development of professional auditing in Great Britain is a good illustration of the way in which antecedent

* A few writers have expressed themselves upon the contributions which accounting has made. For example, *Das Verhältmis der Buchhaltungslehre zur Sozialökonomik* by Oswald; *The Cultural Significance of Accounts,* Scott.

conditions produce subsequent results. It is not sufficient merely to point to the statutory audit as the basis for the growth of professional experts, for the question immediately arises: Why was such a statute passed? There are several answers:

In the early nineteenth century an increasing pressure was apparent in England in favor of freedom of incorporation. The resistance of the government slowly weakened, and an approach was made in the second quarter of the century to permitting incorporation through compliance with a general statute. That constitutes the first point: the pressure of expanding commerce leads to incorporation by statute.

But the companies acts prescribed an audit. The second point therefore is that England's unpleasant experience with stock speculations in the early eighteenth century led to certain safeguarding clauses in the companies acts of the nineteenth century, including an audit, in the interest of the inactive shareholders, of the directors' various activities.

Why was the thing prescribed an audit instead of some other protective device? This, then, is a third point: England's experience in feudal days provided a suitable method for effectively supervising delegated responsibilities—the audit. The idea was easily adapted to the nineteenth-century need and an audit was therefore prescribed for all joint-stock companies.

But an understanding of why there was a statute and why it prescribed an audit does not also produce an understanding of whence came the men who were to grow into professional experts. The men were, first of all, bookkeepers. Hence bookkeeping was basic to auditing; the shareholder's knowledge of his company's affairs had to come from bookkeeping data prepared for him by his own representative. But mere acquaintance with the methods of double-entry bookkeeping does not suffice to constitute "expertness." When the audit committees, consisting only of stockholders, began to realize the complexity of the task assigned to them, they soon sought assistance. They were presently permitted by statute to employ "accountants." No doubt in some cases these outside assistants were simply bookkeepers who were not associated with the specific enterprise. But in many cases someone of more experience and judgment would be needed. Whence came those men? They were found in the ranks of those who had delved into the inner intricacies of accounts in bankruptcies and other litigation and therefore had a deeper knowledge of ways and means than could have been obtained merely from writing up transactions.

This bankruptcy work, in turn, arose from the statutes which sought to protect business creditors when their debtors became insolvent. And since insolvency was directly connected with the long series of financial crises which England experienced, it is evident that business crises of the nineteenth century were contributing factors to the development of professional auditing. It is therefore clear that it is not enough simply to say that auditing was the result of the English companies acts. On the contrary, auditing was the consequence of a complex of many factors, some direct and concurrent, others distant and rather indirect.

The variety and extent in time of these factors are summarized in the following diagram.

THE RELATIVITY OF AUDITING

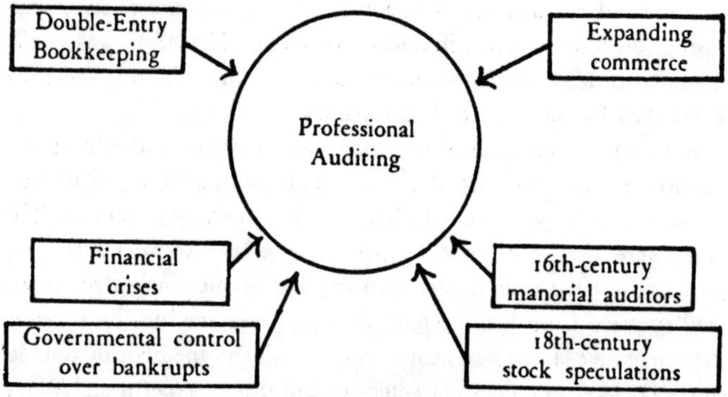

It is noteworthy that the British government played an important part throughout this development. Bankruptcy legislation was passed very early in order to protect creditors as much as possible from unfair losses at the hands of unscrupulous debtors, and it was revised from time to time in attempts to improve the protection given. The publicity sections of the companies acts and the audit provisions also had a similar purpose for they were inserted to protect stockholders (as one type of creditors) from "stock-jobbing" promoters and fraudulent practices by company directors. Here is an excellent example of organized society (government) undertaking to limit individual action in the interest of unorganized society, the latter here represented by creditors and stockholders.

This illustrates well the fact that the development of accounting has been relative to society's own development. It is unlikely that professional auditing would have appeared when and where it did if England had lacked a parliament or had had one which was unresponsive to the social needs of the time. Professional accounting, in the nineteenth-century sense, could not have appeared in fifteenth-century England, for the earlier age did not have the right kind of problems to call it forth. And it would be quite as unreasonable to expect to see fifteenth-century "charge and discharge" accounting satisfying the accounting needs of the nineteenth century.

Another good illustration of the interrelation of surrounding conditions and the development of accounting is found in the rise of theory. Double-entry bookkeeping, as expounded in a long line of early texts, was singularly devoid of theoretical discussions. The presentation was almost entirely descriptive—a verbal picture of bookkeeping routine. This in later years was supplemented by a multitude of rules of thumb for resolving transactions into debits and credits. But occasionally in the nineteenth century appeared a bookkeeping teacher who perceived the inadequacies of the method of learning by rote and tried to replace rules by reasons. These few men saw in bookkeeping more than a clerical routine and in transaction analysis more than a process of account personification. Practical business experience gave them a consciousness of the ultimate purpose of bookkeeping which the mathematicians and writing masters of an earlier day did not have. And some deep instinct for good teaching seems to have led them to seek ways and means of bringing out the logic which was inherent in bookkeeping.

The clue to bookkeeping logic lay in "proprietorship." When the teacher began to speculate about the nature of proprietor's expense accounts and about the relation of the enterpriser to his enterprise, theory began. Here is the basis for that fundamental distinction between asset and expense which underlies so much of the theory of accounts. Here, too, the situation reveals the necessity for a classification of accounts, a grouping together of like accounts which can be viewed in contrast with other groups having other major characteristics. This is recognized as the foundation of much of the value which financial statements possess; it is the basis of the technique of marshalling an array of figures into an enlightening display.

While much credit for the appearance of accounting theory is due to those teachers who were striving to reveal the intellectual side of double entry, it is not improbable that the many problems raised by corporations have created more discussion—and hence more theory—than did the teachers of bookkeeping.

The corporation's contribution to accounting theory is threefold. Because of limited liability there was a legal obligation to retain in the business the amount of the capital contribution. It became important, therefore, to be able to make an accurate calculation of the amount of assets which could safely be distributed. The necessity for such calculations gave added importance to knowledge enabling one properly to distinguish asset and expense.

Because the incorporation of an enterprise resulted in a definite continuity of economic existence (although with changeable membership), there was an economic obligation to maintain the productive power of the enterprise. Here was a further use for sound theory to guide the management in making periodic calculations of the profits. Here, for example, was the practical justification for the theory of treating depreciation as a necessary cost of production instead of a voluntary reservation of profits.

And finally, because corporations were aggregates of capital under delegated management, it was necessary to substitute "figure knowledge" for direct knowledge of investors. Financial statements became the medium of stockholders' knowledge of their affairs and thus gave added importance to well chosen account classifications which would make the statements clear and comprehensible. Theory, which at one time had perhaps seemed rather academic, had now extended its usefulness far beyond the classroom into the realm of practical affairs.

Various conditions had conspired to improve the logic by means of which business facts were analyzed for bookkeeping records and to increase the lucidity with which financial facts were presented to the understanding. This was theory—a refinement of bookkeeping definitions and concepts. Some of these same conditions, with others which were more deeply social in nature, created a need for expert professional services and at the same time produced a body of men capable of performing these services. This was auditing—a method of scrutinizing bookkeeping data. Still other circumstances brought about a great advance in the technique of bookkeeping itself—this was cost accounting.

Our familiarity with the machine age makes it somewhat difficult to recognize the revolution which is hidden in cost accounting. As double-entry bookkeeping was a revolution in account keeping, so costing, which is a complex process of calculating for one's self the cost-make-up of his product, was a revolution in commercial bookkeeping, in which an article's cost was simply the purchase price.

When double entry was developing, and for many generations afterward, business was commercial rather than industrial; it was trade, not manufacture. Production was handicraft work in the family; it was a way of making a living rather than production for later distribution at a profit over cost. There was "cost," of course—raw materials gathered or grown and the labor of the family—but there were no wages, few employees and little invested capital. There was no need here for cost bookkeeping.

Costing problems began to appear when men began to work for money wages and when enterprising masters brought workmen and material together under one roof. This was the "factory system"; its cost bookkeeping if any was attempted, was mainly in regard to kinds of material and quantities of articles produced. But, there was a real need to ascertain money costs (material prices, wages paid) in order to "test" the adequacy of selling prices. This was satisfactorily done in a general way quite easily, for "wool" and "wages" could still be treated with the account simplicity of trading expenditures.

The germ of cost accounting, therefore, lay in the factory system of production. But it needed the soil of the industrial revolution to help it grow toward its fruition. With the industrial revolution came power machinery—first water wheels, then steam—and with machinery came the costing problems of fixed assets, depreciation, establishment charges (overhead), etc. Later the nature of costing became more evident and its calculations better refined. Methods of allocating cost units to product units were devised with such skill that cost accounting has finally become a veritable symphony of analysis and synthesis. But its origins are the intricate origins of the industrial revolution: the movement away from the land to the towns, the commutation of services into wages, the invention of machines which applied power to productive processes. If we are to understand cost accounting fully, these must constitute the background. Costing therefore, like auditing and accounting theory, was a product of surrounding conditions.

This story of a portion of the evolution of accounting is now ended. It has furnished one more picture of the effects of expanding commerce and changing economic conditions. The high lights are in the fifteenth century, when, under pressure from a rapidly growing commerce and trade, men expanded account keeping into double entry; and in the nineteenth century, when a similar pressure, this time from commerce and industry, led men to expand double-entry bookkeeping into accounting. It is another cross section of the unending stream of history wherein ". . . all events, conditions, institutions, personalities, come from immediately preceding events, conditions, institutions, personalities." (Cheyney).

INDEX